SONG HONGBING

CURRENCY WARS III
Financial High Frontiers

Song Hongbing

Song Hongbing (born in 1968) is a young economic researcher who emigrated to the United States. He worked there as a consultant for the American pension funds Freddie Mac and Fanny Mae that will disappear during the financial crisis of 2008.

货币战争③金融高边疆

CURRENCY WARS III
Financial High Frontiers

Translated from Chinese and published by
Omnia Veritas Limited

www.omnia-veritas.com

© Omnia Veritas Ltd – 2021

All rights reserved. No part of this publication may be reproduced by any means without the prior permission of the publisher. The intellectual property code prohibits copies or reproductions for collective use. Any representation or reproduction in whole or in part by any means whatsoever, without the consent of the publisher, is unlawful and constitutes an infringement punishable by copyright laws.

FOREWORD 13
FINANCIAL HIGH FRONTIER 13

CHAPTER I 18
THE FALL OF THE FINANCIAL HIGH FRONTIER 18
Hunting Hu Xueyan 20
Dongting Mountain Gang: the man behind Hu Xueyan's assassination 25
The Opium Trade: The Battle for the Gold and Silver Standard 33
East India Company: The Empire of a Banker 36
The Sassoon Family: The Rothschilds of the East 42
HSBC: I'm in charge of your turf 44
Ticket Money: Why it didn't grow into an international financial empire . 50
Foreign buyers: China's special phenomenon 57

CHAPTER II 60
THE MEIJI RESTORATION AND THE WESTERN MOVEMENT 60
Wangzheng Retro and the Rise of Money 61
Inoue: Japan's Founding Finance Founder 65
Mitsui Family's Big Boss 68
Japan controls the financial high frontier 71
Why the Meiji Restoration didn't "attract" foreign investment 76
Yen Credit Defense War 79
Meiji Restoration vs. Western Movement 83
Financial poisoned milk cripples Han Ye Ping Company 84
Fission of Fate 90

CHAPTER III 95
"APRIL 12" COUP: CHIANG KAI-SHEK'S "NAME" 95
The hesitation of Chiang Kai-shek in marching to Shanghai and Ningxia.. 95
30 million gold rubles for the Northern War 99
Chiang Kai-shek has a bigger leg 105
Yu Qiaqing and Chiang Kai-shek: The Story That Must Be Told 108
The financial powerhouse behind the April 12 coup 113
Chiang Kai-shek's Refinancing 115
The "recapitalization" behind the "Ninghan Merging" 118
Zaibatsu's board of directors fires the CEO for his nonsense. 124
Chiang Kai-shek is finally on the Growth Enterprise Market 127

CHAPTER IV 131
THE RED CENTRAL BANK 131
Mao Zemin's Financial "Empty City Plan" 132

Paris Commune, starving for gold *136*
The gun in one hand and the money in the other *141*
The world's smallest central bank, the Chinese Soviet National Bank *144*
The Birth of Red Money *148*
The people's money, for the people *152*
Trade "Special Zone" and "Central Enterprise" of the Soviet Union *158*
Money Bags for Guns *164*
"Central Bank" and "Red Army Ticket" for 13 days *167*
The Legend of Red Money *169*

CHAPTER V 173

CHIANG KAI-SHEK'S GOLDEN POWER 173

Chiang Kai-shek beat up Song Ziwen for lack of money *174*
Central bank PK Bank of China *178*
Reorganization and Fingerprinting *183*
The Golden Power Game between Government and Commercial Stocks *186*
Chiang Kai-shek's Financial Concentration: "Abolishing Two and Changing the Yuan" and "Four Lines and Two Bureaux" *189*
I'm gonna sell you a big motherfucker! *195*
The Silver Rush: The First US-China Exchange Rate War *198*
French Currency Reform: The Fuse of Japan's War Against China *203*
After the Yellow Bird, Americans Laugh to the Last *209*

CHAPTER VI 213

ROYAL POWER AND GOLDEN POWER 213

The yen is off the gold standard, and the plutocrats are in the way *214*
Secret Meeting of the Marquis of Kido's Family *216*
"The Taisho Coup" and the Loss of Imperial Power *219*
The Dream of the Emperor: The Rise of Imperial Power *223*
Mitsui fell into the "dollar arbitrage trap" by calling on the Emperor *229*
The "Shanghai War": Japan's "fake war" *234*
The Land of Assassination *239*
Imperial power over golden power *243*

CHAPTER VII 252

THE DREAM BREAKS OF THE GOLDEN MAUSOLEUM 252

Banker's Death *253*
Foreign Exchange Parity Fund: Second Central Bank *259*
Kong Xiangxi's dollar fortune *264*
The financial version of "Lurking" *270*
Bankruptcy of the French currency: the consequences of foreign exchange liberalization *274*

The Last Struggle for the Golden Ticket 280
Why Chiang Kai-shek Lost the Currency War 283

CHAPTER VIII 285

THE BIRTH OF THE RENMINBI 285

The Frontier's God of Fortune 286
The hard rebirth of frontier currencies 290
The "price standard" of the Beihai currency: financial innovation in the Shandong base 297
"Strategic goods" and the trade war 301
The Yuan was born 305
The Battle of the Silver Dollar 310
The Battle of Cotton 314
RMB: currency for the people 319

CHAPTER IX 325

FINANCIAL HIGH FRONTIERS AND THE INTERNATIONALIZATION OF THE RMB 325

Currency wars: the reincarnation of history 326
The RMB Dilemma 329
Broad price standard: alternative to the yuan 334
Important features of a good currency 337
Lousy creditors and arrogant debtors 340
Clearing centre: the "router" of the financial network 343
The Global Financial Network of the RMB 347
The infrastructural dangers of the financial high frontier 352
The advent of the "Spring and Autumn and Warring States" era of money 353

CHAPTER X 358

THE GLORY AND DREAMS OF SILVER 358

September 18, 2008, 2:00 p.m., the world financial system almost collapsed! 359
Silver: The World Currency of the Past 362
Can dollar bills keep their value? 366
The Fed's "magic plan": let the gold soar 370
Gold and silver 1:16 historical super-stable structure 376
Silver on the shoulder: both a monetary and industrial metal 379
Application of silver in the field of new energy 380
2017, 25.9 billion RFID chips will use silver 380
U.S. timber protection field will consume 2,400 tons of silver per year in the future 381
Apparel applications will be one of silver's biggest future needs 382

What did the price find? *383*
Silver Market: The Game of 1 Bottle Cap and 100 Bottles *389*
Silver manipulation investigation *392*
Silver market on the verge of a massive run *396*
People's War in Silver *401*

Acknowledgements and Reflections 405

OTHER TITLES **409**

FOREWORD

Financial High Frontier

As I have been researching around the history of money in the United States and Europe, a vein has become increasingly clear, and that is that the issuance of money is one of the most important powers of human society. The coveting and contestation of this key power has been woven throughout recent European and American history. This perspective on the political, economic, cultural and military changes in the world will give an X-ray-like effect. It turns out that the root of all social contradictions lies in the uneven distribution of benefits, and that the most important means of distributing benefits is money issuance.

As American monetary historian Jack Weatherford said,

> *"To control money is a great struggle, to control the issuance and distribution of money is to control wealth, resources, and all of humanity."*

While *The Currency Wars* focuses on how the repeated struggles for the right to issue money in the United States have affected American society and world history, *The Currency Wars 2* focuses on how the fierce competition around the right to issue money in European countries has shaped wars and peace, as well as the formation and shifting of global power. During this six-year-long "research expedition", the following questions came to my mind from time to time: What kind of influence did the game of currency issuance have on the formation of modern Chinese society in the history of China, especially in the recent modern history of China? How does the power of this money differ from its influence in European and American countries? Is there an inextricable and intrinsic link between the monetary gaming taking place on the Chinese mainland and the global battle for monetary power? What would you see when you look at China's history with the X-ray of money?

With these question marks, I began to revisit what I had previously known, but not thought about, about China's modern history.

Currency is far less prominent in China's historical literature than it is in politics, culture and the military. People are often familiar with the military tactics of the emperors of the successive dynasties, and are familiar with the deeds of their generals and courtiers, as well as the anecdotes of the poetry of the literati and the writers. Money seems to be a long-forgotten science in China.

Currency, which has been overlooked by historians, is precisely the key to unlocking many historical puzzles, the compass to discern the maze of today's reality, and the telescope to discover the road to the future.

From the Opium War in 1840 to the founding of the People's Republic of China in 1949, these 100 years were the most thrilling period in China's history; it was the 100 years when the Chinese nation was almost destroyed; it was the 100 years when the self-confidence of Chinese civilization almost completely collapsed; it was the 100 years with the most tragic and passionate feelings in China's history; it was the 100 years when the will of money and the power of money rose and exploded!

Currency Wars 3 will gradually unfold the picture of China's modern history along the main axis of money. A familiar image will appear in a very different vein through the perspective of the currency "developer". Why is the opium trade and opium wars only in China? Why did Japan's Meiji Restoration succeed while China's foreign affairs movement failed? Why did Chiang Kai-shek, who finished the Northern Expedition with Soviet rubles, suddenly turn his face against the Communists? Why do both parties have to "hold the gun in one hand and the money in the other"? Why was Chiang Kai-shek able to unify the currency but not maintain monetary sovereignty? Why did the Kuomintang's French currency reform anger Japan, tempt Britain, but eventually swoop into the arms of the United States? Why is there a dispute between Imperial and Golden power in Japan? Why does the Japanese army always go down and up? Why do coups continue and assassinations become common in Japan? Why did the KMT's French currency reform stimulate Japan and accelerate its war of aggression against China? Why did the Kuomintang's French currency end up in collapse while the Communist Party's renminbi came out of nowhere?

These historical doubts have forced me to think more deeply and to come to realize the enormous influence of the right to issue money on China's recent modern history. The constitution and exercise of money-issuing rights require a whole set of systems and structures to support them, a new understanding of money-issuing rights that I call in this book the "financial high frontier".

The "high frontier" doctrine is a new thinking on national security put forward by Lieutenant General Graham of the United States Army in the early 1980s, who, following Mahan's "sea power theory" and Duhay's "air power theory", proposed that space is also the "high frontier" that sovereign States must defend, and formed the theoretical basis of the United States Star Wars programme.

In the course of studying the financial history of Europe, America, China and Japan, I have a growing feeling that finance is the "fourth dimensional frontier" that a sovereign country must defend. The concept of the frontiers of sovereign states does not only include the three-dimensional physical space constituted by the land, sea and air frontiers (including space), but in the future it needs to include a new dimension: finance. The importance of the financial high frontier will become increasingly important in the coming era of cloudy international currency wars.

From the path of financial evolution in Europe and the United States, it can be clearly found that the currency standard, central banks, financial networks, trading markets, financial institutions and clearing centers together constitute the system architecture of financial high frontier. The main purpose of this system is to ensure efficient and secure resource mobilization for currency pairs. From the source of the central bank to create money, to the customer terminal that eventually accepts money; from the dense network of money flow, to the clearing center of funds remittance; from the trading market of financial instruments, to the rating system of credit assessment; from the soft regulation of the financial legal system, to the construction of rigid financial infrastructure; from the huge financial institutions, to efficient industry associations; from complex financial products, to simple investment instruments, the financial high frontier protects the monetary blood from the heart of the central bank, to the financial capillaries and even the whole body economic cells, and eventually back to the central bank's circulation system.

This provides a frame of reference for the future internationalization of the RMB. The internationalization of the RMB is not simply a matter of releasing the RMB for extracorporeal circulation. Free exchange of the RMB, deregulation of capital items, RMB settlement of cross-border trade, currency swap and construction of offshore RMB centers are only the initial stages of RMB internationalization, and these efforts must be coordinated with a set of frameworks to achieve the desired results. For the yuan to go out, it has to be both visible and manageable. In the future, wherever the renminbi exists in the world, it is in China's national interest. To this end, effective and reliable monitoring is necessary to ensure that these overseas circulating renminbi are in the realm of "legitimate" use.

A dark thread that runs throughout the book is silver. As a currency in circulation, silver has become an essential and key element in the lives of Chinese people over the last 500 years. It was once the real world currency and played a leading role in driving East-West trade for 400 years. It is also a widely used industrial metal and will play a more significant financial and industrial dual function in the future as the dollar dwindles. "Scarcity is precious" is the natural order of investing, and silver fits this principle perfectly. As silver becomes increasingly scarce, the process of discovering its value will unfold at an alarmingly fast pace, making it the long-term investment of choice for the average person.

Just as the book was being finalized, the leader of a country made a high-profile declaration that an international "currency war" had broken out. In October 2010, I was invited to participate in the "World Knowledge Forum" held in Seoul, South Korea, which was called "Davos Asia". As the only speaker from China, I experienced a "war of words" in the face of Western voices accusing China of manipulating the RMB exchange rate.

The term "currency war" has been widely circulated in the Western media since 2007–2009, when "Currency War" and "Currency War 2" were released. The author and the new term "currency war" have been widely reported in the British *Financial Times*, German weekly *Der Spiegel*, American *New York Times, Washington Post, The Nation, Foreign Policy, The New Republic, Forbes, Business Week*, Salon, Spanish National, Indian Pioneer, as well as in dozens of countries and regions around the world, including Romania, Finland, Poland, Australia, Switzerland, the Czech Republic, Israel, Japan, Korea, Singapore, Vietnam, Peru, etc.

This round of international media to "currency war" concept of speculation again, in my opinion, only because of the "currency war" series of books in China and the influence of the Asian region, malicious people try to take the opportunity to imply that China manipulated the RMB exchange rate, launched a "currency war" to the world, in order to achieve the purpose of leading the scourge to China, so as to alleviate the pressure of the world's discontent with the second round of dollar printing plan. However, the eyes of the world's people are shining and there is a growing consensus that the irresponsibility of the dollar is the root cause of the world's "currency wars".

Whether people are willing or unwilling, the dollar printing scheme has been "undeclared war" on the world's currencies, as long as this behavior does not stop, the smoke of the world currency war will be difficult to dissipate.

The purpose of studying and preparing for monetary warfare is not for war, but for peace! The better prepared and more determined you are, the less likely a currency war will occur. General Kim Il Nam had a quote that struck me:

> *"What does it mean to be a strategic deterrent? One, you have to be strong, two, you have to be determined to use that strength, and three, you have to convince your opponents that you dare to use your strength!"*

By learning from history and building its own solid financial high frontier, it is strengthening this strength. Only with such a strategic deterrent is there no fear of others waging currency wars.

As the "Currency Wars" book series continues to grow in young readers, more and more people are leaving me messages to bring the content of "Currency Wars" to life online. We are planning China's first financial online game, "Currency Wars" series, to let young readers understand the world of finance in the virtual world.

Due to time and capacity constraints, there are inevitably errors in the book's ideas, and I sincerely hope that readers will understand and correct them.

Author. December 2010,

Xiangshan, Beijing

CHAPTER I

The fall of the financial high frontier

Who is the real culprit in the assassination of Hu Xueyan? Why did the Opium War only happen in China? Why did China's silver standard lose at the feet of the British gold standard? Why didn't China's money banks and ticket numbers develop into a world financial empire? Why is China the only country with a lot of foreign buyers?

It is impossible for the Western powers to turn China into a semi-colony by means of a strong ship and a sharp cannon and the Industrial Revolution alone, nor can they stifle China's economic potential by ceding land for compensation and opening ports of trade. The real reason for the decline of the Qing Empire was that the Western financial capitalist forces first breached China's financial high frontier.

The primary strategic goal of the opium trade was to subvert China's monetary system, and this strategy was developed and implemented in the Financial City of London. The Opium War was actually a strategic showdown between Britain's gold standard and China's silver standard, and the victory or defeat of the war would determine the prosperity of the East and the West for centuries to come!

For the bankers of the British Empire, its highest strategic objectives are: to take London as the financial centre of the world, to take gold as the world currency standard, the British Empire through the Bank of England to export sterling credit to the world, to turn the major European and American countries into the core members of the gold standard, to turn the peripheral countries of the world into the vassal areas of the pound, to maintain the operation of this system with war and violence, to use money to maximize the control and mobilization of global resources, and finally complete the control of the world wealth and all mankind.

The British financial capital's assault force is far more powerful than the imperial navy, which will be the first to defeat China's silver standard, seize the central bank as the strategic high point of control over the silver roots of the Qing empire, infiltrate and encroach on China's financial network, master the channels of capital and credit flows in China, and complete its total control over China's financial high frontier.

With the loss of financial high frontier control, China's right to trade pricing, the right to locate industrial autonomous development, the government's right to fiscal taxation, and the right to spend on military and defense will gradually be lost. China will inevitably become a lamb to be slaughtered by the Western powers.

In fact, with the demise of the Qing Empire, finance preceded the military.

In the late 19th century, Mahan, an American, first proposed the concept of the "right to control the sea", believing that "to control the sea is to control the world", and in 1921, Duhe, an Italian, proposed the concept of the "right to control the air", saying that "to control the air is to win". Sixty years later, Lieutenant General Graham of the United States Army has again introduced the "high frontier" doctrine of the "right to space", believing that "control of outer space will lead to world domination".

Graham has extensive experience, having served as Deputy Director of Intelligence, Deputy Director of Central Intelligence and Director of Defense Intelligence for the United States Department of Defense and, in 1980, as a defense adviser to the Reagan presidential campaign. In 1981, shortly after the Reagan administration took office, Graham formed the High Frontier Study Group with funding from the Heritage Foundation. The group consists of more than 30 prominent American scientists, economists, space engineers and military strategists. After more than seven months of careful research, the study was presented on March 3, 1982, under the title "The High Frontier – A New National Strategy". The "High Frontier" strategy was immediately brought to the attention of the United States Government, the military and the public, and had a significant impact on the economic, political, military and high-tech development of the United States and the world situation. At the heart of the "high frontier" strategy is the idea that the United States, with its historical tradition of expanding its borders, should in the future undertake new expansions in the Earth's outer space, using space as the new strategic frontier and sphere of control for the United States.

Whether it is the right to control the sea, the right to control the air, or the "high frontier" doctrine, the ultimate emphasis is on the scope of control and the ability to control. From the point of view of Western civilization, areas where there is human activity but not control are "frontiers" to be conquered.

The physical space in which human activity takes place, from continents to oceans, from land to sky, and even from space, is basically tightly controlled by the great powers. And the financial sector is increasingly becoming the main battleground for big power gaming.

The country's frontiers are not only the three-dimensional physical space made up of land, sea and air frontiers, but the future also needs to include a new dimension: the financial high frontier.

Hunting Hu Xueyan

In early November 1883, Hu Xueyan experienced the most painful ordeal of his life, and his financial empire, which he had painstakingly managed all his life, was about to crumble to the ground. This is a superlative myth created with 20 million taels of silver, and if the purchasing power of food is estimated, one or two taels of silver is roughly equivalent to 200 yuan today, which means that Hu Xueyan's financial empire has roughly 4 billion yuan in total assets. However, at this time, Hu Xueyan is facing a deadly "perfect" storm.

In early November, he had a 500,000 taels HSBC debt that had to be repaid, a debt that made him feel doubly anxious. Under normal circumstances, with the scale of Hu Xue Yan's wealth, he would never be overwhelmed by a mere 500,000 taels of silver. Unfortunately, his opponents had already set a net in the sky, and Hu Xueyan could not escape the fate of being hunted. He had a vaguely ominous feeling: "The market is too bad, the foreigners are too powerful, I don't know how to turn over?"

Hu Xueyan's frontal enemy was the British firm of Jardine's, and at this time the two sides were engaged in a fierce battle over the dominance of the raw silk business.

In the whole 1870s, foreign companies firmly control the pricing of China's raw silk exports, under the oppression of foreign companies, raw silk prices are getting worse and worse, in ten years has fallen by half, the silk farmers around Jiangsu and Zhejiang are in dire straits, the local silk merchants are miserable business, high profits are swallowed by foreign companies.

When Hu Xueyan began to intervene in the raw silk business, he felt the pain of the high pressure of the foreign company. Seeing that the silk farmers are being sucked into bankruptcy by the foreign banks, he secretly made up his mind that he must seize the raw silk trade pricing rights, forcing the foreign banks to make concessions on prices. He began to look carefully for the brokenness of the foreign bank's price control system. With its control over raw silk trade financing, international exchange, export channels and shipping insurance, backed by the gunboats of the British Empire, Ocean Bank seemed invincible. However, Hu Xueyan still keenly captured the dead end of the Yanghe line – the difficulty of controlling the source of raw silk production.

Hu Xueyan is determined to occupy the source of raw silk as a strategic high point of control, and in one fell swoop to break the hegemony of foreign banks over raw silk pricing.

The opportunity finally came in 1882. In early spring, Hu Xueyan went deep into the silk production area to conduct a careful investigation, and at the same time, in the exchange with local silk merchants found that the silk harvest that year was reduced, there will be a serious shortage of supply. He immediately seized this rare opportunity, began to act quietly, in Jiangsu and Zhejiang silkworm breeding villages and towns around the purchase, widely distributed deposit, control the source of goods.

Sure enough, the market in May raw silk harvest is estimated to be up to 80,000 bales, however,

> "in August, it is becoming clear that the harvest was overestimated by 20,000 bales".

Hu Xueyan, who had already completed the control of the raw silk supply, immediately deployed a general attack. He mobilized every copper plate in his vast financial empire and plunged tens of millions and twenties of silver into a showdown unprecedented in Chinese business history. By the summer of 1882, he had hoarded nearly 20,000 bales of raw silk,[1] accounting for more than 1/3 of the total stock. In order to completely control the price, he invited his silk industry counterparts to form a raw silk price alliance and insisted on selling at a high price in an attempt to take over the pricing rights of raw silk in one fell swoop.

They tried to break through the fence, but Hu Xueyan's fence was so tight that silk dealers of some size were told to abide by the agreed price. "The finest raw silk sells for only 16 shillings and 6 pence a packet in London, but in Shanghai the price of silk, thanks to the acquisition and manipulation of Hu Xueyan, amounts to 17 shillings and 4 pence in sterling."[2] The logic of the foreign firms is that their own organized suppression of raw silk prices is not manipulation, while organized resistance in China is. This logic continues to prevail to this day, with the United States printing dollars in a frenzy not counting exchange rate manipulation, while China's countermeasure response was judged to be exchange rate manipulation.

Jardine's was forced to ask the General Department of Customs and Excise of the Qing Dynasty and the Englishman Hedder to intervene. Yes, we all read it right, it was the British who took a hand in the Chinese customs. Rather, it was the British who, after defeating the Qing government, forced the Qing government to cede land and pay compensation, and in order to ensure that China paid on time, directly appointed the British to look after China's customs, and all customs duty revenue was taken directly by the British to offset the compensation.

He was in charge of the Great Qing Customs at the age of 28, a typical juvenile successor, but much younger compared to Hu Xueyan. He used the invitation to Hu Xueyan to run a silk factory as a bait and offered "commission in addition to the market price" in an attempt to persuade Hu Xueyan to make price concessions. Soon, Japanese merchants also came to the market and offered an additional 8 million taels of silver at the prevailing market price, which, after negotiations, was agreed to be increased to 10 million taels of silver. As long as Hu Xueyan nodded his head, the equivalent of today's gross profit of

---

[1] British Consular Report, Shanghai, 1883, p. 230.

[2] British Parliamentary Papers, China, 1884.

RMB 2 billion would be in hand. The situation is great. However, Hu Xueyan refused, asking for a higher price.

It was at this point that "European silkworms saw a bumper crop, and the London and continental markets were able to defy China's poor harvest".[3] YCB turned to the acquisition of native European raw silk. By the end of 1883, silk prices had plummeted, half of the silk merchants delayed settlement, and several large silk houses went bankrupt. Hu Xueyan tried to invite the silk merchants to collect all the new silk in the coming year to force the foreign houses to give in, but no one responded.

The Shanghai market for raw silk sold lightly, with buyers and sellers in a standoff for a full 3 months. At this point, the two sides are fighting over the strength of the funds.

Jardine Matheson is no ordinary foreign bank, its backstage boss is the earliest and most powerful of the 17 largest international banking families, the Bank of Bahrain in the UK. In the 19th century, the Baring family was known as the "sixth most powerful power in Europe", predating the Rothschilds and being the undisputed leader in international finance. With this strong support, Jardine's is always in an undefeated position against Hu Xue Yan.

And Hu Xueyan's situation was starting to look bad. You should know that maintaining price control requires high costs, compensation for franchisees' interests, high prices for raw silk, increased deposit ratio, high warehouse costs, huge financing costs, transportation, insurance, labor all cost money. The staggering tapping of funds has put Hu Xueyan's cash flow in ever more fragile danger.

The Beijing faction cadre general Sheng Xuanhuai, who had already taken this into account, began to act. He is plotting to "abolish" Hu Xueyan.

Hu Xueyan and Sheng Xuanhuai do not have any deep personal grudges, just their own. In 1867, Hu Xueyan was the first to borrow money from foreign banks and foreign banks with customs tariffs as collateral, and in 14 years, he financed 16 million taels of silver for Zuo Zongtang's military operations.

---

[3] British Consular Report, Shanghai, 1883, p. 230.

In Sheng Xuanhuai's background was naturally Li Hongzhang, a minister of the Beijing dynasty. The conflict between Li Hongzhang and Zuo Zongtang is well known, and in the 1860s and 1970s, China experienced a serious frontier crisis. In the northwestern direction of China, the Central Asian Agypas took advantage of the ethnic and religious conflicts in northwestern China at that time and, with the support of the British, Russian and other powers, invaded Xinjiang and established the so-called "Hohan State". Soon, the Russian army occupied the border town of Ili, the northwestern defense situation is as dangerous as the eggs. At the same time, in the southeast of China, Japan has provoked a serious invasion of the Taiwan region, and war between China and Japan is on the verge of breaking out. "After the Fourteen Years War of Taiping Heaven, the Qing Dynasty's treasury was so poor that the country's finances could no longer afford to win two wars at the same time. However, the "naval defense faction" represented by Li Hongzhang advocated the strengthening of the navy as a priority and abandoned Xinjiang for this reason, while Zuo Zongtang insisted that the "defense of the sea" could never be invalidated and should not hesitate to launch a military conquest of the Xinjiang rebellion. If the imperial court decided to give priority to "sea defense", huge sums of money would flow into the Beijing faction's sphere of influence, while the establishment of the national policy of "stuffing defense" would inevitably increase Zuo Zongtang's strength. It was a sharp contest of national and personal interests.

Eventually, Zuo Zongtang regained all of Xinjiang and his prestige and status overwhelmed Li Hongzhang. At this time, the Sino-French War was again overcast, with Zuo Zongtang once again leading the battle and Li Hongzhang once again leading the peace. Li Hongzhang was afraid that large sums of money would once again flow into the hands of the main warring factions, resulting in insufficient sources of funding for the Beijing system, so he decided to launch a "reverse left" offensive. In order to stop Zuo Zongtang, Hu Xueyan, the "money bag" of Zuo Zongtang, must first be abolished.

Sheng Xuanhuai's efforts to bring down Hu Xueyan would not be simple, and his energy would be limited to cutting off the 500,000 taels of money that the Beijing-controlled Shanghai Road had paid to Hu Xueyan, which was the money the court owed to HSBC. And since Hu Xueyan used the credit of the Fukang Money Bank to borrow money from HSBC for the imperial court, he had to advance the money if the imperial court was late. However, Hu Xueyan is a financial player after all, in the center of the capital market in Shanghai, whether it is to extend the loan to HSBC, or other foreign banks to split the bill, or to the Shanghai money bank ticket number interbank loan, or nearly ten million dollars worth of raw silk for mortgage loans, moreover, he also has more than ten thousand mu of land, manor and other real estate, as well as more than 20 pawnshops, chain ticket number and Hu QingYutang pharmacy and other huge operating assets, it is not too difficult to raise 500,000 taels of silver.

Therefore, Sheng Xuanhuai not only needs to cut off Hu Xueyan's official sources of funding, but also to cut off all of Hu Xueyan's access to capital market financing, which Sheng Xuanhuai can never handle. He had to unite the real big players in the Shanghai financial market to make this fatal stab at Hu Xueyan's back.

Dongting Mountain Gang: the man behind Hu Xueyan's assassination

In Shanghai, Hu Xueyan's credibility was good, and he had the backing of Zuo Zongtang, the governor of the two rivers in charge of Shanghai, who also made friends in the business community, otherwise he would not have formed a powerful silk merchant alliance to challenge the foreign banks. How about being able to sway the decisions of all the foreign banks, and at the same time control the fate of all the money bank numbers and pawnshops in Shanghai, so that we can all refuse to finance Hu Xueyan?

This is the founder of the most powerful financial buying empire in China's modern history: Xi Zhengfu from Dongting Mountain, known as the "Dongting Mountain Gang" in his circle. As with the international bankers, the Xi family can be described as rather low-key, and except for a few historians, most Chinese are extremely unfamiliar with this name. Da Dao invisibility is exactly what they are!

When foreign foreign firms first entered China to do business, they did not speak the language, were not familiar with the place of life, the business environment and government relations were not in the same light, so they had to borrow the local Chinese to expand their business. Foreign buyers often "cooperate" with foreign foreign banks as independent businessmen who are required to pay exorbitant "deposits" to the foreigners and to compensate them with deposits in case of loss of business. It also enjoys a share of the income from the business. They were doing their best to expand the business of the foreign bank for their own benefit. In addition to the government's access to government resources, there is also a need to network with the business community to reach out to all corners of society. They weave a network of relationships and money, unblocking the channels of wealth and interest. It was through them that foreign capital infiltrated China's economic bloodline, foreign goods flooded China's big cities and towns, foreign spirits subverted China's consciousness, and foreign interests bound China's powerful elite. It can be said that without foreign buyers and agents, the business of foreigners in China will be difficult to do, and the power of foreigners in China will also achieve nothing.

When Hu Xueyan led the local financial and commercial forces to start challenging the foreign banks, he threatened not only the commercial interests of the foreign banks directly, but also the vital interests of the foreign buying class.

In 1874, Xi Zhengfu became a foreign buyer at HSBC, and after paying a deposit of 20,000 taels of silver, he bought an "express ticket" to control the financial market in Shanghai. XI Zhengfu's ability certainly did not disappoint HSBC, just arrived at HSBC, he took care of the Qing government to salt tax as collateral, to HSBC for political borrowing 2 million taels of silver, a large order, 8% annual interest, divided into 10 years to repay. XI Zhengfu's first shot was fired, and from then on it was out of control. Under the operation of the Xi family, HSBC successively managed the Shanghai-Nanjing, Guangzhou-Kowloon, Shanghai-Hangzhou-Ningbo, Jinpu, Jingfeng, Huguang, Puxin and other railway loans, from which it obtained a high share.

In the issuance of banknotes, but also effective, HSBC banknotes circulation can be called the most foreign banks, circulation throughout the Yangtze River, Pearl River basin, in southern China, HSBC banknotes almost replaced the status of the Qing government currency, became the instrument of valuation circulation. 1893, the foreign school intellectual Zheng Guanying in his "Sheng Shi Jian Jian" pointed out:

> "If the foreign merchants use silver notes (banknotes), not by Chinese and foreign officials to check the reality, no matter how much, do whatever they want. It is known that the Bank of England and Wales has made a profit of over two million on the Oval Office."

The family has made a sweat equity contribution to HSBC's possession of China's physical wealth with a white bar.

The Xi family is also extraordinary when it comes to deposits. China's powerful officials and dignitaries have deposited capital in the government's difficult to govern the HSBC account, preferring to get only very low interest, but also willing to figure a "safety insurance". According to statistics, among the long-term customers who opened an account with HSBC, there are five people with fixed deposits of more than 20 million taels, 20 people with more than 15 million taels, 130 people with more than 10 million taels, the level of million taels and hundreds of thousands of taels is more difficult to estimate.[4] The commissions that the Seers received were even more astronomical.

Under Xi Zhengfu's struggle, HSBC's total business in Shanghai is much higher than that of the Hong Kong head office, and the British themselves admit that "HSBC's head office is in Hong Kong, but generally speaking, the Shanghai branch does more business". When Xi Zhengfu and the British side of the Taipan (the old term for managers of foreign companies and foreign firms, referring to the brokerage of Chinese and foreign trade at that time. – (Editor's note) In the event of a conflict of opinion, the final decision at headquarters was based on Xi Zhengfu's opinion, for which the British Taipan was removed at all costs.

He is not only the first to speak at HSBC, but also the first to speak at Shanghai's money bank.

At that time, it was difficult for the bankers in Shanghai to expand their business because their own funds were only tens of thousands of taels of silver. Xi Zhengfu has taken the lead in the ticket splitting business, providing a collateral-free credit loan model to money banks and ticket numbers, greatly improving the financing capacity of local financial institutions. These powerful bankers with their own credit issued forward bills of exchange, in a period of 5 to 20 days, to HSBC or other foreign banks to carry out short-term financing secured by bank notes. In this way, only seventy to eighty thousand taels of silver can be pledged to HSBC with banknotes, thus lending a large amount of capital for commercial trade lending, the scale of which can be as high as seventy to eighty thousand taels. Because of HSBC's huge deposits and

---

[4] Jiang Nan Xi Jia, *Ma Xueqiang*, Commercial Printing House, 2007, p. 78.

low interest costs, in the process of splitting bills to the bank can charge high interest, so as to enjoy the good meal of deposit and loan spreads. 23 May 1879 Zi Linxi newspaper reported that the Shanghai money bank "with foreign bank capital to do business, is already a well-known fact. Nearly 3 million taels of money was lent, the amount necessary to maintain normal turnover in Shanghai".[5] When the silver root falls below this figure, the entire business activity is immediately and significantly affected.

Through the ticket splitting business, HSBC effectively controls the source of funds for the Shanghai money bank and ticket numbers. When HSBC's hands are loose, the market's silver roots are loose, and conversely, the silver roots are tight. The huge amount of cheap Chinese savings obtained by HSBC has greatly enhanced its control over the Chinese financial system and has in effect become the "Bank of England in China".

It is precisely because HSBC controls the entire Shanghai and even the whole country's silver roots are loose and tight, and Xi Zhengfu has the right to sign loans from HSBC, so the Shanghai money bank industry scrambles to pull him into the shares, to achieve the benefits of bundling. In 1878, Hu Xueyan borrowed 3.5 million taels from HSBC for Zuo Zongtang, in the same way that Xi Zhengfu had done.

Not only did Xi Zhengfu hold the position of HSBC's buyer for three generations, but he also used his influence to place other children of the Xi family into the foreign banking system one after another. Whether it is the British system of Macquarie (Standard Chartered), Leigh, and Deutsche Bank, or the French system of Orientale, Sino-French Industrial and Commercial Bank, the German system of Bank of Wales, the Russian system of Bank of Russia, the Belgian system of Bank of Belgium, the American system of Citi, Amex, and Bank of America, the Japanese system of Yokohama Shinkin, Sumitomo Bank, etc., all are under the control of the XI family. According to incomplete statistics, during the 75 years from 1874 to 1949, there were more than 20 foreign banks opened in Shanghai, of which 13 were bought by the Xi family.

As Xi Zhengfu's power expands, even Li Hongzhang and Zuo Zongtang compete to enlist him. Li Zuo and their two must see Xi

---

[5] *The Linsey Gazette,* May 23, 1879

Zhengfu when they go to Shanghai, after all, is a great god of wealth, whether it is "sea defense" or "stuffed defense", leaving money is nonsense. Both of them are devoted to Xi Zhengfu, and they both guarantee Xi Zhengfu's appointment as a government official, but Xi is not at all interested. Later, on Li Hongzhang's repeated recommendation, Xi Zhengfu was only able to accept the second prize. It's at odds with his deliberate low profile. The nearly reclusive Xi Zhengfu never even attends the Dongting Dongshan business community events, and his name rarely appears in Shanghai media reports. He adheres to the belief that it takes a behind-the-scenes operation to make something great.

XI Zhengfu's relationship with Sheng Xuanhuai was even closer. When Sheng Xuanhuai set up China's first modern bank, the China Merchant Bank, after defeating Hu Xueyan, Xi Zhengfu was the main backer behind it, and the two men had an ironclad relationship in business. Whenever Xi Zhengfu asked, Sheng Xuanhuai was always satisfied, and a large number of family members and friends of the Xi family were placed in Sheng Xuanhuai's system. A complete interlocking of interests was achieved.[6]

When the Qing government was about to set up a joint government-business central bank, the Bank of Japan, the Xi family, who knew the huge benefits of a private central bank, was ahead of the curve. A total of 40,000 shares were issued, of which half were officially subscribed and the other half were privately subscribed, and several of Xi Zhengfu's sons took shares in the Bank. Among them, XI Ligong, the son of XI's parents alone, owns 1,320 shares in various capacities. When the Bank of China changed its name to the Bank of China, the Xi family placed four sons in key positions, and when the Bank of China changed its name to the Bank of China, the Xi family became its major shareholder and took charge of the foreign exchange business, becoming an ally of the Song Ziwen family. When the Central Bank of the National Government was established, the Xi family became a direct investor in government stocks and represented the government stocks on the Board of Directors of the Central Bank, while the Xi family also held key positions such as Director of the Bureau of Foreign Exchange of the National Government and Director of the

---

[6] Jiang Nan Xi Jia, *Ma Xueqiang*, Commercial Printing House, 2007, p. 80.

Central Mint. It is believed that the vast network of the Sejong family, which covers a wide range of financial fields in China, is unparalleled in China's nearly 100-year history in terms of the influence of foreign banking systems, official banking systems, the Shanghai Money Bank system and government financial authorities. Because of the powerful Chinese and foreign financial resources at the disposal of the Xi family, the impact on the entire modern history of China has been profound and will be continued in the following chapters.

If Hu Xueyan doesn't challenge the core interests of the Yanghe Bank on the raw silk issue, Xi Zhengfu's relationship with Hu Xueyan should hold up well. However, the shareholders of HSBC are these big foreign banks, the original purpose of setting up HSBC is for foreign banks to have their own "central bank" in the colonies, Hu Xueyan has challenged the core interests of HSBC's major shareholders, causing the shareholders to cause trouble, Xi Zhengfu can not tolerate him!

In fact, it is HSBC and Xi Zhengfu's manipulation of Shanghai's and the country's banking sector that is behind the foreign banks' suppression of raw silk prices and monopoly of pricing power.

According to the Declaration of August 28, 1878, by the 1870s, the amount of foreign banks' splitting of the Shanghai Money Bank had reached about 3 million taels. By the 1890s, the amount of 7 to 8 million taels of divestment had become commonplace. This has made money banks increasingly dependent on foreign banks for the turnover of their funds. And once the Shanghai monetary tightening, its effect will immediately spread to the whole country.

It is strange but not surprising that since 1878, whenever raw silk and tea are available in China, there is a "strange phenomenon" of silver crunch. The one that can create a shortage of money supply, and with obvious intent, is HSBC. Maintaining normal trade turnover in Shanghai requires about 3 million taels of silver, and HSBC often in the season of the purchase of silk tea to collect the silver root to less than 1 million taels, resulting in silk tea merchants can not raise enough funds, silk farmers, tea farmers have to sell their products at cheap prices, while HSBC's foreign bank shareholders were able to cheaply take advantage of the bottom, to reap huge profits!

> *"Every currency panic has been caused by a deliberate contraction of silver roots by foreign banks, led by HSBC, From the beginning of 1878 onwards, the Yingen was in a state of tension, so much so that by the end of the year, the Shanghai*

money bank for bad debts accumulated no more than twenty or thirty traders. The currency panic of 1879 occurred in May, when the demand for silk tea was so great that the city, which often needed 3 million taels of cash, was in short supply with 900,000 taels of foreign banks. This amount does not at all fit the normal needs of local trade. But the foreign bank did not stop there; it further complicated matters by increasing its stock of silver bullion to 600,000 taels."[7]

In 1883, history repeats itself again.

Just when Hu Xueyan and Yihe Yanghe in the raw silk war in a state of stalemate, Shanghai's silver root is being tightened day by day, a large number of silk merchants cut out of the warehouse, silk prices plummeted. early September, the price per package of top quality raw silk can still maintain at 427 taels; in October, down to 385 taels; early November, further down to 375 taels. At this point, the foreign banks in Shanghai completely stopped acquiring the new silk, and Hu Xueyan's financial chain was on the verge of collapse.

By November 9, public concerns about Hu Xueyan's funding had finally exploded into full force. The Fukang Bank was run over in Hangzhou and Shanghai. The 500,000 taels of silver debt owed to HSBC is due and cannot be extended, and the Shanghai Road "coincidentally" does not have to pay to HSBC's debt, Hu Xueyan had to pay the debt with the only remaining family money in Fukang Bank. The unbearable financial empire finally fell on December 1, 1883. Hu Xueyan's business in Beijing, Shanghai, Zhenjiang, Ningbo, Fuzhou, Hunan, Hubei and other places of Fukang branch closed down at the same time.[8] Hu Xueyan's financial empire, which he had painstakingly run for decades, collapsed. In the end, the raw silk was copped by Jardine's.

Hu Xueyan could not stand the foreign bank's price suppression and resisted, but behind the struggle for pricing power is actually the struggle for financial power. It is a pity that Hu Xueyan did not

---

[7] *General History of Chinese Finance*, Volume II, by Zhang Guohui, China Finance Press, 2003

[8] The Ministry of Household Affairs of the Guangxu period, November 12, Guangxu 11, Official Records of the Guangxu Period (3; present), Finance, vol. 2, Shaanxi Department of the Ministry of Household Affairs, Guangxu 11, vol. 8, pp. 44–48.

understand until his death that, with the loss of the central bank as a financial high point, it was futile to rely solely on the hoarding of raw silk to try to compete with the foreign banks in trade, and once the silver root was tightened, his capital chain would be immediately on the verge of collapse. This counterattack by China's indigenous financial forces against international bankers, led by Hu Xueyan, ended in total failure. What he is caught in is an internal and external pincer of foreign financial capital forces and domestic financial buyer forces, whose failure is already strategically irreversible.

Hu Xueyan's defeat was based on the same reason as Foreign Bank's victory, which was that whoever could control the silver root would gain the strategic initiative in the commercial war. Neither the Qing government, nor the Southern Money Bank and Shanxi Bills, represented by Hu Xueyan, were sober enough to realize the enormous power of the central bank. When HSBC took that position, the fate of the entire Qing Empire was completely in the hands of international bankers. If there is no financial independence, there is no economic independence; if there is no economic independence, there is no political independence. The decline of the Qing government's financial high frontier was the beginning of a deep disaster for the Chinese nation!

How did the Qing government's central banking position fall from grace? The crux of the problem is that the native currency, silver, is controlled by international bankers. Once the national currency has been shaken, finance, the country's circulatory system, will inevitably be paralysed, followed by the exhaustion of the vital organs of the economy, the disintegration of the country's political and warfare immune system's ability to mobilize and thus to resist aggression, and finally the fate of being left to the mercy of others.

For international bankers to conquer China, they must first conquer the Chinese currency. The core of the Opium War was not so much a trade war as it was a silver war! This is the real reason why the Opium War did not happen in India, America, Africa, nor in Japan, Korea, or Southeast Asia, but only in China! The target of the opium trade crackdown is precisely China's home currency: silver!

The Opium Trade: The Battle for the Gold and Silver Standard

China was at a distinct advantage in international trade before the UK began its massive opium trade against it. China's tea, porcelain and silk constitute an unbreakable export "iron triangle" that breaks through the barriers of the world market. The true picture of the Chinese market at that time was: the export of tea along the coast of Fujian brought unprecedented prosperity to the local economy, due to the market monopoly in production and processing, Wuyishan became a mecca for tea traders from all over the world; in the middle and lower reaches of the Yangtze River, silk and cotton is the most important handicraft products, hundreds of thousands of silk and cotton production and textile professional army created excellent quality and competitive prices of goods, hit the world market unbeatable; in the Pearl River Delta region, formed the Jingdezhen-Guangzhou industrial chain, the luxury porcelain into the rich living rooms of European royalty in a steady stream; at the end of the 19th century, the Englishman in charge of the General Department of Customs and Excise of China, Herder said in his "Chinese anecdotes":

> "China has the best grain in the world – rice; the best drink – tea; the best clothing – cotton, silk and fur. They don't have to buy a penny's worth of stuff from somewhere else."

From the 16th century to the early 19th century, China's nearly 400 years of marketization and developed monetary economy far surpassed that of Europe. The result was that 138,000 tons of silver found in Europe from the Americas ended up with 48,000 tons being shipped to China. The basic structure of international trade is that China has created a major part of the world's traded goods, the West has plundered a major part of the world's resources, and in the continuous flow of silver from the West to the East has accompanied the rolling westward movement of Chinese goods.

The constant flow of silver to the East has created a serious imbalance in the world financial scales.

Because of the long-term net export of silver to China, to the end of the 17th century, the European silver shortage, the phenomenon of a general decline in prices, while trade began to shrink. 1649 to 1694, the annual average amount of silver in circulation in Europe decreased sharply, than 1558 to 1649, the annual average amount of circulation decreased by more than 50%, while the amount of gold circulation increased by nearly 50%.

A decrease in silver is par for the course, but how can gold increase?

Originally, at the beginning of the 17th century, the price ratio of gold and silver in Guangzhou, China was 1:5.5 to 1:7, while the British ratio was 1:16, transporting silver to China not only can be exchanged for a large number of highly profitable commodities, but also can take advantage of the price difference of gold and silver ratio more than 1 times, with cheap silver in China, Japan and India for expensive gold. Even John Locke once complained:

> "I was told that they (East India Company) could make at least 50% more profit by importing (gold) from certain parts of India... But the real wealth of Britain is buried in the Indian Ocean and it is time for people to speak frankly about why on earth we are facing a silver shortage unheard of in our time."[9]

When gold poured into Britain in large quantities, bankers bought the quasi-life certificates of the Free Minting Act of 1666 by means of huge bribes. This act was essentially an important turning point in the history of money, which "changed the monetary system of the world, the concrete effect of which was the abolition of the monopoly of the king over the issuance of money".[10] The bill gives any person the right to take gold ingots to the mint and demand that legal gold coins be struck free of charge.

This bill is fundamentally in the interest of the gold ingot bankers and commercial capitalists, who will have actual control over the money supply. Being in possession of large amounts of physical gold chips, they will be able to determine the money supply according to their own interests. When they are creditors, they mint less money, creating a deflationary effect that raises the gold content of their claims; when they are debtors, they increase the money supply, eliminating the debt incurred with inflation. This was the first time that the West had essentially transferred to private individuals the right to issue money that would have belonged to the government. Since then, the legal basis

---

[9] Commerce and Diplomacy, Sargent, p. 49.

[10] Remarks Upon a Late Ingenious Pamphlet by an Impartial Hand, John Locke, p. 19.

for the private central bank's power to issue money has been laid and the door has been opened to control the distribution of wealth by controlling the money supply of a country and the world at large.

At this point, that famous Rothschild quote suddenly rang in my ears:

> *"I don't care who makes the laws as long as you let me control the currency issue of a country."*[11]

In the view of the bankers, controlling money is a great struggle, and to control the issuance and distribution of money is to control wealth, resources, and all humanity. To control the world, one must first conquer money; to conquer money, one must first conquer gold; and to conquer gold, one must first conquer silver.

Just as silver was coming east in Europe, it was accompanied by gold going west in Asia. The end result of this is that the UK is hoarding gold and China is sucking up silver. The crux of the matter is whether it is gold or silver that will eventually become the hegemon of the world's currency, which will be a major watershed in the rise and fall of the East and West for centuries to come!

With the unprecedented growth of the British Empire since the Industrial Revolution, the conditions for the establishment of gold as the standard currency were fully in place in 1717. Although it was not until 1816 that the gold standard was legally finalized, Britain had been under the de facto gold standard for the previous hundred years.

For the bankers of the British Empire, its highest strategic objectives are: to use London as the centre of world finance and gold as the world currency, the British Empire to export sterling credit to the world through the Bank of England, to turn the major European and American countries into core members of the gold standard, to turn the peripheral countries of the world into vassal regions of the pound, to maintain the functioning of this system with war and violence, to use money to maximize the control and mobilization of global resources, and finally to complete the control of world wealth and all mankind!

---

[11] *The Creature from Jekyll Island*, G. Edward Griffin, p. 218.

To establish the hegemony of the gold pound as the world's currency, the silver currency nation must first be defeated. The biggest, and most difficult, of these is China.

After years of trying, international bankers finally chose opium as a weapon against the Chinese silver standard. The agency specifically responsible for implementing this strategy is the East India Company.

East India Company: The Empire of a Banker

It is difficult for the average person to imagine that a company could recruit an army, plunder land and mint money, administer justice, declare war and make peace, but the East India Company actually did it. Who could have had such great energy to start such a powerful company? The answer is the international bankers of the Financial City of London!

The East India Company, founded by a partnership of bankers in the Financial City of London and in which the British Crown had a stake, was an empire in itself. Under the authority of the British Parliament, the East India Company monopolized all trade from the Cape of Good Hope to the Straits of Magellan, and had the right to recruit land navies, occupy territory, impose taxes, issue currency, legislate and administer justice, declare war and conclude peace treaties within such a vast area.

In the Seven Years' War between England and France from 1756 to 1763, the British defeated the French in the Indian subcontinent and established a complete system of governance and plundering in British India, including present-day Pakistan, Bengal and Burma. 50 years after 1750, the East India Company extracted £100 million to £150 million from British India, compared with £9.2 million a year in the British treasury in 1750.[12] This does not include the huge international trade gains from the monopoly of Indian trade. The astonishing wealth that flowed like a tide into the pockets of London's financial city bankers and the British Crown was never short of capital in the 18th and 19th centuries as a result of huge colonial plunder and the accumulation of

---

[12] Silver Capital, by (de) Frank, Central Compilation Press, 2001, p. 393.

commercial trade, which was an important prerequisite for Britain to begin the Industrial Revolution in the 18th century.

The Baring family, one of the world's 17 largest international banking families, had already dominated the financial world since the early 19th century and was known as the "sixth power in Europe".[13] From the time he joined the East India Company, he became a leading representative of the Bankers of the City of London in the East India Company and was recognized as the heart and soul of the company. He was chairman of the board of the East India Company from 1792 and ran the entire East India Company, a vast colonial empire. It was under his leadership that the East India Company's opium trade to China grew spectacularly.

From 1790 to 1838, the amount of opium smuggled into China by the East India Company skyrocketed from hundreds of boxes to tens of thousands of boxes every year, and the total amount of opium imported into China reached more than 400,000 boxes, with an average price of about 750 silver dollars per box and a total value of more than 230 million taels of silver!

The East India Company's opium trade followed a rigorous system: first, it established a monopoly on opium in the British Indian colonies, bought and sold opium from both India and Bengal, opened only the Calcutta area to centralized opium auctions, and authorized the trade in opium to retail traders with whom the Company had an agency relationship. At the same time, the company has a resident management committee in Guangzhou, known as the "Taipan", which is responsible for the unified management of all trade with China. This management committee, in turn, was the "central bank" for all trade with China, which had to deal with all foreign exchange operations and provide credit support to retail merchants and, later, to the 13 banks in Guangzhou that did business with them. The entire proceeds of the bulk traders' trade with China, including the proceeds from the sale of opium, must be deposited in a silver bank under the Commission, which issues bills of exchange for London, India and Bangladesh, and the bulk traders may exchange them locally for cash silver. The company then used the stock of silver in China to buy gold, silk tea and other bulk commodities to sell to Europe for huge profits.

---

[13] *Currency Wars 2: The Power of Gold*. Omnia Veritas Ltd, 2021.

The East India Company is structured more like an opium trade chain under a financial umbrella monopoly. If the independent retailer has to bear some trade risk, the company providing monopoly financial services is a "rain or shine".

The East India Company's profits from the "financial services" of the opium trade were large enough to cover most of the administrative costs of British imports of tea and raw silk from China, imports of cotton from the United States and India, exports of British industrial manufactures to India and British colonial rule in India. Throughout the 19th century, the British Empire's opium monopoly held a strategic position in international trade comparable to the oil hegemony of the United States today. The basic state policy of the East India Company empire was to control financially all links in the chain of the opium trade, with production, distribution, warehousing, transportation and marketing channels firmly in its own hands.

Among the bulk merchants of the East India Company, three major foreign firms were formed: Jardine, Baoshun and Chichang.

The Jardine and Madison partnership was established in July 1832, and it was the Bahrain family who provided them with the financing. With the support of the most powerful banking family in the City of London, Jardine Matheson quickly became the "king of foreign banking" in the Far East. Hu Xueyan was defeated in the battle with Yi He for the raw silk hegemony, and I am afraid he did not know the origin of Yi He. Maddison went on to become governor of the Bank of England and the second largest landowner in the UK. Hugh Matheson, heir to the Matheson family, used the proceeds of his family's opium trade to buy tin mines in Spain in 1873 and set up a mining company called Rio Tinto, which is known today as Rio Tinto Group.

The family of the famous opium trafficker, Tideland, is the family behind him. Later, as direct involvement in the opium business was detrimental to the "reputation" of the leading banking family in the Financial City of London, Bahrain, he retired to the background and became the second largest opium trader in China after Jardine's.

The American-owned company, Cichang Yanghe, traded opium, tea and raw silk between Guangzhou and Boston. Its senior partner, John Murray Forbes, the great-grandfather of 2004 U.S. presidential candidate John Forbes Kerry, has been acting as Bahrain Brothers' agent in the United States. The head of business, Warren Delano, Jr. was none other than the maternal grandfather of U.S. President Franklin

D. Roosevelt. William Huntington Russell, a cousin of the owner, founded the famous "Skull and Bones Society" at Yale University. In addition, several major banking families in Boston were involved in the opium trade through the Flagship Foreign Bank. It was the lucrative opium dividends that nourished these banking families, forming the later Boston syndicate and the Roosevelt family dynasty.

These three big ocean houses, which dominated half of China's opium trade, had close ties to the Baring family, which remotely controlled these "giant retail merchants" in the Financial City of London and launched an attack on the Qing government's silver currency with opium in the decades before and after the Opium War.

The Financial City of London, through the East India Company, also established a little-known but effective underground marketing system in China, consisting of four parts: missionaries, triads, businessmen and Manchu bureaucrats. This system would later shape the course of modern China's history.

Missionaries in China, on the one hand, befriended the rich and powerful and the triads through missionary work, and learned about various aspects of Chinese society, economy, and military intelligence, in order to establish modern church schools, hospitals, and the media, and became an important force in shaping the pro-Western Chinese social elite class.

The Triad was originally a secret Chinese folk society whose purpose was to oppose the Ching and restore the Ming, and many of its members later embraced Christianity. The Triad's anti-Qing armed campaign also required large-scale financial support, so many members joined the East India Company's opium sales network to China through the Church's intermediary, becoming the mainstay of opium smuggling along the Guangdong coast. The Triad, with its anti-Qing motto, was tantamount to receiving indirect financial subsidies from the Financial City of London. The future development of the Triad has deep roots in Hong Xiuquan's Worship of God Society, the secret association of Kang (Yau-wai) Liang (Qi-chao) Tan (Zhutong) Tang (Cai-chang) and the Alliance Society. Hong Xiuquan's right-hand man, Feng Yunshan, who was in charge of ideological work, worked under the Christian Huafu Society in his early years; Yang Xiuqing, who was in charge of the military struggle, was also involved in the Triad's opium smuggling business in the Pearl River Valley; and the Liangguang Triad participated directly in the Jintian Uprising. After the failure of the reform of the Wuxu Law, Tan Zutong was killed, and Tang Caichang, a leading general of the Tan family in the Restorationist faction, launched an uprising of the Hubei-Guang Triad to hold a self-reliant army. The early uprisings of the Union against the Qing dynasty were all based on the strength of the Triad. The Shanghai Youth Gang of the Triad played an important role in Chiang Kai-shek's "April 12" coup and consolidation of power.

It is a special agency authorized by the imperial court to deal directly with foreign businessmen and is a trading company, which also performs certain diplomatic functions and must guarantee its foreign business partners. After the Opium War, Thirteen Banks mostly turned into foreign buyers and were the source of the modern Chinese buying class.

The East India Company also controlled and manipulated a portion of the Manchu bureaucrats through bribery and drug addiction. Start with China's superstructure to protect and open up the opium trade. The company penetrated the Beijing imperial court through the northern opium trade network centered in Tianjin. By the time of the Opium War, a considerable number of high-ranking Manchu officials were already in control and at their disposal. Among them were Mu Chang'a, a university scholar, Qi Shan, the governor of the Zhili province, and Jie Ying, the head of the Dzongren government. In response to this, Marx had an eloquent argument:

> "The British bribed the Chinese authorities, the customs officials and the officials in general, and this is the latest result of the Chinese legal boycott of opium. Together with the opium box, bribery invaded the bureaucratic lungs of the 'heavenly dynasty' and undermined the pillars of the patriarchal system."[14]

This group of people formed the source of the Western faction of the later Qing government.

In 1839, when the ambitious Lin Zexu came to Guangdong as a minister of imperial affairs to enforce the prohibition of smoking, the great national hero was confronted with such a well-organized, financially strong, armed and powerful opium empire. As soon as Lin Zexu took office, he severely cracked down on the Triad's underground

---

[14] *Opium Trade*, Marx.

FINANCIAL HIGH FRONTIERS

smuggling and drug trafficking network, ordered foreigners to surrender opium, and carried out a world-shattering campaign to stop smoking. But Lin Zexu would never have imagined how powerful his opponent was, challenging the entire British Empire and the core financial strategy that mattered to the life and death of international bankers!

The opium trade led to a massive outflow of silver from China, triggering a serious "silver is expensive and money is cheap" currency crisis in China. For more than 100 years, from the establishment of the Qing Dynasty to the early 19th century, China's silver and copper dual currency mechanism worked well, and the ratio was basically stable at 1 tael of silver to 1,000 yuan of copper. By the eve of the Opium War, silver had soared to 1,600 cents on the dollar. The peasants, craftsmen and ordinary people usually receive copper money, but the payment of various taxes is converted into silver, thus adding to the economic burden. Due to the people's difficult life, the payment of taxes was naturally delayed, as a result of which the provinces defaulted more and more on taxes, causing the Qing government's financial capacity to decline sharply. Before the opium trade began on a large scale, until 1781 during the Qianlong reign, the state stockpile of silver reached 70 million taels, and by 1789 it was about 60 million taels. With the flood of opium, by 1850 there were just over 8 million taels left, no longer enough for a war.

It was the opium that destroyed the silver-money standard, the cornerstone of the financial high frontier of the Qing Empire, and with it a large trade deficit, declining fiscal revenues, hardship for the people, a serious division between rich and poor, and increasingly acute social conflicts. The international bankers, on the other hand, took the huge amount of silver from the opium hedge and established the "Bank of England of China", and seized the high financial frontier of the Qing Empire: the Central Bank.

The establishment of HSBC marked the beginning of a financial colonial era in China's modern history. In the course of HSBC's seizure of the central bank of the Qing Empire, a new Sassoonian empire emerged, replacing the East India Company as the latest manipulator to execute an opium financial strategy.

The Sassoon Family: The Rothschilds of the East

Sassoon belonged to the same Sephardic Jews as the Rothschilds and lived on the Islamized Iberian Peninsula (present-day Spain) since ancient times, engaged in the business of goldsmithing and coin-exchange, and often acted as an agent for the Genoese banking family, doing credit checks, collecting and lending. In the process, it gradually established itself as a commercial credit and financial network, and in the 1590s, as Iberian Christians drove out the Islamic regime, Sephardic Jews were expelled from Spain and Portugal.

The Rothschilds went into exile in Germany to pursue their old business and later became "court bankers" of the German royal family. Another Jewish financial family fled to the Netherlands, Belgium, and soon made a comeback with a network of business relationships that had accumulated over the years, and was involved in the establishment of the Bank of Amsterdam, ABN AMRO and the Dutch East India Company. It was with the financial support of Dutch Jewish bankers of 2 million Dutch guilders that William III of England landed in England from the Netherlands in 1688 with 15,000 men and began the "Glorious Revolution". The Sassoon family, on the other hand, moved all the way east to Baghdad, the center of commerce and trade in the Persian Gulf region of the Middle East. There, the Sassoon family, with its unique Jewish financial acumen and experience, took advantage of Islamic teachings prohibiting usury and provided financial lending to Middle Eastern commerce with Jewish facilities not subject to Islamic regulations, and soon became the premier financial family in the Persian Gulf region, serving long as the chief financial officer of Baghdad and becoming the patriarch of the entire Jewish community in Baghdad, known as "Nasi", the King of the Jews.

But the good times were not long, at the end of the 18th century and the beginning of the 19th century, the anti-Semitic sentiment in the Baghdad area was high, the Ottoman Turkish officials in Baghdad, began to mass expulsion of Jews, as the "king of the Jews" of the Sassoon family bore the brunt, had to move the family to Bombay, India in 1832. David Sassoon, the founder of the Sassoonian Empire, has started a new saga in India.[15]

Due to the late arrival of the Sassoon family in India, the huge cake of the opium trade was long left. While the East India Company has disintegrated, the three foreign-owned giants, backed by the Baring family, continue to monopolize China's opium imports and India's opium supply chain. In the whole chain of the opium trade, production, transportation, insurance, sales, financing, exchange, almost all of them are in the hands of JIHUA, the needle can't get in, the water can't get out. In the opium empire, tightly controlled by the Baring family, the new Jewish Sassoon would have been more than capable of intervening.

In London's Financial City, the emerging Rothschilds had already overwhelmed Bahrain, and the Rothschilds also wanted to cut their own piece of the opium business, suffering from Bahrain's high degree of control over the East India Company's bulk traders. Sassoon's presence fits perfectly with the strategic development plan of the Rothschilds, who are also Sephardic Jews and whose ancestors might have been better off as a family, so the two sides hit it off right away. With the powerful financial backing of the Rothschilds, Sassoon was ready to shake off his bladder and go big.

After careful research, Sassoon found a glaring loophole in JIH's opium control over India, namely JIH's failure to control the poppy plantations in the Indian hinterland. Sassoon seized the opportunity to capitalize on his strong capital power by lending up to 3/4 of his money to Indian opium traders in the interior. Purchasers from all over the world heard about it, and Sassoon took control of the source of opium cultivation and monopolized the source with a swift and unprecedented force. In fact, Hu Xueyan's thinking is almost identical to Sassoon's, the difference being that Sassoon is backed by the international financial hegemon Rothschild family.

By 1871, the situation was clear, and JIH was defeated in the battle for the source of opium against Sassoon, who was recognized as the main holder of the entire stock of opium in India and China, controlling

---

[15] *Sassoon Group in Old China*, by Zhang Zhongli and Chen Zengnian, Shanghai Academy of Social Sciences, 1985, pp. 3–5.

70% of the total amount of all kinds of opium! That's the power of a monopoly!

Backed by this strength, Rothschild's daughter married into the Sassoon family, and from then on the commercial alliance relationship was consolidated and maintained by the patriarchal forces of Jewish tradition. The Sassoon Empire shook the Far East. From this point on, the Far East's ocean voyages entered the Sassoonian era.

The Jewish super-sensitivity to money is no exception in the Sassoon family. When the Sassoons completed their opium monopoly, they were so well capitalized that they began to think of a central bank as well, and enjoyed the super thrill of controlling the issuance of money. There was no central bank in the Far East at this time, and this opportunity was again seized by Sassoon.

HSBC: I'm in charge of your turf

> *"Of all the elements of political economy, money is the most crucial; of all monetary systems, the power to create money is the most central. But few economists can be found with a single word on the divine power of this country."*
> —American monetary historian DeMarr.

In early 1864, two business plans for the establishment of a bank in China were laid out on the desk of old Sassoon. One is a "Royal Bank of China" for the Chinese financial market, started by a local British businessman in Mumbai, and the other is a "Bank of Hong Kong and Shanghai" proposal by a young Scottish shipping businessman. It was the plan of that young man with no banking experience that finally struck old Sassoon. This Scottish lad, Thomas So Shi Lan, was already in his thirties as the Director of Operations of the famous British Steamship Company in Hong Kong and Chairman of the Whampoa Dockyard Company in Hong Kong.

Old Sassoon instantly liked the idea. As a bank headquartered in Hong Kong and Shanghai, it would be more convenient to have information links than foreign banks with branches only in Hong Kong and Shanghai, which was especially important in the 19th century when transportation and communication were not yet developed. The market is fast approaching, and those banks that need to turn to their head offices across the ocean will be at a disadvantage in their future competition with HSBC.

FINANCIAL HIGH FRONTIERS

Old Sassoon approved the project immediately.

Among HSBC's major shareholders are, in addition to Sassoon, Baoshun and Chichang Yang Bank. However, Baoshun Yang-Hang went bankrupt during the cotton bubble crisis that swept the world in 1866, and Qichang Yang-Hang was also hit by the crisis and faded out of the Chinese market in the early 1870s. So Sassoon's Bank, which had become the new hegemon of opium, became the mainstay of HSBC. HSBC actually became a key pawn in the Rothschild-Sassoon alliance's financial layout in the Far East.

Such a bank would inevitably lead to a firm boycott by the Baring-owned Jardine Matheson Bank, based both on the rivalry between Bahrain and Rothschild forces in the financial city of London and on a real conflict of interest.

HSBC was born just in time for the financial crisis brought about by the end of the American Civil War.

The core strategic industry of the world industrial system at that time was the textile industry, the main raw material required by the textile industry was raw cotton. The world's major cotton-producing regions are in India and the southern states of the United States. With the outbreak of the American Civil War, the North, which held the right to regulate the sea, imposed a naval blockade on the South, whose supply of raw cotton to the world market was immediately interrupted. The British cotton industry turned to Indian cotton, and the price of Indian cotton soared. The cotton markets of Mumbai and Kolkata immediately became casinos for speculators large and small. The cotton bubble spawned an even bigger financial bubble. From 1862 to 1865, 19 banks were born. There were as many as seven colonial banks registered in 1864 alone. In Hong Kong and Shanghai, the number of new British banks has also increased dramatically, and these shell banks have far less in their vaults than they claim in their prospectuses.

Just then, the "bad news" came that the American Civil War was over! The cotton crisis that rocked the global financial sector has begun. The Financial City of London bore the brunt, with 17 banks failing in one year in 1866.

The shock waves of the financial tsunami quickly spread to the Far East, and in 1866, Hong Kong, Shanghai, the first financial panic in more than 20 years, a series of foreign banks and local money banks closed down. When the waves of the financial tsunami receded, the only ones still standing on the beach were the veteran banks, such as L'Oréal Bank, Le Meridien Bank, Standard Chartered Bank, Banque de France and HSBC.

However, a wave has not yet subsided, it is in the second year of the financial tsunami, HSBC's pillar – the old Baoshun Bank was "drowned", at this time the Baring family in the financial crisis and the Rothschild family under the double blow has its own insecurity, unable to take care of the Far East's little brother, can only watch Baoshun Bank was dragged into the cotton crisis. The collapse of Baoshun hit the fledgling HSBC hard.

At this point, it was Sassoon & Yang-Hsing that stood up to the crisis. From 1866 onwards, the Sassoon family remitted all profits from the opium trade in China through the HSBC Bank. In the face of the world's financial tsunami, the only business that still had excess profits was the opium trade. This "currency", which maintains the economic lifeline of the Financial City of London and the British Empire, once again saved the financial circulation system of the Far East of the British Empire with the economic blood of the Chinese people, and became a bargaining chip for the international bankers to complete the reshuffling of the Far East's interest pattern.

At a time when the major banks were struggling to hold on to the crisis, HSBC, supported by Sassoon's huge opium profits, seized the great opportunity to start sweeping Hong Kong and Shanghai's financial peers.

In June 1866, Far Eastern banks, such as Dahlia, convened foreign banks such as Standard Chartered Bank, Bank of France and Bank of France to discuss the financial risks of the "post-crisis era", and finally decided to shorten the six-month commercial promissory note, which was normally used, to four months. One is to reduce the bank's own risk and the other is to adapt to the new business trading environment. As of January 1867, no more bills of exchange were bought and sold in Chinese branches that were due more than four months.

The history of commercial promissory notes dates back to around the 13th century AD. With the development of the Crusades and the naval trade, a huge market for trade and cargo shipping rapidly developed in the Italian region of the Mediterranean, and Italy pioneered the commercial promissory note based on the demand of the naval trade. The most important feature of the bulk maritime trade is the long distances and the long hours, which comes with certain risks, so buyers and sellers are hesitant to pay and ship. Buyers who pay cash right away worry about what to do in case the distant seller doesn't ship or the goods go awry while sailing, while sellers think that if they ship first, they'll end up in big trouble if they don't get paid. There are only two ways to break this impasse, one is for the buyer to be reputable and never to default, and the other is for a reputable guarantor to guarantee the success of the transaction. Since everyone does business in Italy, a local with a family and a business is naturally the best choice for a sponsor. Thus, merchant bankers sprang up in large numbers in Italy to secure payment from the buyer, who simply wrote a note of indebtedness stating when and how much to be paid in the future, which the Italian signed and drew. If the buyer is overdue, the Italians will pay the full amount on their behalf, turning back to the Italians for the buyer theory. The seller got this indebted note and happily shipped it. This note of indebtedness is an early commercial promissory note. The Italians are sitting on a guarantee fee.

When a seller is in desperate need of cash and the bill of exchange has not expired, he can take it to a merchant banker to sell it at a discount, which is called a bill of exchange discount. The merchant banker eats the bill of exchange at a discount and then sits back and makes a profit by waiting for the bill of exchange to become due for the full amount. This discounted price is actually hidden interest, and the deeper the discount, the higher the interest. The Catholic Church at the time strictly prohibited usury, so bill of exchange discounting became a workaround for loan sharking. When paper transactions are active, bills of exchange are essentially readily realizable and function almost as if they were cash. In England in the 18th and 19th centuries, money orders actually became an important part of the money supply before new instruments such as bank notes, cheques and lines of credit began to circulate on a large scale.

The term of a commercial bill of exchange often matches the time of transportation of the goods, and if the goods have arrived for a long time and the term of the bill of exchange has not yet arrived, it is equivalent to the buyer's credit for a long time, taking up the seller's funds, and at the same time, the risk of the bank assuming the buyer to pay the guarantee increases accordingly.

In view of the fact that the sea time between Europe and China has been greatly reduced due to the increased speed of ships, and the reluctance to take too much risk, the bank proposed to compress the term of the bill of exchange. However, compressing the term of the bill of exchange equates to shrinking the size of credit and raising the funding and credit threshold for buyers, with the effect of turning away many customers.

This inter-industry agreement creates a huge opportunity for HSBC to expand its customer resources. When other banks refused to buy bills of exchange due six months, HSBC reversed course and received large sums of money under the protection of Sassoon's huge funds. Merchants with 6-month money orders in hand have no choice but to go to HSBC to do discounting, and naturally the discount is more. HSBC only needs to hold a bill of exchange to maturity to receive the full amount of funds, and of course the benefits are even more substantial. At the same time, HSBC throws the high price of its own four-month promissory note to rivals rushing to receive the goods, thus gaining arbitrage room to buy low and sell high. In half a year, HSBC's foreign exchange business quickly rose from 9.2 million taels of silver to 13 million taels of silver. In less than 10 months, several other banks will have to "surrender" to HSBC and go back to the old path of 6-month promissory notes.

In the war of money orders, HSBC won the flag, indicating that the title of "China's Bank of England" has changed hands. HSBC has since become the new leader of the foreign banking community in the Far East.

Another unique trick of HSBC is to absorb large amounts of deposits from Chinese depositors, especially the huge deposits from China's elite class of officials. In the late Qing Dynasty novel, "The Current State of Officialdom", there is a story about a clan of the Qing government that was ordered to Shanghai to investigate a case in which a bureaucrat had deposited stolen money with HSBC. As soon as he arrived in Shanghai, he was dressed in official attire, sitting in a sedan chair with eight carriers, and came straight to HSBC with some of his entourage. But when he came to the door of the bank, he was blocked from driving. The gatekeeper says you have to enter through the back door. The feudal lord had to walk to the back door of the bank on foot and stand there for half a day, but still no one paid him any attention. Later, he learned that HSBC kept the deposits of Chinese depositors there strictly confidential and refused any investigation by Chinese officials. He had no choice but to reply to his superiors with "no foreigners allowed to check the accounts" and the matter was closed.

Relying on the power of the British Empire, HSBC refused to allow the Qing government to investigate any of its customers' money. Because of this privilege, many warlords, bureaucrats and landowners at the time used HSBC as the safest vault of wealth, sending in all the loot from the years.

In 1872, the British Hong Kong Government gave HSBC permission to issue small dollar bills of $1. Subsequently, HSBC's small amount of banknotes, and quickly circulated throughout South China, in March 1874, Shanghai "Zi Lin Xi" published in February 1874, the four major British banks – Li Ru, Standard Chartered, Li and HSBC's banknotes issue amount, in the actual issue of 3.5 million yuan banknotes, HSBC's banknotes accounted for more than 51%.

At this time, HSBC had become the largest bank in Hong Kong, the cashier bank of the British Hong Kong government, the settlement bank of all its counterparts in China, becoming the veritable "Bank of England in China".

Jardine's expulsion from the opium trade by Sassoon became more realistic at this point, and in the face of the strength of HSBC, Jardine's new leaders, the Keswick family, had to consider their relationship with HSBC more positively. In the later joint campaign to eliminate Hu Xueyan, the two sides reached more tacit understanding.

However, the Rothschild Sassoon Group's expectation for HSBC is not just that it will act as a bank to manage foreign banks in China, but that it will become a bank to manage the entire Chinese financial system, a true "central bank".

In order to perform the functions of a central bank, it must be able to manage and control financial institutions in China, which is the Chinese system of money banks and ticket numbers. The Qing government at this time was able to rely on its own bank and ticket system to keep it going. Both the money bank and the ticket number also provide substantial financing for China's foreign trade and control the source of wealth for China's vast private economy. International bankers can only truly achieve financial colonization of China if they also control the Chinese system of money banks and ticket numbers.

Ticket Money: Why it didn't grow into an international financial empire

The most distinctive of the financial institutions that have grown up in China are the Shanxi Gang's ticket numbers and the Ning Shao Gang's money banks. To put it colloquially, ticket numbers play with tickets, and moneychangers play with money.

In the early days of Venice and Genoa, and later in the Netherlands and England, finance and trade were almost twin brothers, mutually reinforcing and borrowing from each other. Almost all of Europe's earliest financial institutions had their origins in firms, and the growing demand for financial services in business activities eventually led to the separation of professional financial services from commercial trading activities. China's ticket number development is no exception.

The fact that the ticket number originates from Shanxi, rather than the economically developed and shipping-friendly coastal region, is indeed odd, but it makes sense when you think about it. The Jin merchants are known as one of China's top ten merchant gangs, and their drive to travel south and north and their tenacity to endure hardship made them stand out early on in China's business landscape. The Jin merchants were all over the world, and as early as the early years of the Qing Dynasty, two major trading systems were formed – the grain ship gang and the camel gang. The former runs around the provinces and river ports, while the latter travels far and wide, reaching Mongolia and Moscow, becoming the largest trader of tea, silk, cloth, grain, iron and other commodities in China, establishing China's earliest and most extensive trade network.

Unlike the rise of the Jewish financial family, the Jin Shang's bill exchange network is derived from the vast domestic international trade network spanning tens of thousands of kilometers and employing hundreds of thousands of people, while the Jewish financial network originated from pure money exchange, deposit lending, bill trading and other pure money business. What the two have in common is the scale effect and quick and convenient advantage of a strong network radiation capability. Once the network advantage is established, it is almost impossible for later competitors to step in. This is also the core reason why the later southern money banks have not been able to overtake the Shanxi ticket in the field of remote exchange business. The lack of a sufficiently large network has led to the general small size of the money banks, which ultimately makes it difficult to form a large international financial empire similar to the Jewish financial industry.

The financial network forms the third pillar of the financial high frontier, after the money standard, the central bank.

Due to the huge coverage of the Jin trading network, in the era of extremely underdeveloped transportation, funds were often turned over only once a year, severely limiting the expansion of business. At the same time, the remote delivery of cash is too long and the road is not safe, so there is an objective need for a convenient way to transfer funds remotely, which is the core business of the ticket number from its inception: remote money exchange.

The initial foreign exchange business was just for convenience. For example, the "Xiyucheng Pigment Zhuang" in Pingyao, Shanxi, has set up branches in Sichuan, Beijing, Shanxi, etc., and relatives and friends in Beijing want to remit a sum of silver to Sichuan, they just need to hand the silver to the Beijing branch, then the Beijing branch writes to inform the Sichuan branch, and relatives and friends in Sichuan can get the silver at the local branch. Little did I know that this exchange model would immediately attract a lot of business and people were willing to pay a 1% fee for such a service. The owner of the pigment bank, Lui Hetai, perceptively discovered this potentially powerful business model and immediately abandoned the traditional pigment bank business and set up the first ticket number "Rishengchang" in China around 1823.

Before the Opium War, China's total trade amounted to 300 million taels of silver per year, and if 100 million taels of silver had to be exchanged remotely, its profit would be as much as 1 million taels of silver. After several years of operation, Rishengchang Ticketing has made huge profits in the specialized business of money exchange and deposit. It is said that during the 50 years from Daoguang to Tongzhi, the Zaedong Li family received more than 2 million taels of silver in dividends from the Rishengchang Ticket Company. Encouraged by the success of the Rishengchang ticket number, Shanxi merchants set up or changed their ticket numbers, greatly promoting the development of commercial trade at that time. In the following nearly a century, the Shanxi ticket number basically monopolized the exchange business of the Qing Dynasty, gained the reputation of "the world of exchange and communication".

The main business of the ticket number is remote money transfer. Its development shows the basic posture of expansion from north to south and radiation from west to west. Due to the increasing trade between North and Central China and Mongolia and Russia, the number of tickets was set up in more than 30 towns inland with more than 200 in accordance with the economic situation, with the center of gravity in the north and the semicolon centered on the capital. In the medium term, land and sea were combined, with the frontier and coastal areas being set up with the four major centres, Beijing, Tianjin, Shanghai and Han, becoming the four major centres of ticket numbers. During the pre-Guang Hsiu period, the total number and semicolon of ticket numbers reached more than 400, forming a huge financial network. Funds, whether commercial, governmental, or private, end up flocking to this financial highway system that radiates across the country due to the quick, safe, and convenient nature of the ticket numbers. By the beginning of the 20th century, the total amount of money exchanged by the 22 major bills in the country was about 820 million taels of silver[16] and the total profit was about 8.2 million taels of silver, which is about 1/10th of the total revenue of the Qing government for a year!

On the basis of this, it was hoped to develop into a "financial highway system" similar to that laid down by Jewish financiers in the West, thus monopolizing the arteries of credit and capital flows. The fundamental reasons for its decline are twofold: first, the lack of location, the failure to establish its own headquarters in Shanghai, the center of international and domestic trade, thus distancing decision-making from the center of trade financial services with the greatest potential for growth, and the loss of opportunities to dominate the emerging commercial bill of exchange transactions and other financial markets; second, the failure to create a financing system similar to Europe's war bonds and national bonds, confining the business to the field of exchange, and the self-imposed encroachment of foreign banks and official banks gradually eroded the exchange business, which is essential for survival.

Financial markets, especially those that form the core of state financing – the trading market for treasury bonds and various types of instruments – form the fourth cornerstone of the financial high frontier.

---

[16] *History of Shanxi Ticket Numbers*, by Huang Jianhui, Shanxi Economic Press, 2002, p. 341.

China's local financial institutions, both ticket numbers and money banks, have failed to fulfill this great historical mission.

The origins of the Qianzhuang are very similar to the main business of the Jewish financial family of the same period: currency exchange.

The core of the world's Jewish financial family can almost always find their source in Germany. There is a reason why Germany is the birthplace of the modern financial family. Geographically, Germany is the connecting point between the east and west of Europe, especially Berlin, which is the geographical centre of Europe and a transport hub, with businessmen coming and going from south to north and from east to west. The result was a situation where all the currencies of Europe were concentrated in Berlin. From the beginning of the Roman Empire, Berlin was the center of currency exchange. By the time Napoleon occupied the area, the demand for currency exchange had become even stronger. The accumulation of 2,000 years of experience in the buying and selling of money, combined with the urgent need for real currency exchange, made Germany a natural fertile ground for the Jewish financial family to flourish.[17]

The rise of the Chinese money bank is no exception. Since the establishment of the silver standard in the Ming Dynasty, there has been a parallel circulation of silver and copper money, the ratio between silver and copper money to follow the market. Since silver taels were too valuable for ordinary people to use directly in the market to buy goods, copper money was the real currency in circulation in daily life, while silver taels were mainly used for large transactions, official salaries, soldiers' pay and fiscal taxes. At the same time, the silver itself is also very complex, with different weights, shapes and colors of silver in different places, coupled with the influx of various foreign silver dollars, creating a huge demand for silver money exchange and the evaluation of the color of silver.

Especially after the Opium War, Shanghai, as the intersection of international and domestic trade, the demand for currency exchange is more urgent, with Ningbo-Shaoxing-Shanghai as the center, the Ning Shao Gang money bank was born. In order to solve the problem of

---

[17] *Currency Wars 2: The World of Jin Quan*, by Song Hongbing, China United Publishing Company, 2009

conversion of silver taels by domestic merchants and the problem of valuation of silver dollars by foreign merchants, from 1856 onwards, the Shanghai Money Bank industry began to adopt a virtual unit of accounting for silver taels, called "guiyuan". This invention has greatly facilitated the commercial bookkeeping of merchants everywhere.

In addition to the basic business of currency exchange, Ning Shao Gang's money bank business takes full advantage of the Shanghai International Domestic Trade Center to creatively develop a Chinese-specific commercial money order system that integrates foreign financial capital and China's trade market into a flexible and effective platform between domestic and foreign trade.

At the beginning of the Five Kou business, foreign banks entered Shanghai to purchase Chinese specialties and sell foreign industrial products. The first big problem they encountered was a lack of business trust in Chinese suppliers and buyers. The fear of not receiving payment for sourcing Chinese goods and the fear of not receiving payment for selling foreign products is exactly the same as the problem experienced by Italian traders in the 13th century. Seizing this great business opportunity, the money banks of the Ning Shao Gang created the "banknote", a bill of exchange instrument, which greatly contributed to the rapid expansion of domestic international trade.

Banknotes have appeared in Shanghai in the early 19th century, but at that time the banknotes are essentially silver notes, "banknotes, the bank because of the lending or merchant's request, and issued in bearer form, payment and the holder of the note also".[18] Its main feature is immediacy, rather than the deferred payment based on real trade in commercial drafts.

A true commercial draft stretches the term of payment on a timeline and can be discounted, so when a commercial draft is used as a means of payment, it amounts to an expansion of the size of the credit within its term. Most importantly, it is an expansion of credit based on real trade.

The essence of a commercial bill of exchange is that it is a short-term trade currency issued against trade, which is different from a debt

---

[18] *Outline of the Financial Organization of Shanghai*, by Yang Yinpu, Commercial Press, 1930, p. 46.

currency issued against debt. Commercial bills of exchange constitute the most important means of credit expansion in the era of commercial capitalism. This was followed by the credit expansion of colonial capitalism, secured by national debt, industrial capitalism, secured by industrial debt, and the credit expansion of the post-industrial era, secured by personal debt.[19]

The banknotes invented by the Ning Shao Gang were bills of exchange that were cashed in 5 to 20 days by Chinese merchants applying for "trade-based" banknotes, and were paid for by the banknotes when purchasing foreign goods. The foreign banks generally do not trust the Chinese merchants, but they are still quite recognized by the money banks, especially the powerful ones. The reason for this is the foreign buyout system commonly used by foreign banks. Not only are they familiar with the strength of the local bank, but they also have unlimited liability in the event of an accident. If the Chinese businessman can not pay for the goods when due, the bank is responsible for advances to the foreign bank, and then the bank will go to the Chinese businessman to settle accounts, or the bank can pay directly to the foreign bank, and then collect from the Chinese businessman. In this way, the foreign bank's goods are sold well, the bank issued by the bank is to charge interest, so the bank's profits were expanded and new business was added. Chinese businessmen, on the other hand, obtained short-term financing to expand their business. It's a financial innovation with the best of all three worlds. Moreover, the holders of these banknotes can get cash at any time by discounting at many money banks or foreign banks.

When HSBC entered Shanghai, it was faced with a situation where foreign banks coexisted with local money banks. Foreign banks have the advantage of being well capitalized and having complete control over international exchange operations. The advantage of the money bank is that it knows the market and occupies the position of a credit intermediary for the issuance of commercial bills of exchange for domestic trade, especially the lucrative and irreplaceable operation of the money exchange base based on the domestic monetary system, and therefore also has a place.

---

[19] *The Lost Science of Money*, p. 271.

Since HSBC has the ambition to dominate the financial world, it will certainly use its strength to subdue the local financial lords. When the bill of exchange battle that swept other foreign banks ended with HSBC's victory, it turned its attention to the homegrown money bank. Thanks to its ability to pull in deposits from the wealthy Chinese at a very low cost, and the high profits from financing the opium trade, HSBC's total assets reached HK$211 million by the end of the 19th century, establishing itself as the leading financial hegemon in the Far East. HSBC took full advantage of its own strong capital and began to use ticket splitting on a large scale to control the money bank's funds.[20]

With limited bank-owned capital, there is more than enough to eat more of the commercial money order cake. It is this weakness that HSBC sees, and only then lends the cheap excess funds to the bank in Shanghai, which only needs to give the banknote as collateral to HSBC, can get a credit loan. As a result, Shanghai money banks have borrowed large amounts of money from HSBC. HSBC can also directly acquire discounted banknotes in the market and re-discount them, taking advantage of the spread between the deposit and the re-discount. The bankers in the discounted acquisition of other bankers' banknotes, could have held the maturity of the gains, but in order to speed up the turnover of funds to obtain more profits, as long as HSBC offers the right price, will not hesitate to resell these banknotes to HSBC, pocket the profits and then go to do new discounted trading.

In this way, while Shanghai's money banks can access HSBC's capital to make their business bigger, they also have to become subsidiaries of HSBC as the source of their capital is controlled by HSBC. HSBC can tighten its monies by refusing to split the notes or raising the split rate, or it can raise the rediscount rate, which is a deep discount on the notes that the bank wants to resell to HSBC, making it unprofitable for the bank to get the spread between the two discounts, thus forcing them to slow down or stop the first discounting. This will result in the entire money bank having to reduce its financing of the trade due to the slowdown in the turnover of commercial drafts. The ultimate consequence is that the lack of capital prevents Chinese merchants from acquiring local products such as tea and silk farmers, and farmers and craftsmen are forced to sell the fruits of their labor at

---

[20] *The Formation and Development of a Modern Financial Centre in Shanghai,* by Chen Zengnian, Shanghai Academy of Social Sciences Press, 2006, p. 17.

lower prices. And at this time, HSBC behind the foreign bank shareholders "just" to be able to eat cheaply, and then in the international market, high prices thrown out, get a big profit.

While the Chinese financial forces represented by Hu Xueyan are engaged in a deadly struggle against foreign financial forces, HSBC can easily defeat any trade resistance by tightening the taps on the money supply and creating a monetary crunch.

With HSBC holding the reins of the Clear Empire central bank, it is unlikely that any home-grown financial institution will develop into a competitor sufficient to challenge the core strategy of international bankers.

Foreign buyers: China's special phenomenon

The word "buyer" comes from Portuguese and originally meant a servant in southern China who was responsible for purchasing in the market for European merchants. It later evolved to refer specifically to local businessmen who help foreign banks expand their business in China. In order to qualify as a buyer, they were often required to pay a certain amount of deposit, which would be deducted by the foreign bank if the business did not reach the expected size or incurred a loss. Likewise, if they do well, they will enjoy a share of the profits of the foreign bank.

From a purely commercial point of view, a buyer is a normal commercial agent and there is nothing wrong with it. However, the nature of the problem changes when foreign banks are not engaged in fair trade, but in oppressive trade; when foreign banks are not engaged in ordinary financial services, but in manipulative behaviour that controls the money supply. The more powerful the foreign banks and foreign banks are, the larger the scale of their business, and the deeper the harm to the Chinese economy. In the process, foreign buyers, who help foreign financial capital expand its sphere of influence, become important accomplices in harming domestic interests.

From the case of Hu Xueyan's hunting, one can clearly see that the foreign buying class has a major lethal effect on China's economy, finance, trade and livelihood. Without the dedicated efforts of foreign buyers, foreign and domestic banks could not have gained that much control in China.

Is it equal business dealings, or control and manipulation? The correct determination of the intentions and actions of foreign financial capital is at the heart of all historical judgments of merit and right and wrong.

Throughout the world, the phenomenon of foreign buyers and agents is almost a Chinese characteristic. Neither in Asia, in India, in Japan, in Korea, nor in the American continent has such a special class emerged. This is a phenomenon unique to China's semi-colonial state. In the course of Western expansion, the Americas, Africa were first colonized, India in Asia and Southeast Asia were conquered later, and in these thoroughly colonized areas, Western ruling powers could exercise direct vertical domination without the need for local middlemen to take control, so there was no need for a buying class. The situation in China is relatively unique in that the Western colonists arrived too late and China is relatively strong to rule vertically and completely for a short period of time, so it has to rely on a middle class to take over control, a class of bureaucrats and buyers.

On a deeper level, however, where the ruling colony has to completely destroy the local script, which carries the genes of civilization and maintains a complex national identity and spiritual belonging, and where the conquest of a country cannot destroy its script, the ruler is either assimilated or expelled. The ruled, who identify with the ruler both mentally and emotionally, are the only ones who can rule successfully, as has been the case in no other colony in the world. The colonial empires of Portugal, Spain, the Netherlands, Britain, France, Germany, the United States and Japan were the first to eradicate the colonial script, causing the ruled peoples to suffer complete and total collective amnesia and to re-accept the spiritual and emotional indoctrination of the colonial empire in order to achieve its "long-lasting peace". In today's world, the widespread poverty and backwardness in the former colonial areas is largely a legacy of the colonial era. What is terrible is not the plundering of the material wealth of these regions, but the extreme disorder of the spiritual world and the total fragmentation of the belief systems caused by the destruction of the writings of the colonial countries, and the rebuilding of faith in one's own civilization is far from being as effective as economic development and material prosperity in the short term.

China's good fortune lies in the tenacity of its Chinese characters and the enormous civilizational system that has been built on them. Neither the cunning of Britain, nor the greed of Russia, nor the arrogance of Japan, could have completely conquered Chinese civilization. It was in this reality of helplessness that Western colonial empires had to borrow and rely on foreign buyers to achieve the plundering and control of wealth.

Under the circumstances of the total fall of the financial high frontier, neither the foreign movement, nor the Hundred Days Reform Act, nor even the overthrow of the Qing dynasty, could fundamentally change the state of China's semi-colonialization.

Japan was also faced with the colonial ambitions of the Western powers, and the door to commerce was also broken down, but it suffered the opposite fate to China. The fundamental difference between the success of the Meiji Restoration and the failure of the foreign affairs movement was that Japan held its own financial frontier and foreign financial forces failed to effectively control the Japanese monetary system. Of particular importance is the fact that Japan did not form a strong class of foreign buyers. As a result, it is difficult for foreign banks to do business in Japan, let alone control its financial lifeblood.

Even after the success of the Meiji Restoration, Japan's total bank capital was less than half of that amount until 1900. However, with the exception of HSBC, which is still operating, other foreign banks have failed. The number of domestic banks in Japan, on the other hand, soared from zero to 1,867 in 1901. The Meiji Restoration, which was preceded by the Meiji Restoration, modernized industry almost entirely with the support of credit from the country's banking system, making Japan the only successful model in Asia to emerge from the colonization of the Western powers on equal footing with them.

It was Japan's firm grip on its high financial frontiers and its constant supply of credit for its industry, defence and trade that gave rise to a rapidly rising industrial power.

CHAPTER II

The Meiji Restoration and the Western Movement

Why did the Meiji Restoration succeed and the Foreign Affairs Movement fail? Why is there no foreign buying class in Japan? Why did foreign banks land in Japan with powerful capital and end up almost completely destroyed? Why is Japan able to hold on to its financial high frontier?

History has left China with too many painful memories, and has raised many very pointed questions for later Chinese. The success of the Meiji Restoration in Japan and the failure of China's foreign affairs movement, as well as the outcome of the Sino-Japanese War, brought more excitement and entanglement to China than the defeat of the British Empire.

The history of Japanese finance is far older and more advanced than most Chinese people think. The Mitsui family's financial experience predates the Bank of England by 10 years, and the Shanxi Bills by more than 100 years; the establishment of the modern banking system in Japan, more than 30 years ahead of China; the formation of the central bank of Japan, 28 years ahead of China; the unified currency of Japan, the yen, more than 70 years ahead of the French currency of China; Japan established the first monetary cornerstone of the gold standard in Asia; Japan's financial network, complete control of the country's economic system; Japan's Yokohama Shogin Bank, helped the country's traders to regain the right to set prices in one go.

Japan's success in defending its high financial frontier against foreign financial forces was a key prerequisite for the success of the Meiji Restoration.

Japan finally discovered the secret of bank credit and, with limited gold and silver currency, fully mobilized the nation's resources with the high leverage of finance, prying open the doors of modern industrialization, while the amazing wealth created by industry and trade drove the wheels of the Japanese economy into the fast lane of world power.

In contrast, in China, the foreign affairs movement, typified by the Hanye Ping Iron and Steel Union Company, struggled to survive in an extremely harsh financial and ecological environment, and, despite its key advantages and good resources, ended up in Japanese hands.

The experience of history shows that finance is the high point of the modern economy and that the financial high frontier is the second national defense of the modern country!

Wangzheng Retro and the Rise of Money

Late on the night of December 26, 1867, the wind was chilly. At the Mitsui family estate in Kyoto, Japan, the family patriarch, Mitsui Saburosuke, is seated at his feet, and next to him is a wooden box filled with gold and silver. The servants held their breath and listened to the commotion outside the courtyard. The huge living room seemed even more empty in the dark, the sizzling sound of candles burning clearly audible in the silent room. The air seemed to freeze. At this moment, Mitsui was waiting for an important moment that would determine the fate of the family.

He had received accurate information that the Tokugawa Shogunate was mobilizing an army of 30,000 men ready to kill Kyoto. The Choshu and Satsuma clans of the Reversed faction had also recruited a large number of samurai under the banner of the Wangmasa Revival and vowed to abolish the Tokugawa Shogunate, which had ruled Japan for 200 years, and return the power to the Emperor. In a moment, the battle under Kyoto Castle was fierce and the final battle to decide Japan's fate was about to begin.

The Mitsui family, as financial agents of the Tokugawa Shogunate, had made a sweat equity contribution to the Shogunate's rule, and had gained great benefits. However, Japan is no longer the Japan of the lock-state era, the Western powers have knocked on its doors and the whole country is in the midst of a great crisis of being completely colonized. The corrupt rule and harsh exploitation of the Tokugawa Shogunate had already caused the violent popular revolt to burn like a blazing fire, while the Shogunate's weak compromise with the Western powers had stirred up the long-suppressed rebellion of the nobles and samurai of the clans. Mitsui, who has a keen eye on the current situation, has already begun to secretly provide large sums of money to the Reversed Sect. However, he is also unwilling and afraid to publicly express his inclinations.

Tonight, Mitsui will make an important decision that will affect the family's 300-year foundation, placing all bets on the Reverse Shogun faction and making a public break with the Tokugawa Shogunate! A crisp knock suddenly sounded at the door, and the Emperor's envoy arrived.

At the moment, in the palace near Mitsui's house, a smug teenager is pacing back and forth in passion, looking forward to a bright future for Japan. He was the Emperor Meiji, who had just been inaugurated a few months earlier. A few days ago, he issued an edict announcing his acceptance of the administrative power surrendered by the Tokugawa Shogunate and the withdrawal of the emperor's rule, which had been in place for over 700 years. Around the 15-year-old emperor, there were lords from various clans, the most powerful of which were the Choshu and Satsuma clans in the southwest. These people had long been unable to endure the Tokugawa Shogunate's rule, and several times revolted against it, and their subordinates, the samurai, were fierce and courageous, able to conquer the war.

The Meiji Emperor was young, but ambitious and resourceful. The Tokugawa Shogunate has placed successive emperors in the place of Emperor Han Hian, but can you guarantee that these reincarnated factions around you will not become the new Tokugawa family again? Just three years ago, the daring Changzhou clan was even prepared to kidnap his father, Emperor Hyozumi, in order to overthrow the Tokugawa family by "holding the son of heaven hostage to the vassals". The situation of the Ming emperor was very similar to that of the Qing emperor Kangxi who was coerced by Ao-Bai before his pro-regime.

However, the most pressing issue at hand was how to defeat the Tokugawa family, which was unwilling to lose its great power. Their 30,000-strong army would soon fight its way under Kyoto, and the worst part was that his new regime had an empty pouch and could not fight without money. The Meiji Emperor had to turn to the Mitsui family, the richest family in Japan at the time.

Guided by the envoy, Mitsui arrived at the palace with a chest filled with gold and silver, and awaiting him was the Imperial Minister of Finance. After exchanging pleasantries, the minister bluntly told the government that it had no money and that the war would end. Mitsui immediately offered the treasure chest and was immediately appointed as the new fiscal agent of the Empire, with full responsibility for raising funds.[21]

How could the Mitsui family have dared to entrust the survival of the Meiji emperor in a time of crisis?

The origins of this Mitsui are indeed extraordinary. The Mitsui family began building a financial empire 10 years before the Bank of England. His ancestor, Takato Mitsui, started his career in the garment industry and opened the Mitsui Ryotei Store in Edo (today's Tokyo) in 1683, where he engaged in financial services such as money exchange, pawnbroking and lending, and his business model was very similar to that of a Chinese money bank. At that time, Edo was the political center, Kyoto was where the Emperor lived, and Osaka was a thriving commercial city. With the end of the Warring States period in Japan, various industries began to flourish. Trade between the three metropolises is getting closer. Takato Mitsui sensitively saw this opportunity and opened "Mitsui Ryotei" branches in Kyoto and Osaka and began to build a small financial network. Where there was trade, there was financial service, commercial bills of exchange and bill discounting were created, bills of exchange soon entered the financial network of the Mitsui family between several metropolitan areas, capital and credit began to flow remotely, and the Mitsui family's profits climbed by the minute.

At that time, merchants had to buy goods in Osaka, the commercial center, while silver existed in Edo, the political center, and the reverse movement of silver and goods wasted time and money, and at the same time was not safe. The Shogunate had similar troubles, and the commercial taxes collected in Osaka had to be transported long distances to the Shogunate treasury in Edo, which was inconvenient. Seeing this opportunity, Mitsui proposed a solution to the Shogunate, in which Mitsui would collect government taxes in Osaka and then remit the money to Edo through Mitsui's financial network, and a money order would solve the government's dilemma without having to move heavy silver. The Tokugawa Shogunate, of course, was pleased with this simplicity and graciously offered a 60-day term for the money

---

[21] *The House of Mitsui*, Oland Russell, Little, Brown and Company, 1939, p. 142.

order. After a while, Mitsui's services were quite satisfactory to the Shogunate and the period was further extended to 150 days.[22]

That's what Coke did to Mitsui. The government gave such a huge sum of money, almost free, to Mitsui to use for such a long time, and Mitsui could use the shogun's tax money in Osaka to purchase goods for himself and for other merchants, and then pay silver to the shogun's treasury at the branch in Edo. In fact, from Osaka to Edo, it only took 15–20 days for Mitsui to purchase and ship all the goods, which was equivalent to 130 days of a huge zero-interest government loan, which could be used for short-term lending and making huge profits.

Mitsui's remote exchange business is almost identical to Shanxi Ticket's model, and although the financial exchange network is much smaller than Shanxi Ticket, it is more than 100 years older. Before the Western powers entered Asia, the Japanese were probably more financially aware than the Chinese.

More importantly, the Tokugawa Shogunate's trust in Mitsui had reached an unprecedented level. After the Western powers opened the gates of Japan, the Shogunate made it mandatory for all local business of foreign banks to go through the Mitsui family, which made it impossible for foreign banks to have direct contact with Japanese businessmen. The Mitsui family played the role of the Thirteen Banks of Guangzhou in the Qing Dynasty, and the Mitsui family monopolized all trade and financial interfaces with foreign countries, making the Mitsui family's financial and commercial network dominant in Japan.

After more than 180 years of development, by the time of the Meiji Emperor, Mitsui's vast financial empire had already become a key force to be reckoned with by all forces.

At a time when the new Meiji government was faced with the Tokugawa Shogunate's counterattack and the constant riots, Mitsui was ordered to raise 3 million taels of silver for the government as a matter of urgency, the first national debt ever issued in Japan. The Mitsui financial empire immediately mobilized urgently, and all financial networks ran together at high speed. They released a large number of national debt salesmen, each of whom had to master the standardized four-minute speech salesmanship, who ran from businessmen, bankers

---

[22] Ibid., p. 87.

and housewives all over the country, shocking all sectors of society with the passion for the rise and fall of the emperor's country in distress, and the sale ended up being a stunning success, with the amount of 3 million taels of silver in the national debt, which was oversubscribed by 3.8 million taels.[23]

Mitsui saved the new Meiji regime! The sea of money that rushed from the Mitsui financial empire flowed in a steady stream to the frontline barracks that were most thirsty for food and pay.

Very coincidentally, the crates of military pay that Mitsui had expressed his loyalty to Emperor Meiji were being escorted to the front line by a young officer. This person is Xin Inoue.

Inoue: Japan's Founding Finance Founder

At a time when the Western powers were in danger, the Shogunate was in chaos and the country was facing a major crisis, Inoue made a secret determination to go abroad to see why the Western navy was so strong and profitable and how the economy of the Western countries was booming. However, at that time, Japan adopted a strict lockdown policy, and it was a capital crime to leave Japan to study abroad without permission. But Inoue's determination was strong enough that the danger of death was not enough to deter him. He secretly contacted Hirofumi Ito, a fellow Nagasu clan member, and the two of them decided to sneak off to England to study together.

As they were getting ready to leave, they suddenly realised that they had no money on them and didn't know how much it would cost to stay in the UK for a few years. So they went to the British consulate to inquire, and the consul, who had never come across such a rarity, told them that each person needed 1,000 taels of silver a year, which was no small sum for any samurai family. The two men were instantly dumbfounded. But the solution was always more difficult, and they started looking around for money to pull sponsorship. One night in May 1863, they and three other close friends secretly went to Shanghai under the arrangement of the British consul.

---

[23] Ibid., p. 148.

At the port of Shanghai, Inoue looked at hundreds of foreign steamers coming in and out, a busy scene. Inoue feels that if Japan does not open up, it will be abandoned by the world trend. However, he did not think deeply about what would happen to China's economy if foreign ships unloaded whole ships of opium and loaded them with silk tea, gold and silver.

They were hosted in Shanghai by Jardine's Keswick. He asked Inoue and others what they planned to learn in England, and it turned out that Inoue suddenly found another big problem, which was that none of them knew English. Inoue only has one English word, Navigation, and the bad thing is, he pronounced it wrong. Keswick listened to the monk's puzzlement, and finally guessed that they were going to be sailors to learn to sail, so he sent someone to arrange for Inoue to burn boilers and do odd jobs with the sailors. Inoue Xin and others do not understand why guests who have bought a boat ticket still need to do chores, and feel very depressed. Since it is such a tradition in England, Inoue and others had to go with the flow. The gale force winds and waves in the sea had caused both Inoue and Ito Hirobumi to become severely seasick, and the two were vomiting while arguing heatedly about the future of Japan.[24]

The ship finally arrived in England and they began a whole new life. Inoue witnessed the wealth and power of the foreigners, desperately trying to learn English and professional nautical knowledge. He hated to cram all the advanced civilizations of the West into his brain at once. One day, he suddenly read in a British newspaper that the Japanese clan of Changzhou had blockaded the strait and shelled foreign ships, and that the Western powers were ready to form a combined fleet to punish the local "barbarians". Inoue was shocked, because he knew that the strong force of the West could not be resisted by the Japanese samurai, so he immediately decided to set off with Ito Hirobumi to return to Japan, in order to persuade the local daimyo to call a truce before the warships of the great powers hit the Changzhou clan.

The two risked being captured and sentenced to death by the Shogunate and rushed back to Japan to meet the British Consul General. At this point, war was about to break out. Inoue was already able to

---

[24] Ibid., p. 155–156.

express his proposal in English – he was willing to go and persuade the Changzhou clan to stop the war, and the British consul agreed to give them a few days to make peace. After meeting the great name of the Changzhou clan, Inoue Kiritsui Chen the Western powers of the ship's hardness, the Changzhou clan will be defeated in the war. The local warrior class's hatred for the Western powers had reached a point where it was impossible to suppress it, and they fought even though they lost. Inoue had to go back and report the results to the British side. When the British Consul General asked Inoue if she was still willing to return to England to continue her studies, Inoue replied very dryly, "No, sir! If there is war, we will be the first samurai to fall under your fire with katana in hand!" The British Consul General was moved by his determination.[25]

This kind of Bushido spirit was so common in Japan at the time that there was no breeding ground for foreign buyers. It was Inoue and a large number of other Japanese financial samurai who were in charge of the financial and financial power of the Japanese Empire! Foreign financial capital can't be bought!

The brutality of the war made the Western powers realize that direct conquest of Japan was too costly, and that their forces in the Far East were far from adequate. Inoue and Ito Hirobumi were both assassinated and nearly killed when they were mistaken for spies by local samurai for negotiating with the powers. Japan's strong Bushido spirit and national sentiment were indeed the first major difficulties faced by Western colonists. These "barbarians" could not be conquered directly by force, and it was difficult to find a group of foreign buyers who could make a climate for indirect colonial rule.

Later, he became one of Japan's most financially savvy politicians, one of the nine senators of the Empire, and was known as "Mitsui's great master". Ito Hirobumi was the famous iron-blooded prime minister of Japan and the founder of the constitution, and it was during his tenure that the Sino-Japanese War was started.

After the restoration of the king's administration, the Choshu clan, which took the most credit for the fall of the curtain, naturally had the largest share of power in the new government. Among the Choshu clans, it was also the foremost visionary of Inoue and Ito Hirobumi, so

---

[25] Ibid., p. 160.

Inoue was promoted to Daisuke Daizo (the equivalent of the Deputy Minister of Finance) and took charge of the financial and fiscal power of Japan, while Ito Hirobumi went to the Foreign Affairs Bureau and later emerged from the diplomatic field as a prominent politician of the Empire.

Mitsui Family's Big Boss

Inoue's first priority in taking office is to establish a currency standard, which is the most important cornerstone of the financial high frontier. It can be seen that Xin Inoue's vision is quite good, and at a glance, he can see the crux of the fiscal and financial problems.

The reality of the dilemma he faces is monetary chaos. Since the Tokugawa Shogunate, Japan's currency has been depreciating and the currency standard is extremely unstable. By 1869, there were 11 types of gold coins in circulation in the Japanese market, accounting for 54% of the metal currency in circulation, 7 types of silver coins accounted for 42%, and 6 types of copper coins, as well as a variety of paper money issued by the respective clans and towns, which was simply a currency of the Spring and Autumn Warring States period.[26]

At that time, the leading minds in charge of Japan's finances, Okubo Toshimitsu, and indeed the entire new government, were basically ignorant of the finances and finance of modern nations. In the beginning, it was agreed that there should be a silver standard, since silver was the main currency in circulation in Japan. Thus, in February 1868, the government declared silver to be the main currency in circulation and accepted the Mexican silver dollar as a means of payment at the ports of commerce. But at this time, Hirobumi Ito, who had been in the United States as far away as the United States to study the banking system, sent a letter arguing for a gold standard: "Austria, the Netherlands, and some other countries that still have a banking standard, probably because it is too difficult to switch to the old monetary system. If they could choose the money standard again, no doubt they would all choose the gold standard. So for Japan, it would be wise to follow the mainstream tendencies of the West. If Japan

---

[26] *Japanese Banking*, Norio Tamaki, Cambridge University Press, p. 23.

establishes a gold standard, silver can still be used as a complementary currency."[27]

Since Hirobumi Ito is studying the banking industry in the U.S., he is bound to represent the latest thinking in the West, so it is easy for everyone to unify the idea of the gold standard. At the same time, the Japanese currency was called the yen after the "abolition of the Japanese yen". This predates China by more than 70 years.

When the new Meiji government was established, it immediately sent Hirobumi Ito to the United States to investigate the banking system, which showed that Japan was highly sensitive to financial issues, far from being comparable to the Qing Empire. In fact, Hirobumi Ito wasn't well versed in financial matters either; he simply learned some of the basic framework of the local banking industry on the ground in the U.S. and simply didn't have time to digest and absorb it. He sought to replicate the American national banking system in Japan, resulting in the creation of 153 banks, all of which were converted into ordinary commercial or private banks by the end of the 19th century, as a result of the great national banking movement.

But as far as the gold standard is concerned, Hirobumi Ito does have good judgment. Inadvertently, Japan came to the side of the British Empire and belonged to the right side. However, due to the scarcity of gold in Japan at the time, silver was still the main currency in circulation, and the actual realization of the gold standard was delayed until 1897. When the 230 million taels of silver from the Bank of England, in the form of pounds sterling, was paid to the London branch of the Yokohama Shogun Bank of Japan, after deducting 53% of the British war loans and arms purchases, the remaining money purchased British bonds and converted them into gold, which was shipped back to Japan in batches and became the foundation of the gold standard.

With no money in hand, Inoue had to deal with the Mitsui family, Japan's biggest gold masters, and the relationship between the two sides quickly became hot. Since Mitsui had made a great contribution to the establishment of the new government, and had to be greatly rewarded for it, and since there were many more places to ask Mitsui, he gave

---

[27] Ibid., p. 24.

Mitsui the money from the treasury. But just to be fair, Mitsui has to share this big piece of cake with two other old moneylenders.

In 1871, when the National Mint of Japan began minting new coins, Mitsui immediately got another American agent, a government chartered agent, to recycle all the old coins in circulation throughout the country and then promote the new currency.

After all, Xin Inoue had stayed in foreign countries and seen the world, and he strongly suggested that the Mitsui family transform the traditional outdated money bank ticket number into a modern bank in Europe and America. When Mitsui reacted that the bank could issue its own banknotes, he immediately understood the enormous benefits in the middle. With a reserve of 75% to issue bills, isn't the excess just an empty glove white wolf? Mitsui has finally figured out the secret that bank credit money can be amplified. Mitsui immediately applied to the government for the right to issue 1.5 to 2 million yen in banknotes with the effect of national legal tender. Mitsui dreamed of becoming the "Bank of England of Japan"!

In July 1871, Mitsui submitted an application for a license to open a bank. This was Japan's first-ever application for a bank license, and in August, the Ministry of Finance's approval came down, including the timing of Inoue's submission to the Cabinet for approval, which was remarkably efficient. Even better, money already printed by the government in the U.S. would be immediately forwarded to Mitsui, who would issue it directly, saving even printing.

Mitsui was in the midst of ecstasy when the bad news came. As a result of Hirobumi Ito's suggestion, the government suddenly changed its mind about establishing a national banking system, much like the United States. The so-called National Bank is not a government bank, but a joint-stock bank with the power to issue money. However, Mitsui prefers a private banking system that the family can fully control and has little interest in working with others. In order to compensate Mitsui, Inoue gave Mitsui the business of issuing 6.8 million yen in fiscal notes and 2.5 million in colonial notes. Both of these government bills are gold-currencies, but they cannot be redeemed because there is simply not so much gold in Japan. Although Mitsui also made a lot of money, he was still pining for the great lure of a bank that could issue money.[28]

With Inoue repeatedly doing the work, Mitsui reluctantly agreed to a joint venture with the two old money houses to establish the First National Bank, primarily responsible for managing the treasury. This is a huge deal, all the country's fiscal revenue has to go through its hands, which is equivalent to getting an astronomical amount of money precipitation, lending or investment, Mitsui's financial strength became super strong. The beauty is that such a great benefit actually has to be shared with others.

The opportunity to eliminate the opponent has finally arrived.

The Japanese Ministry of Finance "suddenly" realized that the country's money was not necessarily reliable in the joint-stock First National Bank and was prepared to conduct a surprise inspection to see if the three major shareholders had sufficient capital. Mitsui had prepared the money in advance because of Inoue's tipped-off letter, while the other two immediately showed their horses' feet. Unable to come up with enough cash, it was forced to close its doors by the government.

With Inoue's help, Mitsui finally reigned supreme as treasury manager of the First National Bank.

It is no wonder that in Japanese political circles, the nickname "Mitsui's Boss" is the nickname of the company.

Japan controls the financial high frontier

The Meiji oligarchy, consisting of the four clans of Nagashima, Satsuma, Hizen, and Tosa, held the power of the Meiji government. Although the Meiji Emperor's treatment was significantly better than that of the Tokugawa Shogunate, he was still the famous "Choutenko". The Meiji oligarchs held the Emperor as a god and gave him up on high, but the real power was firmly in their hands. Although they overthrew the Tokugawa Shogunate, there were still more than 300 small lords in the country, and if they were not completely eradicated, there was no guarantee that another Tokugawa family would emerge one day. At the

---

[28] *The House of Mitsui*, Oland Russell, Little, Brown and Company, 1939, p. 168–169.

same time, feudal domination was undoubtedly a serious impediment to Japan's modernization if it was to stand on equal footing with the Western Powers.

But how to cut the clan? History is littered with the resultant wars.

The Meiji oligarchs eventually negotiated the "abolition of clans and counties" approach, somewhat like the Song Dynasty's Taizu when "a cup of wine to release military power" thinking. It was up to the central government to raise the lords of the vassals and their subordinates, as well as the vast class of warriors, all at their expense. Once the lords counted, it worked out very well. Previously, their nominal annual income was 100,000 koku of rice, or about 64,000 pounds, and after the abolition of the feudatories and the establishment of the prefectures, the government gave them an annual salary of 50,000 koku. This is quite generous treatment, to know that the income of the lords is not stable, the food harvest is at the mercy of God, another war riots, but also to pay money and people to suppress, perhaps even lose money. At the same time, they are no longer burdened with the livelihoods of the samurai class who have lost their land, and the State provides for them with a sense of well-being. So, the work is moving forward very well. A British journalist could not help but lament that the feudal lordship system, which had taken hundreds of years to abolish in Europe, had been completed in Japan in only three months.

The situation is far from optimistic. The clan was abolished and the Tokugawa Shogunate's hidden dangers were completely eliminated, but at the cost of a huge financial burden on the nation, which supported a clan class of 2 million people who were like the "eight banners". The lords and samurai spent almost one-third of the central treasury on their salaries, and the huge vassal debt of 78 million taels greatly exacerbated the financial crisis of the new Meiji government.

When the Meiji oligarchs first came to power, money was needed to fix both internal and external problems, the new government had no money, and the fiscal taxes didn't work overnight, so the only contingency was by printing money. This is similar to the binge printing of colonial paper money in the American colonies during their rebellion against the British Empire.

During the first two years of the new government, beginning in 1868, a total of 48 million yen of paper money was issued, more than half of which was used to keep the government running, 12.7 million yen was loaned to the vassals who supported the new government, and the remaining nearly 10 million yen was used to develop industry and commerce, including banking. From the third year onwards, three additional banknotes were added: a 7.5 million yen worth of auxiliary currency issued by the Ministry of Internal Affairs to support government bonds, a 6.8 million yen Treasury bond issued by the Ministry of Finance to cover the fiscal deficit, and a 2.5 million yen "layoff bond" to settle the laid-off samurai class and help them re-employ in Hokkaido.[29] With this massive currency printing spree and the proliferation of counterfeit currency, Japanese society entered a state of hyperinflation, the credit of government paper money declined sharply, and the regime was in danger.

The new government is short of money, the binge printing of money is only an emergency, and in the long run, revenues must be increased. So the new government embarked on a reform of the monetization of ground rents. At that time, all taxes in Japan were paid in kind, and farmers had to bear the burden of labor. This is precisely the problem that China solved 300 years ago, with the "one whip law" of Zhang Juzheng, head of the Ming Dynasty cabinet. The success of the land rent reform has significantly increased stable government revenues.

When the economy gradually stabilized, the salaries of the warlords became a matter of great concern to the Meiji oligarchs. The bigwigs negotiated over and over again and finally came up with a trick called the "Golden Locks Public Bond". Rather than paying out huge sums of cash to the warriors each year, the government bought out their future salaries in a lump sum, as in "buying out years of service", but instead of paying cash, it paid out a public debt of gold. For those with a high salary, a lump sum of 6 to 7 years' total income is paid at 5% interest; for those with a low salary, a lump sum of 10 to 12 years' total income is paid at a higher interest rate. The future government will only pay interest each year and the financial burden will be significantly reduced. The principal of the bond is repaid by lot starting in the sixth year after issuance and is repaid within 30 years. This is a much better approach than the fiscal reform of the Yongzheng emperor in the Qing dynasty, when he forced the eight banners to cultivate land in the capital

---

[29] *Japanese Banking*, Norio Tamaki, Cambridge University Press, p. 24.

suburbs, and the level of fiscal and financial management in Japan during the Meiji era was truly astonishing.

In this way, large sums of money can be freed up for the development of industry, and the return on investment from industry can be used to pay the principal and interest on the Golden Locks bonds. Since then, these two million people have been thoroughly marketed by the government.

In August 1876, the government began issuing the Kinloo Public Bond, which amounted to 174 million yen. You know, the total amount of Japanese currency in circulation at that time was only 112 million yen! At the same time, the government amended the National Bank Act to allow the Golden Locks public debt to be invested as bank capital. The lords, who had become rich overnight, immediately took the millions of bonds they had received at once in their hands and put them into banks. It can be seen that the financial intelligence of the Japanese lords was also quite good, and they already knew what kind of benefits they would get from taking a stake in a commercial bank. The shareholders of the famous Fifteenth National Bank were almost all of these prodigies, who succeeded in converting the income from their salaries into financial capital, which they in turn invested in the most prosperous industrial projects, thus reaping huge returns and becoming the new aristocracy of the future. In the three years following the issuance of the Jinlu public bonds, the number of national banks in Japan soared to 153. The lower and middle class warriors have nothing to do but fight, they can't fight the merchants in the mall, and as a result, the Jinlu bonds are swindled away in large numbers. Except for a few who succeeded, the vast majority of the samurai who went "down to the sea" were reduced to the poorer classes.

Mitsui has accelerated its application for bank licenses as the volume of financial business has increased as major policies in these countries have advanced. Mitsui has not given up, despite its previous rejection by the government. When Inoue returned to the Treasury again in 1876, Mitsui's application for a bank license was immediately approved. But with the addition of the article that unlimited liability must be assumed, on July 1, 1876, the Mitsui Bank was officially established, the first private bank in Japanese history. Mitsui's dream of issuing banknotes has finally come true.

The 31 branches of Mitsui Bank, which were formerly part of Mitsui's clothing chain, are now officially divorced from their original business to specialize in financial services, and Mitsui Bank immediately has the largest financial network in Japan. Old masters are becoming customers of Mitsui Bank in droves. Total deposits for the year of opening alone amounted to 11.37 million yen, with a further 2.28 million yen in deposits. The government's abolition of the prefectures, the monetization of land rents, and the Kanroku public debt greatly increased fiscal revenues, and half of the central fiscal revenues were deposited in the Mitsui Bank.[30]

In this way, Mitsui Bank was able to obtain a huge, interest-free, unsecured deposit of funds from the Meiji government. With such strong financial strength, Mitsui began to invest heavily in industries, such as railways, textiles, paper making, shipping, and coal mining, forming a super plutocracy with finance as its core and various industries as its backbone, interdependent and mutually leveraging.

In 1882, the Bank of Japan, the first central bank in Japan's history, was officially established under the planning of Masayoshi Matsukata, Katsumi Inoue and others. It is a joint-stock company, with the government and private financiers each holding a corresponding stake, and the Mitsui family, as major originating shareholders, sends representatives to the central bank's board of directors to participate in decision-making.[31] Although Zaibatsu, representing the interests of all parties, has diluted some of Mitsui's power, no one in the Japanese financial industry is yet on the same level as Mitsui.

Subsequently, the Bank of Japan, as the only legal bank issuing money in Japan, gradually withdrew the right to issue money from 153 national banks and took full control of the strategic heights of Japanese finance.

Another important function of the Bank of Japan is to provide substantial financing directly to priority industries in the country. The Bank of Japan has opened a special discount window for collateralized financing of stocks and bonds of key enterprises, which is unthinkable in other countries, and which amounts to direct monetization of the debt and stocks of enterprises, with the development costs of key enterprises

---

[30] *The House of Mitsui*, Oland Russell, Little, Brown and Company, 1939, p. 183.

[31] *Mitsui: Three Centuries of Japanese Business*, John G. Roberts, Art Media Resources, 1989, p. 126.

shared by society as a whole. This has also created extremely important conditions for Japanese industry to take off.

With the mobilization of the Bank of Japan, the nation's financial resources were effectively consolidated, the entire banking system was fully engaged in the expansion of credit, and large-scale capital was continuously injected into the industrial system. It should be particularly noted that the reason why Japan did not engage in large-scale external debt financing from the Meiji Restoration until the Sino-Japanese War is that Japan witnessed the dangerous trend of increasing colonization by China and other countries under the oppression of foreign debt. Japan's Meiji Restoration was mainly financed by the consolidation and mobilization of financial resources in the country and, more importantly, the creation of credit in the banking system.

Under the guardianship of the Bank of Japan, Japan's financial system has enjoyed unprecedented development. By 1901, there were thousands of financial institutions of all kinds in Japan, with 1867 commercial banks alone and a financial network that spanned both urban and rural Japan. In the following decade, the banking system tripled the size of credit to industry and commerce and quadrupled the size of total deposits, and Japan's railways, shipping, mines, textiles, military industry, machinery manufacturing, agriculture, trade, and other industries soared like a rocket, stimulated by huge amounts of money.

Why the Meiji Restoration didn't "attract" foreign investment

The fact that Japan was able to come up with the idea of using the Kanroku bond as the core capital of the bank at the beginning of the Meiji Restoration shows that Japan's deep understanding of the nature of modern finance was already far beyond that of the Qing Empire at that time. Note that Japan's industrialization during the Meiji period did not bring in large amounts of foreign capital and foreign debt, because Japan had thoroughly discovered the secret of bank credit. Under modern banking and credit money mechanisms, legal tender is never scarce and money can be created by its own banking system. If that were the case, there would be no need for foreign capital to enter the Japanese banking system at all. Japan needs international hard currency for the sole purpose of bringing in foreign technical equipment and resources that Japan does not have!

That is why the Meiji Restoration in Japan never engaged in "investment promotion". Japan only needs foreign technology, machinery and equipment, and raw materials, and Japan has practiced itself better than foreign countries in managing the work. Hard currency can be obtained by exporting raw silk, tea and porcelain from Japan. Foreign funds? Sorry, no need! Because Japan can create its own currency! Foreign foreign firms can participate in international trade and help Japanese products open up world markets and buy what Japan needs. Domestic trade is shared by Japan's own firms.

The digestion of Western technology is a Japanese specialty. It is a Japanese specialty to make a dojo in a snail shell by carving various things to the extreme. When the Russian fleet arrived in Japan, curious Japanese came aboard for a tour, and the Russians showed the Japanese a toy model of a steam train. The first time I saw a small smoky train running up the track, I was completely thunderstruck on the spot. The group never thought about it again and studied carefully why the train could move. Soon, the Japanese also came up with small model trains, and soon they were more elaborate than the Russians.

The fractional reserve system of modern banks is a highly leveraged financial system. A dollar of provision can create a $10 amplification effect. Japan's entire banking system even used nearly 20 times the leverage to create money on a large scale before 1882. The creation of a currency of this magnitude has greatly stimulated the leap forward in Japanese industry and commerce, but it has also laid the risk of inflation.

Japan began to borrow extensively during the Sino-Japanese War and the Russo-Japanese War, when Japan's domestic financial unification had already been completed and industrial modernization had basically taken shape, so that foreign debt would not destroy Japan's political and economic autonomy. The foreign debt of the war was equivalent to venture capital, and Japan gained huge profits in both the Sino-Japanese War and the Russo-Japanese War, simply by sharing profits with the great powers.

In Japan's rapid expansion of domestic financial strength, the influence of the dominant foreign banks is greatly reduced, 1863–1868, the first six foreign banks landed in Japan with a total capital of 200 million taels, far more than the total strength of the Japanese banking system at that time. Until 1897, the total capital of the Japanese banking system was only 133 million yen, which shows the strength of foreign banks.

After the Meiji Restoration, despite the super strength of foreign banks, the development of markets in Japan has been difficult. By the early 20th century, the first six foreign banks to open in Japan, with the exception of HSBC, had all failed or withdrawn from the country. HSBC uses the huge profits from the opium trade in China, there is still a place in Japan, but also has been squeezed into the foreign trade and international exchange and other narrow areas, not only unable to control Japan's currency issuing power, even the general business of entering the Japanese market is difficult.

In addition to the fierce rivalry and siege of Mitsui, Mitsubishi and Sumitomo, Japan's lack of basic soil for the survival and development of the foreign-buying class is also an important reason. It is inconceivable that a foreign bank would want to expand into the Japanese market without the strong cooperation of local people. The Mitsubishi family has publicly vowed to all employees that foreign shipping companies will be eliminated from the Japanese shipping market. With the help of two major power groups, government and finance, Mitsubishi has fulfilled its vow.

The Meiji government, which was formed with the samurai aristocracy of the Nagasu and Satsuma clans at its core, had a completely different mentality towards the Western powers than the Qing government, which was controlled by politicians and civilians, especially in the financial field. The Ministry of Finance was at the heart of the Meiji government's power, and many of its financial officials were of samurai descent from the Choshu and Satsuma clans, who saw finance as the arena for samurai to fight. The first hurdle that foreign banks have to cross if they want to control Japanese finance is this group of financial samurai.

When Japan took complete control of its own financial system, it also had a firm grasp on the country's destiny. Although financial dislocation had caused severe inflation and austerity in the course of intense industrialization, Japan as a whole, in just one generation, had leapfrogged from a backward country on the verge of colonial peril to a modern industrial powerhouse, with its financial high frontier firmly in place!

Immediately afterwards, Japan began a fierce attack on HSBC's still dominant international trade and exchange business.

Yen Credit Defense War

Japanese Finance Minister Shigenobu Okuma established the Yokohama Shogun Bank to save the credit of the rapidly depreciating paper currency. Under his "quantitative easing of money" policy, credit expanded rapidly and the economy overheated, resulting in a significant depreciation of paper currency against silver currency. Monetary credit is severely impaired, inflation is difficult to control and the economy is in chaos. In desperation, Okuma Shigehide offered to borrow 50 million yen from a foreign country and use the foreign silver money to recover the over-issued paper money. As a result, his proposal was drowned out by a storm of cursing.

Many of the Meiji oligarchs traveled abroad, as well as to China, India and other colonial countries, and witnessed firsthand how foreign debt gradually brought these countries under control and eventually reduced them to colonies or semi-colonies. The oligarchs pointed out that the Meiji Restoration was not to avoid becoming a colony of the Western powers. Is it not a repeat of China's mistake to borrow money from foreign countries when the foundation of industrialization is not yet complete and the capacity to repay the debt is not sufficient, but to mortgage tariffs and other government revenues, thereby losing fiscal tax sovereignty?

In desperation, Okuma Shigenobu proposed the establishment of a purely "gold, silver and metal bank" in Yokohama, the commercial center of Japan. It is called Yokohama Shojin Bank because it is a purely real gold and silver business. It does not issue banknotes, but its main purpose is to activate the "good coins" (gold and silver), which have been expelled by the "bad coins" (banknotes), from their state of storage and return them to circulation in society. However, the devaluation of paper currency continued to accelerate, and by 1880, the paper currency was devalued to 45% of the silver currency, and Japanese gold and silver coins disappeared together from all corners as if overnight. The "proper gold" banks are paralysed by the inability to find "proper" gold and silver coins. The devaluation of the paper currency snapped Okuma Shigehide's position as a financial cattleman.[32]

---

[32] *Japanese Banking*, Norio Tamaki, Cambridge University Press, p. 46–48.

Next in this mess is the deflationary righteousness of Matsumata, who has long been extremely unhappy with Okuma Shigenobu's "quantitative easing" policy. The number one priority for Justice Matsumata to take office is to rebuild the credit of the yen paper currency. This meant that the government had to exchange the over-issued paper money in the hands of the people for as much as it could be exchanged for real money, until the people were fully convinced that the government was stockpiling "a great deal" of gold and silver, and no longer demanded to exchange it. At that time, the total amount of money in circulation throughout Japan was 153 million yen, while the gold and silver reserves were only 8.7 million yen, representing only 5.7 percent of the total amount of money in circulation. It's a bloodbath of confidence, and confidence alone is not enough, first and foremost, real money.

He and Yokohama Shinkin Bank have repeatedly discussed a plan that would solve the bank's operational difficulties, reverse the depreciation of paper currency in one fell swoop, and regain the pricing power held by foreign banks in the foreign trade sector.

Justice Matsubata ordered the Ministry of Finance to immediately set aside 3 million yen for Yokohama Shojin Bank for foreign exchange trading. The money will be used to support Japan's export trade, using exports to generate foreign exchange to solve the domestic gold and silver shortage. Since there is a shortage of gold and silver in the country and the paper currency is severely over-issued, finding gold and silver in the country alone will not solve the problem, but we should go all over the world to find gold and silver and stabilize the paper currency with gold and silver from outside.

Japan's foreign trade structure at this time was similar to that of China's, with raw silk and tea being its main exports. Among them, the raw silk industry has been the most important traditional industry and export industry in Japan, accounting for about 30 percent of Japan's exports. Since foreign banks, with the support of foreign banks, had a complete monopoly on the pricing of commodities, Japanese raw silk and tea were often forced to be sold to foreign banks at jump-sale prices. The Japanese Ministry of Finance has long been furious about this, but there has been little that has worked.

When Yokohama Shojin Bank began to act quietly under the orders of Justice Songfang, it was just as Hu Xueyan began to stock up on raw silk in Shanghai, preparing to challenge the foreign banks. But in the end the fate was diametrically opposed.

Japanese silk and tea merchants are also short of money, and foreign foreign banks pay commercial drafts that are due for six months before they can withdraw money from foreign banks. If there is an urgent need for liquidity, one has to get a foreign bank to discount it, but the discount rate can be as high as 20%, which equals a loss of 20% of trade profits! If one is unwilling to lose, one has to wait. However, silk tea is a commodity that can't wait and will go bad over time. As a result, the shortage of funds has led to a slow acquisition of silk tea, and silk farmers can't afford to wait, so they have to sell it at cheap prices. The oceanic trade is profitable.

The emergence of the Yokohama Shojin Bank immediately broke the foreign bank's pricing power over trade. When the foreign bank negotiated a contract with the merchants and issued a commercial bill of exchange, Shojin Bank immediately intervened, paying the merchants immediately in Japanese currency to buy the bill of exchange at a very favorable discount. These yen notes are the very funds that Matsumata Justice authorized the Ministry of Finance to lend to Shojin Bank at a very low interest rate. In this way, merchants no longer have to wait for the long maturity of commercial bills of exchange, nor do they have to take them to a foreign bank to do a very damaging discount. The money orders are now held by CZK Bank to maturity, assuming full risk. Upon maturity of the bill of exchange, all payments made by foreign businessmen are made in the form of gold and silver coins directly into the Ministry of Finance's account at CZK Bank.

In this way, a virtuous circle is formed, the Shojin Bank borrows yen notes cheaply from the Ministry of Finance, then purchases foreign bills of exchange in the hands of Japanese exporters at a discount on the notes, holds the bills of exchange when they expire, the foreign gold and silver coins are paid to the Shojin Bank, which then flows into the Ministry of Finance, and the Shojin Bank makes a profit from the spread between the government borrowing money and the discount on the foreign bills of exchange. At this time, the Ministry of Finance obtained a large amount of gold and silver coins to recycle yen paper money and rebuild yen credit. Japanese exporters will immediately get the money, then go to acquire silk tea, accelerating the speed of capital turnover, the acquisition of a large increase, silk farmers tea farmers benefit. The merchants won more bargaining power in their negotiations with the foreign firms. At the same time, Yokohama Shojin Bank has seen an unprecedented expansion of its business and has begun to open branches in major overseas financial centers.[33]

Yokohama Shojin Bank's financial innovation has been an unprecedented success. It was the emergence and great success of the Shogin Bank that reversed Japan's monetary system on the verge of collapse, consolidated the major economic achievements of the early Meiji Restoration, and solidified the financial bubble created by the monetary expansion.

When the Bank of Japan was established, Shinkin Bank worked closely with the Bank of Japan. The Bank of Japan's ultra-low interest rate loan of 2% to Shinkin Bank provided strong support for Shinkin Bank's expansion into the global market. In turn, the positive gold and silver act of the Bank of Japan to provide a constant supply of gold and silver coin reserves, helping the Bank of Japan to establish an unbreakable monetary credit, 1881 to 1885, the gold and silver reserves behind the yen notes, from the poor 8.7 million yen to 42.3 million yen, accounting for 37% of the total currency in circulation.[34] By around 1890, Japanese paper money was finally restored to the same price level as silver, and the credit defense of the yen ended in victory.

The Western powers were astonished that such a violent inflation could be completely subdued, and that such an over-issued paper currency could restore credit without any devaluation. This shows that Japan's financial mastery has improved by leaps and bounds in just 20 years. From a country that has no idea what modern banking is all about, to a world-class player ready to lay out its financial network to the world.

From the failure of Hu Xueyan's challenge to the foreign bank's raw silk pricing power and the dramatic increase of Japanese silk tea merchants' pricing power, we can see that Japanese officials such as Matsumata Justice were trying every possible means to help exporters regain their pricing power, while Qing bureaucrats like Li Hongzhang were trying to bring down Hu Xueyan; Japan had financial giants like Mitsui and Mitsubishi with a strong sense of nationalism, while the Qing Dynasty was full of financial foreign buyers like the Dongting

---

[33] Ibid., p. 58–60.

[34] Ibid., p. 61.

Sejong family, Yokohama Shinkin Bank was Japan's financial pointer into the world, and the Shanghai financial market was HSBC's colonial weapon to control China.

In China, which has lost its financial frontier, neither the foreign movement, nor the Hundred Days Reform Act, nor even the overthrow of the Qing Dynasty, can truly realize the dream of China's industrialization and wealthy country and strong military.

Meiji Restoration vs Western Movement

> *"Some of the buyers have established links with the foreign bureaucrats through foreign aggression and participated in the political and economic activities of the foreign bureaucracy, and the buying class has become increasingly influential in politics and economically powerful, forming an important reactionary social force. The large bureaucratic group of foreigners led by Li Hongzhang became increasingly visible as political representatives of the buyout forces."*
>
> —Guo Moruo

At the same time that the Meiji Restoration swept through Japan, China was also pushing forward the foreign affairs movement with great vigor. China and Japan, with almost identical motives, in almost identical positions, and facing almost similar problems, ended up with vastly different results, with the Meiji Restoration a complete success and the Foreign Affairs Movement a complete failure.

Is it that Japan's initial conditions are better than those of China? Although China lost the two opium wars to Britain and France and ceded the land, the overall losses did not seriously shake the country's capital, and although the Taiping Heavenly Kingdom Movement from 1851 to 1864 caused great damage to the Qing Empire, it was even more unstable at the beginning of the Meiji Restoration in 1868, with more than 300 clans and towns still to be divided, the central government's revenue was almost zero, and the monetary system was in chaos, there was no fundamental difference between the two.

Is the Japanese system more advanced? The Meiji Restoration in Japan eventually resulted in a bourgeois dictatorship of the Meiji oligarchy, with the Nagasu, Satsuma, Hizen and Tosa clans at its core, and a bureaucratic plutocracy and bourgeois dictatorship in which the interests of the three plutocrats, Mitsui, Mitsubishi and Sumitomo, were interlocked, and the political representatives were the "Meiji Three

Masters" and the "Ninomoto". The Qing Empire, on the other hand, was a bureaucratic buying class formed by the bureaucrats at the core of Li Hongzhang and the foreign buying power groups represented by Sheng Xuanhuai and Xi Zhengfu. The biggest difference between the two is that plutocrats and foreign buyers have different interests.

Such comparisons can go on without limit, but the point is in finance!

The opium trade destroyed the stability of the Qing empire's native currency; the absence of a central bank led to the perpetuation of monetary disunity; HSBC controlled China's banking system; foreign banks infiltrated China's financial network; foreign buyers monopolized the financial market; the secrets of credit creation were not deeply understood by China, leading to the late opening of the modern banking industry; huge reparations and large foreign debts led to the collateralization of the main revenues of China's three central finances, namely, customs duties, salt tax and cents, to foreign banks; China's fiscal and taxation sovereignty was lost; the government's financial resources were depleted and reliance on foreign debts was deepened.

The complete loss of China's financial frontiers has led to the loss of political independence, the lack of funds for economic development, the accumulation of poverty and weakness in military and national defence, and the degradation of China into a semi-colony with no food, science and technology, education and culture to be slaughtered by others.

All this is the essential difference between the Chinese foreign affairs movement and the Meiji Restoration in Japan. The fate of the Hanye Ping Company is a typical example of this comparison.

Financial poisoned milk cripples Han Ye Ping Company

In 1894, in Hanyang, Hubei Province, a large steelmaking, iron smelting and coal mining enterprise was established. With a blast furnace volume of 470 cubic meters, it was the most powerful and advanced steel combine in the entire Eastern Hemisphere at the time. In May 1894, the Hanyang Iron Works was successfully tested, two years ahead of Yawata Iron Works (later the predecessor of Nippon Steel, Japan's largest steel company). By the eve of the Xinhai Revolution, the company had more than 7,000 employees, with an annual output of nearly 70,000 tons of steel, 500,000 tons of iron ore, 600,000 tons of coal, accounting for more than 90% of the annual steel output of the Qing Empire, becoming a model project of the foreign affairs movement.

It is the first new type of steel joint venture in China and has the full potential to become the world's leading steel trust. If Hanye Ping can succeed, then the upstream and downstream industrial chain driven by Hanye Ping will greatly pull China's economic structure and bring about a real industrial revolution in a series of heavy industries such as railways, ships, military industry, machinery manufacturing, metallurgy, mines and so on, which will completely change the tragic fate of China in the early 20th century and even the course of world history!

The steel industry is the backbone of all industries, and countries that lack it are not straight in the ranks of modern nations. The foreigners of the Qing Empire also understood this, and Zhang Zhidong, the governor of Huguang, was the main figure who was instrumental in opening the Han Ye Ping Company.

Unfortunately, in the absence of effective protection of the financial high frontier, the Hanye Ping Company could not escape its tragic fate.

In 1889, Zhang Zhidong, the governor of the two provinces of China, asked the imperial court to prepare an ironmaking plant, but six months earlier he had sent someone to England to order ironmaking equipment, and the British asked about the nature of ore and coke to decide which type of furnace to use. The British had to supply the corresponding steel furnaces according to the British standard of acid steelmaking, and as a result, Hubei Daye Mine contained high phosphorus, and the steel produced by the Hanye Ping steel furnace contained too much phosphorus and did not meet the requirements of track steel, resulting in a large backlog of products. Zhang Zhidong, the author of the theory of "Chinese body and Western use", has neither kept the "body" nor done the "use".

What is Western use? That is, to learn from the West how to achieve a concrete approach to rise in the economic sphere. Such learning must be down-to-earth and conscientious and must not come in the slightest sham. In 1895, after the Ninth Reichstag decided to establish the Hachiman Iron Works, the Government instructed the Minister of Commerce to organize a study on iron ore, pig iron, steel, coke, refractory materials, production costs, and the selection of a plant site before finalizing the budget and plan after 11 rounds of tests and investigations.

The second hidden problem is the problematic location of the plant. The Hanyang Iron Works should be located near a coal or near-iron mine to reduce transportation costs. However, Zhang Zhidong strongly suggested that the factory site must be located under the Dabie Mountain in Hanyang so that it could be supervised nearby. Hanyang is about 120 kilometers away from the iron ore base of Daye and about 500 kilometers away from the Pingxiang coal mine. Each ton of pig iron costs a significant additional freight cost. Hanyang is again a low-lying land, and to prevent flooding, more than 90,000 square meters of earth were filled before the plant was built, costing 300,000 taels of silver, which led to the high price of the product.

The third is the fuel hazard. When preparing for the construction of the ironworks, Zhang Zhidong had a hazy concept of "China is so big that there is no coal" in his mind. After building the plant, Zhang Zhidong spent several years to send people along the middle and lower reaches of the Yangtze River to explore the coal mines, but the result was nothing. The Hanyang Iron Works was unable to produce normally due to lack of fuel, and the first steel production was opened in June 1894, but the furnace was closed in October of the same year due to lack of coke supply. The only option was to buy open-pit coal at a high price, even Japanese and German coke. At that time, the market price of pig iron was 20 taels per ton, while the Hanyang CIF price of Kaiping coal had reached 18 taels per ton, and foreign coal was more expensive. The cost of coal coke at the Hanyang Iron Works was almost three times that of foreign steel mills at the time, and the pig iron and steel that was refined was not competitive in the market. The steel is made in the open furnace at a loss, the closed furnace is not made, and the monthly fixed expenses are 80,000 taels, also at a loss. What a dilemma, a desperate situation.[35]

By 1896, Han Ye Ping had consumed 5.68 million taels of silver, and Zhang Zhidong could no longer hold out. He had to beg Sheng Xuan Huai to clean up the mess.

---

[35] Lessons Learned from the Introduction of Foreign Investment in Old China from Hanye Ping Company, Wang Xi.

At that time, I am afraid that the only one who had the strength to take Han Ye Ping was Sheng Xuanhuai, who controlled the four major foreign enterprises of the Qing Empire, namely, shipping, telegraph, mining and textile. As a representative figure of the Foreign Buyer's Office, Sheng Xuanhuai's ability is indisputable and he has a knack for running businesses. Sheng Xuanhuai, who had long coveted the Hanyang Iron Works, received a strong invitation from Zhang Zhidong and made a counter-offer that the Hanyang Iron Works would have to be taken over by a railway, because with the railway, he would have the market for steel. Zhang Zhidong was forced to agree. And railroad financing is bound to be borrowed through foreign banks, in which Sheng Xuanhuai will have a great deal to gain.

On May 24, 1896, Sheng Xuanhuai arrived in office.

The most pressing difficulty facing the Hanyang Iron Works is coke, which cannot be produced without fuel. In order to do this, it was necessary to introduce a new law on coal mining in Pingxiang, and at the same time to build a railway to transport the coal out, which required 5 million taels of silver, the renovation of the blast furnace adapted to the Daliye iron ore mine, the establishment of rolling steel, steel rails, steel plate factory, etc., another 3 million taels of silver was spent. It was not until 1909 that Hanye Ping really produced qualified steel, which was the "first steel made by the Chinese" in the true sense. This was a valuable time for the large-scale construction of railways in China, and a large number of orders for steel rails and railway equipment flew in like snowflakes. Guangdong-Hanzhou, Beijing-Hanzhou and other railway tracks are used in the "Hanyang-made". That was the time when Han Ye Ping realized a profit. By 1912, Han Ye Ping had assets of 9.4 million taels of silver, but liabilities of 24 million taels.

Clearly, Hanye Ping needs to refinance. It was at this point that the fatal question arose.

In 1913, when the situation in Japan had stabilized, Mori Xuanwai, led by Yoko Mitsui, borrowed 15 million yen from the Yokohama Shogin Bank. As with previous yen borrowings, the conditions were very harsh and became more severe. Unreasonable conditions such as extending the loan period, allowing only raw materials to repay the loan, using mines as collateral, supplying ore and pig iron to Japan at very low prices and locking it in for a long time, and allowing future loans to be provided only by Japan were proposed.

Japan is a country with very poor iron ore resources, and the demand for ore and pig iron is increasing as the country's steel industry grows. Almost all of the ore and pig iron supplies in the early years of the Yawata Iron Works came from the Hanyang Iron Works and the Daye Iron Mine. Japan's strategic goal is clear: to use Hanyeeping as a raw material supply base for Japanese steel and to ensure that Yawata Steel produces high value-added steel. Thus, until the 1930s, 56.40% of Hanye Ping ore production and 54.87% of pig iron production were exported to Japan. The supply of Hanye Ping pig iron and ore played a huge role in the Japanese military steel industry. During the Russo-Japanese War, most of the raw materials for steelmaking for Japanese warships and weapons came from Hanye Ping.[36] Similarly, how many of the guns and ammunition used to slaughter the Chinese in the war of aggression waged by Japan came from China's own iron ore and pig iron?

In 1914, World War I broke out and international steel prices soared several times. Since the borrowing from Japan locked the price of pig iron and ore, Hanye Ping could not adjust it to the market price, and during the war, the pig iron and ore sold to Japan was equivalent to a free contribution of 115 million silver dollars to Japan! Enough to pay off the Japanese loan a few times! Despite this, during the war, Han Ye Ping made a profit of 24 million taels of silver. After World War I, however, steel prices plummeted and Han Ye Ping returned to losses.

In 1915, in its "Article 21" on the extermination of China, Japan specifically raised the issue of Hanye Ping:

> "Once there is a chance that Hanye Ping will be a joint venture between the two countries in the future, the Chinese Government shall not dispose of all power and property of Hanye Ping without the consent of the Japanese Government, nor shall it dispose of Hanye Ping at will. All mines in the vicinity of the mines belonging to the Hanye Ping Company are prohibited from being mined by persons other than the Company without its consent."

Since the purpose of the Japanese loan was so sinister, didn't the shrewd Sheng Xuanhuai understand? Of course he understood, but he helped the Japanese side actively think and come up with ideas. His

---

[36] Ibid.

starting point was how to protect his huge family business from being seized by the revolutionaries, and for this reason he did not hesitate to draw the wolf into his house and hold himself hostage.

In 1913, Yuan Shikai had thought of nationalizing Han Ye Ping, but Sheng Xuanhuai resolutely opposed it. He couldn't wait to send a secret telegram to the Japanese side, hoping that Han Ye Ping would be handed over to them as soon as possible. Japan was "concerned" about Sheng Xuanhuai's health, estimating that he was "bleeding from a lung disease and would only live five years later", and feared that five years later, "don't replace it with a sudden change in relations and the purchase of iron ore would fall through."[37] Therefore, he strived to finalize the loan while Sheng Xuanhuai still had his breath. He was caught in the Japanese debt, and was eventually completely controlled by the Japanese.

The facts show that a foreign movement dominated by a bureaucratic buy-in class would be unimaginable to succeed. As Mao Zedong argued,

> *"In economically backward, semi-colonial China, the landlord class and the buyout class are entirely subordinate to international capitalism, and their survival and development are subordinate to imperialism."*

Steel companies need large-scale financing, and with the loss of financial sovereignty, they can only take on large amounts of foreign debt and end up in the hands of others. If Hanye Ping were in Japan, its bonds and stocks could be financed directly to the special discount window of the central bank, or loans could be made by zaibatsu banks, and the government would use tariffs to block competition from foreign steel, such an important core business that the government would fully support in any case. And in China? The central bank of the Qing Empire, the Great Qing Bank, established in 1905, had no will, much less the ability, to help Han Ye Ping. At the time, China's currency was not yet unified, and the paper money issued by the Qing Bank could not have been credible. The commercial banking system is in its infancy and capital accumulation is far from strong. Shanghai's stock market is a world of speculators, and no one is interested in a super-heavy stock of this size. The money bank is too small to make it work, the ticket

---

[37] Source: Ibid.

number is not thinking of aggressive, but the old way. In the harsh financial ecology, it is difficult for Hanye Ping to survive.

Industry is the most important core sector for the creation of social wealth, and a massive expansion of bank credit, if not combined with the most productive industry, is bound to explode into inflation sooner or later. Japan's experience and China's lessons once again show that finance is the core lifeblood of a country and that it is impossible to retain control of national sovereignty and economic lifeblood without financial sovereignty!

The success of the Meiji Restoration caused Japan's national power to soar and, more importantly, greatly stimulated the impulse to expand. China's foreign affairs movement, while seemingly lively, could not stand the test of war at all. When China and Japan collided head-on, the "Western mirror" of the foreign affairs movement immediately shattered into the slag of history.

The Sino-Japanese War left an indelible mark on the history of both China and Japan. China is no longer the arrogant, high-minded superpower of the former dynasty, but has quickly become a lamb for the slaughter of the great powers; and Japan is no longer the small, isolated island of peace of mind it once was.

Fission of Fate

China's defeat in the Sino-Japanese War was a surprise to the world, but a certainty to China. The problem was not the disparity in national power, but the negative strategy of the foreign buy-side.

At the time, China still had an economic and military advantage over Japan. From an economic point of view, although the Meiji Restoration was very effective, Japan's heavy industry was still weak, and only the textile industry was more developed among light industries. Steel, coal, copper, kerosene, and machine-made production are all much lower than in China. At that time, Japan had a total industrial capital of 70 million yen, bank capital of 90 million yen, imports and exports of 260 million yen, and fiscal revenue of 80 million yen, all of which were not as good as China except for the volume of imports. From a military point of view, from the Meiji Restoration onwards, Japan, out of the instinct of an island nation, did everything in its power to increase its military strength, and before the war, it had 55 warships with a displacement of 61,000 tons, comparable to the Chinese

Beijing fleet. Japan's standing army of 220,000, with a total strength of less than half of China's, is not too far apart in terms of weaponry. Obviously, China still has a slight advantage over Japan in terms of military power.

As the saying goes, "If one soldier is a bear, he will be a bear in a den". It would have been a miracle if the "strong brigade" under the leadership of Li Hongzhang, the Minister of Foreign Affairs, had won the war.

Li Hongzhang boasted of the "world's eighth fleet" of the Beijing navy, ranked ahead of the United States and Japan, but in the Sino-Japanese War, not even a single Japanese ship was sunk, and he ended up with a total loss of his army. The Army is even more ridiculous, having won dozens of battles without a single victory, and the rest can be summed up in the words "fleeing in the wind". The battle of Asan, Ye Zhichao not only fled hastily, but also falsely reported the battle, and later in Pyongyang, North Korea again staged a victory in the Great Escape stunt, running 500 miles wildly to escape back to the Yalu River, if Ye Zhichao to participate in the world marathon, will be the second choice for the gold. On the Yalu River Line, Li Hongzhang arranged 40,000 "strong brigades", more troops than the Japanese, but in less than three days the whole line was defeated. The Japanese attacked Yizhou and fired only one platoon of guns before the "strong brigade" abandoned the city and fled. When the Japanese attacked Dalian, Commander-in-Chief Zhao Huaiye hoisted the flag and left the city, which may have broken the Guinness World Record. The family's gold and silver had been shipped out in advance, but more than 130 cannons, 2.4 million rounds of shells and bullets were seized by the Japanese army. The Japanese attacked Lushun again, the "strong brigade" with 70,000 troops to escape, to deal with the Japanese army of 20,000 labor division expedition, the commander in chief Gong Zhaoma did not even see the shadow of the Japanese army, and then absconded by boat to Weihai the night, the result of the group is leaderless, the military heart disintegrated, the Qing Empire spent tens of millions of two silver to build the Lushun fortress was captured in an instant. In the words of Li Hongzhang's staff, "The Japanese used to say that China was like a dead pig lying on the ground and being slaughtered.

Li Hongzhang could not fight a war, but negotiation was his strong point. As a result, the DPRK entered Japan's sphere of influence and ceded Taiwan, the Penghu Islands and the Liaodong Peninsula with the

Treaty of Shimonoseki, which paid 200 million taels of silver. Subsequently, through the mediation of the conspiratorial powers, Japan agreed to return the Liaodong Peninsula, but the compensation was increased by 30 million taels of silver.

How could the defeated Qing Empire have the money to pay its debts? The international bankers have been waiting for this big foreign debt bill. The financial vultures of the nations swarmed on, and the Great Qing Empire was immediately pecked to death.

The Qing government borrowed 200 million taels of silver and borrowed such a large amount of foreign debt was unprecedented. Before the Sino-Japanese War, the Qing government also borrowed foreign debts, but the amounts were not large and it was not very difficult to pay the principal and interest, and they were basically paid off before the war. The foreign debt required for the huge compensation of the Treaty of Ma Guan mortgaged almost all of the revenue of the Qing dynasty and foreign monopoly capital began to control the finances of the Qing government. The Qing government's inability to make ends meet was getting worse. It was to secure these loans that the Qing government was forced to let Germany lease Jiaozhou Bay, Russia took the port of Dalian in Lushun, Britain seized Weihaiwei, and France borrowed Guangzhou Bay. The loan is conditional on no early repayment or accelerated repayment, and the loan is secured by almost all of the customs, salt and cents taxes of the Qing government. To put it simply, this foreign debt was to take the tax revenue of the entire Qing dynasty as collateral. The defeat of Awu left the Qing Empire completely bankrupt.

Japan suddenly acquired such amazing wealth that the desire for aggression soared and began to set its sights on Russia.

Looking at the Japanese victory in the Russo-Japanese War through the eyes of the British Empire, it was actually in line with their strategic layout around the world, "our illustrious, spirited, little protector of the East, the Japanese, determined to defeat the Russians for us". And what Japan has bloodied is 1.5 billion yen of foreign debt and huge war consumption, nearly four times what it got from the Sino-Japanese War! At this point Japan was so mad that it could not pay such a high debt without going out and looting. Whether it was the Sino-Japanese War or the Russo-Japanese War, in addition to the bloodshed between the winners and losers, there were also international bankers who ate the big cake of foreign debt underwriting and laughed behind the scenes.

Li Hongzhang also had another, bigger piece of the cake for international bankers, which was financing China's rail network. It may not have occurred to the Great Qing Empire that it was the railroad boom that buried its rule.

Railroads are certainly a good thing, the key is who controls them.

In the words of the Meiji oligarchs, they saw with their own eyes that in India, wherever the British Empire's railways were built, they were reduced to miserable colonies. The Great Qing Empire was long on its last legs, and it was simply impossible to come up with the silver to build a nationwide rail network, and the international bankers were desperate.

The first railway loan went to HSBC and Jardine Matheson, the line from Tianjin to Fengtian and Niuzhuang, and the guarantee was the entire railway assets of the Beijing to Shanghuang line. In other words, if the loan isn't paid, the UK will have to rent Beijing. All railroad tracks, wagons, locomotives, etc., went to Jardine's. Jardine, which started out as an opium business, has finally upgraded its industry and is now doing decent business.

The second rail business was the Shanghai-Nanjing line from Shanghai to Nanjing. The Yangtze River basin was supposed to be a British sphere of influence, but the Russians, dissatisfied with the threat to their docks from the British mountain customs railway, jumped in to stir the pot. The result was that Russia went away in a huff. In this way, HSBC and Jardine's monopoly on rail transport in the richest part of China, the Shanghai-Nanjing Line, allows them to set arbitrary rates without fear of competition, as the terms of the loan prohibit further rail construction in the same area.

After the Russo-Japanese War, Japan took over the South Manchurian railway system, but had no money to maintain and repair it, and Japan simply owed too much money. Yokohama Shojin Bank can only turn to HSBC for help, and Shojin Bank can be the only one in Japan, but it is still a minor player in the international financial market.

Railways were mortgaged to foreign banks as if a chain was firmly attached to the Great Qing Empire.

Finally, the once glorious giant, its decaying, decaying body filled with Western financial vultures, sometimes fighting each other, more often pecking at the dried up flesh, met the cold, wary eyes of its back, looking around for potential threats.

CHAPTER III

"April 12" coup: Chiang Kai-shek's "name"

Why did the Soviet Union spend 30 million gold rubles to support the Northern Expeditionary War? Why did Chiang Kai-shek turn against the Communists? Why was there a coup d'état on 12 April? Whose lap did Chiang Kai-shek take? Why does Ninghan "merge"? Why did Chiang Kai-shek, who was in power, go to the field? Why did Chiang Kai-shek make a comeback?

Both revolutions and wars are organized violence, and mass violence requires mass financing. What role did money play in the history of China in 1927, and who were the people who exerted the dominant influence? And whose will do these people represent?

As we follow the will of money, the flow of money, and the effect of money, and observe the cooperation of the Communist Party, the war of Northern Expedition, and the coup d'état of April 12th, a line of money gradually becomes clear.

Chiang Kai-shek, with strong nationalist sentiments, was tempted by power and money to throw himself, step by step, into the arms of the Western powers and the buying classes, whom he had loathed and been hostile to. To do so, he had to submit willingly to the "petition of submission": the "April 12" coup d'état.

Whether it is the "Ning-Han merger", Chiang Kai-shek's downfall or even his comeback, all are interpreting a huge force that has been ignored, which is the will of money!

The hesitation of Chiang Kai-shek in marching to Shanghai and Ningxia

In November 1926, on a late autumn day when the maple leaves were drifting, Chiang Kai-shek was still pacing back and forth in his office at the General Headquarters of the Northern Expeditionary Force in Nanchang. At the moment, his mood was anxious and tangled. The closer the Northern Expeditionary Force approached Shanghai and Nanking, the more restless he felt.

In military terms, Chiang Kai-shek fought well. Since July 1926, when Guangzhou swore in the Northern Expedition, the army has been marching high and mighty. The revolutionary melody of "Down with the Powers and out with the Warlords" resounded throughout China, and the fierce wave of national revolution quickly swept across the Great River, defeating the seemingly powerful Beijing Warlords in a crushing defeat, and the Northern Expeditionary Force reached Wuhan in just three months, destroying the armed forces of Warlord Wu Peifu. The Kuomintang Central Committee and the Kuomintang government also subsequently moved from Guangzhou to Wuhan. Immediately after, in November, the Northern Expeditionary Force Commander-in-Chief Chiang Kai-shek led his troops from the Two Lakes area into Jiangxi, defeated another warlord, Sun Chuanfang, and conquered Jiujiang and Nanchang, pointing his troops directly at Nanjing and Shanghai.

Politically, however, the situation was very much against Chiang Kai-shek. His main political opponent, Wang Jingwei, went to Wuhan. Since Sun Yat-sen's death in 1925, Wang Jingwei, as the successor to the Prime Minister, has become the main leader of the Kuomintang, with strong political power within the party, backed by Soviet politics, military and money. With Wang Jingwei's alliance with local powerhouse Tang Shengzhi in Wuhan, coupled with Soviet advisor Borodin, who was deeply hostile to Chiang Kai-shek, Wuhan had become the nucleus of the KMT's internal opposition to Chiang. By this time, most of the KMT central committee members had arrived in Wuhan and political power was dominated by Wang Jingwei. Wang Jingwei repeatedly urged Chiang Kai-shek to come to Wuhan without delay, and Chiang was in deep trouble. If you go to Wuhan, you are likely to be hollowed out, and if you do not go, you are in danger of being cut off from the party state. What's more, his Northern Expeditionary Force was consuming large amounts of food and rations every day, and the financial power was not in his hands. If Wuhan cut off his wealth, his Northern Expeditionary Force would immediately lose its fighting power.

Chiang Kai-shek's ideal was to unify the country through the Northern Expedition, and then become the Caesar of China. Fortunately, he had to rely on Soviet money to achieve his ideals, and it was Stalin's eye and right-hand man in China, Borodin, who stuck his financial lifeline. After the "Zhongshan Ship Incident", although he weakened the Communist Party's power in Guangzhou to some extent, he had to hold back temporarily for the sake of Soviet armaments and money, and for the sake of his great cause of unifying China.

When the May Fourth Movement broke out, Chiang Kai-shek was so shaken that he wrote in his diary,

> *"This is the first demonstration by the Chinese people, and it is an unprecedented feat... The people are not yet discouraged, the people's hearts are not yet dead, and the Republic of China should be revived one day."*

On 23 June 1925, when the masses in Guangzhou supported the Hong Kong workers' strike and staged a demonstration past Shaji, near the British tenancy, the British army brazenly massacred more than 50 people and injured more than 170, resulting in the "Shaji Tragedy". Chiang Kai-shek wrote in his diary:

> *"The country to this point, not to Chinese lives as a matter of business, let their British imperialism killed by the traitors, heard the heart is broken, a few do not know how to people! Since birth, grief has not been greater than it is today."*

The angry Chiang Kai-shek wrote in his diary a daily slogan of "cynicism" against Yingde, which amounted to over a hundred entries.

> *"All British prisoners can be killed! You'll have to put up with it! It's not a man who can't be destroyed! Have you forgotten the enemy of the British? The revolution will never end! ..."*[38]

In 1926, Chiang Kai-shek severely criticized the foreign policy of the United States,

> *"denouncing the errors of the United States foreign policy and the hypocrisy of Christianity".*

Chiang Kai-shek was not only angry with the great powers, but also hated the foreign buying class, hating them for helping the foreigners control China's economic lifeblood.

---

[38] *Finding the Real Chiang Kai-shek*, by Yang Tianshi, Shanxi People's Press, 2008, p. 20.

> "The abomination of foreign slaves goes beyond that. Any foreign slave in the tenancy sector, the Office and the Yangtze Company may be killed."

The weird thing about history is that who would have thought that Chiang Kai-shek, the head of China's largest bureaucratic buy-in class, would have hated in his bones the forces on which he relied! Absurdly but paradoxically, as a politician who puts personal power first, the ideal is subordinate to reality and he is very conscious of who can bring him power. When the Soviet Union was available, he used Soviet money and weapons to achieve a northern expedition and unification, consolidating and strengthening his power. When the Soviet Union tried to control and command him, he would not hesitate to kick him out of the way. In later days, this was true of the powers he hated, such as Britain, the United States, Japan, etc., and also of the foreign buyers he loathed. He positions himself as the incarnation of revolution and the ultimate interpreter of truth, and to oppose him is to oppose revolution, to oppose truth! Whoever stands in his way of power "can be killed"!

In Chiang Kai-shek's view, the world is full of rats and males. The Fengtian warlord Zhang Zuolin, who has no idealistic beliefs and has Japan as his backing, is in possession of the northeastern part of the country, and although he is powerful, he is a bandit, while Wu Peifu and Sun Chuanfang, who are directly under his command, have many internal contradictions, and although they occupy a large area, they only need to be defeated individually. It was still the Communist Party that gave him the most headache.

Chiang Kai-shek had visited the Soviet Union and witnessed a party with the doctrine and belief system of proletarian dictatorship, well organized and deeply embedded in the army. The Soviet Red Army was unified and united in action, and its fighting strength was very different from that of the Chinese warlords. Chiang Kai-shek, who was greatly inspired, vigorously promoted "One Party, One Doctrine" upon his return to China, saying,

> "If China is to have a revolution, it must also concentrate all its forces and follow the example of the Russian revolution, for it is not possible to have a revolution without the dictatorship and autocracy of one party."

It was for this reason that Chiang Kai-shek's general policy of "United Russia, United Communist Party and support for agricultural workers" for Sun Yat-sen was, in his heart, a stopgap measure to gain

Soviet aid and increase the strength of the Kuomintang. Therefore, the situation of the Communist Party joining the Kuomintang as a "party within a party" is very much resented. In particular, the Communist Party's ability to mobilize the masses and organize them was far more powerful than that of the Kuomintang, and it fought hotly with the leftists in the Kuomintang, greatly increasing the difficulty of Chiang Kai-shek's centralization of power in the Kuomintang. A large number of Communists held key positions in the National Government during the "Great" period of the Kuomintang.

On the issue of the Northern Expedition, Chiang Kai-shek insisted on speed, while Borodin seemed to see through his personal agenda and suggested a delay, consolidating the revolutionary regime in Guangdong first and mobilizing the masses until the time was right. Chiang Kai-shek understood very well that the day when Borodin's "time was ripe" was when he would be driven out. So he had to seize the moment and be bigger and stronger. Against his best efforts, Borodin finally made concessions and Chiang Kai-shek's northern expedition began.

Chiang Kai-shek's Northern Expedition progressed at a breakneck pace, thanks in large part to the Soviet Union's constant supply of arms and financial support. So why did the Soviet Union support the Nationalist Party? This needs to be said of the international environment of the Soviet Union at the time.

30 million gold rubles for the Northern War

In Vladivostok in February 1920, on a dark and windy night, a carriage loaded with wooden crates and escorted by soldiers drove into the compound of HSBC's Vladivostok branch. The bank staff immediately carried the unloaded wooden crates laboriously into the bank's vault, whereupon branch manager Wood opened the first crate with two assistants to inventory the goods. Wood opened the lid to reveal a box full of neatly arranged gold bricks, still glowing in the darkness. So they reached in, took advantage of the little dim light of the candle, and fumbled carefully for the gold nugget, counting the quantity.

> *"The floor is piled high with boxes. We stepped on boxes, holding candles in one hand and fire paint in the other, opening*

> each box, examining the contents, sealing them with fire paint, and sending them off for loading."[39]

The gold, which originally belonged to the Tsar, was lying quietly in the treasury of the Central Bank of Tsarist Russia two years ago, and is now in the vaults of HSBC as trophies. What's going on?

After the Russian October Revolution, the Tsarist army in Siberia, led by Admiral Gorczak, marched on Moscow and seized Kazan, the treasury of the central bank of the Tsarist government, with a whirlwind attack on the gold reserves worth £80 million. He was then defeated under Moscow and fled east along the Great Siberian Railway with the gold. In winter, the cold in Siberia completely destroyed the morale of this defeated army, which had just run to Irkutsk and was in disarray. In order to stay alive, the mutinous soldiers made a deal with the Soviet government in which they handed over Kolchak and the gold to the Soviet government, which in turn guaranteed their personal safety and let them return home. These mutinous soldiers were mainly European mercenaries who, in order to return to Europe by boat from Vladivostok, secretly withheld some of their gold and sold it to the HSBC Vladivostok branch.

The Soviet government, which had been so poor that it was clanging, got hold of the gold reserves left by the Russians and stiffened its loins at once. At that time, the £1 was about 10 taels of silver. The gold from the Russian treasury was sold by European mercenaries to HSBC, and the remaining gold worth about 50 million pounds fell into the hands of the Russian government, which was a huge sum of 500 million taels of silver! Back then, the Japanese extorted 230 million taels of silver from China through the Sino-Japanese War, and after exchanging it for gold in Britain, succeeded in establishing a gold standard yen system. The Bolshevik Politburo, which has no shortage of financial currency masters, used this gold as a reserve to reform the ruble's currency system and introduce a gold standard. So the Russian economy, which had been destroyed by the war, gradually stabilized and got back on track.[40]

---

[39] *A Centennial History of HSBC*, (English) by Maurice and Corliss, China Books, 1979, p. 109.

[40] *A Study on the Transformation of the Russian Banking System*, by Xu Xiangmei, China Finance Press, 2005, pp. 33–37.

The Soviet government, which was on firm footing, had just taken a breather and looked around with palpitations and found itself in a really bad situation. The West is a world dominated by capitalist powers, the East and the South are colonies and semi-colonies under imperialist control, and the powers can launch a surprise attack at any point along Russia's long borderline to subvert the Soviet regime.

In this situation, it is useless to bide one's time, only to attack and build a buffer zone along the border against imperialist aggression. And with China having a long borderline with the Soviet Union, how to prevent imperialism from using China as a springboard to attack the soft lower belly of the Soviet Union became a strategic issue of concern for the Russians. Specifically, to achieve two basic strategic objectives in China: first, to promote independence or autonomy for Outer Mongolia and establish a pro-Soviet regime as a buffer zone between China and the Soviet Union; and second, to maintain exclusive rights and interests in the Middle East railway in northeast China (Manzhouli via Harbin to Suifenhe).

To achieve these two goals is difficult without the backing of the Chinese government. So the Soviet and Russian governments sent the veteran diplomat Yuefei on a mission to China to make a mapping of the various forces. As soon as Yue Fei took office, he immediately discussed cooperation with Wu Peifu in Beijing, but Wu Peifu, backed by Britain and the United States, simply ignored it, not to mention ceding the Outer Mongolia and Middle East Railway. After spending most of the year in Beijing, nothing was accomplished except for catching up with Wu Peifu's general, Feng Yuxiang, on this line. Just when Yue Fei was at a loss, Sun Yat-sen of the southern Guangzhou government took the initiative to come to the door.

To survive, to revolutionize and to unify the country, one must have money and "pull the wind". The British did not look favorably on Sun Yat-sen, who bet his treasure on Yuan Shikai when the Xinhai Revolution was just won. The U.S. JPMorgan consortium sent someone to talk to Lamont, a JPMorgan representative, who asked how "peace between North and South" could be achieved in China. Sun Yat-sen exclaimed,

> *"Peace between North and South? It is possible, Mr. Lamont, and all you have to do is give me twenty-five million dollars, and I can equip a few legions, and then we shall soon be at peace."*[41]

Lamont shook his head darkly, not even a solid piece of ground, without anything of value as collateral, twenty-five million dollars a mouthful, possible?

At this point, the Soviet delegate Yue flew out to embassy China. In early 1923, Yue Fei went to Shanghai for 10 days under the pretext of recuperating from illness, and had a long talk with Sun Yat-sen almost every day. By 26 January, the Sun Moon Yat-Fei Declaration was publicly released, with the following main points.

—The Northeast China Railway will be under the joint control of China and the Soviet Union for the time being and the Soviet Red Army in Outer Mongolia will not have to withdraw immediately.

—Both sides agree that China's immediate priority is to carry out a national revolution and complete national unity and independence, rather than to rush into communism.

Sun Yat-sen's national revolution "could have been dependent on Russian aid".[42]

In March 1923, the Politburo of the Soviet Communist Party met and voted to aid Sun Yat-sen with the first financial aid of 2 million gold rubles.[43] Of course, since the Soviet economy had just stabilized and could not get so much money at once, the two million gold rubles were purely empty-handed wolves. The original Yuefei and Sun Yat-sen signed a good contract, immediately went to Japan, and signed a fisheries cooperation agreement with the Japanese, Japanese fishermen can go to the Soviet Union coastal areas to fish, on the condition that the Soviets pay a large protection fee, the Soviets are using this money

---

[41] *J.P. Morgan Consortium*, (English) Chernow, translated by Jin Liqun, China Financial and Economic Press, 1996, p. 248.

[42] *Middle Zone Revolution*, by Yang Kui-Song, Shanxi People's Publishing House, 2010, pp. 50–51.

[43] Mikhail Borodin (1884–1951), *The Eminent Soviet Communists – Participants in the Chinese Revolution*, by R. A. Mirovitskaya, pp. 22–40.

to complete the financing of a phase of the Chinese project.[44] Shortly after the Soviet Union's economic recovery began to take effect, a second phase of financing was carried out, allocating 3 million gold rubles, 8,000 rifles, 15 machine guns, 4 artillery guns and 2 armoured vehicles to assist China in establishing the Huangpu Military Academy.[45]

According to Wang Bo-ling, director of the Huangpu Military Academy's professorial department, Sun Yat-sen gave 300 Guangdong-made Mauser guns to the academy before it opened. However, the arsenal at that time was so bent on appeasing the warlords that it did not give priority to the military school, and as a result only 30 units were issued at the beginning of the school year, barely enough for the guards. Liao Zhongkai's repeated negotiations were to no avail. At this point, the Soviet aid gunboat arrived ashore with 8,000 rifles, all armed with bayonets, each with 500 rounds of ammunition, and 10 pistols, to the cheers of the cadets. Wang Bo-ling recalled that it was "a great joy, and the whole school, from the governor to the students, was overjoyed" and that "we will have no worries in the future, the revolution will have money".

Before the start of the Northern Expeditionary War in 1923–1926, the Guangzhou National Government received a total of about 3 million gold rubles worth of Soviet arms, including 26,000 rifles, 16 million rounds of ammunition, 90 machine guns and 24 guns. In addition to this, the Soviet government provided the KMT with 100,000 gold rubles per month for party affairs since November 1924, and even gave the KMT 10 million gold rubles for the creation of the KMT Central Bank.[46]

In the North, Soviet advisors also trained and equipped Feng Yuxiang's National Army. According to receipts signed by Feng Yuxiang, between April 1925 and March 1926, the Soviet Union provided him with arms and ammunition worth more than 6 million

---

[44] From "Diplomacy in Writing" to "History as a Lesson" – *A Historical Study of Sino-Japanese Relations in Modern Times*, (Japan) by Ihara Sawazu, China Books, 2003, pp. 413–415.

[45] *The Soviets in World Affairs*, Fisher.

[46] *Middle Belt Revolution*, by Yang Kui Song, Shanxi People's Publishing House, 2010, p. 67.

gold rubles, and in March 1926, Feng Yuxiang visited the Soviet Union after his fall from power and signed an arms loan agreement for about 11 million gold rubles.[47]

Thus, the Soviet Union's arms and financial assistance to the Kuomintang accumulated over 30 million gold rubles over three years. It was through the strong blood transfusion of the Soviet Union that the Northern Expeditionary Force of the Kuomintang rapidly grew into a decisive force in China's political landscape. When the Soviet advisor Borodin was passing through Zhengzhou, he lamented to Feng Yuxiang:

> *"The Soviet Union had spent more than 30 million dollars, and I personally spent a lot of effort and spirit to make the National Revolution a success."*

Chiang Kai-shek, in November 1926, was indeed faced with a major choice: to turn his back on the Soviet Union would lose huge financial support and supplies of military equipment; but to take orders from Borodin and go to Wuhan would again bury his power and political life.

To go, or not to go, that's the question!

Chiang Kai-shek had no choice but to stall for time and patiently approach the various venture capitalists. After much activity, Bank of China Shanghai provided him with 1 million silver dollars and British American Tobacco loaned him 2 million silver dollars, but the money was a drop in the bucket and did not help the overall situation. The only way to make a big project is to pull in a large and stable venture capital. So Chiang told the British Consul General in Guangzhou, through the foreign journalist Norman Norman and the foreigner who had served him, about the impending break with the Communist Party and asked whether "the powers could give Chiang some assurance of support".[48]

However, at this time, a man rushed from Shanghai to Chiang Kai-shek's Nanchang Northern Expeditionary Force General Headquarters, and asked to be interviewed, when the deputy officer informed the

---

[47] *History of International Relations in the Far East*, (English) by Ma Shi, Shanghai Bookstore Press, 1998, p. 692.

[48] British Diplomatic Papers, FO, 405, Vol 1 .252, pp. 311–313, 398–400, 113–115

man's name, Chiang Kai-shek was suddenly overjoyed, cleared his face of many days of worry, and rushed to Yuanmen to meet him personally.

The person who came was none other than Yu Qiaqing.

Chiang Kai-shek has a bigger leg

When Chiang Kai-shek was in the doldrums on the Shanghai Bund, he speculated in stocks and futures at the Shanghai Stock Exchange, which was founded by Mr. Yu, a financial tycoon. After being beaten up, it was Master Yu who took care of the situation and introduced Chiang Kai-shek to Du Yuesheng and Jinrong, two of Shanghai's top gangsters. Chiang Kai-shek had a great friendship with him.

Yu Qiaqing also did not treat himself as an outsider, as soon as he entered the living room, a brief exchange of pleasantries, then straightforwardly threw two key questions to Chiang Kai-shek:

> *"You say that the United Russia, the United Communist Party, help the agricultural workers, is really to help the poor? So what do we do?"*

Chiang Kai-shek laughed,

> *"How can poor rednecks be trusted?"*

Yu Qiaqing asked again,

> *"Then the Northern Expeditionary Force wants to defeat the great powers, I have worked with the foreigners, and I am still doing business with them."*

Chiang Kai-shek sighed,

> *"How can a foreigner beat that?"*

Upon hearing this, Old Master Yu nodded his head and had the bottom of his heart, further probing,

> *"Then how can I help you if I go back?"*

With a fierce wave of his hand, Chiang Kai-shek said,

> *"I will conquer Shanghai soon and arrive at Nanking, you talk to Mr. Du (Du Yuesheng) and Mr. Huang (Golden Rong) and help me maintain good security in Shanghai."*

Yu Qiaqing nodded:

"This is no problem. What can I do?"

Chiang Kai-shek heard it and moved in his heart, leaned forward, stared at Yu Qiaqing, and said in one sentence,

"Money, help me raise money, the more the better, it will cost money to get to Shanghai."

This is clearly a deal. The purpose of the Northern Expedition is to defeat the great powers and support the agricultural workers, but Chiang Kai-shek now can not control so many principles, between power and principle, he did not hesitate to choose the former.

In fact, as early as the beginning of 1926, the British Foreign Office had organized a discussion on China's countermeasures to the war of Northern Expedition, in which embassy and consular officials, naval and military commanders, and the British authorities in Hong Kong offered five options: the use of force, international blockade, assistance to northern warlords, pressure on the Soviet Union and Huairou. It was argued that the first two options were counterproductive and counterproductive, and that it would be difficult to gain the support of the other powers; that the third option would be difficult to find someone with an iron fist of British interest; that the fourth option would be ineffective; and that only the last one, Huairou, seemed feasible and "constructive".[49]

In 1925, the British side of Hong Kong openly supplied the Kuomintang's internal warlord, Chen Jiongming, with arms and cash to revolt against the Kuomintang government. As a result, Chen Jiongming's rebellion was suppressed, and the Northern Expeditionary Army, armed with gold rubles, largely defeated the various warlords of the Beijing, originally supported by international bankers. The speed with which these Beijing warlords collapsed made their backstage bosses jaw-dropping and fumbling. The biggest question before imperialism is, where are the new agents?

At this point, Chiang Kai-shek, the commander-in-chief of the Northern Expeditionary Force, became a good candidate to cultivate. However, the political situation in China is too confusing, and it has always been a good judge of the direction of investment in the Financial

---

[49] W. R. Louis, *British Strategy in the Far East, 1919–1939*, Clarendor Press, Oxford 1971. pp. 129–130.

City of London and Wall Street in the United States, which is also a big one and two. What if this man doesn't do his job or doesn't do his job well after taking the money? In order to get to the bottom of Chiang Kai-shek, the U.S. government even sent someone to look into the criminal records of Chiang Kai-shek in the files of the Bureau of Industry of the Shanghai Public Tenancy.[50]

But it is clear that a mere side investigation is not enough, and one must speak to the face of the gong to get to the bottom of it. Then there was the big buyer Yu Qiaqing ran to Nanchang to personally "interview" Chiang Kai Shek. After the initial detection of Chiang Kai-shek's backing card, Yu Qiaqing went to Nanchang in February 1927 to "retest" Chiang Kai-shek. This time, a secret agreement was reached: Chiang Kai-shek could get a loan of 60 million yen after his arrival in Shanghai and Nanjing, on the condition that Chiang Kai-shek would submit a "declaration" – a knife against the Communists.[51]

60 million ocean temptation! At that time, a courtyard in Beijing was only 200 foreign dollars! The Soviets almost won the Northern Expeditionary War by throwing 30 million gold rubles, or about 27 million ocean, into the Kuomintang over a three-year period from 1924 to 1927.

That's 60 million dollars. It's not said. Fuck! Chiang Kai-shek is going to turn the knife on the Communist Party.

The Soviet Union's three-year investment of 30 million gold rubles went up in smoke after two meetings between Yu Qiaqing and Chiang Kai-shek. Of course, this is not because of how great Yu Qiaqing's personal energy is, much less because of how deep his personal friendship with Chiang Kai-shek is, but because the forces behind Yu Qiaqing are more wealthy than the Soviet Union and more afraid of the Communist Party than Chiang Kai-shek.

Chiang Kai-shek finally clasped a thicker thigh!

---

[50] U.S. Department of State Files (Micro), RDS, NA, M. No. 329, 893.00/8005, 893.00/8312.

[51] The establishment of the Jiangzhe zaibatsu and Chiang Kai-shek's reactionary rule, Ling Yu, "Party History Research Materials", No. 7, p. 49.

Yu Qiaqing and Chiang Kai-shek: The Story That Must Be Told

Yu Qiaqing is a famous figure on the Shanghai Bund, a true financial bigwig. He was a buyer of the ABN AMRO Bank, and also ran a money bank, investment bank, shipping company, and befriended all three schools of thought, even Gold Rong and Du Yuesheng had to respect his predecessors, and even the foreigners in the rental sector gave him three points.

ABN AMRO has a very special place in the international bankers' landscape, with its founders being the old Jewish banking family, the Mendelssohn family. In 1640, after the English bourgeois revolution, Mendelssohn, Sassoon and Rothschild belonged to the Sephardic Jews, and in the 1590s, Spain saw a wave of anti-Semitism, with the Rothschilds in exile in Germany, where they became court bankers for the German royal family; Sassoon went to the Middle East, where he became chief financial officer of Baghdad; and Mendelssohn fled to the Netherlands, where he founded the Bank of Holland and the Dutch East India Company. By the Victorian era, he was known as "the Queen's favourite Jew" and became the British Crown's most trusted court banker. in 1812, Mendelssohn married the Rothschild family and manipulated stock investments for the Rothschilds, and the two families formed a bloodthirsty alliance. During the Second World War, all of the Rothschild family's investments in continental Europe were handled by the Meng family's Dutch bank. To this day, the Rothschild office in Hong Kong, China, is still named after ABN AMRO Rothschild.

It was for this banking family that Yu Qiaqing worked for 30 years, so diligently and conscientiously that the Queen of the Netherlands, who knew nothing about Chinese customs, gave a royal clock in recognition of his achievements.

The Shanghai Chamber of Commerce, founded by Yu Qiaqing, had its own armed forces and played a major role in the battle for the restoration of Shanghai during the Xinhai Revolution. At that time, this merchant group took the Shanghai Tao County Office and then took the Jiangnan Manufacturing Bureau. The Shanghai Chamber of Commerce under Yu Qiaqing's control also raised a total of 3 million taels of silver for the subsequent establishment of the Shanghai Military Governor's Office of the Allied Association, which raised 1.8 million taels of silver.

At the end of 1916, in order to raise funds for the revolution, Sun Yat-sen, who was very economically minded, discussed with Yu Qiaqing and others to set up a securities and goods exchange in Shanghai to deal in securities, yarn, gold and silver, miscellaneous grains and furs, and applied to the Ministry of Agriculture and Commerce of the Beijing government. However, the Beijing warlords were so nervous about the "Sun Cannon" that they refused to approve it, and because of the economic downturn at the time, the matter was shelved.

Later, it was Chiang Kai-shek who took the matter further down the line. In the early years, Chiang Kai-shek followed Chen Qimei, the leader of the Shanghai Allied Association, to carry out the anti-ching revolution, when the Allied Association attacked the Qing army's fortified Jiangnan Manufacturing Bureau, Chiang Kai-shek and Chen Qimei carried guns together, is the battlefield to fight together out of a life of friendship, later the two became kowtow brothers. Chen Qimei was Sun Yat-sen's number one confidant, and after the success of the revolution, he became the governor of Shanghai. Yu Qiaqing worked as a financial advisor to Chen Qimei and raised large sums of money to maintain his operations. Because of his special relationship with Chen Qimei, Chiang Kai-shek also got into a hot fight with Yu Qiaqing. Later, when Chen was assassinated, Chiang Kai-shek lost his backing.

Sun Yat-sen's idea of using the stock exchange to fund the revolution was still insightful; both revolution and war require money, and a lot of it. When Chiang Kai-shek accepted the organization's commission to continue to promote the Exchange, he felt that he had found a direction for his career. He first organized a secret society called "Xiejingsha" in Shanghai with his old friend Dai Jitao, Chen Qimei's nephew Chen Guofu, and Zhang Jingjiang, a wealthy warlord in Jiangsu and Zhejiang, to carry out specific organizational planning work. Then La Yu Qiaqing came to mobilize the Shanghai business community to apply to the Ministry of Agriculture and Commerce in Beijing to create the Shanghai Stock Exchange.

On July 1, 1920, China's first comprehensive exchange, the Shanghai Stock Exchange, was officially opened. The chairman of the board is Yu Qiaqing, and the items traded are securities, cotton, cotton yarn, cloth, gold and silver, grain, oil, hides and skins, etc. On the same day, Shanghai "Declaration" published an advertisement:

> "Shanghai Stock Exchange No. 54 broker Chen Guofu, I trade in securities and cotton on behalf of my clients, if entrusted, we sincerely welcome. Office: Room 80, 3rd floor, No. 1 Sichuan Road Phone: exchange 54."

This No. 54 brokerage office is the "Hengtai" set up by Chiang Kai-shek, the specific business is handed over to Chen Guofu to operate. The scope of business of "HMS Hang Tai" is to trade in various securities and cotton yarns on behalf of customers with a total capital of 35 shares of 35,000 silver dollars. Chiang Kai-shek had 4 strands in it. Later Chiang Kai-shek failed in his opportunistic business and was forced into debt, or Yu Qiaqing introduced him to the head of the triad society, Gold Rong, and was under Gold Rong's tutelage, and Gold Rong stepped in to clear the debt, and funded for him to go south to Guangzhou to defect to Sun Yat-sen.

In March 1927, immediately after the liberation of Shanghai by an armed uprising of the Shanghai working class under the leadership of the Communist Party, the British ambassador to the United States told Secretary of State Kellogg:

> "A retreat there (Shanghai) would be impossible, and our position and rights at the ports of commerce would be all but lost, and our government would consider defending with all its might the leased territory of Shanghai, which was a concentration of British interests. We warmly welcome U.S. cooperation on all fronts in Shanghai and Nanjing Wenwu."[52]

Just in March 1927, in order to defend the "Shanghai Tenants", where the interests of the (international bankers) were concentrated, there were more than 17,000 British troops, 4,000 Japanese troops, 3,500 American troops and 2,500 French troops gathered in Shanghai, together with the Tenants' Bureau of Industry armed with the "Tenant's Business Corps" and patrols, etc., the total number of imperialist forces reached 30,000.

At the same time, sophisticated international bankers are well aware that it would be costly and counterproductive to simply and brutally intervene directly in the face of the Chinese people, who have been inspired by the patriotic enthusiasm of the Revolution. To stabilize

---

[52] U.S. Diplomatic Papers (1927-vol. 2), edited by the U.S. Department of State, translated by Zhang Weiying et al., China Social Science Press, 1998, p. 164.

their vested interests in China, it is also up to the direct agents of the international bankers in China – the buy-side class.

At this time, the biggest interest of the Chinese buyout class is to demand power from the international bankers. The international bankers' interests in China are concentrated in the Shanghai public rented sector, where the highest authority is the Bureau of Industry. Due to the special status of the tenancy, many big buyers, Jiangsu and Zhejiang plutocrats have settled in the tenancy, to the Bureau of the Ministry of Industry to pay taxes according to regulations. However, the lackeys were not destined to sit at the same table as their masters, and these big buyers and plutocrats had no place in the Bureau of the Ministry of Industry, while the interests of "no one in the court" could not be guaranteed. In accordance with the bourgeois republican principle of "no representation, no taxation", these bought-and-paid classes are already discontented.

On March 18, 1926, members of the board of directors of the Bureau of Public Tenants of the Ministry of Industry in Shanghai had a dinner with the big shots of the Chinese bourgeoisie in Shanghai at the Dahua Hotel. According to Chinese tradition, problems are solved at the dinner table. This event is called "another milestone in the history of Shanghai ... the convening of such a conference is a first in the history of the city".[53] The American Director of the Works Bureau, speaking on behalf of his British and Japanese colleagues, said:

> "We are the hosts of all of you, and I am very glad to have a group of Chinese gentlemen of such a high reputation come to this meeting today... We are joined by a group of representative figures, all of whom are capable of regulating and guiding a huge and astonishing force, which is known to the world as public opinion".[54]

Mr. Felton Fei, Chairman of the Board of Directors of the Ministry of Industry and Commerce, who gave the keynote speech at the dinner, got right to the point: in the face of the prairie-salting forces of revolution, it is necessary to "figure out how to cope". If force were to

---

[53] *Millers Review*, March 27, 1926.

[54] *North China Express*, 20 March 1926.

be used, it could "quickly lead to an extremely serious international situation".

> "Shanghai workers seem to have become easy victims of 'third parties' (referring to the Chinese Communist Party) who induce them to undermine the safety of the factories. So why not exploit this extreme gullibility of the Chinese working class ... to their advantage and ours? Why not create another kind of leader to differentiate themselves from the ones they are already familiar with? They need to be at least as receptive to this new leadership as they are to any other leadership... I mean, there needs to be some people like we gathered tonight (to lead them)."

Yu Qiaqing immediately stood up and replied:

> "We (referring to the Chinese businessmen present) are all well aware of this very tense situation... We do not exaggerate, and at the slightest provocation, flames will immediately break out... For our mutual benefit, we must prevent it (referring to the revolution) by all means." Time is running out and it's dangerous to take orders from God. "The most important thing we can do now is to meld local initial work with concerted action on a national and international scale to bring about the fastest and most satisfactory resolution of our major problems." Immediately afterwards, Yu Qiaqing's words turned, "But frankly, we don't want to get it at 'any cost'." The principle of "racial equality" and "sovereignty" must be somewhat recognized by the foreigners. Especially at this moment, they should let the Chinese bourgeoisie participate in the administration of Shanghai.

Three weeks later, the Shanghai Public Tenancy Foreign Taxpayers' Annual Meeting passed the Chinese participation in the municipal case, and the Shanghai Public Tenancy Board had a record three Chinese directors. Since then, Yu has held a seat on the Board of Directors of the Ministry of Industry, and other Chinese directors include Xu Xinliu, Managing Director and General Manager of Zhejiang Industrial Bank, the flagship bank of the Jiangsu and Zhejiang zaibatsu system. It was clearly a deal, and the big Chinese bourgeoisie in Shanghai, the big buyers, and the Jiangzhe plutocrats sold their souls to the international bankers at such a price.

For the international bankers who were eager to suppress the Chinese revolution, Yu Qiagqing, who was so clever and had so many hands and eyes, was the right person to "interview" Chiang Kai Shek.

The financial powerhouse behind the April 12 coup

On March 26, 1927, the Northern Expeditionary Force led by Chiang Kai-shek finally drove into Shanghai. As soon as Chiang Kai-shek arrived in Shanghai, he immediately approached Yu Qiaqing and others to implement the previously agreed deal. Yu Qiaqing immediately took the lead in organizing the Shanghai Business Federation, which included all the important banks, money stores, banking houses and commercial and industrial groups in Shanghai, to prepare financing for Chiang Kai-shek.

One of the most important organizations in this federation is the Shanghai Yin Lou Guild, represented by Xi Yunsheng. The Xi family of the Dongting Mountain Gang is the top pillar of the Jiangxi and Zhejiang plutocratic system, with significant influence in foreign banks, government-run banks, commercial banks, money banks and business circles in Shanghai, and has woven a huge network of people.

Since 1874, when Xi Zhengfu became a buyer of HSBC, three generations of his grandchildren have held the position of HSBC's buyer for more than half a century. All of HSBC's business with China, including the splitting of bills for the Shanghai Money Bank, political loans to the Chinese government, railway loans and advances to the opium trade, have all been operated by HSBC's "buyer's office", which is controlled by the Xi family. The senior officials of the Qing dynasty's foreign affairs faction, from Zuo Zongtang and Li Hongzhang to Sheng Xuanhuai, would inevitably ask for help from the Xi family once they needed financing, and without exception they became close friends of the Xi family. Shanghai bankers, which need to raise funds on a regular basis in their day-to-day business, are more than willing to listen to the Xi family.

The other three of the four brothers were not simple either. The oldest, longevity, had been a buyer at the Standard Chartered Bank Shanghai Branch in the second year of its establishment and was the bank's patriarch. The old man was a buyer for the Bank of England, Derby Bank and Sino-Russian Dawson Bank. Old Fourth was passed on to Shen Er Yuan, a relative of the Xi family and the first buyer of the new Sassoon Foreign Exchange, who succeeded him as the buyer of the Sassoon Foreign Exchange, known as "Sassoon Old Fourth".

In addition to acting as a buyer for international bankers, the Xi family also used its monopoly on foreign banks and the connections of government officials to create China's official banking system, such as the Ministry of Foreign Affairs Bank, the Bank of China, and the Bank of China, with its strong financial resources, and became a major shareholder.

It can be said that the entire financial industry in Shanghai, from foreign banks, to government-run banks, to private banks and ticket numbers, are all within the power of the Xi family. At that time, the Xi family only made a small attempt and beheaded Hu Xueyan, who was the richest man in China.

The Xi's children gradually entered the family's network of buyers, becoming buyers of 13 foreign banks, and more in-laws, fellow countrymen, and classmates gradually entered the system, and a powerful network of financial and social relationships was formed. For example, Xi Zhengfu's grandson, Xi Dezhang, was a classmate of Song Ziwen's when he was in the United States, and Xi Dezhang's older brother, Xi Dezhang, married his daughter to Song Ziwen's younger brother, Song Ziliang. Siddhartha went on to become director of the National Government's Central Mint, while Siddhartha became general manager of the Bank of China.

By choosing to support Chiang Kai-shek, the XI family is tantamount to a vote of confidence in Chiang by the international bankers. In China, the time has come when it belongs to Chiang Kai-shek.

On March 29, 1927, a delegation from the Shanghai Chamber of Commerce visited Chiang Kai-shek, claiming to give financial aid whenever he broke with the Communist Party. On March 31, Yu Qiaqing and the Shanghai Commercial Federation took the lead in formally setting up the "Jiangsu and Shanghai Finance Committee", with the participation of Chen Guangfu, General Manager of the Shanghai Commercial Savings Bank, Qian Yongming, Deputy Director of the Joint Reserve of the "North Fourth Bank", and representatives of the two largest Chinese-funded banks, Bank of China and Bank of Communications, bringing together almost all the leading figures and representatives of major institutions in the Chinese financial industry.

The banks and money banks in Shanghai gave Chiang Kai-shek a financial aid of 3 million silver dollars from April 1 to 4.[55] On April 8, the U.S. Consul General in Shanghai, Gao Si, learned that the Jiangsu and Zhejiang plutocrats had offered Chiang Kai-shek 3 million silver dollars on the condition that they "insist that unless Communists are purged from the Kuomintang, they will no longer give him support."[56] Bankers are, after all, the highest of businessmen, and although they painted a 60 million dollar pie for Chiang Kai-shek, they can only get a down payment before the job is done, and only after the job is done beautifully will they continue to give.

Only a week after Chiang Kai-shek got the money, he staged the world-shaking "April 12th" coup! massacres of communists, workers, peasants and left-wingers.

Chiang Kai-shek put forward the bloody slogan of "rather kill 3,000 by mistake than one" to the Communists, and the banker felt very "generous" and immediately provided another 7 million silver dollars to Chiang Kai-shek.[57] At once, the river was so big that heads rolled and blood flowed! With the heads of a large number of communists, Chiang Kai-shek paid a bloody "declaration of defection" to the international bankers' power group for himself!

Chiang Kai-shek's Refinancing

At this time, Yu Qiaqing, who completed the "project inspection" and "financing" of the first phase, retired behind the scenes, "Chiang Kai-shek project" director of the investment committee, replaced by Chen Guangfu, the representative of the middle generation of the Jiangzhejiang and Zhejiang plutocrats. After graduating from the Wharton School of the University of Pennsylvania, he founded the Shanghai Commercial Savings Bank, which is unique in Chinese financial history. The company started with a deposit of 18,000 silver dollars in 1915 and reached an astonishing size of 33.3 million silver dollars in 1933, making it a financial wizard.

---

[55] Declaration, 28 March 1927, 11th edition.

[56] United States Department of State Archives, 893.00B/276.

[57] *Shanghai Money Bank History*, People's Bank of China, Shanghai Branch, p. 207.

In addition, Chen Guangfu had a close relationship with the Kong Xiangxi and Song Ziwen families. When Chen Guangfu founded the Shanghai Commercial Savings Bank, he raised a total of 70,000 yuan in equity, of which Kong Xiangxi had a stake of 10,000 silver yuan, the Song family also invested 5,000 silver yuan in the name of the old Madam Song Ni Guizhen, before the Northern Expedition, Kong Xiangxi wrote to Chen Guangfu several times, inviting him to go south. With this relationship, Chen Guangfu became Chiang Kai-shek's most relied upon banker.

Chen Guangfu was not ashamed of his mission and launched the "Jiangsu and Shanghai Finance Committee" to underwrite public debts for Chiang Kai-shek and to finance Chiang Kai-shek's serious shortage of money on a large scale, which was the famous "Jiangsu Customs Erwu Tax-Subsidized Treasury Bills". At that time, the Chiang Kai-shek regime, under the banner of the "national revolution", in order to highlight its "revolution", inherited the policy of the previous national governments of Guangzhou and Wuhan and imposed an additional 2.5 per cent surtax on top of the 5 per cent customs tariff controlled by foreigners, that is, the so-called "25 per cent surtax" in order to protect national industries. Of course, until the foreigners agreed, the "2.5 with tax" was just a slogan, but it did not make sense for the bankers to issue the government bonds of Chiang Kai-shek as collateral for this "unwarranted" future income.

Shanghai's financial and industrial sectors subscribed to the "Jiangxi Customs 25 Tax-Subsidized Treasury Bills" in order to "protect against warlords and the Communist Party". Politically, they chose the Nanjing National Government and financially supported Chiang Kai-shek. The issuance of bonds is expressly debt service and establishes government debt credit. In order to supervise the issuance of public debt funds to be used rationally, Jiangsu and Zhejiang plutocrats also set up a special "Jiangsu Customs Twenty-five with tax treasury securities fund custody committee", the director by another giant of Jiangsu and Zhejiang plutocrats, Zhejiang Industrial Bank Shanghai branch general manager Li Fusun. This fund's custodial committee strengthened the cooperative relationship between Chiang Kai-shek and the financial and business communities in Shanghai.

The total amount of the "Jiangxi Customs Second and Fifth Treasury Bills with Taxes" was 30 million silver won, with a monthly interest rate of 7 per cent, to be amortized over 30 months starting in July of the same year. This public debt is shared by the Shanghai financial community, the business community and Jiangsu and Zhejiang provinces, in addition to the two Huaihai salt merchants 3 million silver yuan. Of all those who subscribed to the Chiang Kai-shek regime's public debt, the Jiangsu and Zhejiang plutocrats accounted for 80 percent, with the Bank of China taking the largest amount.[58]

The managing director of Bank of China is another financial wizard, Zhang Jiajiajie. Zhang studied at Keio University in Japan, and in 1914, at the age of 28, he became the Deputy Manager of the Bank of China Shanghai Branch. Under Zhang Jiahua's leadership, the Bank of China refused to cooperate with the Beijing government and raised nearly 6 million silver yuan in equity from the major banks, exchanges and enterprises of Jiangsu and Zhejiang, and bought 5 million silver yuan in official shares of the Beijing government in 1923.

The famous Zhang Jiawu became a close friend of Li Fusun and Chen Guangfu, who were the most influential figures in Shanghai's financial industry. In order to unite the banking industry in Shanghai, he initiated the establishment of a Friday dinner party for managers to exchange financial information, emotions and opinions. Zhang Jia Miao used the gathering to make friends, analyze information and disseminate scientific business practices, which soon opened up the situation, and the gathering gradually expanded into the Shanghai Banking Association. The Shanghai Banking Association has three people at its core: Zhang Jiajiajiajie, who finances the most for Chiang Kai-shek, Chen Guangfu, who organizes the financing and Li Fusun, who supervises the funds.

In just two months from April to May 1927, Chiang Kai-shek received 40 million silver dollars in financing, much more than the 30 million gold rubles that the entire national government received from the Soviet Union between 1924 and 1927. Chiang Kai-shek's "speculative business" seems to have triumphed.

He "divested" the Soviet and Communist "dangerous assets" within the Kuomintang and brought in a much larger and more sophisticated venture capital – the Jiangsu and Zhejiang plutocrats and the international bankers behind them. However, he also faces the great

---

[58] Chiang Kai-shek's relationship with the Shanghai financial community and businessmen in Jiangsu and Zhejiang in 1927, Wang Zhenghua.

challenge of the Wuhan National Government, still controlled by the left wing of the Communist and Kuomintang parties.

The "recapitalization" behind the "Ninghan Merging"

April 9, 1927, the Shanghai Municipal Federation of Trade Unions, the chief of the workers' pickets, Wang Shouhua received a postage sent by Du Yuesheng, invited Wang Shouhua to Du Gongguan on April 11 to go to the banquet, have important business to discuss. On April 11, at about 8 p.m., Wang arrived at the Du Gongguan and had an ominous feeling that Du Yuesheng did not appear. The surrounding beaters, who were approaching, showed a killing look. Wang Shouhua secretly screamed in disbelief and turned around to leave, but it was too late. A few beaters swarmed him, skillfully knocked him to the ground, cleanly put him in a sack and put him in a car to be buried alive in the suburbs of Long Hua.

Immediately afterwards, at 3 a.m. on the 12th, the Green Gang hooligans under Du Yuesheng, armed with pistols, formed a detachment with a specific target, dressed in workers' clothes with the word "Work" on their sleeve, and rushed out of the French Concession, the main camp of the Green Gang, by car. At the same time, several hundred soldiers of Bai Chongxi's army similarly disguised through the public rented area, went to Zhabei, Nancheng, Huxi and other places, and attacked the quarters of the Nancheng workers' pickets. Zhou Fengqi's troops of the 26th Army had taken up positions close to the workers' pickets and the headquarters of the General Workers' Union during the night, when they forcibly disarmed the workers' pickets on the pretext of maintaining order and regulating the conflict.

At noon that day, the Shanghai General Workers' Union launched a general strike of workers in the city, demonstrating against the atrocities. As a result, Chiang Kai-shek's "National Revolutionary Army" began to shoot at the marching "nationals" and the massacre began. In two days, 300 workers were killed, 500 were arrested and 5,000 "disappeared". This was followed by a massive and bloody crackdown in Nanjing, Suzhou, Wuxi, Hangzhou, Guangdong, Changzhou, and other places, in which some 25,000 communists and left-wingers were massacred. The whole of China knew that Chiang Kai-shek, Commander-in-Chief of the National Revolutionary Army, had openly betrayed the National Revolution.

The news reached the Wuhan National Government and immediately triggered a major political earthquake. In the name of the Kuomintang Central Committee, Wang Jingwei, Chairman of the National Government of Wuhan, announced the immediate dismissal of Chiang Kai-shek from all positions, expelled him from the Kuomintang, and issued a warrant for his arrest. The Wuhan National Government was then faced with a major strategic choice: either to continue the Northern Expedition and destroy the Beijing warlords who still dominated the Yellow River region and north and northeast China, or to conquer Chiang from the east and the National Revolution would be divided.

The Wuhan government's military forces, such as Tang Shengzhi and Zhang Faqui, are mostly at odds with Chiang Kai-shek, and thus advocate the Eastern Expedition in order to get rid of Chiang Kai-shek and annex the richest area in China, Jiangsu and Zhejiang. The Soviet Union's political advisor, Borodin, and Chinese Communist leaders Chen Duxiu and Zhou Enlai advocated the continuation of the Northern Expedition and the defeat of the Beijing warlords before turning the gun on Chiang Kai Shek.

Borodin argued that

> *"it is impossible to advance eastward with our present strength ... an eastern advance would not only prompt Chiang Kai-shek to make an open alliance with imperialism and even the warlords of the North, but we would be defeated and eliminated."*[59]

Borodin's concerns were valid.

As far as the military situation is concerned, the Wuhan Government is at a disadvantage on all sides. To the north are the direct line warlords who have not been defeated and the Feng line warlords who are still strong, to the east the richest provinces are occupied by Chiang Kai-shek and his allies Li Zongren's army, and to the south the two provinces are held by Li Jishen's Gui and pro-Chiang forces, all these enemies are sharpening their knives and ready to pounce. The army under the command of the Wuhan government was mostly on the

---

[59] Statement by Borodin at a meeting of the Political Bureau of the Central Committee of the Communist Party with a delegation of the Communist International, 13 April 1927.

side of the Wuhan government because of some practical considerations, either because they needed the Wuhan government's provisions or because of factional conflicts and conflicting ambitions with Chiang, but in fact they mostly identified with Chiang Kai-shek's anti-Communist "Qing Party" and could sell out the revolution at any time, just like Chiang Kai-shek, as long as the price was negotiated. Only one of Ye Ting's divisions could really breathe and share the same fate as the Wuhan government.

As for the economic situation, that's even more difficult. In fact, the Wuhan side is also seeking support from the Shanghai financial and business communities. The National Government of Wuhan sent the Minister of Finance, Mr. Song Ziwen, to Shanghai on 27 March to handle all financial matters, and ordered that all the finances of Jiangsu and Zhejiang provinces should be placed under its auspices, and that all taxation and fund-raising from Chinese commercial banks should be managed by the Minister of Finance.[60] Song Ziwen arrived in Shanghai on 29 March and negotiated with Chiang Kai-shek the next day for the unification of the financial affairs of Jiangsu and Zhejiang. On the 31st, the General Command of the National Revolutionary Army established the "Jiangsu-Shanghai Finance Committee", with Shanghai's financial leaders in charge of specific matters. As a result, when Song Ziwen arrived in Shanghai, the work could not start for a while.

After the "April 12th" coup, Chiang Kai-shek completely turned his back on the Communists and the Kuomintang left, and Song's personal safety was once threatened, not to mention financing the Wuhan government. In the end, even Song Ziwen himself was rebelled by Kong Xiangxi and Song Hei Ling and defected to Chiang Kai Shek.

Subsequently, Chiang Kai-shek formally established the Nanjing National Government on April 18 and began publicly denying the Wuhan government, leading to a proclamation on the 28th stating that he would join the Great Powers in imposing an economic blockade on Wuhan. The Jiang and Zhejiang plutocrats, who hold China's financial lifeblood, have sat on the side of Chiang Kai-shek and cut off all channels of financing to the Wuhan National Government, and

---

[60] Minister Song's Management of Finance and Electricity, 5 April 1927, Shanghai R.O.C. Daily, 2nd edition no. 1.

Shanghai's banks, money banks, and ticket numbers have all stopped sending money to Wuhan, waiting for the government to fall.

At this time, prices in Wuhan had risen to astronomical levels, and the various coins and credits issued by the Wuhan government had fallen by the wayside. The government's monthly revenue is just 1.5 million silver dollars and its expenditure is 13 million silver dollars! With more than one-third of the city's unemployed and their families, plus revolutionaries and asylum-seekers from all provinces, and tens of thousands of wounded in several battles, the entire government of Wuhan has reached a critical juncture, with all sides in turmoil.

Wuhan, whether it was the Soviet Union, the Chinese Communist Party, or Wang Jingwei, actually bet its treasure on Feng Yuxiang's National Army in the north.

After becoming a warlord, Feng Yuxiang was baptized into Christianity, using Christian hymns as his army's song and Christian dogma as his blueprint for formulating military regulations, which led to his being called the "Christian General" by world opinion. In 1924, when he discovered that the Soviets were generous with their subsidies, he joined the Soviet Union.

Now, Feng Yuxiang, cultivated by 16 million gold rubles and arms, is in charge of the Tongguan Pass, with a tiger's eye on the central plains, waiting to bet his chips at the crucial moment when the Chinese political scales are tipped.

The day came quickly.

In June 1927, Feng Yuxiang and Wang Jingwei held a Zhengzhou meeting. At the meeting, Wang Jingwei listed the various vices of Chiang Kai-shek in an attempt to convince Feng Yuxiang to oppose Chiang. The price offered was to give him all the power of the party, government and army in Henan, Shaanxi and Gansu provinces in the name of the Wuhan National Government. Of course Feng Yuxiang is not a fool, the above three places are already under the actual control of Feng Yuxiang's National Army, and Wang Jingwei's price is equivalent to an endorsement after the fact, Feng Yuxiang did not reap any real benefits. It seems there's no way to squeeze any more oil out of Wang Jingwei, so squeeze this old orange peel of Chiang Kai-shek and see if you can wring out some orange juice.

So just one week after the Zhengzhou Conference, Feng Yuxiang held a meeting with Chiang Kai-shek in Xuzhou on June 20. At the meeting, Chiang Kai-shek urged Feng Yuxiang to surrender to the Nationalist Government of Nanjing and to fight against the Communist "Qing Party". Chiang Kai-shek offered a monthly allowance of 2.5 million silver dollars to Feng Yuxiang's men, starting in July 1927. Immediately after the meeting, Chiang Kai-shek returned to Shanghai to implement the payment. In a report on June 30, British Consul General Sir David Baldwin said there had been a massive crowdfunding campaign in Shanghai during the last two weeks of June. He speculated that it was to enforce Chiang Kai-shek's funding of Feng Yuxiang in order to gain his support against the Wuhan National Government's Xuzhou Agreement.[61]

Chiang Kai-shek, who was backed by the Jiang and Zhejiang zaibatsu, had made an extraordinary move, offering 2.5 million silver dollars a month, far more than Wuhan could offer. 2.5 million silver dollars a month! It was as if someone had recited the mantra "Open Sesame Door" in front of Feng Yuxiang, and a treasure so huge that it was beyond imagination appeared before his eyes. Feng Yuxiang, without thinking, immediately decided to throw away the gold ruble and pounced on the big thick leg that Chiang Kai-shek had just held. On June 21, Feng Yuxiang sent an ultimatum-style telegram to Wang Jingwei and Tan Yen-loos of Wuhan.

At this time, Wang Jingwei is very angry. Originally, on 1 June, Luo Yi, a representative of the Communist International, arrived in Wuhan with a copy of the Communist International Executive Committee's Resolution on China (the "May Directive"). Within a few days, Luo Yi conveyed this resolution to Wang Jingwei in his capacity as the "Minister of the Imperial Affairs". The resolution of the Communist International reads as follows:

> ➤ Strongly advocate bottom-up agrarian reform, but must fight against excesses that do not touch the land of officers and soldiers and make concessions to artisans, traders and small landowners.
>
> ➤ To mobilize 20,000 Communists and 50,000 revolutionary workers and peasants in the Two Lakes region to form their own army.

---

[61] Further communication on China, British Foreign Office 405/254, Confidential, No. 13315, July-September 1927, No. 43, annex.

- ➢ To change the current composition of the KMT by absorbing new workers and peasant leaders from the lower echelons into the KMT centre.
- ➢ Expulsion of all those who have old ideas.
- ➢ Establishment of a revolutionary military court headed by prominent Nationalists and non-Communists to punish reactionary officers.

This was not a Communist State cooperation, Stalin was asking Wang Jingwei to surrender completely to the Communist Party. Wang Jingwei looked at it and suppressed his anger, but he bargained anyway. He offered the Soviet Union a loan of 15 million gold rubles, while Moscow agreed to provide only 2 million gold rubles in aid. Stalin went too far, asking people to sell their bodies and refusing to pay enough to do so, and anyone would flip out. At this point, Wang Jingwei received a telegram from Feng Yuxiang urging him to fight against the Communist Party, which really hit the nail on the head.

Immediately afterwards, Song Ziwen, the finance minister of the Wuhan government, who had remained in Shanghai for the previous months, suddenly returned to Hankou on July 12 and, carrying a letter from Chiang Kai-shek, held several rounds of private talks with Wang at his home in Wang Jingwei.

Three days later, the Wuhan National Government staged a counter-revolutionary coup under the slogan "Better to kill 3,000 by mistake than to spare one", and a large number of communists and left-wingers fell to the slaughter.

After the cleansing of the "Communists", the contradictions of principle between the national governments of Wuhan and Nanjing have been resolved, and it is only a matter of time before the "Ning-Han merger" takes place. Chiang Kai-shek, who had won a decisive victory in the Ning-Han struggle, seemed to be going to be the leader of the new government as a matter of course. To everyone's dismay, however, Chiang Kai-shek stepped down less than a month after the "split" in Wuhan.

With such a bizarre political situation in China, it is no wonder that even the British Empire's foreign ministry, which is good at "venture capital", is puzzled by the turbulence of the Chinese political scene. However, the answer is actually very simple. There is an old Chinese proverb: "When the bird has exhausted its bow, the rabbit will die and the dog will cook." Only this time, the "bow" and "dog" became Chiang Kai-shek, and the one who wanted to "hide the bow and cook the dog" was the Zhejiang and Jiangsu plutocrats.

Zaibatsu's board of directors fires the CEO for his nonsense

The original sin of Chiang Kai-shek for the Jian Zhejiang and Zhejiang plutocrats was that the appetite was too big and the appetite too ugly.

Chiang Kai-shek did not have an easy time after the "April 12th" coup. The purge of the unarmed Communist Party was just an "appetizer for dessert" before the main meal. After the formation of the Nanjing National Government, it had to maintain the operation of the state apparatus, deal with the Wuhan National Government, and beware of the Beijing warlords in the north, all without money.

However, Jiangsu and Zhejiang plutocrats, as capitalists, have to calculate investment returns. The front-end financing was forced by the Communist Party, without a little blood, everyone has to play. Now relieved, Chiang Kai-shek's appetite is getting bigger and bigger, which exceeds the plutocrats' budgets, and everyone is starting to shrink back from the position of supporting Chiang.

It does not matter if the Jiangzhe zaibatsu shrinks, Chiang Kai-shek immediately rolled his eyes, it is not stuck in my neck! If you don't want a toast, you'll be punished. So Chiang Kai-shek took what he did to the Communists and the unions and took it out on the capitalists.

On 14 May 1927, the son of a painter living in the French Concession was arrested on counter-revolutionary charges and released on 19 May, after the painter had promised to "donate" 200,000 silver dollars to the State. The king of cotton yarn and flour, Rong Zongjing, was arrested on charges of "being a treacherous merchant and having financed a warlord", and Chiang Kai-shek personally ordered the confiscation of the Rong family's flour mill in Wuxi, which was dropped after Rong Zongjing donated 250,000 silver yuan to the Chiang regime. The 3-year-old son of Sincere's manager, O Byung Kwang, was kidnapped and asked to make a "donation" of 500,000 silver won to the party's cause. The actual result of Chiang Kai-shek's use of this combination of "kidnapping" and "expectation of kidnapping" to extort money from the capitalists, according to the U.S. Consul in Shanghai, "is a definite reign of terror among the wealthy classes … the attitude of the merchant and gentleman classes is constantly developing into an opposition to the Kuomintang, which is unbridled in its tyranny and inflicts great suffering on them".[62] An Australian observer in China, Chapman, reports,

> "Rich Chinese may be arrested in their homes or mysteriously disappeared on the road... The big rich man is arrested as a 'communist'! ... it is estimated that Chiang Kai-shek raised a total of $500,000 in funds by this means, a reign of terror that has never been experienced by Shanghai in recent times under any regime."[63]

Chiang Kai-shek's style of play is almost identical to Hitler's later style. A few years later, Hitler was also on the GEM with Wall Street's venture capital. The Rothschild family had been in the Gestapo's prison. For political strongmen like Chiang Kai-shek and Hitler, consolidation of power is the highest principle of action, and everything else comes second. Bankers and working class people, if they can do what they want, can work for them and get what they need; once the situation changes, they can turn their backs faster than they can read.

The Shanghai Beach moguls are really angry and the consequences are really serious. The tycoons think that Chiang Kai-shek has really not set himself right, and that we are giving you money to work for us. Now you're so arrogant and domineering before you're rich, and you don't play by the rules.

Such dangerous elements must be done away with. The reason for the delay was that there was a pro-communist Wuhan government outside the gates of the Shanghai Bund, and the external pressure had not yet been completely lifted and Chiang Kai-shek had to be tolerated. By the time Wang Jingwei had made a move on the Communists in Wuhan as well, there would have been nothing to worry about.

Thus, Chiang Kai-shek stepped down into the countdown.

In fact, the Nanjing National Government is not a piece of cake. There was a clear conflict of interest between the Gui system, led by Li

---

[62] U.S. Consul in Shanghai, Kningham to Mamouri, U.S. Department of State 893/9195, 30 July 1927; Goss to Mamouri, U.S. Department of State 893/9199, 5 June 1927; Kningham to Meyer, U.S. Department of State 893/9660, 3 September 1927.

[63] *The Chinese Revolution 1926–1927* (London, 1928 edition), Chapman, p. 232.

Zongren and Bai Chongxi, and Chiang Kai-shek's Huangpu system. Even He Yingchen's support for Chiang Kai-shek was unreliable. Chiang Kai-shek's tyrannical dominance had created too many political enemies for his own good, while he himself reveled in the joy of victory.

At this delicate moment, Chiang Kai-shek's army was defeated by the Fengtian warlord's forces in the Second Northern Expedition and even lost the important east China town of Xuzhou. Shanghai and Nanjing were in a state of emergency, and Chiang Kai-shek's prestige fell by the wayside. The Gui forces within the Nanjing government took the opportunity to push the palace, and the Wuhan Wang Jingwei authorities, who negotiated the merger, repeatedly insisted that the precondition for the Wuhan government to move to Nanjing was that Chiang Kai-shek himself must step down, and the Guangdong patriarchate within the Kuomintang and the "princely faction" that supported Sun Yat-sen's son, Sun Ke, also joined forces to push Chiang to the ground. And despite the gangster-style extortionate fundraising in Shanghai, the Nanjing government is still financially unable to make ends meet because of the huge military expenditures. Chiang Kai-shek became a family only to know that the rice is expensive, and for a while without the support of the zaibatsu of Jiangsu and Zhejiang, can only look at the mess and can not do anything about it.

It was only then that Chiang Kai-shek understood that there was a difference between ruling a country and overthrowing a regime, and that he could no longer play rogue tactics as he had done in the past.

Chiang Kai-shek was, after all, quite a clever man, and instead of carrying it hard like this, he might as well rush back and set the others up on the fire in the foreground to roast, and then come back to take over the plate when everyone else is too much to roast.

So, on August 12, 1927, at a meeting of the Kuomintang's Central Military Committee, Chiang Kai-shek proposed that he would resign as commander-in-chief and leave the defense of Nanjing to other generals, and then leave Nanjing for Shanghai. Chiang Kai-shek's statement of retreat was issued on August 13, and he officially went to the field on August 14. Immediately afterwards, the Wuhan government announced its move to Nanjing on August 19, Wang Jingwei also arrived in Nanjing in early September, and Ninghan was formally reunited for the "Ninghan Merge".

Chiang Kai-shek is finally on the Growth Enterprise Market

Seeing that the fruits of victory were so stolen, Chiang Kai-shek savored the bitter taste, thought about the pain and did a deep reflection. To return to the center of China's political scene, it is necessary to enlist the monetary support of the Jiangzhe plutocrats who control China's financial power. Although Wang Jingwei and Li Zongren had their momentary success, he was convinced that only he had the strength and the skills to succeed in China, and that sooner or later the Jiangsu and Zhejiang plutocrats would realize who was the real "true son" of China in the future. It was imperative to regain the recognition of the "capital markets" and find a way to reapply for an IPO.

The key to gaining the support of the Jiang and Zhejiang plutocrats is to dispel their doubts and make them identify with Chiang Kai-shek as "one of their own" from the bottom of their hearts, and the best way to do this is to join forces and tie themselves to the Jiang and Zhejiang plutocrats by marriage. He was going to launch an offensive, an offensive to win the hearts of the beauties, an offensive that would be of no less strategic value than any real war.

His target was Song Mei-ling.

At the time, the Song family's old lady, Ni Guizhen, was recuperating in Japan, and in order to woo Song Mei-ling, Chiang Kai-shek went to Japan on September 28 to get the Song family's permission to marry him. In this way, he is related by marriage to Sun Yat-sen (Song Qingling), Song Ziwen and Kong Xiangxi (Song Anling). The Song family, on the other hand, has very close ties to the Jiangxi and Zhejiang plutocrats and the big Chinese buyout class that represents the interests of international bankers in China.

The grandson of Xi Zhengfu of the Dongting Mountain Gang, the big Shanghai buyer's family, Xi Dezhong, was a classmate of Song Ziwen's when he was studying in the United States, and his elder brother, Xi De Mao, married his daughter to Song Ziwen's younger brother, Song Ziliang, who had a large stake in the Shanghai Commercial Savings Bank of Chen Guangfu, a big banker of Jiangsu and Zhejiang.

The Song family themselves are the Chinese buyouts of American capital. Song, the founder of the Song family, grew up in the United States, had a full American church education and was a devout

Christian. Several of Song's siblings graduated from American universities, and Song himself worked at a Wall Street commercial bank right after graduating from Columbia University. Song's husband, Kong Xiangxi, was also educated in the U.S. and was the general agent for Mobil Oil's North China region. This family is inextricably linked to American capital. As for Chiang Kai-shek's union with Soong Mei-ling, the big headline in the Chinese media at the time, which covered the political marriage, said it accurately, "Chiang and Soong join forces, 'China-US' cooperation" (Chiang, Soong Mei-ling).

It's the perfect combination of a Chinese buyout consortium and a military dictator. Just when Chiang Kai-shek was busy injecting "new assets", "Ning Han merge flow" after the new national government has been close to uncover the pot.

Sun Ke, the Finance Minister of the new government and head of the "Prince Faction" within the Kuomintang, did not have the fundraising ability of Chiang Kai-shek, who had a monthly budget of 20 million silver dollars during his reign, and Sun Ke was completely unable to raise this amount. Until October 1927, when he had raised only 8 million silver dollars, the government was paralyzed and the army refused to take orders because it could not get paid. In a pinch, Sun Ke also followed suit, he issued the "Jiang Customs Second and Fifth Treasury Bills with Taxes" again on October 1, the amount of which was 10 million more than Chiang Kai Shek's 30 million silver yuan, reaching 40 million silver yuan!

In order to mobilize the Jiangsu and Zhejiang zaibatsu to subscribe to their public debts, Sunke also called a meeting with Yu Qiaqing and other top financial figures to mobilize everyone to subscribe, which resulted in a tepid response. The Shanghai Money Bank had given Chiang Kai-shek a loan of 5.6 million silver yuan from April 1 to July 16, 1927, but when Sun Ke asked the Shanghai Money Bank to subscribe to the 500,000 silver yuan Erwu tax-taxed treasury bills on October 26, he raised only 340,000 silver yuan.[64]

---

[64] *History of the Shanghai Money Bank*, Shanghai Branch of the People's Bank of China, p. 207; Kningham to Meyer, U.S. Department of State 893/9660, 12 November 1927.

Without the support of Jiangsu and Zhejiang plutocrats, the new government would have been virtually unsustainable.

At this time, the Jiangzhe zaibatsu, has been on Wang Jingwei, Sunke, Li Zongren the execution of this group of people is quite disappointed, rely on this group can fight over the warlords in the north? The bigwigs began to wait and see, and perhaps Chiang Kai-shek, who had become a "family", was better able to take on the task of unifying the country.

Soon, the armies of Li Zongren and Bai Chongxi of the Gui family within the new government, like the Xiang family of Tang Shengzhi, broke out in a civil war for power, and although the Gui family defeated Tang Shengzhi, both sides lost so much that they were actually unable to fight again.

At this time, the pro-Jiang forces within the Kuomintang took the opportunity to demand that Chiang Kai-shek return to power in order to clean up the mess, the Jiang and Zhejiang plutocrats already regarded Chiang Kai-shek as an insider, plus they were also confident that through the last "recapitalization", Chiang Kai-shek should have learned enough lessons, he should be on the road.

On January 4, 1928, Chiang Kai-shek arrived in Nanjing from Shanghai to take charge of the overall situation, and on January 9, 1928, Chiang Kai-shek officially telephoned the whole country to assume the post of "Commander-in-Chief of the National Revolutionary Army", and then took up the top positions of Chairman of the Military Committee and Chairman of the Central Political Conference of the Kuomintang.

Only 116 days have passed since the end of the year.

When Chiang Kai-shek came to power, under the co-ordination of Finance Minister and Central Bank Governor Song Ziwen, the Jiangsu and Zhejiang plutocrats quickly subscribed to the 40 million silver dollar public debt, which could not be sold with all their efforts. With the renewed support of the Jiang and Zhejiang plutocrats, Chiang Kai-shek finally took his place in the country. In return, the Jiangsu and Zhejiang plutocrats also counted on Chiang Kai-shek to do his best for them.

Yet they have forgotten the nature of a military dictator. Such a person would never be willing to be subjected to anyone, and would have to find a way to control any person or organization that wanted to control him. Cromwell did, Napoleon did, Hitler did, and Chiang Kai-shek was no exception.

For the time being, however, Chiang had to rely on the bankers' moneybags. Because Chiang Kai-shek was facing resistance from his most formidable enemies, the Communists he was trying so hard to eradicate.

Shortly after the coup d'état, the Communists, who had been bloodied by Chiang Kai-shek's butcher's knife, also began to take up arms.

On August 1, 1927, the Communists revolted in Nanchang. Chiang Kai-shek's nightmare draws to a close.

CHAPTER IV

The Red Central Bank

What will be the future after the land is divided up by the landowners? It costs money to fight the siege. How can the Red Army fight without money? Without gold, without silver, how could the Soviet currency work? Fictionalized red money?

In addition to the military and political aspects of the Red Base's survival and development, finance also plays a fairly crucial role. Money was indispensable for the war against the "siege", for the functioning of the Central Soviet regime, for the livelihood and production of the local people, and for the development of market trade.

The Soviet government realized the importance of money and banking early on, and in 1932 created the world's smallest central bank, the Chinese Soviet National Bank. At its inception, it had a staff of only five, and at best, 14. These people don't have a high education, don't have much banking experience, and don't even know how the central bank works. To make matters worse, it lacks even start-up capital. On top of that, to issue currency, there is no special paper, no design drawings, no ink, no anti-counterfeiting, everything has to be taken care of by yourself. Not knowing treasury bookkeeping, not knowing bank accounting, not knowing bill of exchange discounting, not knowing public debt issuance, they have grown steadily from scratch and in practice.

Unifying finances, developing trade, active markets, they mature rapidly in three years. The Red Central Bank has contributed to the victory of the war against the "siege", the consolidation of the Soviet regime, the improvement of people's lives and the prosperity of the market and trade.

Mao Zemin's Financial "Empty City Plan"

One day in 1933, Mao Zemin, President of the National Bank of the Soviet Republic of China, had just returned to his office in Ruijin from abroad and was about to check the accounts when Cao Jüru, head of the accounting section, hurried in and said anxiously,

> "Governor Mao, recently many villagers have come to exchange banknotes for cash. The cash in the treasury is less than half, I think something is going to go wrong, you hurry and think of a way!"

Once Mao Zemin heard about it, he rushed to the business office of the bank. There was a long queue outside the business hall, and the hall was filled with people waiting to exchange their money, and everyone was talking and excited. Someone shouted, "Nowadays, businessmen only take cash, not paper money, and I want to exchange it for cash!" Someone picked up the conversation and said, "Yeah, what's the point of keeping paper money now that it's going to be scrap?"

Mao Zemin frowned without saying a word and turned and walked out of the hall. He turned around in the streets of Ruijin County, and really saw some daily necessities stores, cloth shops and salt stalls with signs that said "cash only". Mao Zemin realizes that the run he feared the most has finally happened!

He rushed back to the Ministry of Finance, reported to Minister Deng Zichuo, and at the same time sought out Qian Zhiguang, who had just taken up his post as Director of the General Administration of Foreign Trade, to discuss with him.

Mao Zemin said:

> "The bank's most taboo is a run, and recently I had a vague feeling about it, but I didn't expect it to come so quickly. After the third counter-'siege', the Kuomintang imposed a tight economic blockade on us, the Soviet region was short of supplies, prices soared, and paper currency depreciated. In addition, the enemy has created a large amount of counterfeit money flowing into the Soviet Union and has spread sabotage and disrupted the financial market in the Soviet Union. We have to come up with a way to stop this situation as soon as possible."

In fact, the reasoning is simple: the credibility of the National Bank and the Soviet currency must be guaranteed, and by preserving the credibility of the Bank and the currency it issues, the credibility of the Soviet government is preserved.

At this point, Mao Zemin was facing a situation similar to that of Japan's Matsumata Justice, where the over-issuance of paper money had led to a dramatic depreciation of paper currency against the silver dollar. There are also a significant number of non-cash yen notes among the paper currency of Matsumoto Justice, so the situation is manageable as the government is not forced to exchange cash for silver despite the depreciation of the paper currency. But Mao Zemin's problem was in trouble, and the hometown demanded immediate cashing, and the credit of the Soviet currency would immediately collapse with unimaginable consequences once the silver dollar reserves were squeezed out.

In those days, in order to rebuild the credit of the yen, Matsumata Justice boldly adopted the method of exchanging as many banknotes as possible for as many silver dollars as possible, all at a ratio of one to one, until the market was fully convinced that the government's gold and silver reserves were sufficient. However, at that time, Matsubata Justice solved the problem of the influx of gold and silver coins from overseas by using the innovative method of foreign exchange drafts of the Yokohama Shojin Bank, while Mao Zemin could not solve the problem by the idea of increasing the reserves of gold and silver coins.

In any case, the credit of the Soviet currency must not be allowed to go bankrupt. Mao Zemin insisted that all those who came to request the exchange of foreign currency, the bank should guarantee the exchange, and strictly stipulated that the exchange of a dollar note for a dollar of foreign currency, no one should raise the price of foreign currency!

Determined, the National Bank immediately brought in a large quantity of cash from the treasury for public exchange of banknotes. Two days have passed, the number of people coming to exchange for foreign currency has increased, and the line at the bank door is getting longer and longer. Cao Jiru said to Mao Zemin,

> "Governor Mao, there's not much left in the foreign currency, should we stop the exchange?"

Mao Zemin replied,

> "Now the people are exchanging coins with high enthusiasm and cannot stop. The purpose of exchanging the light yang is to improve the credibility of the paper currency, and only by

> *improving the credibility of the paper currency can financial stability be achieved!"*

Cao Ju Ru sighed,

> *"It is this reasoning. But if Chief Money they don't come back tomorrow and the day after tomorrow, there will be a lot of trouble."*

Mao Zemin bowed his head and pondered for a while, then suddenly his eyes lit up and he said,

> *"It seems that we have to learn from Mr. Kong Ming and sing the 'empty city trick'. In the middle of the night, you guys..."*

The next morning, the streets of Ruijin County appeared by the Red Army guards to open the way, Cao Jüru led the basket transport team. Some baskets were filled with gold bricks, gold bars, gold necklaces, gold rings, gold earrings and silver bracelets, silver collars, silver dollars, silver ingots, and others were neatly stacked with koyos. The snake-like convoy of transport passing through the downtown area and through the streets was spectacular. More and more townspeople on both sides of the street are blocking the street.

The transport squeezed its way through the crowd, picking stretches of jewelry and koyo into the bank. Every time a quart is passed, some villager counts it while excitedly exclaiming, "The bank is so rich!"

In the national bank business hall, gold and silver jewelry piled up a gilded "gold and silver mountain", people who came to exchange silver dollars after seeing, exclaimed:

> *"I have never seen so much gold and silver in my life, the bank in the Su area is really generous!"*

The exchange crowd dispersed quite a bit, and Mao Zemin was able to wait patiently for the return of the light of money, after his anxiety was lessened.

On that day, Qian Zhihong finally brought back the silver yuan, cotton cloth, salt and other materials seized by the Red Army during the anti "siege" as planned, Mao Zemin praised them for saving the Soviet bank and the Soviet government. Mao Zemin also told him that the "Empty City Plan" had used all the gold and silver in the vault. If the light of money doesn't come back, the "Empty City Plan" will come to fruition.

With the supplies brought back from the front, Mao Zemin immediately ordered a halt to the exchange. The cooperative sells daily necessities in large quantities, and the price tag reads, "Paper money only, no cash."

People have commented,

> "Who says paper money has to expire and who says it's worthless? You see, the government even took out kwan-yang for paper money, and now it only takes paper money for selling things."

The people rushed to the bank to exchange banknotes and buy back what they needed. Some people do not buy the goods and also exchange the cash for paper money.

In no days, more cash was recovered than exchanged out!

In the face of the run-off crisis, Mao Zemin responded wisely by using the gold and silver "empty city ploy" to fight a beautiful psychological war, and took timely measures to ensure the supply of supplies in the Soviet Union, successfully consolidating the credibility of the State Bank and the government. The maintenance of the credit of the National Bank ensured the government's ability to finance and deploy materials, laying the economic foundation for the Red Army's victory against the "siege".

Mao Zemin may not have been aware of Matsumoto's righteous yen credit defense war, and while they faced the same problems, the means of resolution were very different. While Songfang Justice was to ease the credit crisis of paper money by increasing gold and silver, Mao Zemin discovered another great law of money, that gold and silver are not the only credit support for money, and that commodities can be equally effective means of supporting money! The demand for money by the people is in essence the possession of all kinds of living materials can be realized through money, in this case, the credit of paper money can completely bypass the gold and silver reserves, and directly material-based.

Mao Zemin's monetary-price standard practice influenced the monetary thinking of later communists. In the era of revolutionary lack of precious metals and the plight of the liberated areas under economic blockade, the establishment of a red financial high frontier necessitates a major financial innovation in the practice of monetary standardization!

The key to the Red regime's longevity in the face of white terror and its organization of five large-scale military operations against the "siege", as well as its promotion of economic development in the Soviet Union, was that the Communists grasped from the outset two key points: the revolution had to grasp the barrel of the gun and the bag of money in one hand. A gun barrel protects a money bag, and a money bag effectively supports a gun barrel!

Snow made this observation about the Soviet National Bank notes in his Diary of the West:

> "Wherever it is, Soviet currency seems to have acquired its position on the basis of general confidence in the government, and the fact that it does have real purchase value in the market."[65]

The Red Regime's awareness of the extreme importance of money is still a lesson from the blood of the Paris Commune.

Paris Commune, starving for gold

At the end of May 1871, in the cemetery of Father La Scherz in Paris, with a few shots fired, the last soldiers of the Paris Commune fell under the "Commune Wall", their eyes filled with fearlessness, anger, a hint of regret and confusion. The first proletarian regime in human history, the Paris Commune, was brutally suppressed just two months after its birth. What is it that makes the flame of revolution go out so quickly?

A key element is money, Bank of France money!

Any regime that wants to run the state apparatus in an organized way needs money. Without money, resources cannot be mobilized and war cannot be fought. The Paris Commune is a lesson in blood.

> "The Bank of France was founded in 1800 and its 200 shareholders with voting rights are eligible to elect 12 board members. A detailed analysis reveals that the 200 shareholders belong to essentially the same group of people, the 44 main families that control the Bank of France. And the seats held by

---

[65] *Journey to the West*, by Snow, translated by Dong Le Shan, PLA Literature Press, 2002, p. 282.

> *these families are inheritable, and in the midst of this three families whose seats have remained unchanged for a hundred years are Malet, Mirabeau and Rothschild. The first two belonged to the Swiss banking family who were authorized by Napoleon to establish the Bank of France because of their secret financing of Napoleon's 'Fog Moon Coup' in 1799. Rothschild was a representative of the later rise of the Jewish banking family. Through the financial operations of the Napoleonic government, the Bourbons and the Dukes of Orléans, the Law family opened the 'July dynasty', which was in unprecedented power in France, and became a core member of the Bank of France."*[66]

The Bank of France, which they controlled, was at the heart of the financial industry in Paris, then the economic and financial center of not only France, but of the entire European continent. The franc it issues is the legal tender of France, the foreign exchange and gold it holds are the guarantee of the international purchasing power of the franc, the bonds it sells are of the highest credit rating, and it is the main source of funds for the French government.

The bankers who owned the Bank of France believed that the goal of the proletarian regime represented by the Paris Commune was to oppose the bourgeoisie and to fight fundamentally against their core interests. On the other hand, they were concerned with war reparations and financing arrangements for Prussia. Even if the Paris Commune had come to power with no touch for the Bank of France, the proletarian government would certainly have insisted on a hard line on the question of reparations and financing. Not only would the number of payouts be reduced, but the financing would not necessarily be arranged by them, and more likely the Government would borrow directly from the people, thus making the war bond cake they had been dreaming of, but the basket would be empty. Money has no motherland, only profit in the eyes of bankers! Now that the Versailles government is easier to navigate, the bankers' choice is obvious.

The leaders of the faction in charge of the economic policy of the Paris Commune, who naively believed that the objective of the Commune was the local autonomy of Paris rather than the central

---

[66] *Currency Wars 2: The Golden Power of the World*, by Song Hongbing, China Business Federation Press, 2009, Chapter 3.

government of France, did not have the power and the need to take over the Bank of France as the central bank and made the fatal mistake of leaving it in the hands of the old Authority, which had close links with Versailles.

The leaders of the Paris Commune did not realize that whoever holds the Bank of France holds the economic lifeblood of France. This lifeline determines both who the resources are allocated to and who the State apparatus serves. So it's not just an economic mistake, it's a political one. As Engels put it, if the Commune were to take over the Bank of France, "it would make more sense than holding 10,000 hostages".

In the more than two months of the commune's existence, the Bank of France has had billions of francs in cash alone on its books. And the Commune only applied for and accepted a miserable loan of 16 million francs from the bank. Instead of taking over the Banque de France, the result was to starve for gold, and it was impossible to force the bankers, led by Rothschild, to pressure the government of Versailles to make peace with the Paris Commune, instead giving the bankers the opportunity to remit more than 200 million francs to Versailles!

With this large sum of money, the Versailles government was able to "reward the brave with a heavy reward", and in a short time, on the basis of more than 10,000 defeated soldiers, assembled an army of 110,000 to fight against the commune.

At this critical juncture, in order to secure the interests of the bankers, Rothschild intervened directly in the post-Prussian War negotiations between the Versailles government and Bismarck on reparations.

> *"Bismarck's hordes are beginning to rest, but the international bankers are busier. The business of war reparations of up to 5 billion francs is a huge business that everyone salivates over, and if a 1% overhead charge is charged, that alone is a 50 million franc pie!*
> *On the amount of the war reparations, the French Government of Tigre envisaged 5 billion francs, but Bismarck took a piece of paper and wrote down 6 billion francs in a flash! Teiyaer jumped up in a flash like a dog that had taken a bite. The two men began to argue violently.*
> *Finally, Teyyer asked Rothschild to intervene. When Rothschild appeared, Bismarck turned all his anger on Rothschild, and all those present were astonished. Rothschild is indifferent and still*

> *insists that 5 billion francs is a 'sustainable amount of compensation'. Fuming is fuming, Rothschild's position in the international financial markets is unshakeable, and there is no way to raise enough war payouts on the European market without accepting his terms. After weighing the pros and cons, Bismarck had to accept Rothschild's offer of 5 billion francs. What the French government in Teyre couldn't handle, the Rothschild's immediately took care of.*"[67]

With money, everything is easy! Bismarck, the "iron-blooded chancellor", generously promised to repatriate tens of thousands of French prisoners of war and to cooperate in maintaining "neutrality", even including an attack on Paris by the Versailles army through the Prussian lines.

It is sobering to note that while the Versailles government, Bismarck and the international bankers united to destroy their common enemy, the Paris Commune, in an attempt to retake power, the revolutionaries spent their time and energy on such trivial matters as how to improve the treatment of teachers. And so tragedy inevitably ensued.

The power of a bank derives from the commodity it operates on, money, and the power of a central bank derives from its control over the source of money. The most effective way to control an economy is to control the currency of that economy; and the most important way to control an economy's currency is to control the banking system that creates it, especially the central bank.

The lessons of the Paris Commune show how fragile and vulnerable revolutionary regimes are when they do not hold the lifeblood of the economy. And in modern society, banks, especially a financial system with a central bank at its core, are very important for a regime and an economy. Marx and Engels, as early as 1848 in the Communist Manifesto, made it clear that the proletariat, to become the ruling class, was to "concentrate credit in the hands of the State, through national banks with state capital and exclusive monopoly power".[68]

---

[67] Source: ibid., chap. 1.

[68] *Communist Party Manifesto*, People's Publishing House, 1972, p. 272.

Half a century after the failure of the Paris Commune, it was Lenin who turned the ideas of Marx and Engels into reality, and Lenin's understanding and practice of the banking system was very much in place, pointing out that the banks were

> "the centre of modern economic life and the nerve centre of the whole capitalist national economic system".[69]
> "Modern banking is so inextricably bound up with commerce (food and all other commerce) and industry that it is absolutely impossible to do anything significant, anything 'revolutionary democratic' without 'stepping in' to the bank."

It was the Soviet Union's firm control of the banking system that allowed it to miraculously weather the untold odds and go from being a backward, backward country to a world-class superpower and leader of the communist world in just 15 years.

From 1905, when the Russo-Japanese War ended in Russia's abject defeat, Russia was reduced to a pathetic beggar among the great powers, and in 1917, when the Russian October Revolution broke out in the latter part of the First World War, saving its strength for the construction of the Soviet Union, Russia withdrew from the First World War and signed the disgraced Brest Peace Treaty with Germany, ceding 1 million square kilometres of land, losing 90 per cent of coal, 73 per cent of iron ore, 54 per cent of industry and 33 per cent of railways, and paying DM 6 billion in compensation to Germany. This was followed by a civil war in Soviet Russia that lasted for many years, and the situation did not gradually stabilize until 1923. After the establishment of the Soviet Union, economic work was gradually put on track, and the banking system, under state control, immediately exerted great power over the economic recovery and the rise of heavy industry. Just 15 years later, the Soviet Union's gross industrial product jumped to second place in the world and became one of the most powerful countries in the world. In 1939, when the Japanese and Soviet forces collided head-on at Normenhan, on a battlefield of seven square kilometers, hundreds of meters wide, Soviet tanks flooded the sky, the sound of artillery rumbled, and the elite of the Japanese Kanto Army lost everything. During the Patriotic War, strong heavy industrial production capacity

---

[69] *The Complete Works of Lenin*, 2nd edition, vol. 32, p. 189.

ensured that the Soviet Union supplied military equipment to the front in a steady stream until the capture of Berlin.

Without strong financial forces, there can be no strong industry or defense.

The gun in one hand and the money in the other

Without money, the revolution can't move an inch. The later Chinese Communist Party also experienced firsthand, during its own upbringing, the extreme importance of money for revolution, especially for independence and autonomy.

The early Chinese Communists, mostly young people, generally had no fixed occupation or source of income, and a lack of funds was essential to building a nationally influential party in a short time. In the early years of the Party's founding, the main source of funding was simply the money earned by a few intellectuals, such as Chen Duxiu and Li Ta-Chao, from teaching and writing articles, as well as donations from other people. Therefore, the problem of funding became a major problem in the building of the Party, and in the end, it was only with the assistance of the Communist International that the work of building the Party of the Chinese Communist Party was completed.

At first, Chen Duxiu, a scholar, was full of spirit and insisted that the Chinese Communist Party should be independent and autonomous, not subject to the people, and was unwilling to accept the assistance of the Communist International and do as he was told. He repeatedly refused to provide funds from the Communist International, so that after the "Great Day", the CPC Central Committee had difficulty in raising $2,300 per month.

In October 1921, Chen Duxiu was arrested in Shanghai's rented area and faced seven or eight years in prison. Marin, the representative of the Communist International, spent a lot of money and painstaking efforts to break through the joints of the courtroom and invited a famous French lawyer to defend the case, before successfully rescuing Chen Duxiu from prison. Recalling how he could not even get the money to save himself from prison and how he could be independent, Chen Duxiu lamented,

> *"Now that the rulers have oppressed us so mercilessly, we can only establish closer relations with the Communist International and have no more doubts."*

Even so, Chen Duxiu did not fully agree that the CPC should become a vassal of the Communist International; he simply agreed that the various departments of the Party could apply for funding from the Communist International in their own name. In this way, the work of the Party can be carried out quickly.

After Chen Duxiu, another person who wants to be independent and do something big is Li Lisan.

In 1930, when Jiang Feng Yan fought the Great War, Li Lizan believed that the Kuomintang's rule was crumbling and that the Chinese Revolution would become the last class war in the world, and demanded that "the Soviet Union must actively prepare for war". In this blueprint for the riots, the Chinese Revolution was at the centre of the world revolution, the Soviet Union fully cooperated with the Chinese Revolution, and the Communist International was only a supporting actor in the implementation of this plan.

In April 1920, when Wiesenski came to China to help establish the Chinese Communist Party, the first directive given to him by the Communist International and the Political Bureau of the United Communist Central Committee was that "our general policy in the Far East is based on a conflict between the interests of Japan, the United States and China, and that all means should be used to aggravate such a conflict"; the second was to support the Chinese Revolution. That is, the great help given to the Chinese Kuomintang and the Chinese Communist Party, which promoted the powerful development of the Northern Expeditionary Revolution, was also born out of the needs of the Soviet national interest. Now, all of a sudden, Li Lizan jumped out of nowhere, and in a single "riot", he demanded that "the Soviet Union must actively prepare for war", "come out of Mongolia, assist China and attack the enemy", and that the Soviet Union should ignore its own security and cooperate fully with the Chinese revolution.

> "The international intervention was carried out with the greatest speed and by the most fundamental means: the suspension of funding for the activities of the Central Committee of the Communist Party of China. This is the harshest sanction the CPC has received since its founding. Li Li-san, whose funding has been suspended, is left with only Taiwan."[70]

---

[70] *The Brilliance of Suffering*, by Jin Yonan, Hua Yi Press, 2009.

In the end, Mao Zedong, who deeply understood the social situation in China at the time, found an independent and autonomous solution to the problem of financial resources, and only then did he fundamentally lay the economic foundation for the independence of the Chinese Communist Party.

Mao Zedong's idea was to establish the "Red Divide", and in 1928, he asked the question "why the Red regime in China can exist". He noted:

> *"It is never the case that within a country, surrounded by white regimes, there is a small area or areas of red regimes that exist for a long time, something that the countries of the world have never had. There are unique reasons why this kind of wonder happens. The conditions for its existence and development must also be considerable. It cannot take place in any imperialist country, nor in any colony ruled directly by imperialism, necessarily in the economically backward semi-colonial China ruled indirectly by imperialism. For this strange phenomenon must be accompanied by another strange phenomenon, and that is the war between the white regimes... Because of the long division and war between the white regimes, a condition is given which enables a small or several small patches of the red zone, led by the Communist Party, to take place and persist in the middle of the surrounding white regime."*[71]

It was along this line that the practice of the Chinese revolution later succeeded.

Relying on the Red Base, the Communist Party's policy of "beating the bully and dividing up the land" won the support and support of the peasants for the Red Regime, and agricultural production flourished, laying the foundation for the economic independence of the Base.

The lessons of the Paris Commune and the successful experience of the Russian Soviet made Mao and the other founders of the base realize that for a revolution to succeed, it must have one hand on the barrel of the gun and the other on the bag of money. From the very beginning of the Chinese Soviet Republic, the new Red regime decided to create its own independent financial system, creating the Soviet

---

[71] *Selected Works of Mao Zedong*, vol. 1, p. 48.

Republic's own central bank, the National Bank of the Chinese Soviet Union.

The most important work of the National Bank was threefold: first, to unify the currency; second, to unify finance and taxation; and third, to support production and trade in the Soviet region.

Without a unified currency, there can be no reliable fiscal taxation; without fiscal taxation, there can be no stability in the Soviet regime and no victory in a long war. Likewise, a unified currency will strongly promote production and trade, raise the people's standard of living, revitalize the Soviet economy, increase the government's fiscal revenues and consolidate the nascent Soviet regime.

The world's smallest central bank, the Chinese Soviet National Bank

In November 1931, at the First National Congress of the Chinese Soviet Union, Mao Zemin was ordered to establish the National Bank of the Chinese Soviet Union. The following are the five founders of the National Bank.

Mao Zemin, Governor of the State Bank of China. Born a farmer, private school for four years. Work experience: Primary school general affairs (managing daily expenses and food), head of economic unit of An Yuan Coal Mine Workers Club, general manager of An Yuan Road Mine Workers' Consumer Cooperative, manager of publishing and distribution department of the CPC Central Committee (Shanghai), general manager of the Hankou Republic Daily, minister of economy of the military region of Fujian-Ganxi Province.

Cao Ju-ru, Head of Accounting Section, National Bank. Born into a family of shopkeepers, primary school culture. Work experience: Worked as a shop assistant in Nanyang, head of accounting section of Minxi Industrial and Agricultural Bank.

Yonglie Lai, Chief, National Banking Section. Work experience: shop assistant, Red Army soldier, founder of Yongding County Farmers Bank.

Mo Juntao, Chief, General Affairs Section, National Bank. Born a shopkeeper, dropped out of school at the age of 12 to work as a child labourer. Work experience: sand ripper at Hankow Foundry, letter carrier at British Bank, Red Army soldier.

Qian Xijun, National Bank Accountant. Born a farmer, studied at the Shanghai Civilian Girls' School. Work experience: Head of the Publishing Section, Central Publishing Department, Communist Party of China (CPC Central Committee), Traffic Officer.

These people are selected by thousands of people in the Soviet Union who have been "involved" with the bank, including Cao Jiu Ru's dealings with the bank, only to withdraw money for the boss's deposit, while Mo Juntao worked as a blue-collar worker in the bank in Hankou, and never even ordered money. If these 5 resumes were laid out in front of Rothschild or JPMorgan and told that these people can manage a central bank well, their best response would be to snort. These five men had neither an Ivy League degree nor Wall Street experience, and were not even qualified to work as security guards at the Bund Bank in Shanghai.

If they can run a good rural cooperative, some might believe it. Running a central bank, on par with Rothschild or JPMorgan? That's a big joke! Whether it's human, material or financial resources, it's a hundred and eighty thousand miles away from the average person's imagination of a central bank!

The task before these five was to establish an independent central banking system, which was more difficult than ever!

Just think of the number of problems that lie before them.

- How is the bank's start-up capital obtained?
- What is the basis of the currency?
- What is the reserve for paper currency issuance?
- How to establish monetary credit?
- How to unify the currency in the Soviet Union?
- Where is the bank's vault built and how is it kept secret?
- How are the treasury accounts recorded?
- How are banknotes issued? Who will design the pattern?
- Where does the printing paper and ink come from?
- How is paper money anti-counterfeiting?
- How are silver dollars issued? Is it an independent design or an imitation?

> How do you do business with loans, bills of exchange discounting, etc.?

There are endless questions, and it makes you sad to think about it! But it is this "five tiger generals", in an ordinary farming house in Yaping Village, 6 miles outside of Ruijin City, a few tables, a few abacus, began the National Bank of China from scratch the difficult business, laid the foundation of today's Chinese banking system!

At the beginning, the biggest problem facing the National Bank was the lack of start-up capital, and its financial sources were mainly supplies seized during the war. Whenever the Red Army was engaged in major combat operations, the National Bank would organize confiscation collection committees to follow the troops to the front to raise money for food.

In 1932, Mao Zemin also came with the army to Zhangzhou after the great victory of the Battle of Zhangzhou commanded by Mao Zedong. He walked the streets and talked to the merchants, propagating the policies of the Red Army, hoping that the merchants would maintain regular trade contact with the Red Army and communicate with each other about their presence or absence. Meanwhile, the National Bank issued a bulletin on confiscation and collection in Zhangzhou City, where the Red Army does not confiscate stores, but can accept donations from store owners. This policy has been embraced by large and small business owners in Zhangzhou, who have made donations. On this expedition, the Red Army not only received a large amount of military supplies, but also raised 1.05 million foreign currency, and the National Bank was funded!

In order to store some of the money collected in Zhangzhou, the National Bank decided to build a secret vault, and they found a house on a hill in the village of Ruijin, Shicheng County, close to Ruijin, with a cellar on the hill immediately behind it. And this house, in front of the cellar, could be both covered and guarded. The National Bank chose this as the location of the secret vault.

In the interest of confidentiality, no staff of the National Bank was used that day in the vault. The gold to be put into the secret vault (gold bars, goldware, gold ornaments, etc.) was wrapped in sackcloth in advance by the soldiers of the army and placed in five quadrants. Another 20 quintals of silver dollars and silver dollar treasure were also wrapped in advance. There were also three quarters of jewels and two quarters of paper money (foreign currency and Nationalist French currency). The 30 quarts of "treasure" were picked in turn by a platoon of fighters to stop at the bottom of the hill a mile from the house and then released to guard it. At night, another platoon of warriors picked the 30 quads into the house at night and stored them in the cellar behind the house. For fire protection, the 30 stretchers were covered with pre-prepared stone slabs. When these "treasures" were counted and packed, Mao Zemin personally looked them over. After being placed in the cellar, Mao Zemin also personally inspected it. They made an inventory of the contents of the 30 quadrants, two in total, one in the personal custody of Mao Zemin. For the sake of confidentiality, the inventory lists some yellow wine and some white wine. Yellow wine represents gold and white wine represents silver. After those stretchers were placed, the cellar mouths were blocked with stones by the warriors and camouflaged outside. The next day, all the Red Army fighters involved in the storage were evacuated and replaced with a number of other fighters to guard the room in front of the cellar.[72]

In the work of secrecy, Mao Zemin first kept the people of the National Bank out of the way, and then organized four more batches of fighters to transport them, each with only a portion of the information. The ones in charge of transportation don't know where to store the gold and silver, the ones in charge of transportation don't know where to end up, the ones in storage don't know what's inside, and the ones in the last guard are clueless. Not only that, but Mao Zemin also disguised it with yellow wine and white wine in the Qing dynasty, which is really well thought out.

> *"Subsequent practice has shown that the decision was a brilliant one. When the Red Army was later forced to evacuate the Central Soviet Union for a long march, this part of the money that was initially in reserve played a great role."*[73]

When starting a bank correspondent vault business, people don't know how to start bookkeeping. On one occasion, the front-line troops sent a batch of seized cash register, and the agents found that the paper wrapped around the cash register was in fact a four-pack of bills from the tax authorities of the Kuomintang. After careful examination, Mao

---

[72] *From Child Labour to Red Bankers: The Revolutionary Years of Mo Juntao*, by Mo Xiaotao, China Finance Press, 2010, pp. 33–34.

[73] Ibid., p. 33.

Zemin and Cao Ju Ru were overjoyed, as if they had been given a treasure. They carefully analyzed and studied the four links, from which they were inspired to improve the system and process of the treasury, and finally developed the bank treasury management method. In this way, the recipient, manager (the State Treasury), user and disposer of the treasury funds are recorded accordingly, ensuring a rigorous financial system and effectively eliminating corruption and waste at all levels of government and in the military.

Inspired by the quadripartite list, the National Bank immediately issued a notice requesting the Red Army's political departments at all levels, the Ministry of Supply, to pay attention to the collection of books, documents, account books, bills, statements and other physical objects related to the management of financial, banking, enterprise and other knowledge for reference, and not to throw away easily, even if it is just a piece of paper.

With the establishment and improvement of various systems, the National Bank is gradually becoming operational.

The Birth of Red Money

Next was the preparation of the privileged business of the State Bank, issuing the currency of the unified Central Soviet region.

The central revolutionary stronghold was in the economically backward countryside, where there was no industry, only scattered individual agriculture and a few small crafts. Frequent wars, coupled with the intensifying economic blockade by the Nationalist Party, make it extremely difficult to secure a fiscal balance. When it was first established, the market was flooded with all sorts of different kinds of money. Inferior coinage expelled good coinage, making silver dollars rarely in circulation.

Before the establishment of the Soviet National Bank, the currency in circulation according to the territory was: copper yuan coupons from the Jiangxi Industrial and Agricultural Bank, silver yuan coupons from the Minxi Industrial and Agricultural Bank, paper money from the Guanyang and the Kuomintang, and even copper plates from the Qing Dynasty. People buy things, grab a handful of tickets of all kinds, and sometimes they can't even keep score. Not only the common people have headaches, but businessmen are also overwhelmed.

Some Red Army fighters were simple-minded and believed that revolutionary fighters did not use KMT banknotes, and sometimes set fire to KMT banknotes seized on the battlefield, not even knowing that these banknotes could buy many of the supplies that were scarce in the Soviet Union, such as salt and rice. At that time, the Kuomintang's French currency, the miscellaneous coins issued by warlords and the noblemen, and circulating in the Soviet region, undoubtedly gave the Kuomintang the opportunity to destroy the financial market in the Soviet region.

With the establishment of the National Bank, the currency of the unified Soviet Union became a top priority. To issue currency, the first difficulty is, who will design and pattern the paper money?

Someone recommended Huang Yaguang. He studied in Japan, and not only can he write well, but he can also draw. After some inquiries, the mixed feelings are that Huang Yaguang does have painting talent, but the worry is that he is in the movement of the "Su She Party" sweeping through western Fujian, was designated as a social democratic party members in prison. Mao Zemin reported the case to Mao Zedong, who, after much deliberation, decided to risk making a mistake to save the life of Huang Yaguang by personally approving Huang Yaguang.

At that time, the Soviet Union was under severe economic blockade by the Kuomintang, and working conditions were very poor. Mao Zemin secretly bought drawing pens, circular gauges, ink and copper plates from Shanghai, and Huang Yaguang began to work on the monetary pattern based solely on his memory of some of the banknotes he had used.

In the process of designing the currency pattern, Mao Zedong demanded that the design of the Soviet government currency must reflect the characteristics of the industrial and peasant regime. Therefore, when Huang Yaguang designed the currency, he drew scythes, hammers, maps, five-pointed stars and other patterns, and organically combined these patterns to give people both beautiful and generous, but also highlight the characteristics of the base currency under the Communist Party leadership. He originally wanted to draw an image of Mao Zedong's head on paper money, which was rejected by Mao and later changed to an image of Lenin's head. Huang Yaguang copied the head of Lenin on the red booklet, representing the people of the Soviet Union under the guidance of Marxist-Leninist thinking to change the new weather.

The issuance of paper money also has to address the issue of paper and ink. Due to the Kuomintang's blockade of the Soviet region, raw materials for printing were scarce. After going to Shanghai and Hong Kong to photocopy banknotes and purchase printing materials without success, the National Bank could only temporarily print on white cloth while making its own paper. Without raw materials to make paper, we pick up some rotten sacks and broken cotton wool, go up to the mountains to cut wool and bamboo, peel the bark, collect the soles of shoes and rope heads. As a result, the National Bank's "rag-picking" team was often seen at the village street. After the pickup is smashed all over, it is soaked in a lime pond and pounded into pulp for paper making.

Later I heard from my hometown that tea wrappers made from the bark of an old tree on a nearby mountain were both hard-wearing and tough, and the men of the National Bank immediately went up the mountain to collect them. Initially, the paper was not very good, poor toughness, thick and yellow, then added glue and fine cotton to increase the toughness and whiteness, before finally made a suitable paper for printing banknotes.

Buying ink from the white zone is also a struggle. The ink purchased from Ganzhou was confiscated by the Kuomintang on the way back. A Qian Zhuang owner suggested using the traditional pine smoke method to make ink, burning the pine paste of the pine tree into smoke oil, then mixing some tung oil. The ink problem is solved.

After overcoming problems with funding, design, and printing banknotes, the Soviet National Bank printed the first Soviet banknotes on July 7, 1932, just five months after the National Bank was established. Currency is based on the silver dollar, paper currency is the silver coupon, and the silver coupon for one silver dollar is the national currency. With a unified currency, the National Bank, together with the Soviet financial department, announced that all transactions and taxes would be calculated in national currency, that the paper currency of the Kuomintang would be prohibited from circulation, and that the currency issued by the former Soviet banks would be withdrawn on a pro rata basis and would no longer be used.

The National Bank issued silver and copper coins in addition to paper money. At that time, the National Bank Central Mint also minted three types of silver coins, the "Yuan", the "Sun Xiaotou" and the Mexican "Eagle Ocean", which could be circulated both inside and outside the central revolutionary strongholds. The issuance and circulation of National Bank money, the gradual recovery of various miscellaneous coins, and the unification of the currency of the Central Soviet region.

In order to control the issuance of paper money, article X of the Provisional Statute of the Soviet National Bank states:

> *"At least three tenths of the paper money shall be issued in cash, or in precious metals, or in foreign currency, and the rest shall be secured by goods or short-term bills of exchange, or other types of securities, which are readily marketable."*[74]

This ensures that the currency has sufficient cash as collateral and that the effective expansion of the currency is fully realized.

When the National Bank issued the first set of banknotes, due to the limitations of the conditions, both the manufacturing technology and the anti-counterfeiting technology were blank, in order to be able to do the maximum anti-counterfeiting, Mao Zemin used the method of adding his and the Minister of Finance Deng Zizhuo's signatures in Russian to the banknotes. But this method is very easy to imitate. With the currency in circulation, the Kuomintang and the warlords began various sabotage activities, importing large amounts of counterfeit currency and disrupting the financial order in the Soviet Union.

In order to solve the problem of anti-counterfeiting, Mao Zemin thought hard and could not find a good solution. One night, when he smelled the stench of the wool head from the fire when his wife was weaving a sweater, he had a sudden idea to put a certain amount of wool into the paper when making paper, so that he could not only identify the paper money by looking through it, but also tear or burn it by smelling the stench of a kind of wool to identify the real Soviet currency, thus solving the problem of anti-counterfeiting and ensuring the normal circulation of Soviet currency.

By the end of 1932, the Soviet National Bank had printed and issued 650,000 silver notes, while the reserve amounted to 390,000, or

---

[74] *Tracing Mao Zemin*, Cao Hong, Zhou Yan, Central Literature Press, 2007, p. 153.

60 per cent of the total amount issued, twice the rate stipulated in the statute.

Paper money circulated smoothly in the Soviet Union, clearing up the confusion of the former currency market in one fell swoop.

In this way, the founders of the National Bank, through countless trials and tribulations, with strong conviction and tenacity of will, fully utilized their ingenuity and firmly grasped the money bag.

The people's money, for the people

Sixty per cent of China's land is above 2,000 metres above sea level, making it unsuitable for crop cultivation, while much of it receives little rainfall. To make matters worse, floods caused by irregular monsoons often result in severe crop failures, leading to massive famine.

If compared to the United States in 1945, 6.5 million farmers supported 140 million people and arable acreage reached 365 million acres. China's then 65 million farming families supported 400 million people, with only 217 million acres of arable land equivalent.

Such land pressures and increasingly heavy taxes made it difficult for Old China farmers to maintain subsistence levels in normal years. Farmers have had to make full use of all available resources to maintain their increasingly depleted land. They pick up every fallen leaf, every dead grass, every stray eel of wheat, to fuel it. Animal and human droppings are carefully collected to restore fertility to the land.

In China, the goals of agriculture are fundamentally different from those of neo-colonial countries such as the United States, Australia, and New Zealand. Whereas in these countries there is a general surplus of land and a shortage of labour, the opposite is true in China. Thus, China's agriculture pursues the maximum output per unit of land, while the United States pursues the maximum output per unit of population. Whereas Chinese farmers can toughen up on small plots of land with intensive labour, American farmers prioritize labour-saving measures such as agricultural mechanization and chemical fertilizers, which become relatively inexpensive when the inputs are evenly distributed among large per capita occupants of farmland. But with land scarcity per capita in China, this input becomes unaffordable.

The large surplus of agricultural labour in old China and an agricultural economy oriented towards maximizing land output inevitably produced massive poverty and semi-employment. During the non-farm rush hours, the agricultural population has to engage in various handicrafts to supplement its meagre agricultural income. The agricultural economic system of old China can be said to be in a rather fragile equilibrium, with a thin cushion of wealth against natural and man-made disasters, and rural handicraft income as a key pressure reducing valve for this weakly balanced and high-risk economic system.

At this point, the economic forces of the West pressed on with thunderous momentum.

The massive and cheap machine-made commodities created during the industrial revolution are flooding into China like a tidal wave, and local handmade textile products, wood products, ceramics, clothing, shoes and hats are increasingly difficult to compete with Western products in the local market. The rural economic system is on the verge of collapse after the loss of income from handicrafts. China could have resorted to high tariffs to mitigate the devastating impact of Western economic power, but the Western powers would never allow backward countries to adopt policies of self-protection and would not hesitate to use force if necessary. China was forced to accept ultra-low tariffs of 5 per cent and was dominated by Western powers in customs affairs and the financial system.

Between 1900 and 1940, China's rural economy worsened, with 10 per cent of the wealthy owning 53 per cent of arable land and a high degree of land monopoly. The vast majority of farmers are tenant farmers who have to pay 1/3 to 1/2 of their produce as rent each year, and the resulting lack of income forces more than half of them to take out annual loans to survive. At that time, the annual interest rate for borrowing crops in China was 85%, and the annual interest rate for currency borrowing was as high as 20% to 50%![75]

In this situation of high land monopoly, extreme exploitation of rents and high interest rates, the agrarian economic system has been

---

[75] *Tragedy and Hope*, Carroll Quigley, 1996, p. 181.

completely overturned, the peasants have lost any hope of surviving and revolution has become inevitable.

Where there is oppression, there is resistance! What is strange is not why the revolution broke out in rural China, but why it broke out so late!

Mao Zedong looked around at the entire economic map of rural China and found that the rural economy in many places was on the verge of collapse. He saw that it was a fertile ground for revolution where "the fire of the stars can start a prairie fire" and had the potential to establish the "armed separation of the peasants and the workers", especially "in places where the peasants and the workers had greatly risen up during the bourgeois democratic revolution of 1926 and 1927, such as Hunan, Guangdong, Hubei and Jiangxi provinces. In many parts of these provinces, there was once a very large organization of trade unions and peasants' associations, a struggle of the working and peasant classes against the politics of the landlord-rich squire and the bourgeoisie in many economies." His vision of the Red Divide was by no means a theoretical fantasy, but was based on life practice, and he began his Soviet practice in Hunan and Jiangxi, where the rural economic system was weakest.

The land reform movement of the "land grabbing and land division" was first carried out on the land, and land rights changed from centralized to roughly equal. Whereas 80 to 90 per cent of the land used to be in the hands of landowners, now, with the exception of a share of the land according to population, the rest is in the hands of the farmers who are directly involved in production.

At the same time, the Government is also actively campaigning for the abolition of the various debts that have been imposed on farmers. The first is the usury exploitation system, "Workers and peasants should have their debts owed to Tian Dong abolished and not returned". Also, the abolition of pawnshops was an important part of the abolition campaign. In the past, pawnshops mainly took farmers' clothes as collateral for loans with very high interest rates, and the amount of money lent was less than half the value of the collateral, and farmers were subjected to very heavy exploitation. The Soviet government confiscated the pawnshop, and the pawned items were returned to the peasants as cheaply as possible, without the peasants having to redeem them.

While ensuring that farmers have land to grow, they are also exempted from agricultural taxes so that they can fully enjoy the fruits of their labor. These measures have facilitated and ensured the smooth development of the agrarian revolution, with a high level of enthusiasm among farmers for agricultural production and a strong support for the Government. The peasants did not understand high Marxism or Leninism, but they understood very well that the Soviet government had brought them great practical benefits. Any government can only be stable if it brings tangible benefits to the people.

On the other hand, the economic situation in the countryside at that time was very chaotic. One is the outflow of cash, and the lack of trading leverage in rural markets. The main holders of cash, wealthy merchants, gentry and landowners, fearing revolution, have fled with cash, resulting in an extraordinary shortage of cash chips in the market, making it difficult to carry out both large and small transactions. Some landowners don't lend their cash to farmers for fear that the rich will hide it. As a result, farmers are unable to sell their produce for cash, cannot borrow money, and sometimes do not even have the cash to buy their daily necessities, making production and living difficult. Second, the lack of funds for handicrafts and commerce makes it difficult for reproduction and buying and selling activities to proceed normally. Many large industrial and commercial operators have been withdrawing funds, causing cottage industries to cease production and workers and shopkeepers to lose their jobs. Third, the financial market is in serious disarray, no less than a dozen kinds of coins in circulation, metal coins are various silver yuan, copper money, paper money, the Kuomintang Bank, foreign banks and Chinese banks issued various kinds of paper money, and also local merchants and shops issued municipal bills and warlords and landlords issued miscellaneous coins. Among them, metal coins tend to reduce the color and weight in circulation, the name of paper money is many, the value varies, the exchange rate between coins is variable, often the phenomenon of paper money devaluation is like scrap paper. In addition, the farmers often take advantage of the money exchanged by unscrupulous traders, and after several years of exploitation, they have very little left.[76]

---

[76] *An Outline of the Monetary History of the Chinese Revolution*, by Xu Shuxin, China Finance Press, 2008, pp. 15–16.

Farmers are desperate for their own banks and a fair currency!

The National Bank of the Soviet Union, through the issuance of a unified currency, completely changed the situation of numismatic chaos, so that the peasants are free from the exploitation of money changers, but also provides sufficient trading chips for the rural market trade, greatly promoting the development of the economy.

The National Bank has provided strong support to farmers and craftspeople for the rehabilitation and development of industrial and agricultural production, mainly by addressing the financial needs of production and operation, by granting low or no-interest loans such as seed loans, cattle loans, fertilizer loans, etc., and by obtaining loans for the purchase of fertilizers and agricultural implements for intensive cultivation on their land, agricultural output has increased significantly.

In order to prevent the impact of food price fluctuations on farmers' incentives to produce, the National Bank, in cooperation with the Bureau of Food Adjustment, actively regulates food prices.

> *"In order to stabilize the market and prevent a sharp rise or fall in food prices, the National Bank has also granted loans to the Food Adjustment Bureau. In the autumn harvest, it is bought at a reasonable price; when farmers are short of food, it is sold again at a reasonable price, which protects the development of the rural economy and guarantees the interests of the peasant masses."[77]*

These financial measures have solved the difficulties of farmers in terms of land, debt and food marketing, and have allowed agricultural production to resume in a short period of time and the livelihoods of farmers to be greatly improved.

The farmer Xie Rendi, a family of six, did not have a bit of land before the revolution and had very few farming tools. Xie Rendi borrowed 100 quintals of grain from the landowner, due to heavy exploitation, only 10 quintals of grain a year, the family did not have enough to eat, every year had to borrow grain from the landowner, cut the grain, paid the rent, paid the debt, and no rice under the pot, again had to borrow from the landowner ... After the revolution, he shared the landowner's grain, clothes and ploughs and harrows and other

---

[77] *Tracing Mao Zemin*, Cao Hong, Zhou Yan, Central Literature Press, 2007, p. 152.

agricultural tools, when the family divided the field, the family shared 57 quintals of grain, 7 feet 8 feet of vegetable garden land. In the first year after the land was divided, he collected 72 quintals of grain, as well as sweet potatoes, beans, etc. In addition to 40 quintals of rations and 3 quintals of land tax, he also had 29 quintals of grain left. The vegetable garden grows vegetables that can be sold in addition to what they eat, and life has radically improved. At the time, the cloth was expensive, but he had to buy two a year. There are also some additional farming tools to be purchased.[78]

Even in the late Soviet period, as a result of higher military and government expenditures,

> *"the burden on the peasants (including agricultural taxes, public debt, and grain borrowing), although increasing, improved greatly on the basis of productive development, and in 1933 the peasants' lives improved at least twice as much as in the Kuomintang era. Most of the peasants, in the past there were many times when they could not eat enough, and in times of difficulty some of them even had to eat bark and bran, and now not only is there no hunger in general, but life is getting richer year by year. Most farmers used to dress badly, but now they generally improve, some twice as well, some twice as well."[79]*

The establishment and consolidation of the regime and the victory of the revolutionary war are inseparable from the ground. Mao Zedong once made a humorous analogy:

> *"A revolution has to be grounded, as if one had to have an ass. If a man does not have an ass, he cannot sit down. If one keeps walking and standing, it will not last. When your legs go sore and you stand soft, you fall down. It is only when the revolution has a basis that it can have a place to rest, regain its qi, replenish its strength, and then continue to fight, expand its development, and move toward final victory."*

The existence of a local economy cannot be achieved without the development of a local economy, without the support of local farmers and workers, and without monetary and financial security.

---

[78] *History of the Burden of Chinese Peasants*, Volume III, China Financial and Economic Press, 1990, p. 63.

[79] Ibid., p. 92.

As Mao Zedong said,

> "Only when the Soviet Union has made every effort to solve the problems of the masses, has practically improved their lives, and has gained their faith in the Soviet Union, can it mobilize the masses to join the Red Army and help the war."[80]
>
> "To be embraced by the masses? Do you want the masses to put their best foot forward on the battlefield? Then one has to be with the masses, one has to go and mobilize the masses, one has to care for the itching of the masses, one has to work sincerely for the benefit of the masses, to solve the problems of production and life of the masses, the problems of salt, the problems of rice, the problems of houses, the problems of clothing, the problems of giving birth to small children, to solve all the problems of the masses."[81]

It was guided by such ideas that the establishment of the financial system of the Soviet region, everywhere for the benefit of the peasants, from the practical point of view of solving the rural economy, the measures of the State Bank greatly facilitated the life of the peasants, established the credit of the currency of the Soviet region, and the government was more heartily embraced and loved by the peasants. It was because of the popular support, in order to counter the "siege" and large-scale expansion of the Red Army, the Soviet Union can be seen everywhere parents send their sons, wives send their grandsons, brothers compete with the Red Army's moving scenes.

Trade "Special Zone" and "Central Enterprise" of the Soviet Union

As a civilian boat laden with cloth went up the river and approached a place downstream of Ganzhou, the captain stopped the boat on the west bank to wait for a guide. Suddenly, there was the sound of "da da da da" machine guns on the east coast. "Get the ship to the east coast now!" The captain commanded. Shipwrights pulled up Penny

---

[80] Mao Zedong's Rural Investigations, Central Documentation and Research Office of the Communist Party of China, China Jinggangshan Cadre College, People's Publishing House, 1982, p. 308.

[81] Volume 1 of *Mao Zedong's Collected Works*, edited by the Central Document Research Office of the Communist Party of China, People's Publishing House, 1996, pp. 138–139.

just approaching the east bank has not yet stopped, the shore to wait for a long time in the Su district estuary trade branch of the staff jumped on board. After greeting them, the captain hastily shouted, "The Red Army has robbed" and abandoned the ship to "escape" to Ganzhou. When he returned, the captain said to Boss Bu Zhuang, "No good, a boatload of cloth has been 'robbed' by the Red Army!" Instead of being in a hurry, the owner praised the captain for a job well done. In a few days, the money for the ship's cloth was delivered to the cloth shop in no uncertain terms. The boss made a few thousand silver dollars at one count. The captain, on the other hand, was paid hundreds of silver dollars by the Board of Trade as an extravagant gratuity.

This peculiar scene was a common occurrence in the areas adjacent to the Soviet and Nationalist regions. In fact, it was a special form of trade between the Soviet Union and the State Union.

After the failure of the third KMT "siege" of the Central Soviet Union, the KMT intensified its economic blockade of the Central Soviet Union and cut off trade between the Soviet Union and the Kuomintang. Soviet agricultural products and specialties could not be sold, prices fell again and again, and much-needed salt, cloth, kerosene, western medicine, etc. could not be shipped in. At one time, the high prices of some items in the Soviet region, the people were panicked, which directly affected the life of the masses and the Red Army, and affected the people's confidence in the government.

Recognizing that this was a major problem that affected the survival of the Central Soviet Union, the Government established the Central Ministry of National Economy and the General Directorate of Foreign Trade, which was responsible for developing foreign trade. At the same time, a series of flexible policies were put in place that were adapted to the actual situation: incentives for private businesses to operate a variety of goods essential to the Soviet Union; tax reductions on certain daily and munitions items; multifaceted cooperation with State-run businesses using private and cooperative capital to the maximum extent possible; encouragement of businessmen from the Guvuzi district to come to the Soviet Union to do business; secret dispatch of people from the Soviet Union to open shops and purchasing stations in the Guvuzi district, etc.

"Breaking the enemy's economic blockade, developing foreign trade in the Soviet Union, practicing the exchange of surplus Soviet produce (grain rice, tungsten sand, timber, tobacco, paper, etc.) with industrial goods (salt, cloth, oil, etc.) in the White Zone, is a hub for developing the national economy."[82] under Mao's general approach to trade, and Mao Zemin was actively involved. He believes that the Soviet Union's output is cheap and lucrative, and that businessmen in the Soviet Union will not miss this opportunity. Not only that, but he also simultaneously exploited the greed and internal contradictions of the warlords and made underground deals with them. In order to support foreign trade, the State Bank has set aside 1 million of the 3 million yuan of economic construction bonds as foreign trade funds.

One day in the winter of 1931, the people of Ruijin County, the government put up a notice around the people talking: "The area of the Soviet Union, all over the treasures. Once excavated, the country is rich and the people are strong. There is a prize for all. Mao Zemin, Governor of the National Bank of the Chinese Soviet Republic."

Someone said,

> "The county name of Ruijin County, taken from 'He Sheng Rui Qi, digging the ground to get gold', underground treasures must be quite a lot." Another person took the message, "There's a prize for reporting, whoever doesn't want it, get on it!"

A few days later, Mao Zemin received a letter from the Red Army and a dark, shiny stone. The letter said that there is a place called "iron mountain ridge" produced tungsten ore, before the Red Army, there were Cantonese merchants to open mines there, foreigners said how much to ask for. Mao Zemin immediately did a survey, a quart of tungsten sand can be sold for 8 yuan, while a quart of rice only 2, this is simply the Soviet Union's treasure bowl! Mao Zemin was overjoyed that the State Bank was going to be a wealthy man!

Ganan is known as the "tungsten capital", with hundreds of tungsten mines of all sizes. Tungsten steel is a key material in the manufacture of firearms and is highly sought after internationally. During the First World War, the warring nations scrambled to expand their armaments, and tungsten ore became an important strategic material. The foreigners and local warlords monopolized the

---

[82] Report at the Second National Workers' and Peasants' Congress, Mao Zedong, 23 January 1934.

acquisition of tungsten ore, and countless tungsten sands were continuously dumped overseas.

If the Red Army has such strategic materials as tungsten ore, it will have the money to bargain with the Guotong District, will tear a rift in the blockade line of the Soviet Union, bringing huge income to the Soviet Union.

In the spring of 1932, the Soviet Union established the China Tungsten Ore Company to lead and organize tungsten production in the Soviet Union. Mao Zemin is also the General Manager of Tungsten Mines. China Tungsten Ore Company is the first "state-owned enterprise" established in Soviet Union, supporting the financial operation of the whole Soviet Union.

At that time, many of the KMT's military and political dignitaries had their own deals. Mao Zemin then sent someone to get in touch with the trading department store they run in Ganzhou. Guangdong warlord Chen Jitang, who both fried gold and collected tungsten sand. When he heard that there was a new way to get rich, he was overjoyed and immediately sent his cronies to negotiate secretly with representatives of the Soviet Union. Before the trip, Chen Jitang solemnly instructed: "endure the disgrace and humiliation, and only succeed."

Mao Zemin also came to Ganzhou City to personally deploy tungsten sand for export. After several rounds of bargaining, the price of tungsten sand was raised nearly seven times from the original price of 8 pieces per quintal, to 52 pieces per quintal! Soon, the two sides reached a secret agreement on the tungsten sand deal: imports from the Soviet Union were escorted by warlord troops stationed in Ganzhou, and tungsten sand was brought into the Soviet Union from Guangdong, and back from the Soviet Union. Each side gets its own way.

After Chen Jitang got into the tungsten sand business in Ganzhou, the other officers of the Guangdong army were also very red-eyed. The orders of Chairman Jiang had long been forgotten, and one after another, they started to trade with the Soviet Union, exchanging tungsten sand and agricultural products with salt and cloth. The tungsten sand produced by the China Tungsten Mining Company was affixed with a large seal bearing the words "National Defense Materials" and escorted out of the country by the militia in a grand manner, in exchange for much-needed salt, cloth, western medicine, ammunition, etc., and silver dollars.

From 1932 to 1934, the company produced 4,193 tons of tungsten sand and earned more than 4 million yuan in revenue, making it the most important economic source in the Soviet Union and a veritable "first central enterprise". The income from tungsten mines played a huge role in crushing Chiang Kai-shek's economic blockade and the four "sieges" and enriching the national banks.

In addition to making full use of strategic goods to open up trade channels, the Soviet government also established Soviet "special economic zones" at the borders of the Soviet region, where transportation is more convenient, and halved taxes to mobilize and attract Soviet merchants to trade with the Soviet region. By mobilizing and relying on the masses in the Soviet Union, a strong and reliable merchandise purchasing force was established, and the KMT's economic blockade was broken through layers and layers by establishing a secret trade relationship with the Ganzhou Grand Merchant House.

The Soviet Government also provided protection and encouragement in order to fully motivate individual traders to trade. It provides that "freedom of commerce shall be guaranteed without interference in regular commodity market relations" and that "hawkers and peasants shall be exempt from commercial taxation if they sell their surplus producers directly. Business capital under $200 is tax-free." As a result, small traders in the central Soviet Union not only set up stalls in the towns of the Soviet Union, but also often infiltrated the State-controlled area to purchase scarce goods.

At the same time, the Communist Party and the Kuomintang fought over currency and salt.

The Kuomintang was so annoyed by the silver coins issued in the Soviet Union that it sent minting experts to infiltrate the central Soviet Union and command local bandits to mint poor quality counterfeit silver coins using the red copper silver plating method. At one time, the market was flooded with counterfeit coins and merchants refused to accept silver coins minted in the Soviet Union. The Soviet government immediately responded by forming a counterfeit currency detection team, heavy fist attack, completely put an end to the KMT planted in the heart of the Soviet Union counterfeit currency manufacturing nest.

The merchants of Ganzhou found that the silver dollars paid by the Soviet government were made in the Soviet Union and were not of high quality, which made it difficult for them to circulate in the Nationalist

Region. The National Bank, on the other hand, is unable to produce the "Eagle Ocean". Mao Zemin, through enlightened merchants, purchased an "Eagle Yang" coin minting machine and a number of steel moulds from Shanghai, and the Central Mint gave up minting the 1-dollar silver coin, which could only be circulated in the Soviet region, and focused on minting the "Eagle Yang", which was widely used in the Guoming district, and foreign trade began to rise again, breaking the economic blockade imposed by the KMT.

As the saying goes, "The people open the door to seven things, the wood, rice, oil, salt, vinegar and tea." Salt was an indispensable commodity, and was therefore used by Chiang Kai-shek as a "weapon of mass destruction" against the Communist Party. The Kuomintang government established the Salt and Fire Oil Administration in Nanchang, Jiangxi, and set up salt and fire oil public sales committees in the surrounding counties of the Soviet Union, implementing the so-called "salt sales by mouth" method, and punishing those who purchased excessive amounts of salt or knowingly failed to report them as "bandits and enemies".

This move of the Kuomintang is very powerful, because the Soviet Union does not produce salt, and the monthly demand for salt at least 150,000 pounds above, overnight, the Soviet Union salt supply unprecedentedly tight, salt prices soared.

In order to cope with this dilemma, the Soviet government sent a group of people disguised as beggars to the white area to beg for food, bought salt in the bag to bring back. The Soviet government also launched the people to make double-decker buckets, using the opportunity to pick manure to the Guoming district, put the salt on the bottom to pick back, and even change the coffin to double-decker, put some stinky pig intestines on the upper layer, put salt on the lower layer, let some people pretend to be buried, when crossing the border, the KMT soldiers far smell the stench, let the "funeral procession" carrying salt passed.

The implementation of foreign trade and the development of individual businesses in the central Soviet Union has led to a prosperous business scene in the Soviet Union, which has played an important role in breaking the blockade and promoting economic construction in the Soviet Union. Snow exclaims in *The Comic of the Westward Journey*,

> "In 1933, the foreign export trade of the Central Soviet Region, which exceeded 12 million yuan, they broke through the Kuomintang blockade and profited greatly."

The National Bank realized in practice that the credit of the Soviet government and the National Bank depended on the abundance of supplies and the level of prices, and that only by ensuring the supply of materials, the Soviet currency could gain the trust and support of the people.

Money Bags for Guns

In the early years of the establishment of the Soviet Union, the economy had not yet recovered and developed, and fund-raising by the Red Army was the main source of military expenses and fiscal revenue. The first three "counter-siege" campaigns were financed by the army's own fund-raising and seizure of Kuomintang supplies. After the third "anti-siege", the Central Soviet government, influenced by the "left" ideology, hastily cancelled the Red Army's fund-raising mission, cutting off the main sources of finance for the national bank and government. The pursuit of a false and aggressive military course, the adoption of a strategy of "position warfare" and "regular warfare", and the blind expansion of the Red Army. The Red Army's military expenses became the responsibility of the Soviet government's finances.

In order to support the guns, the Soviet government developed a policy of "guaranteeing the sustenance of the revolutionary war and the expenditure of all Soviet revolutionary expenses"[83] and took measures to solve military and government expenses by unifying the finances, increasing savings, raising taxes, and issuing public debt.

In the early years of the establishment of the Soviet Union, the Soviet governments at all levels operated separately, with no fiscal policy to speak of, and were indiscriminately collecting and spending money and wasting it at will, not to mention the absence of plans and budgets. The source of finance is beating the dirt. Due to inexperience, some places collect taxes indiscriminately regardless of class, and some

---

[83] *Selected Works of Mao Zedong*, Volume I – Our Economic Policy, People's Press, 1996.

governments do not pay them as they please. Government spending at all levels is extremely uneven, with those with little income suffering so much that they do not have kerosene to light their lamps, and those with more income reaching several thousand dollars a month.

In order to unify finances and overcome fragmentation and corruption, the central Government has established that all revenues of all levels of government are sent to the central treasury at any time, that expenses must be paid in accordance with the approved budget and that final accounts must be submitted to the higher authorities. Mao Zedong warned government workers by saying that "corruption and waste are great crimes". At the same time, in response to the phenomenon of the accounting system in which governments at all levels collect, manage and use money without distinguishing between them and cannot regulate each other, the National Bank, as the agent of the government treasury, has formulated a unified fund management system with four links to ensure that the receiving party, the management party (the national treasury), the using party and the controlling party all have strict records, so as to eliminate corruption and waste from the system.

The unification of finances allowed the centre to make effective and planned savings on unnecessary expenditure in order to concentrate financial resources to support the war.

The great development of the rural economy in the Soviet region has created favourable conditions for the government to impose land and business taxes on farmers. The tax rate is divided by class into the middle peasant and the rich peasant, with a series of tax breaks. The tax authorities use uniform tax receipts and tax exemption certificates for the collection of land taxes. At that time, many farmers used the taxation and exemption certificates of the Soviet tax authorities as proof of ownership of land.

In March 1933, the central Soviet Union also established a unified customs system, and nearly 30 customs offices were established in 15 Soviet counties, thus giving the Soviet Union an independent and autonomous red "customs".

These taxes, become an important part of government revenue. At the same time, the National Bank also advocated a savings campaign,

> *"informing the Party, political and military organs and State enterprises that they must open deposit accounts with banks and that loans should be processed in accordance with overdraft procedures". "Savings campaigns can encourage the masses of*

> workers and peasants to save in their daily lives by depositing the change they save in the bank, which can be reduced to a large amount and turned into a whole. The banks, on the other hand, generally concentrated and flexibly used these social surplus funds and invested them in various cooperatives, especially credit cooperatives, as well as in the production business run by individual workers and peasants, and vigorously developed Soviet production and expanded foreign trade, so that the problems of expensive salt, expensive cloth and decreasing cash could be solved without delay."[84]

The issuance of public debt is another means for the Government to raise funds, both to avoid excessive currency issuance and to provide investment opportunities for the general population. The Soviet government has issued a total of three public bonds, the first two are war bonds, the amount of 600,000 yuan and 1.2 million yuan, and the third is economic construction bonds, the amount of 3 million yuan. The purchasers of the first tranche of public bonds were able to take the bonds to pay land and business taxes, and as a result the bonds quickly returned to the government, effectively causing a financial loss. Then the government realized it couldn't let the bonds go back into government hands before the redemption period, and it later banned the practice of paying taxes directly on the bonds.

The issuance of public bonds in the Soviet Union, not like the Shanghai Tang, all public bonds sold to banks, by the banks to do securities speculation, but to mobilize the masses, take the road of direct sales. The issuance of public bonds enriched the financial revenue of the Soviet Union and supported the war against the "siege".

These measures effectively raise money for the Red Army without placing a particularly heavy burden on the population.

And all of this, all based on a unified currency!

In the absence of a unified currency, the treasury will be filled with various kinds of miscellaneous coins, which will cause great trouble in management and expenditure, and the conversion of various coins and the allocation of money in which currency, I am afraid, will be too busy to count money and keep accounts every day. In which currency are

---

[84] *The Financial and Economic History of the Central Revolution* (First Edition), edited by Xu Yi, People's Publishing House, 2010.

public bonds issued and purchased, and in which currency are interest payments and redemptions made? It's a nightmare! And it is the unification of the currency that provides the unifying vehicle for these policy measures.

In the late Soviet period, the National Bank, under the influence of the "left" line, violated the important principle that "the issuance of paper money by the National Bank should basically be in accordance with the needs of national economic development, and purely financial needs can only be placed in a secondary position",[85] over-issuance of currency amounted to 8 million yuan.

As the Red Army, under the military leadership of "leftist" tendencies, continued to lose wars and shrink its bases, while the currency issue continued to expand, causing serious inflation, the credit of paper money plummeted, seriously undermining the trust of the people of the Soviet Union in the revolutionary government.

"Central Bank" and "Red Army Ticket" for 13 days

In October 1934, when the Central Red Army was forced to withdraw from its base due to the defeat of the fifth "siege", 14 men from the National Bank, together with a team of guards and nearly 200 transporters, took to the road more than 160 quintals of Central Bank money containing gold jewellery, silver dollars and Soviet notes.

In January 1935, the Central Red Army moved into Zunyi. Zunyi is the commercial town of Qianbei, for the distribution of a variety of local products, is the Red Army since the Long March through the first bustling medium-sized city.

Three months of long trek Red Army commanders, got a good opportunity to recuperate, use Zunyi, a place rich in supplies to replenish supplies, buy living, medical and other supplies, to prepare for the future march to war. The Red Army carried mostly Soviet banknotes issued by the National Bank in the Central Soviet Union, and the people of Zunyi, who had suffered from the war and the depreciation of the banknotes, did not accept the Soviet banknotes in the hands of

---

[85] *Selected Works of Mao Zedong*, Volume I – Our Economic Policy, People's Press, 1996.

the Red Army. After several years of experience in the Soviet Union, Mao Zemin understood that in order for the "Red Army Ticket" to gain the trust of the people, there must be two conditions: first, the "Red Army Ticket" must be able to buy goods and commodities; second, the paper money must have the corresponding material preparation behind.

In order to get "Red Army tickets" circulating in Zunyi, Mao Zemin mobilized Zunyi traders to actively open their doors to provide the Red Army with as many goods as possible. At the same time, he wants to build credit for the "Red Army Ticket". At this point, Mao Zemin held two trump cards in his hands: one was table salt and the other was cigarettes.

In those days, Guizhou warlords, bureaucrats, and gentry gathered in Zunyi, and they opened many cloth shops, salt shops, smoke shops, and money mills. Warlords, landlords, bureaucrats and treacherous businessmen colluded with each other to manipulate the market, hoarding hundreds of thousands of yuan worth of salt and a large amount of soot, which was sold at high prices in the market, and many people suffered from a large neck disease because they could not afford salt. After the Red Army entered Zunyi, it confiscated these materials.

So Mao Zemin sold the salt seized from the warlords and tycoons at a flat price. But to buy these inexpensive table salt, you have to use the "Red Army Ticket".

The compliant masses and merchants began to sell their goods willingly and accepted "Red Army tickets", which they used to buy precious and inexpensive salt. In order to make it easier for people to redeem their Red Army tickets at any time, the State Bank has set up 25 exchange points in the Zunyi commercial centre and at army stations.

The "Red Army Ticket" credit was in full swing and the market was booming like never before. Later, unable to establish a base in Zunyi, the Red Army decided to withdraw. In order to ensure that the interests of the people of Zunyi would not be lost after the departure of the Red Army, the State Bank put up notices in Zunyi, set up exchange offices, and exchanged salt, rice, cloth and other materials and gwangyang for the "Red Army tickets" held by the people. On the night before the Red Army withdrew from Zunyi, they finished redeeming their Red Army tickets overnight.

The practice of the State Bank of issuing and repossessing Red Army tickets in Zunyi has not only livened up the market, guaranteed the supply of the Red Army, but also safeguarded the credibility of the Soviet banknotes, safeguarded the interests of the people, and made the people understand that the Red Army is a good army that protects the interests of the people, thus leaving a good impression on the local scene. The locals are saying, "Reds are good, don't cheat, 'Reds tickets' are worth a lot."

In this way, the State Bank, with only 14 people, in just over 10 days, in Zunyi, with a population of several hundred thousand people, commanded the completion of the issuance, circulation, exchange and return of the "Red Army ticket", which cannot but say a miracle. Through the efficient circulation of "Red Army tickets", they not only replenished the Red Army commanders with rich supplies, but also organized the return of money for the benefit of the masses during the evacuation, fully demonstrating the credit of the Soviet Government and the National Bank and establishing a good image of the Communist Party and the Red Army in the minds of the people.

The Legend of Red Money

In 1921, the Chinese Communist Party was a micro-party with only 57 members, and she had neither money nor guns. However, 28 years later, she led a million troops to sweep the country and seize power in one fell swoop! At the beginning of the founding of the country, the 16-nation allied army was defeated in Korea at a time when the country was in a state of despair. China has not had such a moment of complete independence since 1840. Peng Dehuai's words can represent the heart of all Chinese people:

> *"The history of imperialism, which can conquer a country and a nation by erecting a few cannons in the East, is gone!"*

The CCP's comprehensive political, military and financial victories all stem from the same system of thought and wisdom, which is underpinned by three pillars: service to the people, independence and practical orientation.

The right to issue money is one of the most important powers in human society, and how this power is exercised is the important test for money issuers. There is an essential difference between issuing money for the benefit of the people and issuing money for the benefit of a few.

As the saying goes, "he who wins the hearts and minds of the people wins the world", the people are smart, the people are wise, the eyes of the people are sharp, and the interests of the currency issuers are actually clear at a glance. The issuance of currency in the Soviet Union, including the issuance of "Red Army tickets" in Zunyi, is in the fundamental interest of the people, which is fully consistent with the rationale for the survival and development of the Red regime. The people's currency can only be supported and trusted by the people and have the strongest, longest lasting and most unbreakable monetary credit if it serves the interests of the people!

The currency of the Soviet Union is on a completely independent path, under military "siege" and economic blockade, experiencing enormous pressure that the normal monetary system cannot bear. The founders of the Red Central Bank started from scratch, with no external assistance, no external advisors, no external reference system, completely autonomous, independent and self-contained. This is also in line with the Communist Party of China's practice of "red division". No one, not Stalin or Chiang Kai-shek, believed from the beginning that the idea of "the countryside surrounding the city" would succeed. This is a major innovation that has never been seen before in the world. For the Soviet government, which created this new model, ridicule, suspicion, accusations, suppression from within the party and hostility, sabotage, blockade, "siege" from outside constituted tangible and intangible pressure at all times. The spirit of independence is not a flower cultivated in a greenhouse or in good times, but rather a weed that grows stubbornly in the face of high temperatures and harshness. The red currency of the Soviet Union grew little by little under extremely humble conditions, creating at every step, every achievement born of practice.

"Come from practice, go to practice." This may seem like a very common cliché, but it is a truth that has been refined through a thousand successes and failures. The creators of the red currency had neither extensive monetary experience nor profound theoretical scholarship, but they possessed the courage and wisdom to go beyond the practice of the common man! They are not book-oriented, not foreign, not top-oriented, and all measures are oriented towards solving practical problems. In the process of solving the problem, the genius of acuity and awe-inspiring skill is revealed everywhere. Practice creates experience, practice sublimates thought, practice leads to theory!

From 1932 to 1934, the Red Central Bank of the Central Soviet Union, although it only existed for three short years, took the unique financial thinking and wisdom of the Chinese Communist Party to the extreme. The three years that the State Bank was in the Soviet Union were the first three years that the people of the Soviet Union had their own bank and mastered their own financial rights, and the first three years that the Chinese Communists established an independent financial system.

Reading history, the Chinese Communists understood that the Paris Commune had shed blood in the Lacherts Cemetery for not taking over the Bank of France; seeing the Soviet practice, they understood that mastery of the bank was the only way to consolidate power. When it was their turn to do it themselves, they truly felt that without money it would be difficult to move at all, and without money they would have to obey the will of the "big brother" who gave them money!

Mao Zedong found his way to the establishment of an independent regime in the countryside, the hotbed of revolution, and also began the process of blazing the trail of financial independence. The Soviet Union survived Chiang Kai-shek's "siege" and the Soviet Union's suspicious eyes for 7 years!

The founders of the Red Central Bank went to great lengths for red money. They don't have much culture, much experience, or even start-up capital, but they believe that any difficulty can be overcome by serving the common man, by coming from practice to practice!

The National Bank issues money for very different purposes than the National Party and the banks of the Western powers. The National Bank issues money to facilitate people's livelihood and meet the needs of economic development, not as a means of "shearing the fleece" to rob and scrape the people, not as a "golden ticket" for the Kuomintang to compete with the people for profits, and not as a dollar that can be repaid just by labelling it "quantitative easing"!

The National Bank has a sufficient reserve of silver dollars for the issuance of currency, and through practice they have realized that, with gold and silver as collateral alone and without the corresponding material to prepare, the currency is still just a piece of paper. What the people need for their lives is firewood, rice, oil and salt, not gold and silver. A paper currency that can buy material goods has credibility in the eyes of the masses, and the government that issues it has prestige!

The credit of the currency is the foundation of the nation and the key to sustaining the red regime.

Understanding the fundamental rationale of monetary credit, the Chinese Communists tried repeatedly in the War of Resistance and Liberation, the more they used it, the more mature it became, and finally laid down an independent RMB system and a strong financial high frontier.

CHAPTER V

Chiang Kai-shek's Gold Power

Why did Chiang Kai-shek rely on the moneybags of the Jiang and Zhejiang plutocrats when he was in power? Why was Chiang Kai-shek's central bank unable to compete with the Bank of China in the early days? How did the four great families, Jiang, Song, Kong and Chen, dig the first bucket of gold? Why was the silver rush of the 1930s the first exchange rate war between China and the US? Why was the French currency reform the trigger for Japan's war of aggression against China?

Chiang Kai-shek had mastered the army and swayed the government, but he did not yet control finance. Nothing can be lacking, and in the face of challenges from all sides, what Chiang Kai-shek was most lacking was money. He established a central bank, but for the time being he was no match for the Bank of China, and he issued banknotes, but they were not well received. He finally understood the truth that military centralization is just beginning, political centralization is just learning, and financial centralization is just getting underway.

Thus, Chiang Kai-shek embarked on a progressive plan to take control of China's financial system and thus the lifeblood of the nation's economy.

When the "abolition of the two to change the yuan", "four lines and two bureaus", "French currency reform" was completed one after another, Chiang Kai-shek finally realized the dream of the world of gold power.

At this point in time, with the silver frenzy and the collapse of China's silver standard, where is the French currency going? The three great powers' currency wars were in the dark and finally ignited the fuse of the anti-Japanese war.

Chiang Kai-shek beat up Song Ziwen for lack of money

In the fall of 1933, Chiang Kai-shek was not having a good time. At the beginning of the year, Japan's intentions to wage war against China were made clear when it annexed the Jehol River and looked at northern China. The national anti-Japanese outcry made Chiang Kai-shek, who insisted that "to resist outside, one must first restrain inside", quite passive. The Tanggu Agreement traded a temporary truce between China and Japan at the expense of recognizing the Japanese occupation of the three eastern provinces and the Jehol River, but drowned Chiang Kai-shek in a national outcry.

Between internal and external problems, he understood that he could not "win two wars at the same time", who was his main enemy? He was convinced that no matter how strong Japan was, no matter how powerful the Japanese army was, it would not be possible to completely defeat China and turn it directly into a Japanese colony. In his mind, it was impossible for the British and American powers to allow Japan to dominate China, and without the supply of raw materials and energy from Britain and the United States, and the opening of the world market to Japanese products, the seemingly powerful edifice of the Japanese Empire would collapse in an instant. Therefore, if Japan goes too far, the Western powers will surely step in to stop it. Therefore, external diseases are nothing but scabies.

However, the nature of the "communists" was different. The Central Soviet Region they established at the junction of Jiangxi, Hunan and Guangdong provinces was called the Chinese Soviet Republic, which was the "State within a State"! At that time, Chiang Kai-shek hated the idea that "there was a party within a party", which divided people's hearts and morale, and seriously obstructed his path to centralization. "Since the coup d'état of April 12, it was originally thought that the Chinese Communist Party's "party trouble" would be wiped out, but now it has occupied more than 60 counties in the three provinces of Gan, Min and Yue, with a population of more than 3 million. The "Qing Party" became the "anti-bandit". What particularly shocked him was that from 1930 to 1933, the original thousands of "rogue bandits", the National Army had failed on four occasions, and the "rogue bandits" had become "bandits", and the "bandit force" had grown to over 100,000 people. Chiang understood well that the real threat to the CCP lay in a deadly challenge to its ruling base and core of power, a war between a very few rich people and the vast majority of poor people. When the overwhelming majority of the poor are a scattered mass of unorganized people, it's not a big problem, but when the overwhelmingly well-organized Chinese Communist Party, wakes up and organizes the overwhelming majority, it's an impossible nightmare to revive! Therefore, it is the internal worries of the "communists" that are the main problem.

However, most of the core members of the Kuomintang failed to understand the essence of their own strategy of "resist foreigners before restoring domestic ones", and even his brother-in-law, Song Ziwen, jumped out and openly advocated the priority of anti-Japanese resistance, and even thought that "communist bandits" were a political problem, not a military one, and that the military simply could not solve the problem. Song Ziwen is the recognized leader of the Anglo-American faction within the party, the Anglo-American naturally does not want to see the situation of Japan's dominance in China, his brother-in-law has repeatedly expressed fierce anti-Japanese views, won the praise of public opinion, and trapped himself in the situation of bending the knee to sell the country. What's more, Song Zimin also pushed for a national budget system and, as the Minister of Finance and President of the Central Bank, repeatedly opposed his fifth "siege". At this time, Chiang Kai-shek has long held a bellyful of fire.

In October, Chiang Kai-shek's million-strong "anti-bandit" army had formally launched an all-out offensive against the central Soviet region, and the cost of the war immediately soared. Chiang Kai-shek pressed Song Zimin to hurry up with his military pay, but Song Zimin always pushed back. On this day, Chiang Kai-shek called Song Ziwen to his feet and went straight to the point:

> *"The fifth 'siege' order has been issued, and every five days the Ministry of Finance has to pay 1.66 million yuan for the military!"*
> *"As Minister of Finance, I can't get that much out of it, the Ministry of Finance is planning a national budget system."*

Song was about to unfold, not expecting Chiang Kai-shek to give him no chance to discuss it at all.

A furious Chiang Kai-shek roared,

> *"Whose world is this world? Who's in charge?"*

With a resounding family background and a Western education, Song Ziwen also has a great personality. After becoming Minister of Finance, he often said to people:

> "Don't worry about food, don't worry about flowers, don't worry about poor planning."

In fact, this statement refers to Chiang Kai-shek's persistent efforts to "annihilate the Communist Party" in spite of his financial resources.

Chiang Kai-shek was under great pressure and the war had reached a critical juncture, but Song proposed to establish a "national budget system".

Chiang Kai-shek directly snapped,

> "You are the one who didn't take an active role in the communist struggle and provide the necessary funding, otherwise the communist struggle would have been won!"

Song Ziwen threw down his hat and clapped his hands on the case:

> "Look at you, you didn't win this battle, but you're blaming it on me, it's outrageous!"

"Motherfucker!" Chiang Kai-shek couldn't stand it any longer, and his disrespect for this noble brother-in-law had already accumulated in his heart. A heavy ear scrape went straight to Song Ziwen's face.

Because it came so suddenly, Song Ziwen was stunned by the slap and didn't react for half a day. Song Ziwen was so old, how could he have suffered such an indignity! Once he had recovered, he swung up his stool and smashed it at Chiang Kai-shek.

Chiang Kai-shek, after all, is a soldier by profession and has a slightly better hand, so he hunched over and dodged it.

It was a slap in the face by the head of state to the Minister of Finance, and after the slap was over, Jiang Song was still able to unite closely afterwards, showing how strong the cohesion of the family was.

Song Ziwen was slapped in the face and resigned in a fit of anger, and was succeeded as Finance Minister by his brother-in-law Kong Xiangxi. The official explanation for Song's resignation was:

> "Since the National War, income has plummeted, and military and political expenses are about 10 million yuan a month short

of what they should have been, so they are unable to raise money and want to go."[86]

But the relationship between Chiang Kai-shek and Song Ziwen was "broken bones and still attached to tendons". On the surface, Song Ziwen "class", should be honest at home to reflect, but in fact, his energy is not reduced that year, "load-shedding" after he can be at ease "business straight business".

In fact, Chiang Kai-shek did some injustice to Song Ziwen, Song Ziwen, although dissatisfied with Chiang Kai-shek's "communist annihilation" endlessly wasted money, but it is also considered a dedicated effort to help Chiang Kai-shek raise money. Song Ziwen's dilemma is that every year 900 million yuan of fiscal revenue, half of which goes to war, the country has long been unable to make ends meet, only to the Jiangsu and Zhejiang plutocrats to borrow money, and the plutocrats to Chiang Kai-shek's militaristic poor also has long had grievances.

Kong Xiangxi took office, Jiangsu and Zhejiang plutocrats feel Chiang Kai-shek's appetite for more and more, only endless civil war, it was proposed to Kong Xiangxi, should reduce the bank advances to the requirements of the bank, not the bank as the treasury. I didn't expect this to offend Chiang Kai-shek, who wanted to "use a knife" on the bank.

Chiang Kai-shek, who had been a securities manager, was different from those old-fashioned warlords in that he had always been sober enough to know that for a revolution to succeed, one must hold the barrel of a gun and the bag of money in one hand. At this time, Chiang Kai-shek further recognized, from other people's money bag, always better to take money from their own money bag to come smoothly, convenient! Donkeys, you can make donkeys, or you can make donkeys with fire!

Monetary control is the main contradiction between Chiang Kai-shek and the Jiang and Zhejiang plutocrats, which has been revealed as early as the Northern Expedition period, it is the increasing intensification of this contradiction that made him firmly believe in a centralized power, military centralization is just beginning, political

---

[86] Song Z. Wenzhuan, *Wang Song*, Hubei People's Press, 2006, p. 76.

centralization is learning, financial centralization can unify the Jiang and Lake.

Central bank PK Bank of China

The central bank is the strategic high point of a country's financial frontier. Whoever can control the central bank can control the economic lifeblood and political-military vitality of the whole country, which Chiang Kai-shek knew very well. At the beginning of the Nanjing government, the establishment of a central bank became a major decision of the "party state".

In November 1928, the central bank of the Nanjing government was officially established, and Chiang Kai-shek placed Song Ziwen in the position of the first president of the central bank to watch the moneybags for him fully. However, Chiang Kai-shek and the Kuomintang had just entered the Ning-Shanghai area at this time, Wuhan on the upper reaches of the Yangtze River was not yet fully controlled, the warlords in the north were not yet fully subservient, and the government's financial resources were very limited, while expenses far exceeded revenues. The newly established Central Bank is so poor that it can't even get its capital out, and its $20 million capital is being offset by government bonds.

In fact, Chiang Kai-shek's original design for the central bank was to directly restructure the Bank of China so that the credit and resources accumulated over the years would be used for his own purposes.

However, the Bank of China is not eating this at all.

The Bank of China's "big banker" at this time was Zhang Jiajiajie, who had dealt with Chiang Kai-shek, Song Ziwen and Zhang Jiajiajie as far back as the Northern Expedition. At the time of the Northern Expedition, Song Ziwen raised money from the Bank of China in Hong Kong, first borrowed 500,000 yuan for the Northern Expedition, and sent a telegram to the troops of the Northern Expedition: "Our troops arrive everywhere, be careful to maintain the Bank of China." Song told Chiang Kai-shek that the person in power at the Bank of China was Zhang Jiajiajie, and Chiang Kai-shek reached out to Zhang through his trusted brother, Huang Zhu, for help.

Huang郛 was a key figure in Chiang Kai-shek's liaison with the Jiangzhe plutocrats and gang leaders. Zhang Jia Miao saw Huang Zu, of course, already knew his intention. Although he decided that the Beijing government might not be a rival of the Northern Expeditionary Force, he was cautious, so he had to deal with Huang Zu and send him back first. He then secretly sent men to Guangzhou to check on the situation, while he himself took command in Shanghai and gave "financial support" after deciding that the Northern Expeditionary Force would definitely win.

Later, those who were sent reported that "the Northern Expeditionary Force had successfully fought its way to Jiangxi and that Chiang Kai-shek was already in Nanchang". In 1927, Zhang decided to bet his treasure on Chiang Kai-shek, and sent the precious aid through Huang Cao. In 1927, Zhang secretly ordered the manager of the Hankou branch to borrow one million yuan upon his arrival in Wuhan. It's really a step-by-step approach.

When Chiang Kai-shek arrived in Shanghai, the fund-raising process increased step by step, and finally offered to borrow 10 million yuan. Zhang was unprepared for such a large sum of money and immediately declined the advance, but he also realized that Chiang Kai-shek was up to something big. Zhang Jiajiajie was reluctant to pay the huge sum of money, and Chiang Kai-shek and Song Ziwen invited him to Nanjing several times to discuss the matter, but Zhang Jiajiajie stayed in Shanghai and refused to give face.

At this point Chiang Kai-shek was furious and began to turn over the Bank of China's old records, "Check the Bank of China used to lend five million to Wu Pei Fu, Zhang Zongchang millions, and now when my army salaries are ten thousand urgent, so difficult, the intention is not to ask." In a telegram, he threatened: "I have heard that you have given a large sum of money to the warlords last year to help them in their rebellion against this army, and that you still have a plan to help them. I've heard that Mr. I know that you are righteous, so I don't want your firm to help you anymore." Chiang Kai-shek issued strict orders: 1, the Bank of China pre-purchased 10 million yuan of treasury bills; 2, if not fulfilled, the head of the Bank of China will be wanted; 3, if still invalid, the Bank of China will be confiscated and replaced by the Central Bank.

For this reason, Chen Guangfu, another big man in the financial sector in Shanghai, came to advise Chiang Kai-shek: "The government has to raise money and money on the one hand, and cannot ignore the financial circulation in the city on the other; if it is too hasty, if there are problems in the financial sector, there will be no way to raise money and dangers will arise, which will have a great impact on the military future." Meaning: man, you can't mess with the Bank of China right now! Let's take it slow!

What is it about the Bank of China that is so unconcerned with the government?

The Bank of China's predecessor was the Qing Empire's central bank, the Great Qing Bank, founded by Sheng Xuanhuai. Sheng Xuanhuai himself was a typical pro-Japanese, and had "deep involvement" with Japan in business such as Han Ye Ping. Because of its historical background, it has been controlled by the Beijing system, and its successive presidents have all been pro-Japanese figures. Bank of China's "big banker" Zhang Jiajiajia, a graduate of Keio University, is passionate about Japanese culture and superstitious about Japanese strength, so much so that he wears kimonos and speaks fluent Japanese in a totally oriental style. Later, Song resigned as president of the Central Bank and founded the China Construction Bank Corporation (CCB), which was strongly opposed by Japan, and the Bank of China's boycott of Song's CCB was a sign of the influence of Japanese forces over the Bank of China. In addition to the Japanese backstage, the powerful backstage of the major shareholder of the Bank of China is HSBC, behind which the British Empire can not be underestimated, and Britain and Japan was an important anti-Russian alliance.

When Sheng Xuanhuai was preparing for the establishment of the Hoba Bank, Xi Zhengfu, the head of the Dongting Mountain Gang, "directed" Sheng Xuanhuai's Hoba Bank with his extensive experience in monopolizing 15 foreign banks and foreign buyers' positions. Sheng Xuanhuai had been friends with the Xi family for decades and had joined forces to get rid of Hu Xue Yan. The head office of the Ministry of Finance is located in Beijing, and its equity department subscribes to half of the shares, while the other half is privately owned and is a government-business joint venture bank. After the establishment of the Bank's Shanghai Branch, Xi Zhengfu's three sons, Xi Yuguang, became the Bank's deputy manager.[87]

Later, Hoba Bank changed its name to Qing Qing Bank, with Xi Yuguang as the Associate Manager of Qing Qing Bank in Shanghai, Xi

---

[87] Jiang Nan Xi Jia, *Ma Xueqiang*, Commercial Printing House, 2007, p. 97.

Yukun, the second son of Xi Zhengfu, as the Manager of Yingkou Branch, and Xi Yukui, the sixth son of Xi Zhengfu, as the Manager of Hankou Branch, and later as the Deputy Buying Office of HSBC for 10 years.

After the Xinhai Revolution, the Qing Bank was reorganized as the Bank of China. At this time, the Xi family became one of the "owners" behind the Bank of China, and the "owner" behind the Xi family is HSBC. In addition to the British system, the Xi family also had an unusual relationship with the Japanese banking power, Xi Zhengfu's sixth son Xi Yuqui became the third largest Japanese plutocrat Sumitomo Bank in 1916 to buy the bank, reigned for 15 years, Xi's son-in-law Ye Mingzai served as the buyer of the Japanese Yokohama Shogun Bank for 21 years.

The XI family not only held the position of HSBC's buyer for three generations, but also used his influence to place other children of the XI family into foreign banking systems. Whether it was the British banks such as McGarry, Leigh and Derby, or the French banks such as Orientale and ICBC, or the German banks such as Dwight Bank, or the Russian banks such as Doddson Bank, or the Belgian banks such as Warby Bank, or the American banks such as Citi, Amex and Shinki Bank, or the Japanese banks such as Yokohama Shinkin and Sumitomo Bank, all of them were under the control of the XI family. According to incomplete statistics, during the 75 years from 1874 to 1949, there were more than 20 foreign banks opened in Shanghai, of which 15 were bought by the Xi family. In addition, the Xi family is also a significant shareholder in other banks in Jiangsu and Zhejiang, and the only money bank in Shanghai is the Xi family.

The deep roots and influence of the XI family in China's banking system are unparalleled in recent Chinese history. It can be said without exaggeration that the Xi family is the main pillar of the plutocratic system in Jiangsu and Zhejiang, and behind the Xi family is a powerful force of international bankers.

In China's banking system, XI Jia is not only the "owner", but also directly controls the important business sectors of Chinese banks, especially the foreign exchange sector.

The Bank of China had been the equivalent of a central bank during the late Qing Dynasty and the era of the Beijing government, a full and independent national capital bank. In an era when Britain, Japan and other powers have already tightly controlled China's financial high frontier, how can it be possible to become an independent central bank?

Wasn't it a daydream when Chiang Kai-shek tried to move the brains of the Bank of China? Chiang Kai-shek had neither the strength nor the guts to call out to the great powers, after all, to fight a dog is to see its master. In the end, Chiang Kai-shek had to abandon his original idea of restructuring the Bank of China and retreat to establish a central bank himself.

Under Chen Guangfu's guidance, Chiang Kai-shek understood his situation, and he had to ask the Bank of China.

In the meantime, it was just in time for the death of Zhang's mother. It is important to know that before this, Chiang Kai-shek and Zhang Jiawei had not met, but Chiang Kai-shek had spent time in Shanghai financial circles, plus he was also a native of Jiangsu and Zhejiang, and also had some contacts with the various channels of Jiangsu and Zhejiang plutocrats, so Chiang Kai-shek decided to visit the condolence in person.

On the day of the condolence, Chiang Kai-shek suddenly came to Zhang's mother's funeral home, and without saying a word, he worshipped with his head upside down, which could be described as a shock to the four seats, and also gave face to Zhang Jia Miao. This move touched Zhang Jiawu so much that he did not expect Chiang Kai-shek to pay so much attention to the "Zhendong friendship". However, he did not know that for Chiang Kai-shek, who had mingled with the "pier", this set is not difficult at all, at this time Chiang Kai-shek's "waistband" is not hard enough to raise money to solicit people, this is just the standard action of "enter the door to the pier".

At that time, Chiang Kai-shek's Nanjing National Government was unstable and needed to be recognized by the Great Powers, and the only recourse in this matter was to Zhang Jiawu. Zhang frequently met with the Japanese, British and American consuls in Shanghai to bridge the diplomatic gap between the Nanjing government, and even the diplomatic negotiations between Nanjing National Government Foreign Minister Huang Zhu and the British and American governments were held at Zhang Jiajiajie's home.

And the "advance" matter, Chiang Kai-shek finally sent a full team of people, by Zhang Jingjiang and Chen Guangfu mediated in the middle, said the government will soon issue public debt, is indeed capable of repayment. Zhang Jiaxiel thought that Chiang Kai-shek might be able to take advantage of Chiang's unstoppable power to become bigger and stronger, and finally agreed to pay 10 million yuan in instalments by the Bank of China.

> *"Before the April 12th Incident, the Bank of China has provided high amounts of sponsorship for the Northern Expedition, it can be seen that the Bank of China has made a "sweat equity" for the Northern Expedition. And the Bank of China's Hankou branch at the time gave the Wuhan National Government a huge sum of 16.5 million yuan. It is not hard to imagine that the plutocrats are not all gamblers, and the eggs cannot be put in one basket! The Bank of China also played a role in the subsequent "Ninghan Merging".*

In fact, Zhang Jia Miao is just a front desk runner, the person with his back to the big tree is not a big tree himself. It was not Chiang Kai-shek who begged, but the powers behind him. Later, the Jiang and Zhejiang plutocrats, who forced Chiang Kai-shek into the wild, were also behind the energy of the great powers.

However, just as Hitler had borrowed the power of the international bankers when he came to power and began to seize the power of the German central bank under the control of the international bankers step by step once the power was in his hands, it took Chiang Kai-shek more than six years from the establishment of the central bank in November 1928 until 1935 to seize control of the Chinese banks and formally establish the authority of the central bank of the Nanjing government. And it took Hitler a full six years, starting in 1933, to finally seize the power of the Central Bank.

Reorganization and Fingerprinting

After the establishment of the central bank of the Nanjing government, nominally established the status of the "true dragon and son of heaven", the original two giants – Bank of China and Bank of Communications, was designated as a specialized bank of international exchange and development industry. However, as late as 1935, the central bank was still far behind the Bank of China in terms of issuing only as much money as the Bank of Communications. As a central bank whose main function is the issuance of money, how can it be?

The Bank of China's banknotes have a history that explains their high reputation in the market.

There were three important figures in the Jiangzhe zaibatsu – Chen Guangfu, General Manager of Shanghai Commercial Savings Bank, Li Fusun, General Manager of Zhejiang Local Industrial Bank, and Zhang Jiajiajia of Bank of China, who were known as the "Three Dingjia" of the Jiangzhe zaibatsu. At the age of 28, Mr. Zhang was appointed Associate Manager of Bank of China Shanghai Branch. During the period of the Beijing government, the two semi-official banks, the Bank of China and the Bank of Communications, were the two most important Chinese-funded banks, and to some extent played the role of central bank. The Bank of China and the Bank of Communications were responsible for issuing "silver dollar coupons", the volume of which had increased seven or eight times in two years alone.

At the time, Liang Shiyi was the secretary general of Yuan Shikai's presidential administration, and seeing the rising prices, he came up with a bad idea: to merge the two banks of China and transportation. The idea is presumably to have a "downsizing merger" in order to issue more banknotes. As soon as the news spread, it immediately caused a panicked run on depositors. In desperation, the Beijing government made the Chinese and Jiao Tong banks stop cashing in.

Zhang Jiajiajie, the young deputy manager of the Bank of China in Shanghai at the time, believed that "if the order is complied with, the credit of the Chinese banks will be ruined and there will be no hope of recovery". Then, together with Bank of China Shanghai Branch Manager Song Hanzhang, he made a bold decision: disobey! But it's not easy to disobey! By defying the government's orders and openly confronting the government, the Beijing government could immediately put them "off the job". At the same time, if the Bank of China's treasury is opened to cash, the Shanghai branch alone does not have the strength. At that time, there was just over two million silver in the vault, and the exact amount of silver needed to open the exchange had to be predicted with precision. But at this moment, Chang had a plan in mind and was ready to put on a good show!

Zhang Jiahua and his partner Song Hanzhang made no secret of the fact that they had first found several of the big bosses of Zhejiang's zaibatsu – Chen Guangfu, General Manager of Shanghai Commercial Savings Bank, Jiang Honglin, Managing Director of Zhejiang Industrial Bank and Li Fusun, General Manager of Zhejiang Local Industrial Bank. These three are the three most famous Southern private banks in the banking industry during the Beijing period, also known as the

"Southern Three Banks". Zhang asked them to sue himself in court on behalf of shareholders and depositors respectively!

According to the law at the time, the authorities could not arrest and replace the current manager or deputy manager during the proceedings, thus sealing the "cave" of the Beijing government first. Immediately afterwards, Zhang hired the Englishman Cooper and the Japanese Murakami to help him sing a wonderful duet. Cooper and Murakami took over the Bank of China on behalf of the shareholders, after which they, on behalf of the shareholders, issued shareholder's letters to Zhangjiajie and Song Hanzhang directing them to continue presiding over the business of the branch and to conduct business as usual. (The British and Japanese were still hard buddies during the North Sea era, only gradually parting ways after the 1930s.

For the cash bank, Zhang contacted the "South Three Banks" and foreign banks to support the Bank of China. Most of the "South Three Banks" are shareholders of the Bank of China and have related interests, at the same time, foreign banks are well aware that the Bank of China is the mainstay of Chinese finance, once the Bank of China collapses, the whole situation is unmanageable and not good for foreign banks, and very quickly entered into an overdraft contract with the Bank of China for 2 million.[88]

The formal implementation of the Government's "cease and desist order" immediately led to a run on the money. The bank door was crowded with people, "scrambling to be first, banging on doors and climbing on windows, almost without regard to life or death". The Bank of China Shanghai branch was well prepared and cashed in, but the runners were still crowded. By Saturday, it was only open for half a day as usual, but Zhang decided to stay open in the afternoon and put a notice in the newspaper.

On Sunday, the bank took out another newspaper ad announcing that it was still open for cash. The public found that Bank of China is a "trustworthy" bank, there is no need to go to the run, so the people's hearts are settled, and the run was completely calmed. In the aftermath of the storm, the reputation of the Bank of China surged, and Zhang Jiajiajie and Song Hanzhang were called "bold and resourceful

---

[88] Zhejiang Xingdian: Board of Directors Meeting Minutes, 17 May 1961, Shanghai Yindian

bankers" by the press of the time. If there were no great powers behind them, Yuan Shikai would not have let these two daring bankers go.

Later, Zhang Jiahua became the Vice President of Bank of China Head Office, where he actually headed the Bank of China's business. As soon as he came to power, he proposed that Chinese banks recruit commercial stocks, reduce government stocks and get rid of government control. Relying on the strong friendship with Chen Guangfu, Li Fusun, Yu Qiaqing, Song Hanzhang, Jiang Honglin, Qian Xinzhi and others, Zhang Jiawu launched the "Friday Dinner Party" in Zhangfu, which gradually expanded and became the Shanghai Banking Association. The Zhejiang Zaibatsu controlled 14 of the 22 member banks of the Shanghai Banking Association, which by 1925 held 84% of the total funds of all member banks.

Bank of China has repeatedly expanded its shareholding in commercial stocks to increase the power of commercial stocks in the Bank of China, with the Jiangsu and Zhejiang plutocrats raising 6 million yuan in shares. Later, the Beijing government ran out of money and sold another 5 million yuan in government shares. The proportion of commercial shares gradually increased to 97.47% by 1923, when the Bank of China was already controlled by commercial shares.[89]

By the time Chiang Kai-shek entered Shanghai, the central bank was established in 1928, the national government implemented the reorganization of the Bank of China, the Bank of Communications, etc., and forced the capital increase and expansion of shares, although it was a small shareholder, the government finally occupied a place in these two main banks, into a very important wedge of official shares.

The Golden Power Game between Government and Commercial Stocks

If the Kuomintang wants to reorganize the Bank of China, it obviously cannot do so without the Xi family, and if the Xi family does not cooperate, neither will the great powers. The new head of the XI family once again "friendship" deep involvement. He is the grandson

---

[89] *The General History of Chinese Finance*, Volume 3, by Hong Jia Guan, China Finance Press, 2008, p. 127.

of Xi Zhengfu, the old master of the Dongting Mountain Gang, who was involved in the establishment of the Tobu Bank that year.

In 1928, the Central Bank was established, and Song Ziwen was the Minister of Finance and President of the Central Bank, and because of his "deep friendship" with Song Ziwen, once the Central Bank was established, he joined the Central Bank as the Director of the Foreign Exchange Department, and was soon promoted to the Director of the Bureau of Foreign Exchange and the Director of Business.[90] Xi Meiying, the youngest daughter of Xi De Mao, married Song Ziwen's younger brother, Song Ziliang, and Xi De Mao's younger brother, Xi De Shou, became the director of the Central Mint and ruled the Kuomintang government's power to issue currency.

By restructuring the Bank of China, the Nationalist government was actually making a deal – Chiang Kai-shek took a stake in the Bank of China and the Xi family forces intervened in the central bank. Both parties' interests are reciprocated and exchanged, and the sale is reasonable.

The head office of the Bank of China moved from Beijing to Shanghai and became a "government-licensed international exchange bank", which gave the Bank of China a competitive advantage in foreign exchange operations and has been accumulated and improved to this day. He is an "expert" in foreign exchange work in China, which he could not have done without his extensive family tradition of buying and selling.

In November of the same year, Bank of China held a general meeting of shareholders and decided on the directors of commercial and government shares. At this time, despite the increased government control over the Bank of China, its leadership remained in the hands of the merchant stocks, as they remained in the majority. The director of the Bank of China and the director of the Bank of Communications, in terms of capital formation, has increased the weight of the official shares. From the "Bank of the Household Ministry" to the "Bank of the Qing Dynasty" to the "Bank of China", we can see the evolution of the government's shareholding thinking, and in the process, the successful transformation from "buying and managing" to "bureaucratic buying

---

[90] Jiang Nan Xi Jia, *Ma Xueqiang*, Commercial Printing House, 2007, p. 100.

and managing" to "bureaucratic" is really a distinctive growth path that is different from private capital.

It is not difficult to see from the series of competitions between the official and commercial stocks of Chinese banks that the competition between bureaucratic and private capital is escalating in the development of the banking industry in China in recent times. Although Zhang Jiajiajie is a countertop figure, he represents the private capitalist side of the Jiangsu and Zhejiang plutocrats, with the great energy of foreign capital behind him, hoping to take control of China's financial power and further control of Chinese industry through the holding of commercial stocks.

And the bureaucratic capital represented by Chiang Kai-shek has a strong desire to control China's financial system, and with power in hand, it is imperative. While bureaucratic capital does not dare to flirt directly with the foreign capital behind private capital, the power of encroaching on private capital to dismantle it is strengthening.

Most embarrassing of all is private capital, which lacks clear independence, or is dependent on foreign capital, fighting against bureaucratic capital, or throwing itself into the arms of bureaucratic capital in exchange for autonomy for the right to distribute dividends. Pure private capital has no future in China; they are either subsumed by bureaucratic or foreign capital, or they are completely marginalized.

When bureaucratic capital meets foreign capital, there is again a marked dependence. Chiang Kai-shek had to rely on European and American forces in order to fight the war, especially in the face of Japan's increasingly pressing aggressive pressure.

Of course, at the beginning of the Chiang Kai-shek era, the Nanjing government has just been established, the central bank is still weak and can not play the functions of a national bank, the Bank of China, Bank of Communications continues to undertake the central bank business of currency issuance, public bond issuance, national debt advances, treasury revenue and expenditure, Chiang Kai-shek actually still take the banking system controlled by the private capital of the Jiangsu and Zhejiang plutocrats as a money bag, and the Bank of China, Bank of Communications, the most powerful bank in China at that time is still held by the private capital of the Jiangsu and Zhejiang plutocrats.

Chiang Kai-shek and the Jiangsu and Zhejiang plutocrats reached an agreement, the national government issued public bonds, led by the

Jiangsu and Zhejiang plutocrats to buy several large banks, subscribed to part of their own, the rest of the banks then put up for sale in the securities market. In this regard, the Public Debt Fund's Board of Trustees was also established, the chairman of which was Mr. Lee Fusun, the old partner of Mr. Cheung. In October 1928, the Bank of China was reorganized and Zhang Jia Miao became General Manager.

As the national government gradually wiped out the major forces that were entrenched in China, the banks controlled by Jiangsu and Zhejiang plutocrats, each with its own door, were naturally rich, and the big brothers at the "small dining table in Zhangfu" were making a fortune. Chen Guangfu's Shanghai Commercial Savings Bank not only did a good job in underwriting bonds, but also because of his "good relationship" with the U.S. banking industry, he was responsible for most of the National Government's dollar loans.

After the reorganization of the Bank of China, Zhang Jiajiajie made overseas visits to raise foreign exchange funds and set up overseas institutions. By 1934, the total assets of Chinese banks had reached 970 million yuan. During his tenure, the government has issued more than 2.6 billion yuan in domestic debt, and his "service" to the government is noteworthy.

By the early 1930s, China's financial system had formed a kind of balance of power, with bureaucratic capital and private capital and the foreign capital behind it moving towards a "merger", with mutual equity participation and mutual wealth.

However, this was only a brief transition, and the ultimate goal pursued by Chiang Kai-shek was financial centralization.

Chiang Kai-shek's Financial Concentration: "Abolishing Two and Changing the Yuan" and "Four Lines and Two Bureaux"

Chiang Kai-shek understood that central banks alone were not enough to achieve financial centralization; the key was to unify the currency. Without a unified currency, there will be no unified treasury, and no unified political and military power base. And the premise of a unified currency is that the monetary standard must be established first.

In order to achieve the unification of the monetary standard, the Nanjing government resolved to implement the "abolition of the two yuan", changing the monetary standard from silver and two yuan to silver yuan, and the value base of all paper money was unified into silver yuan.

In China at that time, silver was available in a variety of colors, weights and sizes, and the conversion of silver in transactions was very difficult. The various silver dollars are also very complex, common silver dollars in the market, there are early foreign merchants brought into China Spanish silver coins – when called "Hongyang", the British people initially did business, used to receive this "Hongyang". Later on, the business of the "Yangzhuang" became bigger and bigger, so the Mexican silver coins, then called "Eagle Yang", also gradually passed in China.[91] A number of "Long Yang" similar to "Ying Yang" were also cast in various provinces of China, which, together with various imitations of silver dollars, were a dazzling sight.

In circulation, the conversion between various kinds of silver, silver dollars, and copper money is quite troublesome, and it is up to the banker to decide how to convert it. To abolish all silver in the market, resistance mainly comes from the money bank, the money bank is dry silver, silver dollars and copper money exchange business, unified currency, the money bank will lose the right to exchange, and also lose the right to financial discourse. Of course, Chiang Kai-shek later to engage in financial unification, the money bank these "small shrimp" is naturally to be reunited.

The national government was also aware of the issue of the silver dollar as a monetary standard, and had organized a special study, led by Song Ziwen, that the abolition of the silver dollar in favor of the silver dollar required a step-by-step approach. Song Ziwen began to reform the monetary system, and Side-Mao again "friendship" to participate in the "abolition of the two to change the yuan".

The "abolition of two yuan" is a very difficult systemic project, involving not only Chinese banks and money banks, but also foreign banks and foreign exchange. As a representative of the Central Bank, Mr. Szeto is a key member of the Shanghai Silver Dollar and Silver

---

[91] *The History of Money and Finance in the Qing Dynasty*, by Yang Duanliu, Sanlian Bookstore, 1962, p. 261.

Exchange Management Committee, which is responsible for the design, implementation and coordination of all parties.

On the eve of the fifth "siege", under the personal supervision of Chairman Chiang, in April 1933, the "abolition of the two sides for the new yuan" finally came to fruition.

The unification of the monetary standard made a crucial step in Chiang Kai-shek's monetary unification. Next, he would completely control the Bank of China and the Bank of Communications, establish the authority of the central bank and complete the full layout of financial centralization.

So, Chiang Kai-shek called Finance Minister Kong Xiangxi and said harshly:

> "The country and society are on the verge of bankruptcy, and the key is the two banks of China. The finger is pointed straight at the Bank of China, and the Bank of Communications is nothing more than a sidekick."

On 27 March 1935, the Legislative Yuan of the National People's Government approved the issuance of 100 million yuan of financial bonds to be used to finance the capital increase of the Central Bank, Bank of China and Bank of Communications. Then the Bank of China was forcibly "reformed", changing the general manager system to the chairmanship, and directly appointing Song Ziwen as chairman, with Song Ziliang and Du Yuesheng on the board. At the same time, the forced addition of 15 million yuan of government shares, the total share capital expansion of 40 million yuan, the government and business in half, so that the government shares increased from the original 5 million yuan to 20 million yuan. Chang's transfer to vice president of the Central Bank actually shelved Chang, leaving him with only a title. I didn't know anything beforehand about such a big event. Subsequently, Chiang Kai-shek "took over" the Bank of Communications in the same way, and in April, the Bank of Communications amended its constitution, and the proportion of government shares was changed to 63%, and the Bank of Communications was also "officially run".

The Japanese side is extremely dissatisfied with Chiang Kai-shek's "perverse act" of expelling the pro-Japanese medical device Zhang Jiawu. In a confidential telegram from Kawagoe, Consul General of Tianjin, to the Wakayoshi Counsellor in Beijing, it is stated that

> *"According to a confidential conversation with a dignitary, Zhang Gongquan (Zhang Jiaquiao) was expelled from the Bank of China because Chiang Kai-shek, in order to crush the Communists and expand armaments, had caused a monthly deficit of 25 million yuan and an annual deficit of 300 million yuan for the Nanjing government. This was planned by Kong and Song to strengthen Chiang Kai-shek's regime... In the final analysis, what they plotted was to seek (the right to issue currency) unification in the name of financial control and currency rectification, so that the forces of the Nanjing government could issue non-convertible paper money in a unified manner... At a time when the air of Sino-Japanese friendship is rising, it is a great joke to drive away Zhang Gongquan, who had close ties with Japan, just for Kong and Song, etc..."*

After taking over the two banks, the "four banks and two bureaus", controlled by bureaucratic capital, formed a new pattern of China's financial industry. The four banks were the Central Bank, the Bank of China, the Bank of Communications and later the Chinese Farmers' Bank; the second bureau was the Central Trust Bureau and the Postal Reserve and Banking Bureau. From this day on, Bank of China's general manager, Zhang Jiaqi, was forced to resign and disassociate himself from the Bank of China, which was reduced to an instrument of bureaucratic capital, marking the end of the era of free capital in China. Given Zhang's social influence and the sentiment on the Japanese side, Chiang Kai-shek had his doubts. In order to win the hearts and minds of the people, Zhang Jia Miel was appointed as a cabinet member and a minister six months later, but he resigned from the ministerial post due to his ill health and went to the United States on a "study tour".

The cleansing of private capital had just begun, and Chiang Kai-shek, who had completed the first step of "taking over" the Bank of China, had caused the three banks, namely, the Central Bank, China and the Bank of Communications, to accumulate a large amount of banknotes from the Bank of China, the Industrial Bank of China and the Si Ming Bank, and to cash them all at once, creating a run on the bank.

The last of the three banks to experience a run on the bank, the chairman and general manager of the Bank, Fu Xiaoan, was Sheng Xuanhuai's innermost boss that year. He had anticipated that Chiang Kai-shek was going to come and begged Du Yuesheng, a director and "personal friend" of the Bank, to help "clear the way".

Du Yuesheng was pained: "With us to back you up, don't be afraid." In fact, Fu Shinan had fallen into the trap of Du Yuesheng precisely.

Du Yuesheng patted his chest and said: "How many positions are missing, just come and tear it down, it's a small favor, you should help as a little brother, but you still have to be fully prepared. As for the top, do your best to see the opportunity."

Fu Shinan decided to sell the soon-to-be-completed "Bank of Commerce Building" at a price of 1.8 million yuan for the paid part of the "Friendship". He asked Du to pass on to "above" to take it over and Du Yuesheng agreed.

Immediately, the building was purchased by Song Zilian, the brother of Song Zilian, on behalf of the Shanghai Postal Savings and Finance Bureau. Song Ziliang immediately changed the name of the building to "Construction Building" and started work overnight to change the signboard of the building.

It was immediately rumored that the China General Chamber of Commerce was going to collapse and even the building was sold. At this time, the Central Bank informed Song Ziliang that the money for the purchase of the building would first be repaid to the Central Bank, before Fu Xiaoan could touch the money for the sale of the building, it was transferred to the Central Bank by Song Ziliang, and the Bank of Commerce and Industry of China was taken out of the pay.

On the eve of the Dragon Boat Festival, Fu Shinan scraped together some marketable securities and asked the central bank for a mortgage of 3 million yuan. Unexpectedly, after the Dragon Boat Festival, we suddenly received a phone call from the Central Bank informing us that we had no more positions on our books. Fu Xiaoan then hurried to the Treasury, kneeled down and bowed, pleaded, and still pleaded in vain. At this time, Du Yuesheng continued to spread the word outside that the China Merchant Bank was about to collapse and depositors were withdrawing money in droves.

Fu Shinan could only go begging Du Yuesheng again to help keep the mess going. Du Yuesheng was falsely polite again. In the end, Fu Shinan held the Bank's asset inventory in both hands and handed it to Du Yuesheng, who stepped down in disgrace.

The Bank of Commerce and Industry of China was reorganized as a "government-business joint bank", and the old shares were discounted. After some bargaining, the Ministry of Finance only agreed to discount the old shares by 15%, that is, every 100 yuan was discounted by 15 yuan into new shares. The Bank of Commerce and Industry of China has only 525,000 yuan in old shares, and the Ministry of Finance has added 3.475 million yuan in official shares. All government shares were financed by the Ministry of Finance with the same amount of the "Revival Bond", with Du Yuesheng as Chairman. This was supposed to be part of the reward given by the party state to the Qing Gang, but the Jiang and Zhejiang plutocrats, who failed to "keep up with the times" and still fought against the government, were completely "played" by Chiang Kai Shek.

After this pile of banks, there's still one farmer's bank left, and it's in a special situation. The Chinese peasant bank was reorganized by the peasant bank of four provinces, Chiang Kai-shek himself was the chairman, private shares are in the hands of Chiang himself or Chiang's immediate family, the act of Chiang's need to issue banknotes at any time, and the issue of reserves is not among the supervision, Chiang Kai-shek built the peasant bank into his own "back garden". Later, when British financial adviser Liz Ross came to China and asked for an inspection of the Chinese banking reserve fund, Kong Xiangxi informed the peasant banks to cooperate in the process, to no one's surprise Chiang Kai-shek was furious and shouted, "Don't I even have this right anymore?"

According to a report by Snow, farmers' banks may secretly have opium income. The National Bureau of Tobacco Control earns nearly 200 million yuan a year, part of which is held by youth gangs and other triad organizations, and part of which is handed over to the government is directly controlled by Chiang Kai-shek's military commission. Because of the "ambiguous" nature of the Peasant Bank's business, it was not given the right to issue banknotes at the time of the currency reform, but the Agricultural Bank was soon placed alongside the three major banks with the right to issue banknotes, and it was clearly Chiang Kai-shek who was behind this rapid change.

The key figure who pushed the government to further manipulate the private economy was Song Ziwen, who, after resigning as Minister of Finance, retained the position of the National Economic Council, a body whose basic policies were determined by Chiang Kai-shek and whose "day-to-day work" was undertaken by Song Ziwen. Later, Song became chairman of Bank of China and wielded almost a quarter of the capital domination of the Chinese banking industry. Song, in turn, established the China Construction Bank Corporation, which was based in China, and invested extensively in industry and commerce, including all aspects of the cotton trade, the chemical industry, and automobile manufacturing, and Song used his authority to increase private investment by himself and his relatives, eventually taking control of a large number of businesses.

After the "slap incident", Song Ziwen resigned as Minister of Finance and was succeeded by Kong Xiangxi, who also held the positions of Vice President of the Executive Yuan and President of the Central Bank, and was identified by Chiang Kai-shek as "the man on the side". The Central Bank Board had adopted a plan to sell 40 million of the 100 million shares to commercial stocks, and Kong had "solicited" private subscriptions from Chiang, but in fact the Central Bank shares had never been sold to "private individuals". How could Chiang Kai-shek, whose intention was to centralize power, possibly reduce his control over this key institution.

Kong Xiangxi's central banking system controls the insurance industry, so he naturally wants to set up his own land. He established the prestigious Central Trust Authority, which specializes in trusts and investments. In his capacity as president of the Central Bank and chairman of the board, Kong appointed his eldest son, Kong Lingkhan, as the executive director, and actually held great power over business and personnel, making the Central Trust Bureau a specialized institution for the Kong family to deal in arms, smuggle and embezzle, and scrape foreign exchange.

The Chinese banking system under Song's control and the central banking system under Kong's control complement each other in important decision-making. China's financial system, after a dazzling reshuffle, became the purse strings of bureaucratic capital with the "four great families" at its core, which, of course, also included Chiang Kai-shek's first-string henchman, Du Yuesheng.

I'm gonna sell you a big motherfucker!

With the unification of the four major banks, the Government can justifiably ask the four major banks to borrow money and no longer be "exploited" by commercial banks and money banks. The Government is preparing to consolidate old public debt and issue new public debt. In order to promote the exchange of new public debt, it is planned to give appropriate concessions to old public debt on the grounds that, after the exchange, the interest rate will be increased to the benefit of those who "supported the Government" at the critical time, in order not to make it worse for those who had previously purchased public debt.

It was Kong's turn to dominate, and of course, Song got the news right away, so she immediately arranged to eat into the old public debt. At first, the Kong family sent people to buy them quietly, and when they were almost done, they spread the news, and the price of the old bonds soared immediately, and in a few days, the old bonds became the "hot investment" in Shanghai.

Du Yuesheng did not get the first handful of news, and when he saw that the price of the old bonds was rising strongly, he immediately went to the Kong family to ask for information. Du Yuesheng calculated that the old national debt should still be rising, and at the same time, he sent people to spread rumors that the country's economic situation was improving and that those who supported the government in difficult times should be benefited. But the price of the old public debt has risen so far that paying interest on the old public debt at the fabled price will only bring down the government finances. Du Yuesheng is still waiting for another rise, and Song霭ling is already quietly "closing the net" on shipments.

By the time Du Yuesheng found out, the old public debt had already begun to plummet, and Du Yuesheng was furious. The characteristic of triad society is "black", there is no reason to be dumb, otherwise, how can we walk in the rivers and lakes in the future! Du Yuesheng has decided he wants to rob Kong Xiangxi!

He asked Kong Xiangxi out to dinner, Kong Xiangxi arrived at the dinner party, saw a large turtle on the table, thought it was going to be a "big dish", so rushed, quickly stewed. But Du Yueh-Sheng was not sure how to tell him about the old information about the old public debt, and how he had suffered a big loss, and forced him to give half a million dollars to "buy" the big bastard.

Kong Xiangxi understood this and replied, "You've lost out on the public debt, it's only your own fault! No need for that!" The more Du Yuesheng heard it, the angrier he became: "Then isn't Mrs. Kong's source still you? You're on this job and you're pretending!"

"What a load of nonsense!" Kong Xiangxi was just about to lose his temper when two of Du Yuesheng's beaters simultaneously drew their guns and aimed them at Kong Xiangxi's head. Kong Xiangxi fought a cold war, but after all, he was an old juggler, so he quickly calmed down, Du Yuesheng was so bold, after all, he did not dare to really kill himself, just wanted to swindle a few money, so calmly pointed to his own head and said: "If you think that a gun eye on my head is worth half a million dollars, then shoot, fight here!" Kong Xiangxi didn't even bat an eyelid.

The original thought to deal with Kong Xiangxi, using the triad on the means of a scare, he is not yet a mess, did not expect to come out of the Shanxi compound of Kong Xiangxi, not eat this.

Du Yuesheng hurriedly turned his face away and scolded, "Get off! We're talking business with Dean Kong, not kidnapping. Go! Why would the Minister of Finance rely on us for such a small sum of money to send this big bastard to President Kong's family? Send the guests off!"

Kong Xiangxi is "driven" home by Du Yuesheng's men, and Song is confused when she sees a large sea turtle being carried in behind her. The story is told by Kong Xiangxi, who is so angry that she yells at Du Yuesheng for daring to go to the Kong family. He said he would go to Chiang Kai-shek for comment. The company is still much more sophisticated, and if this matter is to be stirred up, how can he still have the face to be the finance minister?

The next morning, the guards ran in in a panic and reported that whoever had placed the large black-painted coffin at the door was unknown. Of course Kong Xiangxi understood that it was Du Yuesheng who was disgusting him.

Kong Xiangxi then called a special meeting of the Central Bank's Board of Directors and solemnly declared a patriot who had made outstanding contributions to the cause of public debt, which the Central Bank's Board decided to reward. Of course, this patriot is Du Yuesheng! Du Yuesheng was immediately relieved of his anger and felt that Kong Xiangxi had done a very "decent" job, as a result, the two of them "no fight, no deal", Kong Xiangxi and Du Yuesheng became closer "war buddies".[92]

---

[92] *Kong Xiangxi, the richest man in Shanxi*, by Chen Tingyi, Oriental Press, 2008, pp. 317–323.

The Silver Rush: The First US-China Exchange Rate War

At a time when the various domestic capital systems are in full swing, the international environment is also undergoing major changes. When the Great Depression of the 1930s swept the world, major capitalist countries such as Britain, Canada, Japan and Austria abandoned the gold standard and began to devalue their currencies in an attempt to open the doors of other countries' markets and find a way for their economies.

In 1933, President Roosevelt of the United States, in order to emerge from the economic crisis, began to implement the New Deal, which increased government spending and stimulated economic growth. At the same time, in order to combat deflation and falling prices, the Silver Acquisition Act was passed, authorizing the U.S. Treasury to acquire silver in domestic and foreign markets until the price of silver reaches $1.29 per ounce,[93] or until the value of silver in Treasury reserves reaches 1/3 of the value of gold reserves, as a Treasury reserve.[94] The policy attempted to achieve two strategic objectives: first, the increase in reserves naturally broadened the base of the money supply in an attempt to mitigate the worsening deflation by expanding the money supply; second, the United States hoped to drive up the price of silver and increase the purchasing power of the silver standard countries by purchasing silver in the market, in effect forcing the currency of China and other silver standard countries to appreciate in order to dump excess commodities on them.

History is surprisingly similar! The Silver Takeover Act of 1933, promoted by Roosevelt, and Obama's attempt to force the yuan to appreciate in 2010 are arguably identical in thinking!

Roosevelt's two main objectives were clearly unlikely to succeed. The central problem with the Great Depression in the US was the excessive debt-to-GDP ratio, which was as high as 300% in 1929! Highly indebted U.S. industry is expanding at a rate that far exceeds the

---

[93] *China's Financial and Economic Situation from 1927 to 1937*, by Yang Ge, China Social Science Press, 1981, p. 224.

[94] *Monetary History of the Republic of China*, Second Series, edited by the General Staff Office of the People's Bank of China, Shanghai People's Publishing House, 1991, p. 119.

increase in U.S. domestic purchasing power, with the result that domestic consumption capacity is inadequate, triggering a severe oversupply of products by industrial firms, massive defaults on corporate indebtedness, and consequent stock market crashes and widespread bank failures and failures. The default crisis forced banks to tighten their credit, with the result that more businesses closed, a large number of workers lost their jobs, domestic consumption power was drastically reduced, and the problem of excess industrial products worsened, leading to a vicious cycle of deflation, falling prices, mass unemployment and economic depression. This is exactly the same as the essence of the 2008 US financial tsunami! In 2008 the US total debt-to-GDP ratio was nearly 400%, and Obama's governance of the crisis is also highly similar to Roosevelt's. (See *The Economics of Liquidating Lies: Roosevelt, Greenspan, and Obama, None Can Save America*, by Thomas Woods, China Business Federation Press, 2010.1)

It is a dead end not to start by reducing the size of the debt, but only by increasing the currency and credit! Roosevelt's New Deal didn't fix the Great Depression for 8 years, and Obama's luck may have been worse.

If the size of the debt is too large at the heart of the crisis, would increased provisions for currency issuance be useful? The conclusion is necessarily negative. The increase in reserves will not solve the problem of no one willing or able to borrow money in the face of high indebtedness, and credit must rely on borrowing to flow into the economy. Roosevelt's first purpose was simply impossible to achieve.

Will pushing up the price of silver and forcing the Chinese currency to appreciate solve the problem of US exports? Rising silver prices in the U.S. are bound to trigger China's metal currency outflow arbitrage and seriously shake China's home currency. The result is a severe recession in China's economy, with a significant drop in consumption capacity and an inevitable reduction in imports.

Roosevelt's Silver Takeover Act played a role that was necessarily the opposite of what he envisioned. There is no onstage explanation as to why Roosevelt's detrimental approach came about. In fact, the ruling elite in the US are thinking entirely of a higher strategic level! That is, how the dollar replaced the pound as the new hegemon of the world's currency!

When Chiang Kai-shek completed financial centralization and monetary unification, and established the silver standard, the current monetary hegemon, Britain, and the potential monetary hegemon, the United States, as well as the tiger-ridden Japan, created a powerful sense of crisis. If Chiang Kai-shek is allowed to consolidate China's financial high frontier, then China may become another Japan, with economic, political, and military strength gradually gaining independence and autonomy. No one in the three great powers wants to see a truly strong and independent China appear on the Asian continent!

If China's silver standard is to be subverted, the first target to be struck is China's monetary cornerstone – silver! This is not unlike the British opium strategy of that year, which subverted the monetary standard of the Qing Empire. Only, this time, it was the United States that did it, and in a more covert and "civilized" way. Artificially raising the world silver price will lead to a massive outflow of Chinese silver, no silver currency in circulation, and the silver standard will not be broken! When Chiang Kai-shek was unable to achieve monetary independence, he had to rely on one of the three great powers. After overturning China's silver standard and monetary autonomy, China's monetary future has only three paths: first, pegged to the British pound and join the British pound alliance, becoming a monetary vassal of the British pound; second, tied to the Japanese yen and integrated into the "Greater East Asia Co-Prosperity Sphere", becoming a Japanese economic colony; third, allied with the US dollar and jumped on the American ship, becoming the largest US market and raw material supply base in the Far East.

No matter which currency is pegged, China is bound to lose its monetary sovereignty! China's currency standard will become a foreign currency exchange standard, with foreign currency as a reserve, or based on a fixed exchange rate of some sort, to issue Chinese currency. In order to maintain exchange rate stability, China had to stockpile large amounts of foreign currency in order to intervene in the market when the exchange rate fluctuated. In this way, the foreign exchange issuing country is equivalent to creating a piece of overseas reserves "mint tax" of its own land, the larger the amount of overseas foreign exchange reserves, the more amazing the "mint tax" income of the issuing country! Not only that, but the issuing country can indirectly control the credit expansion and contraction of all overseas reserve countries through monetary policy adjustments by its own central bank. It's that same famous line: "If I can control the currency issue of a country, I don't care who makes the laws!"

Thus, China's currency has become the main battleground for the U.S., British and Japanese currencies, which currency is pegged to.

Silver prices soared as the U.S. government made large purchases of silver in the New York and London markets. Attracted by rising international silver prices, China's silver is "exported" in large quantities. In 1934, in just over three months, the outflow had reached 200 million silver dollars.

The US kept buying silver and by 1934, the price of silver in the London market had risen twice as much as before! The bankers, seeing such a market, have long since discovered the opportunity here, and can make a considerable profit by selling the silver by sea from upward to London or New York, how can they let such an opportunity go! Shanghai at this time stored most of China's silver, especially the Shanghai Tenancy is considered the safest place, and landlords, warlords and corrupt officials from all over transported their silver to the Tenancy for storage, as it was protected by the extraterritorial jurisdiction of foreign powers.

At that time, the major banks rolled their books every night, and if the general treasury lacked a position, they informed the treasury to transfer the stored reserves to foreign banks and the central bank treasury. This can be very busy for the bodyguards, the warehouse boxes of silver yuan, a hundred taels of silver bars and big yuan was carried on the "ironclad car" to transport out. The silver that enters foreign banks, but does not enter, is shipped away. On August 21, 1934, the HSBC banknotes were delivered to the British postal ship HMS LaPuren for export from Shanghai, which amounted to 11.5 million yuan of silver.[95] Led by foreign banks, Shanghai's financial markets were in a frenzy of silver outflows.

The description of the silver tide in the American journalist Hosse's book, "Betrayal of Shanghai Tang", is perhaps a good illustration of the situation in Shanghai at that time: on the Xiffei Road, at midnight in a ballroom, Mr. Shanghai would apologize to the dancers sitting with him, go to the telephone booth, call his agent, ask about the silver market of the day, take care that if the market is better than yesterday, he can sell some more, then go back to his table and ask the cichlid to open a bottle of champagne to celebrate a little. Whether it's

---

[95] Declaration, 22 August 1934.

in the office or in the playground, there's nothing but silver hovering over their heads. They have abandoned their old businesses, the letters that they should take care of on a daily basis, all their friends, and all they can think about is silver.

Foreign banks hold the most silver in Shanghai, and since they can move freely and the national government can't interfere with their decisions, they naturally become the mainstay of silver exports. Silver inventories in foreign banks changed dramatically during the silver rush, with silver stocks dropping as much as 85%! Foreign banks in China transported a large amount of silver accumulated during the previous years of "gold and precious silver" to the international market for sale, while the amount of silver deposited in Shanghai dropped sharply from a high of 275 million silver yuan to a low of 42 million silver yuan.[96]

Silver outflows, China's currency is "appreciated", the foreign trade deficit is growing, foreign goods flood the Chinese market, Chinese exports are increasingly difficult. Silver outflows also caused deflation, bank credit decreased, interest rates rose, at that time in Shanghai was almost as high as the interest rate could not borrow money. Silver outflows, silver root shortage, lack of market chips, prices plummeted, resulting in industrial and commercial bankruptcy and collapse.[97] By the end of 1934, house prices were plummeting, and the price of rented property in Shanghai fell by 90%! People's hearts are floating in the market, bank runs are widespread and banks and money banks are failing.

In order to stem the flow of silver, the national government introduced a silver export tax, which in turn spurred an even greater wave of silver smuggling, with more than 20 million silver dollars smuggled for export in the last few weeks of 1934. In 1935, the amount of silver smuggled reached 150 million to 230 million silver dollars. The massive outflow of silver has had disastrous financial and economic consequences for China.

---

[96] *China's Foreign Trade and Industrial Development (1840–1949)*, by Zheng Youkui, Shanghai Academy of Social Sciences Press, 1984, p. 104.

[97] *Economic History of the People's Republic of China*, edited by Zhu Sihuang, 1947 edition, p. 408.

The dramatic changes in the financial ecology have panicked the hearts and minds of the entire society. The national government begged the United States to lower the price of silver purchases on the world market to mitigate the serious harm caused to China by the rising silver price, but the United States refused. At that point, the national government had to offer to sell China's remaining silver to the United States at a mutually agreed upon price to meet the U.S. silver purchase needs.

Eventually, China was forced to abandon the silver standard in order to escape the economic crisis. Chiang Kai-shek's dream of monetary independence was soundly awakened by Roosevelt.

French Currency Reform: The Fuse of Japan's War Against China

The "four big families" because of the uneven distribution of the loot, fighting constantly, while the silver tide in the market continues to spread, the national government imposed a silver export tax, silver smuggling is increasingly rampant. It was only then that Chiang Kai-shek recognized the US silver policy and aimed directly at China. China adopted the silver standard, while the pricing power of silver was firmly in the hands of the Americans. The sharp rise in the price of silver triggered a serious economic crisis, forcing Chiang Kai-shek to consider a currency reform.

At this time, the United States, Britain and Japan had long been engaged in a fierce battle to seize control of the Chinese currency.

Japan's invasion of northeast China is expanding its power in northern China. In the Teneba Declaration, Japan stated that it had "special responsibility" for East Asia and China, and that other countries could not interfere in China's affairs without Japan's consent, and that China had become Japan's main meal. Britain has the largest investment in China and the largest commercial interests, in the face of the former "jianghu junior" Japan's aggressive, the British Empire can not swallow this breath? It was only that Nazi Germany in Europe, which was under increasing pressure from the British Empire and was intent on packing up Japan, was clearly outgunned.

The only one who has the strength, the motivation and the means to take Japan down is the United States, and it is also the United States that Japan fears, fears and is most helpless. The U.S. controls Japan's oil and steel lifeblood, and as soon as the hand tightens, Japan is immediately out of breath. The main reason why the United States did not start it was because it wanted to sit on the mountain and watch the tiger fight. On the one hand, they wanted to take Germany's hand and get rid of the biggest obstacles to hegemony, Britain and the Soviet Union, and at the same time, they didn't want to be the villains and wait for Britain, Germany and the Soviet Union to lose a few times before they would take a shot at the world. On the other hand, it is hoped that Japan will fall deep into China's quagmire, greatly depleting Japan's strength, and eventually deal a fatal blow. By that time, looking at the world's major powers, who else could compete with the United States when the Anglo-French, German, Japanese and Soviet powers had all been hit hard?

The national government, so overwhelmed by the recession, could only offer to sell the United States in silver and abandon the silver standard, but the Americans were rather lukewarm on the surface; they were waiting for a better time to kill the price. The national government also went to beg HSBC, Standard Chartered Bank's loan to China, Song Ziwen presided over the collection of foreign debt, to HSBC proposed a loan of 20 million pounds, in the main to China to take an "active" foreign policy of the British financial sector under the urging of the British said agreed to "conditional" loan to China. In this round of battles, the U.S. is older than the U.K.

The British government asked George, the acting commercial counsellor of the British Embassy in China, to convey to Kong Xiangxi and Song Ziwen the British conditions: loans can be made, but the future French currency of China must be separated from the silver standard and pegged to the pound exchange rate.[98]

At the same time, the United Kingdom suggested that Japan, the United States and France should jointly convene an international financial conference to discuss "collective assistance" to the Chinese Government. Britain understood that without the participation of the United States and Japan, I was afraid that these two men would be secretly working to undermine the beauty of the British Empire, and that the best case was that, under British leadership, the countries would

---

[98] *The History of the Central Bank,* edited by Hong Jia Guan, China Finance Press, pp. 318–319.

listen to British arrangements, and once the Chinese French currency was tied to the pound sterling, they would all join together to support the cause. The British are clearly too naive on this issue.

Although France expressed a willingness to cooperate with Britain, this was because it had to rely on British support in the face of Nazi Germany, which swore revenge. However, the Japanese side categorically rejected the initiative, while the United States adopted a "wait-and-see attitude". Fearing that Britain would take control of China's finances and finances once it dominated the country's currency reform, the United States finally decided not to send a representative to the meeting for discussion. The United Kingdom, seeing no one, announced a visit to China by the government's chief financial adviser, Liz Ross, to "offer advice" on China's currency reform.[99]

Ross wanted to "check" a deal in the United States before he left, but the United States Government did not want to invite him to stay in Washington, so he went to Japan. Ross came to Japan in the hope of bringing about Anglo-Japanese cooperation, and when he met with Foreign Minister Hirota of Japan, he proposed that if "Manchukuo" could pay customs duties to the National Government, Britain could use its good offices to get the National Government to recognize "Manchukuo". If the Manchurian issue is resolved, the dispute between Japan and China over North China will be solved. If the Manchurian tariff is added to the national government's tariff, then the ability to guarantee the national government's loans will be strengthened, which will stabilize China's currency, and Anglo-Japanese trade with China will be effectively protected, and won't that be a beneficial outcome for everyone? If the currency reform is successful, trade will develop with it, and Japan will be the country that benefits the most by then.

The Japanese were furious that Rose had made a fool of herself as a three-year-old child! The Manchukuo has been in the bag for a long time, and Ross wants to take Japan's loss of Manchurian tariffs to help Britain sell favors in front of Chiang Kai Shek? This is outrageous! What's even more pathetic is that Ross would trade a small trade favor in exchange for Japan's huge interest in giving up control of China's currency issue? The Japanese were pissed off.

---

[99] *Monetary History of the Republic of China*, Second Series, ed., Counsellor's Office, General Bank of China, Shanghai People's Publishing House, 1991, p. 164.

In the end, neither Japan nor the United States cooperated, and Britain was left on its own. Ross arrived in China in September 1935 as a senior adviser, stating that one of his "important duties" in China was to investigate the feasibility of managing currency in China.

He conducted this "study" with Patsy at the British Treasury, and Rowlands at ABN AMRO. As expected, contrary to the Japanese view at the time, they came to the conclusion that it was "quite feasible". The "study" found that, although there had been "disruptions" in the transportation of silver in northern China, a large amount of silver had been concentrated in the National Government banks in Shanghai and Nanjing, so that a system of managed inflation had been implemented and there was enough silver to maintain the stability of the foreign exchange market and thus ensure the stability of inflation. So the UK thought it could provide loans to China and bring about currency reform.

Later, according to the recollection of Dai Mingli, Director of the Department of Numismatics, he was ordered to travel from Nanjing to Shanghai to participate in the drafting of a proclamation on the reform of the currency system. The main elements of the programme were translated from English into Chinese, and the translation of the provisions of Article 6 of the programme was always inappropriate, with Song concluding that "it is sufficient to state that the Central Bank, the Bank of China and the Bank of Communications will trade in foreign exchange without restriction, and the rest need not be said." In fact, the "technical content" of this sentence is quite high, indicating that Chiang Kai-shek, in the process of balancing the countries, also wants to seek the maximum benefit. The drafting of the Ministry of Finance's monetary reform bulletin was completed by midnight, and staff rushed to Kong's residence, where it was signed by Kong and issued overnight.[100]

Sadly, the most important monetary reform documents of the Nanjing National Government were all drafted by the British, so how can such a government talk about the possibility of monetary independence?

On 4 November 1935, the National Government announced its policy on French currency, stipulating that banknotes issued by the

---

[100] *The Old Financial Dialects*, edited by Hong Jia, China Financial Press, 1991, p. 129.

Central Bank, the Bank of China and the Bank of Communications were "French currency", i.e. they had unlimited legal tender capacity. The circulation of silver dollars in the market is prohibited, and silver dollars deposited by financial institutions and private individuals are restricted to be collected by the Central Bank. After much "secret planning", Kong Xiangxi and Liz Ross finally determined the exchange rate of French currency to the pound sterling, the French dollar to the pound sterling one shilling and two and a half pence, so that the French currency is linked to the pound sterling through the exchange rate.

From this day on, the French currency of China became an appendage to the foreign currency.

HSBC was a key factor in the "monetary consensus" reached between Chiang Kai-shek and Britain. When the silver rush hit China, only HSBC had the strength to keep Shanghai afloat, its pivotal position in China's financial markets and its vast capital power made the authors of The History of HSBC exclaim:

> "It is incredible that HSBC can keep the currency of a large country stable for most of the year."[101]

After the monetary reform, in compliance with the Emperor's decree, HSBC took the lead in handing over tens of millions of silver dollars in its inventory to the National Government's central bank in exchange for Chinese banknotes and French currencies, and banks such as Standard Chartered immediately and unconditionally agreed to hand over silver, and at the same time supported the monetary reform.[102]

The British Minister to China issued a circular to British nationals saying:

> "It shall be unlawful for any legal person or persons of British nationality residing in China to pay all or part of their debts in cash."

The nationalization of silver made the national government obtain about 300 million yuan of silver, the Nanjing government then shipped a large amount of silver to London to sell in exchange for the pound

---

[101] *A Centennial History of the HSBC Bank*, (English) by Corliss, China Books, 1979, p. 129.

[102] *History of the Central Bank*, edited by Hong Jiabang, China Finance Press, 2005, p. 333.

sterling in the United Kingdom as a reserve to maintain the stability of the French currency. Initially, the National Government had a Bank of England French currency reserve of around £25 million.

The sterlingization of French currency has greatly stimulated the nerves of Japan. The UK's blatant challenge to Japan's sphere of influence and the sterlingisation of French currency means that the alliance between China and the UK is completely locked at the monetary level and a split between Japan and the UK will be inevitable. At the same time, Japan began to intensify its aggressive expansion into northern China. Since the French yen has become a bubble, soft can not come hard.

Chiang Kai-shek also had to give an "explanation" in order to quell the anger of the Japanese side. On the same day that the Ministry of Finance issued its monetary reform, the Executive Yuanliang of the National Government formally agreed to resign as mayor of Beijing on his own initiative and to abolish the Beijing Military Committee Branch. Both were requests made by the Japanese North China Garrison to Chinese officials in North China. Chiang Kai-shek took a low profile and met the Japanese demands, hoping to ease the pressure on the Japanese side. But Japan was not buying it, and the Kanto Army and the Japanese North China Garrison argued that the implementation of the currency reform would deplete the economy of North China and that Britain would be in economic control of the whole of China. This prompted Major General Tufeihara to propose the line: "Let North China be economically cut off from the Nanjing regime."

At the same time, the Japanese embassy in China issued a statement by the military attaché Isotani, categorically refusing to transport the silver from North China to the south and opposing the currency reform.[103] Japan's Ministry of Foreign Affairs spoke out, blaming Japan directly for the currency reform. In Beijing, Japan instructed ronin and hooligans to buy goods in foreign currency in the market, and if shops used French coins for change, they claimed they could not cash them and forcefully refused. This reciprocity has discouraged firms from accepting French currency again. For a while, the people of North China were on edge. To the outbreak of the war of resistance, Japan simply began to do it themselves, "DIY" French

---

[103] *China's wartime inflation problem*, Tadao (Japan) Miyashita.

counterfeit banknotes, the counterfeit French currency in reverse into foreign exchange, and then purchase materials.

The printing of counterfeit currency in Japan was done by Kenzo Yamamoto of the Japanese General Staff. He had dreamed of making counterfeit coins since he was young, and finally realized his "dream of counterfeit coins" as a teenager with the French coins of the national government. At first, Yamamoto selected 5 yuan French coins and printed hundreds of thousands of yuan, but when the counterfeit coins arrived in China, there was a "bad news" that the 5 yuan French coins had been scrapped in China.

Later, he finally succeeded in counterfeiting low-denomination counterfeit currency from the Chinese farmers' bank and purchased a large amount of supplies from China. "In World War II, the German Navy intercepted a United States merchant ship in the Pacific Ocean and seized a semi-finished 1 billion French francs printed by the United States Mint for the Bank of Communications of China, with only numbers and symbols missing. After Japan purchased this batch of semi-finished products, it finally mastered all the secrets of French currency printing, Japan made a total of 4 billion yuan of counterfeit French currency before and after.

Chiang Kai-shek attempted to counteract Japan by fighting for Britain and the United States, and set up a National Defense Design Committee to study China's monetary reform and incorporate the issue of China's monetary reform into the "National Defense Design". This shows that Chiang Kai-shek, in the process of considering the French currency reform proposal, had already developed the intention to close in on Britain and the United States and guard against Japan.

It was in the struggle for control of the currency with China that the Japanese, who had successively lost, became "furious" and thus accelerated the full-scale war of aggression against China. It can be said that the French currency reform became the fuse of Japan's war against China!

After the Yellow Bird, Americans Laugh to the Last

In fact, the proposal for China's currency reform was prepared long before Ross came to China, with the secret involvement of Kong Xiangxi, Song Ziwen and three U.S. financial advisers. Ross was not the architect of the 1935 monetary reform, and his arrival as the British representative eventually led to a compromise with the established interests of the United States.

When Leez Ross arrived in Shanghai, the National Government first arranged for the American advisor, Yang Ge, to brief him secretly in Nanjing on the whole situation and the idea of monetary reform, so that Britain and the United States could "touch" the basic principles on the Chinese currency issue first! It was only afterwards that Kong Xiangxi and Song Ziwen "informed" Ross of the contents of the monetary reform proposal.[104]

In a secret meeting, Kong did suggest again to Ross that the currency peg was open to discussion, but instead of continuing to discuss the peg to the pound, Ross suggested that the exchange rate be lowered to an appropriate level and then announced that it would be stabilized at that level, which seemed "more natural".

At the same time, in Washington, Shi Zhaoji, the Minister of the National Government to the United States, also made some progress in negotiations with the U.S. Secretary of the Treasury, Morgan Soh, whose "hatred" of Japan's aggression in Asia finally overwhelmed his suspicions about Britain.

Morgenthau promised to buy 100 million ounces of silver, but demanded to know what would happen to the foreign exchange after China sold the silver and offered to have a "firm link" to the dollar. Kong immediately replied that although China was cautious in its wording of the currency reform, Japan was already extremely annoyed, and could the US help China explain to Japan if it was pegged to the dollar? The U.S. at this point, while promising China, is still not actually moving.

Kong Xiangxi had to play the last card to power the U.S.:

> *"Even in the worst case, we can always sell silver on the open market in London, but that would just be bad for both China and the U.S."*

The telegram did the trick, and after Morgenthau consulted Roosevelt and agreed that the French currency must be pinned to the dollar, the Chinese and American treasuries reached an agreement that

---

[104] *China's Fiscal and Economic Situation from 1927 to 1937*, by Yang Ge (USA), translated by Chen Zexian and Chen Xiaofei, China Social Science Press, 1981.

China would sell 50 million ounces of silver to the United States. The 50 million ounces of silver, tendered for shipment to the United States by Chase Bank in Shanghai and Citibank in Citibank, N.Y., were sold in dollars, as agreed, and were deposited at the Chase Bank head office in New York.[105]

For China to stabilize its currency, it urgently needs to sell its acquired silver dollars for more foreign exchange reserves. The National Government decided that Chen Guangfu would go to the United States to negotiate. As a result of the negotiations, the Chinese central bank will take the approach of pegging the higher side of the Anglo-US exchange rate, that is, when the Anglo-US exchange rate changes significantly, the Chinese central bank will adjust the exchange rate of the lower side of its currency.

Thus, the "China-US Silver Agreement" was formally signed, and the U.S. Treasury Department purchased 50 million ounces of silver from China at a price of 50 cents per ounce, in order to maintain the French currency exchange rate, and determined that the exchange rate between the French currency and the U.S. dollar was 100 French dollars equal to 30 U.S. dollars, so that the French currency and the U.S. dollar "linked" through the exchange rate.

China then sold several batches of silver to the United States, and the dollars received as China's foreign exchange reserves were deposited with the Federal Reserve Bank of New York or other American banks. The file shows: to Japan launched the "July 7 Incident" before the national government foreign exchange reserves, the U.S. dollar $ 073.9 million, the pound reached $92 million, the yen only a fraction. This further strengthened the financial control of the national government by the United Kingdom and the United States, while the French currency became a common vassal of the pound and the dollar, and firmly "excluded" the yen.

In fact, the national government's financial dependence on the United States has grown as a result of the economic strength of the United States and the growing reserve for French-dollar dollars, which later has actually been pulled into the dollar group.

---

[105] *History of the Central Bank*, edited by Hong Jiabang, China Finance Press, 2005, p. 359.

The end of the French currency reform is that the British "mantis is catching the cicada" in front, while the United States is the "yellow bird is behind", French currency is finally tied to the dollar chariot.

The French currency reform allowed Chiang Kai-shek to tighten his control over commercial banks and complete his monopoly over the nation's finance. The "Four Great Families" directly controlled China's industry and commerce under the "Four Row and Two Bureau" system. The bureaucrats and buyout capital have merged completely to share China's pie of wealth.

Song Ziwen and Kong Xiangxi made a large amount of silver business in the process of French currency reform, and the British and American bought a large amount of silver, Kong Xiangxi also made a lot of money from it. And Song exaggerates even more, as the Asian Wall Street Journal once made a selection of the 50 richest people in the world over the past thousand years, including His Majesty the Sultan of Brunei, Haji Hassan Naberja, and Bill Gates. Of the 50 people selected, six were Chinese: Genghis Khan, Kublai, Heshen, Liu Jin, a eunuch, Wu Bingjian, a Qing businessman, and Song Ziwen.

When Chiang Kai-shek finally completed the French currency reform, he had already laid down the golden world of the Chiang dynasty. However, Japan's aggressive expansion into China is intensifying, seriously threatening China, which has just completed monetary reunification.

CHAPTER VI

Royal power and golden power

Why did the "Taisho Coup" mark the retreat of the Emperor's power? Why were there repeated coups in Japan in the 1920s and 1930s? Why is it that the Japanese army, which has always been highly ranked, is often seen as a strange phenomenon of "down and up"? Why was the "Shanghai War" a "fake war" launched by Japan? Why did Japan's gold power ultimately lose to the imperial power?

There has always been a fierce struggle between the imperial power and the golden power, and Japan's recent history is no exception. From the "King's government retro" to the "Meiji Restoration", from the "Taisho coup" to the "226" mutiny, all reflect the fierce game of imperial power and gold power.

Since Emperor Taisho was forced to compromise and back down in the face of the golden power, depression began and Japan's imperial power has been in serious crisis. Since his accession to the throne, Emperor Hirohito has been plotting every moment to bring back the royal power. And his main opponents are the plutocratic forces and their politician surrogates.

Since the Meiji period, the four clans of Nagasu, Satsuma, Hizen, and Tosa have gradually formed a political power center of the Meiji oligarchy, represented by the Meiji Kau Genros. Behind them is the dual support of warlord forces and plutocratic forces. They made the emperor a god and then "borrowed" the name of the emperor to influence the general policy of the country. The will of the Emperor must and can only be carried out through them.

For the Emperor to truly dominate Japan's destiny, he had to defeat the patriarchal-zakuri-warlord alliance. Emperor Hirohito was brilliant in his strategy of "unleashing the grassroots to fight the top", tacitly accepting and encouraging the phenomenon of the army's "lower hand

and upper hand", and gradually taking back imperial power. Finally opening the Pandora's Box of the Great War.

The yen is off the gold standard, and the plutocrats are in the way

Saturday, December 12, 1931. Three months after the "September 18" Incident, the Japanese government abruptly announced the abandonment of the gold standard, which was officially implemented from Monday. The Japanese financial market was immediately hit by an 8-magnitude earthquake, which caused an outcry in the political arena, and the business community was in an uproar, leaving the Japanese public in a state of panic.

The yen, a strong yen issued on the security of gold, will become "no one to depend on" from now on!

Although there were rumors in the market a month ago, the official announcement from the government still leaves the common man with his hands full. The salesmen in Tokyo department stores are working overtime to adjust the prices of various commodities; the housewives in the market are frantically snapping up the necessities of life, and the thought that in two days' time the prices of various commodities will be generally increased gives the housewives heart palpitations. With the Great Depression, ordinary people's incomes were precarious and life was increasingly stressful. At this point, the news that the yen had lost its gold conversion guarantee undoubtedly pushed the public's unease to the edge of panic.

But not everyone is in a state of panic, and a few are bouncing their crowns.

Foreign exchange traders are celebrating with champagne in the glitzy offices of Mitsui and Mitsubishi in Tokyo and New York. More than two months ago, concerned government officials, who have been "underwritten" by the plutocrats for years, revealed to them that Japan was about to follow Britain in abandoning the gold standard and that the yen would depreciate by at least 30% against the dollar after Japan abandoned the gold standard!

The plutocrats certainly don't miss this big pie that falls from the sky.

The Mitsui Zaibatsu family alone, immediately went out and hoarded $100 million and shorted the yen in the foreign exchange market. Mitsubishi and other plutocrats were not to be outdone, and everyone was buying dollars and throwing yen around. At one time, the Tokyo foreign exchange market was in a frenzy of smoke and confusion.

The plutocrats have been waiting for the government's announcement of the decoupling of the yen from gold every day, and now it's finally come true! They make a fortune. With the Mitsui family netting at least $20 million, the traders' year-end prizes must be missing!

At this moment, the office of Sumitomo Zaibatsu, the third largest plutocrat in Japan, is silent. These two months, foreign exchange traders have been holding a breath in their hearts, watching the huge profits within reach not to make, and do not know if the company's headquarters executives are taking the wrong medicine. Although Sumitomo also got the same insider through connections, the head office has repeatedly ordered foreign exchange traders not to participate in the yen speculation business.

Two months later, on 9 February 1932, the former Minister of Finance, who had announced the abolition of the gold standard, was shot three times, and on 5 March, the president of the Mitsui Zaibatsu was assassinated. The people finally realized that something was wrong, and it turned out that the large sums of money earned by Zaibatsu Mitsui were to be exchanged for blood! Why didn't the equally well-informed Sumitomo wade into this mess?

It turns out that the Sumitomo Zaibatsu heeded the advice of Nishionji Kouwang – never get involved in dollar speculation, because it was an elaborate trap devised by Emperor Hirohito!

He was a member of the Fujiwara family, and in Japanese history, he was honored as the "Meiji Kuken" along with Hirobumi Ito, Masayoshi Matsukata, and Katsumi Inoue. As the "Nine Senators" faded, Nishionji Kouwang finally became the most powerful figure in Japanese politics. In the Taisho and Showa eras, when the government was more powerful than the others, the prime ministers of the successive governments had to win general elections, but they had to be recommended by them. His descendant, Koichi Xiyuanji, was once hailed by Zhou Enlai as the "China-Japan Civil Ambassador". For three generations, the Nishionji Kouwang family has been politically influential in Japan for a hundred years, making it the most prestigious family of nobles in modern Japanese history.

At the age of 19, Nishionji Kouwang served in the Meiji government as a close minister to the Emperor and held a key position of "senator". In the face of the Tokugawa Shogunate's rampant "clear-side" army, he resolutely rejected the compromise views of some ministers, and urged them to unite and fight the enemy together. He then took part in numerous battles to overthrow the Shogunate, and did many outstanding feats. After the stabilization of the Meiji regime, Nishionji went to Europe to explore Japan's path to lasting peace and stability. He stayed in France for ten years, examining the political system and customs of the country, meeting many liberals and constitutional scholars, and was deeply influenced by Western liberal civil rights thinking. Politically, he opposed the deification of the emperor and insisted on the path of the rule of law and constitutionalism. He assisted his teacher, Hirobumi Ito, in drafting Japan's first constitution and served in his cabinet.

Later, Nishionji Kouwang joined Hirobumi Ito in founding the Masatomo-kai, which restrained the imperial power, and served as president of the Masatomo-kai. Masatomo's money came mainly from the Mitsui Zaibatsu, and the brother of the Nishonji Kouwang passed to the Sumitomo Zaibatsu, so the Sumitomo Zaibatsu sided with the Nishonji Kouwang.

It was Nishiyuanji's hope that it was Emperor Hirohito who had the earliest insight into the "dollar arbitrage trap" and warned Sumitomo Zaibatsu not to fall for it, or else the consequences would be unthinkable.

Why would the yen's departure from the gold standard and the plutocrats' arbitrage through the strengthening of the dollar and the depreciation of the yen be a huge trap laid by the emperor?

Secret Meeting of the Marquis of Kido's Family

On September 23, 1931, just five days after the September 18 Incident, members of the Eleventh Club were holding an emergency meeting at the home of the Marquis of Kido in Tokyo. The "Eleven Club" is a small secret circle founded by Kido on 11 November 1922, consisting of a group of clan nobles and a few trusted diplomats and officers. This club was the "supernumerary think tank" that Emperor

Hirohito could rely on the most, apart from his own ministers. They meet on the evening of the 11th of each month to discuss the policies and implementation plans of the emperor and his close ministers for governing the country.

Five days before the September 18 Incident, the Japanese Kanto Army had launched a military operation to occupy China's three eastern provinces, immediately stirring up strong public opinion against Japan in China and around the world, and the League of Nations had severely condemned Japan's actions. At the same time, domestic political parties, plutocrats and capitalist power blocs have expressed serious dissatisfaction. Once the League of Nations decides on sanctions against Japan's economy, the country's economy in a severe depression will suffer even more, to the detriment of the plutocrats and capitalists.

In order to calm international opinion and appease the various forces in the country, the "Club of Eleven" urgently convened this meeting and had to come up with a response for the Emperor as soon as possible. First, avoid any sanctions introduced by the international coalition to boycott Japan's trade, the global recession has hit the Japanese economy hard and any international sanctions would be a nightmare for Japan. Secondly, efforts must be made to appease and control the "short-sighted" bankers and industrial capitalists so that they continue to finance the military development of the Empire.

The meeting, which lasted until late at night, identified three viable proposals, three major events that would shape the history of Japan and China for the next eight months.

The first big thing, the "dollar arbitrage trap" was proposed by the financial experts in the club. Two days ago, the UK abruptly announced without warning that it had abandoned the gold standard, leaving the pound to depreciate by 20% overnight and the Bank of Japan to lose heavily on foreign exchange. The good thing is that the British government seems to be treating its bankers equally and without prior notice and they are losing even more. If such a thing happens in Japan, government officials will certainly give the news in advance to the relevant households, bankers will certainly in the months before the abolition of the gold standard to exchange the yen for foreign exchange, when the yen depreciates sharply and then exchange back to the yen, making a fortune out of nothing. For Japanese bankers, who are good at the government route, this is the natural "industry practice", while the British approach is simply unbelievable and stupid. At this point, the Emperor held a trump card in his hands, and if he agreed to allow the yen to be devalued by that magnitude as well, and revealed it to the plutocrats beforehand, their profits could be as high as about $100 million! That figure was enough to bribe any Japanese zaibatsu, including the largest, Mitsui, into aligning themselves with the Emperor's thinking.

If the plutocrats really buy a lot of dollars and short the yen based on insider information about the imminent devaluation of the yen, they will be held by the emperor to this major leverage, that is, the plutocrats are rich in national disaster, once the information is revealed, it is a major scandal for the plutocratic capitalists, the emperor holds them in this short position, not afraid of plutocrats do not cooperate. In this way, the emperor would have a greater say in the policy of the state. If the plutocrats supported the military's expansion plans, emperor could support the plutocrat-funded cabinet, plus the additional "bonus" of an approved abandonment of the gold standard.[106]

The second major event was the forceful coercion of Chiang Kai-shek to stage a "fake war" in Shanghai to divert international attention. Japan will create opportunities for Japanese forces to be "forced" into a "self-defense" military conflict in Shanghai that will directly threaten the security of Western powers' personnel and billions of dollars of investment in China. This was a high-handed move to threaten Western interests in China with the Sino-Japanese War, and then at the request of the League of Nations, the Japanese army publicly gave in and withdrew, so that the Western countries would owe Japan a favor, so that the League of Nations would naturally be embarrassed to pursue what happened in Manchuria. At the same time, Japan supported a puppet "Manchukuo" in Manchuria with Pu Yi as emperor, ostensibly independent, but actually a puppet of Japan, and to be recognized by Chiang Kai Shek. Under these circumstances, the League of Nations has even less reason to intervene and condemn.[107]

The third major event was the creation of a "fake coup" in which the military threatened the Emperor. Let the West see that the military is trying to rid itself of the Emperor's control. If pressure is exerted on

---

[106] *The Conspiracy of the Emperor of Japan*, by Bergamini (USA), Commercial Press, 1984, p. 578.

[107] Ibid., p. 579.

Japan, it will lose this democracy, the largest constitutional monarchy in Asia, thus pushing Japan into a fascist centralized state. The League of Nations did not want to create another fascist state in Asia, given that Italy and Germany's fascism had created enough trouble, and that only the Emperor had the ability to regulate the military, which would naturally put a lot less pressure on Japan.

The emperor's think tank, which is well versed in the Three Kingdoms Evolution, has devised a dazzling set of serial schemes. The main idea was to put the plutocrats in a trap, then see if the League of Nations resolution could satisfy Eugene, and if not, start a second "fake war" and get Pu Yi to set up a "Manchukuo", with all costs paid by the plutocrats "already in the trap". If the plutocrats are unwilling to pay, they throw out the scandal of the politicians and bankers who have paid for the national tragedy and make it the object of public anger, while using the third trick of assassination and coup against them and diverting the attention of the League of Nations.

Wasn't the Emperor the supreme ruler of Japan? Why go to such lengths to deal with bankers and politicians? A single edict would have solved the problem, wouldn't it?

The problem is, the Emperor's edict is not always good! Imperial power may not be able to compete with golden power!

"The Taisho Coup" and the Loss of Imperial Power

In 1868, the four clans of Nagasu, Satsuma, Hizen and Tosa joined forces to defeat the Tokugawa Shogunate, raising the banner of the "Restoration of the King's Government" and ushering in the Meiji Restoration era with the establishment of the Meiji Emperor. Japan became a constitutional monarchy, and the Emperor became the "Supreme Head" recognized in the national constitution. So how much power does the Emperor actually have? Who is the real dominant force in Japanese society?

It should be said that the same system, the same laws, different Emperors have different degrees of power! Power is never fully conferred by law, nor is it fully guaranteed by the system; it is the result of a fierce competition of interests.

Since the seizure of power by the four clans, the Meiji oligarchs have gradually formed the core of political power, which is represented by the Meiji Kau Genro. Behind them is the dual support of warlord forces and plutocratic forces. They made the emperor a god and then "borrowed" the name of the emperor to influence the general policy of the country. The will of the Emperor must and can only be carried out through them.

The Meiji Emperor, with his unique personal charisma and political power, effectively integrated his imperial will with the interests of the "Meiji oligarchs", thus gaining the support of all parties, consolidating imperial power and manifesting the Emperor's authority.

However, when Emperor Meiji died and his son, Emperor Taisho, took the throne, the situation changed significantly. Taisho was a typical weak emperor, lacking neither the personal charisma of Meiji nor the political power of Meiji, and his talent, political achievements and prestige were far inferior to Nao's. As the saying goes, people are usually tolerant when one's talent is greater than one's temper, but when temper is greater than one's talent, it often invites a backlash.

This is what is wrong with Taisho, and his tragedy is that he is ignorant of it.

Around the time of the Xinhai Revolution, the second cabinet was formed, during which Emperor Taisho became Emperor. Taisho's sense of imperial power was so strong that it was obvious that all sides resented it, and he did not have the power to bide his time, much less the political hand to lend his strength. His sense of self was that of a super bull man, a bull man who was doubly blessed by God and the Constitution, bull to the extent that at a word, all parties would immediately and unconditionally obey.

As soon as Taisho came to power, he began to expand the army and strengthen national defense, including increasing the number and equipment of the army and navy, so that he would be able to catch up with or even surpass his father, Emperor Meiji, in the opening of new territories and military conquests. His high-mindedness and determination simply overlooked the fact that his power base was not sufficient to sustain his ambitions.

The patriarchs were not buying it in the first place.

Nishionji Gongwang is the obvious opposition, and behind him are the forces of big bankers and industrial capitalists. He relied on his political aspirants to have an overwhelming majority in Parliament, and his cabinet policies were very different from the will of the Emperor.

He worked to cut Japan's massive 1.5 billion yen debt from the Russo-Japanese War and firmly controlled the fiscal budget. The result was a standoff with Emperor Taisho.

The policy of expanding military readiness is of course in the interest of the military, and so the Taisho is allied with it. In order to force Nishionji Gongwang to concede, the Cabinet's Minister of War resigned, which led to the dissolution of the Nishionji Gongwang Cabinet.

How did the resignation of the Secretary of State for the Army lead to the collapse of the Cabinet? Originally, Japanese law stipulated that in the Cabinet, the Ministers of the Army and Navy must be active military personnel, and if one of the two parties was determined not to cooperate with the Prime Minister, they could refuse to send representatives to the Cabinet, thus rendering the Cabinet non-existent.

After the collapse of the Nishionji Gongwang Cabinet, Taisho instructed the Army's Katsutaro to form a cabinet. The government of Xiyuanji immediately returned the favor and united all the civil officials who refused to take up the ministerial post, resulting in the failure of the cabinet. In the end, Taisho had to use his supreme constitutional right to push Katsutaro to the throne of prime minister.

This maneuver of Taisho's was rather raw, sending himself directly to the center of the storm, completely losing the leeway the Emperor deserved.

Sure enough, the Taisho Emperor's approach caused a storm of protest in the council. On the surface, the legislators accused Katsutaro of being "the guy who hides behind the dragon's sleeve," but they were actually complaining about the Emperor's abuse of his power. The Taisho Emperor was furious and directly ordered the council to adjourn for three days to reflect on the matter. However, the Nishionji Temple wished that these civil rights politicians had been "spoiled", and still openly criticized the Cabinet after the resumption of the meeting. In the Meiji era, it only took a frown and a burp from the emperor to put things to rest, but now the emperor himself has given an edict and still can't manage it!

The furious Emperor Taisho summoned the West Garden Temple Gongwang and ordered him to go back to unify his mind and stop resisting the order. He went back and conveyed the holy message. The council discussed it for another two days and still rejected the Emperor's proposal!

The whole of Japan is going nuts! Never in the history of Japan has the Emperor's will been denied so unmercifully! After all, he was a royal patriarch and should be on the side of the Emperor, otherwise how would the people of the world view him who betrayed the Emperor? As a result, Nishionji Kouwang resigned as president of the Jeongyou Association. But his insistence that the emperor was a man and not a god and that imperial power must be tempered by the Constitution did not change anything.

This was followed by demonstrations and riots against the Cabinet in Tokyo and Osaka, the first "constitutional crisis" in Japanese history. The major political parties have also put forward the slogan "Down with the clans and preserve constitutionalism". And the supporters behind it are the bankers and industrial capitalists who want to wrest power from the aristocracy and warlords. Buyers and sellers are first and foremost concerned with ROI, and no one wants to lay down an order when they lose money. If the military adventure fails, won't the investors who have invested huge amounts of money have nothing to lose? No one will do a losing deal.

The Taisho emperor was immediately in the awkward position of extreme isolation, and in addition to the army, with the Changzhou clan at its core, which had benefited directly from the military expansion policy, which was also on the emperor's side, various other forces were on the side of Nishionji prestige.

The situation deteriorated further and Prime Minister Katsura was forced to resign. At this time, the Emperor of Taisho was exhausted and lost his authority. In the end, whether in a mood or under threat of abdication, Emperor Taisho had to make a series of arrangements and concessions in terms of national policy and personnel arrangements.

(a) Withdrawal of most elements of the plan to expand the army.

(b) To abandon for the time being plans to conquer the South Ocean by force.

(c) In the event of a world war, Japan and the Anglo-French and American countries that control the Pacific region.

The oldest adviser to the Emperor was replaced by an official of civilian origin.

Crown Prince Hirohito left the special school of the royal sons to be educated in a Spartan-style school.[108]

This event is known as the "Taisho Coup".

Emperor Taisho was depressed from then on and suffered a sudden cerebral hemorrhage in 1919, after which he became mentally ill. At a military parade, he looked around with the edict rolled up as a telescope in front of a foreign envoy. The ministers decided that the emperor was no longer fit to run the dynasty, and in 1921, Prince Hirohito regented.

Why did Emperor Taisho's concessions implicate Hirohito?

The royal aristocracy believed that the root cause of the "Taisho Coup" was the Emperor and that it was his laziness and lack of decision-making power that led to the crisis of royal power. As a result, Hirohito was placed in the home of a retired naval officer only 70 days after his birth, where he was educated in the "Bushido" and then trained by teachers at the special "Gosakuin Institute," with the aim of creating a qualified authoritarian monarch who would be able to reassert his power in the future.

The Dream of the Emperor: The Rise of Imperial Power

One day in December 1921, the regent, Hirohito, who had just returned from a trip to Europe, received the nobleman and politician, Duke Wang of the West Garden Temple, at the palace. Before he came to the palace, he had heard that the day before, Hirohito had thrown an unpretentious party at the palace to celebrate his return from his honeymoon in Europe and to take charge of the Great Government. Such public gatherings of the Regent and a handful of his cronies were still very rare at the time. This worried and shocked the West Garden Temple Gongwang greatly. There is now speculation in Japan's high society as to whether Hirohito will rely on a secret society or a cabinet after he takes office. Both the Xiyuanji Gongwang and a few of the old courtiers who retired thought that Yujin should be cautious. Hirohito listened very patiently to the advice of the Emperor, apologized seriously for the absurdity of the night before, and then very sincerely asked the Emperor to be his senior advisor.

---

[108] Ibid., pp. 410–411.

He said he was in his seventies and had reached retirement age, so he just wanted to live by the sea, read novels, play the lute and spend his twilight years in peace, and had no energy for such an important position.

Understanding his concerns, Hirohito promised to show his respect for the constitutional monarchy by publicly renouncing his support for the clandestine small group if the Nishikonji Gongwang agreed.

Xiyuanji Gongwang pondered silently for a while. As a member of the noble Fujiwara family, he should keep the family tradition to uphold the emperor system. On the other hand, he feared that he would not be able to stop Yuhito's despotic behavior like that of his father, Emperor Taisho, and that he would be caught up in the struggle between the Emperor and the plutocrats, making himself unpopular and ruining his reputation for a lifetime of fighting for civil rights and freedom. Finally, he believes that the Japanese people have gradually changed over the past decade and may be able to accept the ideals of the rule of law and constitutionalism advocated by his mentor, Hirobumi Ito. If public opinion clashes with the will of the Emperor, it is believed that Yuhito will respect and accept the opinion of the majority of his subjects. Now that the country needs him, it should accept the position. So, he agreed to what Hirohito had proposed.

Hirohito was getting impatient as he waited for the Saiyuanji Gong to reply, but he had to be patient. He served for more than 40 years in the cabinet and the Privy Council, the highest advisory body during the Meiji period, and had a high reputation and extensive contacts among bureaucrats and parliamentarians. He was quick to act and thoughtful, and had the integrity to make a harmonious and careful impression on the Emperor, but was also adept at speaking out of the box and defending the Emperor's overreaching policies and blunders.

After the completion of the Xiyuanji Temple, Emperor Hirohito could hide behind the scenes and fully use his long-sleeved political means and the power of the bowser, to cover up the political situation, to accumulate the imperial power without any pressure, and to wait for the opportunity to move.

With many years in power, Emperor Hirohito is becoming more and more mature. He also had his moments of depression and pain, and whenever this was the case, he would come to the imperial study of the palace. Right in the corner of the room he treasured a beloved bronze bust of Napoleon, which immediately lifted his spirits every time he saw it. It was the only souvenir he bought for himself during his travels in Europe. I remember when I visited Napoleon's tomb in France, he used to stare at Napoleon's Austerlitz sword and imagine himself galloping like Napoleon. "A hero like Napoleon." Whenever he encountered difficulties, he often motivated himself with the air of Napoleon's sweep across Europe. He believed that Zeng Zu Xiao's dream of "Respecting the King and Joining the Barbarians" would be carried forward in his life!

More than 400 years ago, with frequent wars and the fall of imperial power, the Shogunate was so arrogant as not to provide any financial assistance to the Emperor, who was so poor that he often could not afford to host a sumptuous banquet for his ministers. Because of the lack of money, the emperor of Houdu was buried 44 days after his death, and his heirs had to postpone the enthronement ceremony by 22 years. Nara, the later Empress of Heaven, was so depressed that she went to the streets to sell words, and later raised money from King Chin to finally build a new palace to give the Emperor a decent life. Even so, when Westerners came to Kyoto to see Empress Nara, the Empress of Heaven, they were told that the request could not be delivered because the Shogun was absent. Thus the emperor is portrayed as a religious leader reclusive in Kyoto and without power. For the next 300 years or so, not a single foreigner saw the Emperor. In the West, the existence of the Emperor is completely forgotten.

During the Emperor's time of filial piety, the United States coerced the Shogunate into signing a treaty of commerce and navigation, and the Emperor opened his country to the West in humiliation. From then on, it became the dream of successive emperors to "reign supreme". Hirohito's grandfather, Emperor Meiji, began the Meiji Restoration with the financial support of Zaibatsu, including Mitsui, who abolished the Shogunate and restored imperial power.

The lessons of past dependence on the Shogun's handouts made Meiji realize that money was often more important than force in order to maintain the Supreme Lord's power. The Meiji gave the new industrial monopoly on development in Japan and the right to trade in colonial materials to zaibatsu such as Mitsui, Mitsubishi, and Sumitomo, and took a share of the dividends. Mitsui holds the rights to operate Japan's largest coal mine, as well as a franchise for camphor and sugar in Taiwan, China. The Emperor and the Zaibatsu formed a mutually dependent alliance, and with the support of the Emperor, the Zaibatsu controlled the pillar industries of Japanese banking, heavy industry, transportation, trade, etc. In return, the Zaibatsu were loyal to the Emperor and adjusted their industrial and commercial plans according to the Emperor's long-term national policy, becoming a veritable "government and business". By the end of the Meiji Era, the royal estate had grown from a few tens of thousands of dollars when Meiji took power to $40 million.

But as the Taisho era began, the plutocrats who held the nation's economic lifeblood, like the big bankers in the West, increasingly had their own interests at heart and sought to override the emperor. They intervened frequently in the policies of the Empire. When Taisho implemented the imperial program of "perfecting national defense" and carried out a massive enrichment of the army, the patriarchs representing the interests of the zaibatsu, led by Nishionji Gongwang, repeatedly rejected the Emperor's elaborate plan to expand the army on the grounds that the nation was still straining to balance the fiscal deficit left over from the Russo-Japanese War, forcing the Emperor to almost abdicate from the throne, and finally ended up depressed.

Now the plutocrats and politicians, who cannot see the "long-term planning and interests" of the Empire, are pushing back on Emperor Hirohito's plan to occupy Manchuria, making Emperor Hirohito feel very constrained in realizing his dream of a prosperous China.

From the time of Emperor Takashi Tomo, Japan had developed a strategic plan to expel the barbarians and unify the country under the leadership of the Emperor. The first was to increase national strength and modernize; then to fight the enemy by expanding overseas, creating a buffer zone between Japan and the West to keep Japan safe. This gave rise to a dispute between "northward" and "southward". The Northern Progressives advocated the annexation of Korea and the occupation of Manchuria, Mongolia and later the Siberian region, while the Southern Progressives argued for the occupation or control of the southern part of Japan, including the maritime islands and the Southern Ocean region of Southeast Asia.

According to Hirohito, the northward advance is only necessary for national defense and does not in any way solve the key problems of Japan's overpopulation, exports of industrial goods and sources of strategic goods. Hokkaido has been part of Japan for centuries, but it is still very sparsely populated. It did not help that Emperor Meiji conquered the same cold Joseon. The naive and simple-minded Northern Progressives in the Army today, who want to expand further into icy Siberia and sandy Mongolia by using Manchuria as a base, are just crazy!

The warm climate of the South Ocean, the scarcity and laziness of the natives, facilitated Japanese immigration, and the rich oil, rubber and minerals of the East Indies would provide a steady stream of strategic resources for Japanese industrial development, so the future and hope of the Japanese Empire lay in the South, not in the North.[109]

Now Chiang Kai-shek was busy "besieging" the Communist strongholds of China; the Soviet Union was engrossed in domestic construction, and Britain and the United States, beset by economic crisis, turned a blind eye to the "September 18" incident. Manchuria was only the first step in a plan that would then allow imperial powers to move south from Manchuria along the Chinese coastline and eventually take control of the strategic points of the Southern Ocean.

A Western-educated biologist who has carried the dream of "Respecting the King and Joi" for generations, Hirohito believes that his understanding of "Joi" surpasses that of his predecessors. His ambition has gone far beyond just "to resist the Ezo," arguing that Japan can no longer exist in isolation, but will enter Asia and the world with a leadership mindset. Inspired by the achievements of his idols Napoleon, Lincoln and Darwin, he was determined to resist the Anglo-American and Western powers as Napoleon did, to "save" Asia and the world from colonial domination as Lincoln did the emancipation of the black slaves, and to "evolve" other races with the Shintoism of the Yamato people. To attack, to liberate, to evolve, this is what the Divine has given him.

In order for the nation to be united with the outside world, it is necessary to convince the major political forces in Japanese society. Among them, the army and the ronin were very understanding and supportive of the Emperor's intentions, following closely in his footsteps. And plutocrats and the political parties they support often put their own interests ahead of the national interest. In Hirohito's view, the power of the plutocrats would naturally be further developed with the expansion of the Empire's frontiers, and it was annoying that they were now confined to their immediate interests, fearing that the economic sanctions that the League of Nations might propose would affect them,

---

[109] Minamijinomoto, (Japan) Muro Fuchikanobu, 1936.

and unwilling to side with the Empire in long-term planning to provide a steady stream of funds for the occupation of Manchuria and future operations.

Thinking back to his ancestors' poverty due to the fall of power, to his father's forced concessions, and to his own power struggles with plutocrats and politicians today, Yuhito vowed to firmly establish an empire centered on imperial power, where force is the core of all problems, and where necessary, he would not hesitate to use force and never be as kind-hearted as his father.

Over the years, Hirohito has imagined how he would have handled the "Taisho Coup" if he had been in his father's place. His father did not know much about Japan, and his set of laws that united the people in their common struggle and allegiance to the country was stuck in theory and not really felt. Father thought that no matter what, just call the shots. He could not imagine at what point the Emperor would be disobeyed. He didn't know how to exert Emperor Meiji's laid-back charm and careful manipulation of power.

If my father had been a little more determined and powerful like my grandfather, Emperor Meiji, things would never have gone this far. The "Taisho Coup" was a complete regression of imperial power, and now it was his turn to set things right and revitalize the imperial system.

Since politicians and plutocrats do not listen, they can simply bypass them and directly mobilize their subjects at the grassroots level, such as low-level military officers, ronin and peasants, and mobilize them to fight MPs and plutocrats through grassroots organizations, gangs and public opinion that support the royal power. On the other hand, the manipulation of zaibatsu and politicians was left to the public eye of the Nishikonji Temple and he was used to make plans. If the decision is wrong, it's the West Garden Temple's public expectation to bear the criticism of the court, and if things are not done badly, it's Emperor Hirohito's wisdom.

Emperor Hirohito was holding on to his heart to show how he had wrested power back from the plutocrats and politicians who dreamed of "constitutionalism".

The primary issue now is how to deal with the coalition of Zaibatsu politicians, centered on the patriarch Nishienji Gongwang.

On the morning of the second day of the meeting of the "Eleven Club", the cronies who attended the meeting reported the three proposals to Emperor Hirohito, who, after considering them, thought that they were good and ordered them to proceed immediately, first putting Mitsui and other zaibatsu into a "dollar arbitrage trap".

Mitsui fell into the "dollar arbitrage trap" by calling on the Emperor

If Japan achieves a republican government, then Mitsui and Mitsubishi will definitely be candidates for the presidency.[110]

Mitsui had supported the emperor, and the emperor had not treated Mitsui any less favourably. The rapid rise of the Mitsui Zaibatsu after the Meiji Restoration was unthinkable without the support of the government.

In 1888, the Meiji government held a public auction of the Miike coal mine with four private companies, including Mitsui and Mitsubishi, all looking for connections behind the scenes to take the big deal. Finance Minister Justice Matsubata has decided that the auction bid must not be less than 4.5 million yen and if it is not met, he will resign and the cabinet may be dissolved.

Mitsui's ambition for the Sanchi coal mine was to win it, and they brought in Inoue, one of Mitsui's top advisors and a bigwig in politics, to get in touch. Inoue merged his own property company with Mitsui to form what is now Mitsui Products, and the two companies formed an incomprehensible bond. After Xin Inoue gave a greeting to the government department, the coal mine and Mitsui Bank entered into secret negotiations to finalize the details. Then the government suddenly announced that the Miike coal mine had been sold for 4.55 million yen to Mr. Sasaki, who came out of nowhere, and of course Sasaki was representing Mitsui. Mitsui then took over the Miike coal mine for a mere 1 million yen deposit and paid the remaining amount over 15 years.

In less than a year after Mitsui bought the Miike coal mine, it not only recovered 4.55 million yen in costs, but also made a lot of money. If the coal mine can be mined for 50 years according to conservative estimates, it will generate a profit of 450 million yen for Mitsui, which

---

[110] *The Japanese Truth*, by Takeshi Takashi, Hunan Education Press, 2008, p. 220.

is 400 times the initial investment of 1 million yen in a deposit! It's the biggest "loss of state assets" case in Japanese history![111]

The successful operation of the Sanchi coal mine cannot be separated from Sanjing's returnee technical genius team, who are retained with high salaries. A graduate of the Massachusetts Institute of Technology, he rose to the occasion, using the technology of large water pumps he had just learned abroad to solve the problem of coal mine drainage and greatly increase the production of coal. Because of Takuma's management and technical talent, the profits of the Miike Mine surpassed those of Mitsui Bank and were comparable to those of Mitsui & Co. The Sanchi coal mine is known as "Sanji's portable safe". Takuma also quickly rose to become Mitsui's president and became Japan's "King of Part-time Workers" with an annual salary of 300,000 yen. Unfortunately, his brilliant life came to an abrupt end because of the "dollar arbitrage trap".[112]

Following the successful acquisition of the Miike coal mine, Mitsui's business focus shifted from the commercial and financial sectors to the industrial sector, and after the Sino-Japanese and Russo-Japanese wars, it gradually became a monopoly capital conglomerate, and after World War I it became a plutocracy with power in various industries.

The New York Times described Mitsui this way in 1922: there has never been such an organization in Western civilization. The Rothschilds, who were only in the financial business, were very average compared to the Mitsui Zaibatsu. Mitsui was the richest conglomerate in the Eastern world, controlling mines, banks, railroads, shipping, factories and trading companies. "Rich as Mitsui" means as much wealth to the Japanese as it does to the Americans who dream of "Rich as Rockefeller".[113]

The plutocrats not only control the economic lifeblood of the country, but also collude with patriarchs, bureaucrats and warlords to manipulate political parties and sway power. The major political parties in Japan at that time all had their own "gods of wealth" behind them.

---

[111] *The House of Mitsui*, Oland Russell, Little, Brown and Company, 1939, p. 223–224.

[112] Ibid., p. 225.

[113] *The New York Times*, January 8 1922.

The politico-faculty patriarch, Sorin Inoue, was known as "Mitsui's big boss," and the central figures, Taro Yamamoto and Morikori, had close ties to the Mitsui zaibatsu, while Shigunobu Okuma, president of the Improvement Party, and Takamine Kato, president of the Constitutionalist Party, had close ties to the Mitsubishi zaibatsu, who became the son-in-law of Mitsubishi founder Iwasaki. These men have been the most active political figures in Japan since the late 19th century, becoming agents of the Zaibatsu and serving their interests.

In 1927, Japan experienced a financial crisis of unprecedented magnitude and banks went bankrupt due to runs. Finance Minister Isao Kiyoshi Takahashi issued an emergency decree suspending the nation's banks for three weeks and helping the monopoly financial capital through a 2.2 billion yen extraordinary loan from the Bank of Japan to major banks and a 700 million yen government subsidy. Subsequently, the government amended the Banking Law to raise the capital threshold for starting a bank to 1 million yen, forcibly accelerating the consolidation of the banking industry, so that a large number of small and medium-sized banks went bankrupt or were swallowed up by large banks in the financial crisis, while the five largest banks, such as Mitsui and Mitsubishi, took advantage of the opportunity to pick up the slack and grew dramatically, with their total capital leaping to 1/3 of the total capital of banks nationwide.[114]

The monopoly capitalists, relying on the power of the Government to form a financial oligarchy, have instead "reaped the benefits" of the financial crisis and have continued to grow. This is reminiscent of the 2007 US financial crisis, when the US government went out of its way to bail out several "big but not bad" banks, including Goldman Sachs. The same government that lent taxpayer money to the big banks, the same government that let their competitors go bankrupt, no wonder Buffett didn't hesitate to plunge into Goldman Sachs stock in the crisis, with the government on the side of the plutocrats, let's see who can fight the enemy!

After the great success of the "Taisho Coup", the plutocrats, with their alliance of political parties and the remote control of the Cabinet of Ministers, became increasingly unscrupulous and arrogant towards

---

[114] *Japanese Banking*, Norio Tamaki, Cambridge University Press, p155-156.

the Emperor and the military. But this time, they were up against the shrewd and powerful Emperor Hirohito!

The day after the meeting of the "Eleven Club", after learning of the conspiracy of Emperor Hirohito's think tank through his spies, Nishionji Kouwang understood that instead of "stopping and thinking" as he had requested, the Emperor and his coterie were accelerating forward after the occupation of Manchuria. He decided to cancel his plans to return to Tokyo and stay in Kyoto, suggesting to the nation that his absence from the Emperor was due to his disagreement with the country's new expansionist policy.

At the same time, because of his special relationship with the Sumitomo zaibatsu, he warned Sumitomo's bankers not to get involved in the "dollar arbitrage trap" and put pressure on the emperor by discussing the matter privately with those around them.

In early October 1931, the largest of the Zaibatsu Mitsui after hearing the insider, could not resist the temptation to speculate on the foreign exchange market, buying 100 million U.S. dollars, sitting and waiting for the dollar arbitrage into reality, other Zaibatsu also have to follow the wind to buy. The initiative is now in the hands of the emperor, and if the Zaibatsu and Xiyuanji Kouwang take sides and do not finance the occupation of Manchuria, Yuhito will remain on the gold standard and drive the Zaibatsu to the brink of bankruptcy. If they get involved, they can make millions or even tens of millions of dollars in quick money.

When he heard that Mitsui and other Zaibatsu had fallen into the trap, he realized that he, like Mitsui, was in a dilemma, but he still insisted on staying in Kyoto. At the same time, he again warned Sumitomo's management that a financial holocaust was coming, leaving them to weigh in on whether it was worth profiting from. Most executives heeded his admonition, so much so that they lost a lot of money two months later when the yen depreciated.

In Tokyo, the Emperor's coterie was busy organizing political forces with different interests, an alliance that included military officers, politicians, and directors of the Mitsui zaibatsu. Fearing the risk was too great to take on the responsibility, the Civil Affairs Party cabinet on the stage repeatedly asked the emperor to resign. The AGA had to hold its ground because they had already assured Mitsui, the "god of wealth" in the background, that Japan would abandon the gold standard. Mitsui has already bet $100 million to avoid a long night, and they can't wait to get their own AGA in power to cash in dollars and make speculative profits.

Emperor Hirohito did not panic and asked the current cabinet to stay on for a few more days, waiting for a resolution from the League of Nations. But Zaibatsu Mitsui waited more and more anxiously, urging Masatomo every day to find a way. The president of Jeongyoukai was cornered and publicly pledged at a voters' rally in November to make Japan follow Britain's lead in leaving the gold standard. The news out, the foreign exchange market on the yen immediately fell, the Mitsui Zaibatsu dollar against the yen book substantial profit, the pressure immediately reduced. Hearing this news, Nishiyuanji couldn't believe his ears and said, "Isn't this a bank that declared bankruptcy before it even opened?"

On 10 December, the resolution of the League of Nations finally came down, neither condemning nor harbouring Japan, but sending an investigative mission to Manchuria and Japan to determine "what is right and what is wrong". Although the League of Nations was engaged in unprincipled perfunctory evasion, the sending of the mission was, in Hirohito's opinion, extremely unreliable, and it was undoubtedly to cheer up the anti-Japanese fighters in Manchuria and delay the crisis between the League of Nations and Japan indefinitely.

Hirohito decided to immediately launch a break from the gold standard and a "fake war".

A few days later, Zaibatsu Mitsui's "dollar dream" came true, and the Japanese Zaibatsu and the government's Yokohama Shogin Bank together made tens of millions of dollars in book profits. The plutocrats popped their crowns, and once again they compromised the emperor! But they forgot that there is no free lunch in the world, "the mantis catches the cicada, the yellow sparrow is behind", and the money became a leverage in the hands of Yuren forever!

After accepting the resignation of the current cabinet, Hirohito sent someone to inform Nishiunji Gongwang to come to Tokyo for the inauguration ceremony of the new government. The Nishinenji temple's governor in Kyoto finally wakes up to the fact that he has to play this game of "recommend the prime minister and find a scapegoat" with Hirohito more often. He couldn't help but ask, full of sarcasm, "Who did the Emperor's coterie choose?"

When he learns that the next scapegoat is Inuyasha, who was once the president of the Jeongyou Association, he can't help but admire Hirohito's shrewdness, and Inuyasha is the perfect bait to catch Chiang Kai Shek!

The "Shanghai War": Japan's "fake war"

Inuyoue is a veteran of the three dynasties since the Meiji period and has strong ties to leading figures of the Kuomintang. He was a close friend of Sun Yat-sen's revolution and always supported his revolutionary activities. When Chiang Kai-shek was in Japan, Inuyasha took him in and helped him.

Only when someone like Inuyasha told Chiang Kai-shek that the planned war in Shanghai was a play for the League of Nations, would Chiang Kai-shek believe it and even be willing to cooperate in putting on a good show!

On December 13, 1931, the cabinet of Inuyoui officially came to power, and his envoy had been in Nanking for some time in secret talks with Chiang Kai-shek. The two sides agreed that Chiang Kai-shek acquiesced in the "legality" of the Japanese occupation of Manchuria, and in exchange, Japan helped Chiang Kai-shek to eliminate the 19th Road Army stationed in Shanghai. The Nineteenth Road Army belonged to the Cantonese forces that opposed Chiang Kai-shek's dictatorship. Once the "independent" "Manchukuo" was recognized by Chiang Kai-shek, the League of Nations would have no reason to condemn the Japanese government, let alone impose economic sanctions.

On December 15, Chiang Kai-shek called down for the second time, resigning as President of the National Government, President of the Executive Yuan and Commander-in-Chief of the Army, while Finance Minister Song Ziwen and the entire Cabinet resigned en masse, taking all the books with them. When Chiang Kai-shek left, he also placed his own close associates as chairmen of four provincial governments, laying the groundwork for retaking power. In this way, he can sit back and watch the "fake war" take place, avoiding the responsibility of the war and waiting for the opportunity to come back and become a hero to end it.

In order to ensure that the war proceeded as planned, Hirohito sent his granduncle, Kakuninomiya, as Chief of Staff of the Army, and the

Kanto army cadre general Itagaki, who had planned the "September 18" Incident, was transferred back to Tokyo to help formulate the battle plan for the "fake war".

In January 1932, before the League of Nations had even left for Manchuria, the Kwantung Army launched a full-scale and rapid attack on all parts of the northeast, which brought disgrace to the Western powers. The U.S. Secretary of State proposed a recall of the ambassador and economic sanctions, but there were few supporters in Congress and the administration, so they sent Japan a tough note of non-recognition of Manchuria. This has allowed Japan to understand the British and Americans' background cards and to carry out the planned plan with greater confidence.

The United States, Chiang Kai-shek, and the country are all done, it is really "everything is ready, only the east wind is lacking", now we are waiting to create a reason to start a war.

On January 8, Emperor Hirohito went to the outskirts of Tokyo to watch military drills, and his trip was featured in the newspapers five days earlier in a perverse manner. Security was thorough that day, with the Kanto secret police force being flown in from Manchuria to assist in security, and public places in Tokyo and hotels favoured by the Koreans being raided, but somehow "missed" a member of the Korean independence movement from Shanghai. He left Shanghai in December, mysteriously "eluded" the ever-savvy immigration officer when he entered Japan, and took a train to Tokyo under the watchful eye of the railway plainclothes. At this point he carried a grenade in every pocket on his body and waited silently for the Emperor's convoy.

When he saw the Emperor's carriage marked with chrysanthemums passing by, he pulled out a grenade and threw it; unfortunately, the grenade landed under the carriage of an interior minister, and only a small explosion occurred, leaving the minister unharmed. The assassin was immediately arrested, placed on death row in complete isolation and executed by the secret police nine months later.

After the incident, the attacked interior minister calmly informed that there was no need to report Seowonji Gongwang; the Emperor, knowing the identity of the assassin, jokingly said that he must be a member of the Korean Independence Party; one of the Emperor's close associates wrote in his diary that he had a feeling that something would happen that day.

The assassination had generated strong sympathy among subjects who had grown increasingly frustrated with the emperor, and demanded that the Minister of Internal Affairs, who was in charge of the police, cut his stomach and apologize. The Minister of Internal Affairs had to hand in his resignation along with the rest of the Cabinet, and the Emperor returned without a glance and left the entire Cabinet in office.

After hearing all this, Gongwang of Xiyuanji was silent for a long time and said a great treacherous thing: "It is often said that the Emperor is above the Constitution, but where else can the Emperor find a reason to exist besides the Constitution?"[115]

On January 9, the first day after the assassination, in Shanghai, a journalist with ties to Japanese intelligence reported the news and wrote: "Just blew up the car that came with it, it's a shame." Newspapers such as Shanghai's KMT organ, the Republican Daily, carried the story, which caused a riot among the Japanese diaspora. The Japanese consulate in Shanghai then protested and demanded an apology for the newspaper's suspension. Japanese agents seized on the matter and started making excuses for war.

The day after the assassination, the Japanese intelligence in Shanghai received a telegram from Tokyo: "The Manchurian Incident" was developing as expected, but some in the Cabinet were still skeptical due to the opposition of the Great Powers, so please take advantage of the current tensions between China and Japan to carry out the incident you planned, so that the Great Powers would turn their attention to Shanghai.

On 18 January, five Japanese monks went to the entrance of the Sanyou Towel Factory to poke around and suddenly some unidentified beaters disguised as workers rushed out from the side, beating the Japanese monks to death and injuring them. The next morning, the Japanese diaspora in Shanghai held a general meeting to request protection from the Japanese government. Japanese intelligence agents broke into Mitsui's office in Shanghai and forced Mitsui employees with pistols to send a telegram to Tokyo headquarters demanding government protection.

---

[115] *The Conspiracy of the Emperor of Japan*, by Bergamini (USA), Commercial Press, 1984, p. 605.

Members of the Emperor's coterie used the telegram to demand that Mitsui bear the cost of starting the "fake war" because it was to "protect Mitsui's interests in Shanghai". Inuyasha asked Mitsui to donate $8 million to pay for the government to mobilize troops to protect Mitsui in Shanghai. The president's group thought that the government's demands were simply blackmail by the underworld, and replied that Mitsui did not need such protection and could not afford the huge sum. Inuyasha reminded the group that they had heard that Mitsui had just made at least $20 million from the dollar arbitrage, and that people had to be kind, so how could Mitsui have made the money without the help of the government? If Mitsui agreed to provide the funds, the government could negotiate with Chiang Kai-shek to make Manchuria "independent", thus avoiding international economic sanctions and guaranteeing Mitsui's interests.

The group figured out that this was part of the Emperor's plan to establish the empire by force, and that it wouldn't change because of the opposition of these politicians or the Mitsui Zaibatsu. The Emperor will use all sorts of means to force them to compromise, and dollar arbitrage is a trap for the Emperor, and a big fight is coming. He agreed to consider the prime minister's proposal, but could not guarantee that Mitsui and the other Zaibatsu would support the plan.

On January 21, the emperor ordered the parliament to adjourn in preparation for the general election a month later. In this way, during the transition, Hirohito could exercise a constitutional prerogative granted to the emperor – to approve additional expenditures that were not in the budget. At the same time, Hirohito's cronies warned Nishionji Gongwang that if the Zaibatsu did not make up their minds to fund the "fake war" by February 10, bloodshed would shock the nation.

Since January 23rd, the Japanese naval fleet has been dropping anchor in Shanghai, and the citizens of Shanghai have asked the Nanjing government to send troops to reinforce the Nineteenth Road Army in Shanghai, and the Nanjing government continues to remain inactive.

On January 26, the Chief of Staff, Hirohito's paternal uncle, Idle House, convened a supreme military conference and ordered the navy in Shanghai to exercise self-defense powers.

On the night of 27 January, following Chiang Kai-shek's instructions from behind the scenes, the Minister of Defence, He Yingqin, sent three urgent telegrams to the Nineteenth Road Army, asking them to endure the humiliation and to avoid conflict and not to make any move so as not to interfere with national defence events.

At 8:00 a.m. on January 28, a Chinese man who appeared to belong to the anti-Japanese "Save the Diet" threw what appeared to be a bomb into the Japanese consulate, according to official Japanese reports. This gave the Japanese Navy the ultimate excuse to go to war.

At 5 p.m., a *New York Times* reporter who went to the port to interview a Japanese naval commander was told that at 11 p.m., Japanese marines would drive into Zhabei to protect the Japanese diaspora, but that the Japanese who needed protection in Zhabei at the time had been evacuated two days earlier.

At 8:30 p.m., the Japanese issued a so-called "proclamation" calling for "the immediate withdrawal of all Chinese troops and hostile installations in Zhabei by the Chinese side". In order to secure a pretext for the invasion, the Japanese deliberately delayed the notification of the Mayor of Shanghai by letter until 11:00. Only minutes after the briefing, and before it was even certain that the ultimatum had been delivered, the Japanese Marines entered Zhabei. In other words, Japan will not give China any chance at all.

The war of resistance broke out in Shanghai. The Japanese army was resisted tenaciously by the Nineteenth Road Army, and Chief Cai Tingkai said he would fight the Japanese to the last man. Seeing that instead of being wiped out by the Japanese, the Nineteenth Road Army became a hero and could no longer sit still, Chiang Kai-shek immediately ran back to Nanking and announced that he would step forward to lead the government and the army in a time of national crisis.

Chiang Kai-shek had to play two plays at the same time, a dark play for the Japanese to continue communicating with the Japanese envoy, and a bright play for the Chinese with a hilarious plot that ran counter to Chiang Kai-shek's claims of entering the war. The Chinese ambassador attended the ceremony and toasted to the longevity of the friendship between China and Japan with the officers of the Great Japanese Imperial Navy. Where is this like two warring nations? They are like two brothers in the Greater East Asia Co-Prosperity Circle.

The Nineteenth Army rejoiced upon hearing Chiang Kai-shek's promises, thinking that he had finally found his conscience and was no longer confused by the bankers and capitalists around him and began to look out for the national interest. They fought bravely to hold the line, much to the disgrace of the Imperial Army of Great Japan. The marines, the elite of the Japanese army, under the bombardment of aircraft and gunboats, with the help of Japanese expatriates and sailors, were unable to break through the line of the 19th Road Army.

But more anxious than they were was the venerable Emperor Hirohito. In order to prevent the Japanese navy from making false pretenses and expanding the war in order to redeem itself, he ordered the reinforcements to advance slowly and without impatience, and he personally examined every detail of the battle deployment and logistics every day. He knew in his heart that this game was being played too big to deceive not only the international community, but also his subjects and the officers and soldiers who fought bloodily for him. In the end, he was so relieved that he transferred the Queen's cousin to be the Chief of the Navy. Now that the top commanders of the navy and army are all relatives of the emperor, a clear-eyed person can see how important this war is to Yuren!

On the one hand, Hirohito was furious, and on the other hand, Zaibatsu such as Mitsui was taking his time not to pay out money. According to Japanese practice, the country's financial ambitions are subject to the approval of the great zaibatsu. Now that the money isn't there, it's clear that they take issue with imperial policy. This is a blatant appeal to the Emperor! They're in for a treat this time.

The Land of Assassination

In early February 1932, as the targets of the Japanese bombing moved closer and closer to the Western powers' tenancy in Shanghai, the Japanese government sent an offer to foreign envoys in Tokyo to mediate a "misunderstanding" between China and Japan. After two days, the U.S. Secretary of State said it was important to combine the good offices in Shanghai with the Manchurian issue. That way, as long as the West takes a hard line on Shanghai, plutocrats who fear economic sanctions won't pay for the war. Although Japan's national credit is at its lowest point in international financial markets such as New York, which is very unfavorable for future Japanese overseas financing, Hirohito still stubbornly rejects the U.S. proposal, not to mention the Feb. 10 deadline he warned the plutocracy about a month ago. Since they're still holding out on ideas, the plan to punish the bankers kicks in.

This time it was Junnosuke Inoue, the ex-Ozosho, who had coordinated the entry of Zaibatsu, including Mitsui, to hoard dollars, and who knew that the plot was coming from the palace, and who later did a poor job of persuading the Zaibatsu to donate part of their profits to the state. As the saying goes, "A man is like a tiger." Who let Inoue Junnosuke know too much!

On February 9, Hirohito invited the head of the original Chinese intelligence network, who was affiliated in China with the leader of the Japanese right-wing group Blood League, known for assassinating politicians, to lecture at the Imperial Palace. At 8 p.m. that night, Junnosuke Inoue was preparing to give a campaign speech at an elementary school when he was shot three times by a company of the Blood League's most powerful assassins. The first victim of the "triple conspiracy" was born. The assassin was treated with unusual preference at the police station and went to court a few months later, refreshed and red-faced.

Another purpose of getting rid of Junnosuke Inoue is to strike a blow at the ruling Akyu and Inuyasha in the upcoming elections, as dollar arbitrage occurred during the Inuyasha cabinet, and Akyu's moderate advocacy tends to be at odds with the expansionist policies of the emperor and the military, who believe that the empire should pursue economic expansion rather than military expansion and maintain long-term cooperation with China.

The outcome of the general election is worrying Hirohito's small circle. It seems that the common people are not stupid, they know that the current economic policy was inherited by the cabinet from the previous government and so continue to vote for the AFP.

The Zaibatsu, who had just broken out in a cold sweat at the death of Inoue Junnosuke, saw that the voters did not support the war and stood up and prepared to challenge the Emperor again. The plutocrats who had turned their backs on Nishiwon-ji for their own interests, now came to their door to join him in the "Constitutional Defense Movement" and recreate the glory of the "Taisho Coup" period.

The plutocrats had recruited their own security team to fight the Blood League group. Instead of paying for the "fake war" in Shanghai, they came up with the idea of buying off the Kanto army, which was most loyal to the Emperor. A representative of Mitsubishi approached the Commander of the Kanto Army and asked him to accept a "donation" of up to $100,000. The answer they got was that the amount was too small and Mitsubishi should have been more generous and donated directly to the Chief of Army Staff in Tokyo.

The Yuhren coterie recognizes that this is a serious political crisis, with profit-minded plutocrats colluding with politicians, confusing the Emperor's subjects, and now trying to buy off the Army. And politicians, corrupted by the money of plutocrats and the so-called parliamentary democracy of the West, lose their loyalty to the state and the emperor. Therefore, the plutocrats who are the culprits must be dealt a direct blow.

To the relief of the Yuhito coterie, on February 29, when the League of Nations reached Tokyo, the 70,000-strong Japanese elite finally broke through the defenses of the 50,000 19th Road Warriors, and on March 1, the puppet "Manchukuo" was announced with great fanfare, and on March 2, international opinion was completely captivated by the kidnapping of the child of a world-famous American pilot. This string of good news is considered a godsend by them, this can now rest assured to prepare how to deal with the plutocrats.

On that day, Mitsui Bank held a shareholders' meeting to discuss the annual report, which specifically pointed out that the difficulties encountered by the banking business in the past year, the losses caused by the stock market and the devaluation of the pound far exceeded the profits from the dollar arbitrage, which was entirely to hedge the losses from the devaluation of the pound, and in the end Mitsui Bank suffered a net loss of 4 million dollars, and outside criticism of Mitsui for speculating on the dollar to make a lot of black money is completely unjustified.[116]

On March 3, the Ministry of Finance seemed to have completely ignored Mitsui's cries of poverty and announced that it was going to issue about $8 million in bonds in order to repay the debt incurred from the war in Shanghai, hoping that the zaibatsu, including Mitsui, would actively purchase them in the interest of the country. Takuma, the Mitsui president's group, was unconvinced, responding, "The nation's major entrepreneurs are unanimous that the company is in financial

---

[116] *The House of Mitsui*, Oland Russell, Little, Brown and Company, 1939, p. 254–255.

difficulty and lacks the cash to buy the bonds as desired." Both sides are fucked![117]

In 1932, Japan was in the midst of an economic crisis, while the rural northeast suffered the worst food production cuts since 1869. The peasants feed on the grassroots, their daughters are bought to work as courtesans and their sons go to Manchuria to "defend the national interest". The money that should have been used to redeem the daughter had to go to pay rent and taxes. Another tragedy happened to a peasant father whose son was in Manchuria and who wrote a letter to his father before he left for Manchuria, but forgot to put a stamp on it and the father could not receive the letter because he could not afford the four-cent postage. A month later, the father received official notice of his son's death in Manchuria.[118]

The common people have had a very hard time and have complained against the capitalists. The Yuhito coterie saw this as the perfect time to take action against the Zaibatsu, both by targeting them to vent their anger and telling them to obey the Emperor's orders.

On March 5, Takuma was shot down by a Blood League assassin in front of the Mitsui Bank building and died 20 minutes later.

The assassin later told the Asahi Shimbun,

> "My aim is to break the corrupt established political parties, but behind the established parties there must be Zaibatsu giants, so my plan is to start with the assassination of Zaibatsu giants, and the group (Takuma) is the center of the Mitsui Zaibatsu, so I will kill him."[119]

The assassin's criticism of the plutocrats was really spot on and exactly in the Emperor's mind.

The day after the assassination of Takuma, Nishinonji Kouwang returned to Tokyo, but refused to enter the palace to see the Emperor as a matter of protocol. He has been in talks with various parties, trying to preserve the dream of constitutionalism for which he has fought all his life. He wants the Inuye Cabinet to stay in office, to keep a little hope

---

[117] Ibid., p. 255.

[118] Ibid., p. 249–250.

[119] *The Japanese Truth*, by Takeshi Gao, Hunan Education Press, 2008, p. 127.

and confidence in the Constituent Assembly, and to do everything possible to stop the terrorist politics of assassination. In exchange, Xiyuanji demanded that the Great Zaibatsu buy all the $8 million in bonds issued for the Shanghai war, and another $7.5 million as start-up funds for the puppet "Manchukuo".

After everything was agreed upon, the Emperor of the Western Garden Temple made an arrangement with the Emperor. But things didn't turn out the way he wanted, the assassinations didn't stop, and all the forces that stood in the way of the Empire's expansion had to be removed.

On 15 May, an armed coup d'état was carried out by a small group of naval officers and members of a peasant fascist organization. They planned to attack Prime Minister Inuyugae's residence, the residence of the interior minister, the headquarters of the Jeongyou Association and the Bank of Mitsubishi in four separate ways, then occupy the police station and destroy the substation. Except for the killing of former Prime Minister Dog Yang Yi, most of the other targets of the attack were not achieved, and they ended up taking a taxi to the Police Department to surrender.

Eleven of the assassins of Prime Minister Nyi were court-martialed. However, just before the trial, the court received a petition signed in blood by 350,000 people, initiated and signed by sympathetic people from all over Japan, requesting the court to grant clemency. During the trial, instead of confessing their guilt, the killers used the courtroom as a propaganda stage to proclaim their abject loyalty to the Emperor and to stir up more public sympathy and calls for reform of the government and economy. In addition to the petition, another plea sent by 11 young people was sent to the court. They enclosed a finger from each to show their respect for the assassins and asked to die in place of the eleven assassins.

If public opinion is like this, how can the Emperor not have full confidence in his dream of "revering the King and fighting the barbarians" which he is personally in charge of?

Imperial power over golden power

> *"From the beginning, Hirohito was an action-oriented and powerful emperor, but paradoxically, he gave the world the impression of a defensive and passive monarch. The world*

> believes that he plays no decisive personal role in the decision-making process and insists that he be seen as an incompetent, famous and insubstantial head of state, lacking intelligence and knowledge. The truth is, he is shrewder, more cunning, and more energetic than most evaluations. One can read more into Hirohito's careful words than what he actually says and does. In his first 22 years in power, he exerted a high degree of influence and rarely showed incompetence about what he wanted to do."[120]

The background of the Japanese invasion and expansion led by Emperor Hirohito was very similar to Germany. They all had a complete monopoly economically; their cultural traditions of love of force, respect for authority, worship of order, hard work and diligence were profound expressions of conceit and disrespect for their unique values; politically, the model of Japan's 1889 constitution was Bismarck's German constitution, and although both countries were constitutional, it was the army, the landlords and the capitalists who really held power behind the parliament. The only significant difference between the two countries is their industrial strength, Japan is a truly resource-poor country, lacking coal, iron ore, oil, alloy materials, hydro resources, and even food. And Germany is just using it for propaganda.[121]

The congenital lack of resources and Japan's rapidly growing population after the Meiji Restoration created a strong contradiction. The population of Japan as a whole grew from about 30 million in 1873 to 70 million in 1939. They wanted to emulate the European emigration to solve the population problem, but most of the world's colonies had been cleared by the European and American countries. At the same time, Britain, the United States, Germany, France, Russia and other countries were very vigilant and uneasy about Japan's expansion, and in 1921 Britain refused to restore the Anglo-Japanese alliance; in 1922 the U.S. Supreme Court declared that Japanese were not eligible for naturalization as U.S. citizens, which greatly hurt the Japanese people's self-esteem and pride, and increased Japan's hostility towards Britain

---

[120] *The Truth – Emperor Hirohito and the War of Aggression against China*, (U.S.) by Bix, translated by Wang Liping and Sun Shengping, Xinhua Press, 2004, p. 8.

[121] *Tragedy and Hope*, Carroll Quigley, GSG & Associates, 1996, p. 561.

and the United States, and turned to forceful expansion to resolve domestic conflicts.

In the wake of the world economic recession and financial crisis of the 1930s, both Japan and Germany pursued a policy of internal repression and expansion of external aggression and established fascist rule to overcome the crisis by increasing defence spending and militarizing the national economy.

In Germany, due to the collapse of the imperial power, regime change was achieved from the bottom up, through general elections.

In 1929, the economic crisis that swept the world broke out and the German economy took a sharp turn for the worse, with the number of unemployed in Germany reaching 2 million in 1930 and rising to 6 million in 1932. The Nazis immediately seized this historic opportunity to blame the Treaty of Versailles and the war reparations for Germany's economic crisis, and the weakness of the government for trapping the people in deep water. The economic depression and social upheaval caused the German people to completely lose faith in the Weimar Republic and turn to support the Nazis as the first major party in the Reichstag, and the Hitler government came to power.

Many people mistakenly believed that the Nazi regime was a dictatorship with all the power to run a society, that it could dictate all social resources as it wished, and that Hitler could decide the fate of all. In fact, Hitler as a politician had to rely on the cooperation of the four platforms of power in German society in order to run his government.

The social power platform in Germany at that time included the industrial capitalists, the military, the bureaucratic class and the Junker landlord class. Hitler protected the interests of the Junker landowning class and gained their support through a series of measures such as guaranteeing profits on agricultural products, regulating farmers' wages, reducing interest and taxes on loans, and exempting them from unemployment insurance.

Since the historical military power, with the Prussian officer corps at its core, had deep ties to the Junker landlord class, the elite of the Prussian officer corps were from the Junker landlord class, and the protection of the Junker landlord class won Hitler the support of the army.

By requiring early retirement of Jews and anti-Nazis in the bureaucratic hierarchy, large numbers of Nazis became civil servants, strengthening Nazi power.

The capitalists grew in power after the Nazis came to power. This class of people is not organized on a large scale, nor is it controlled and constrained according to a principle such as loyalty to a particular leader. The Nazi government essentially did not interfere with the free operation of industry and commerce, and the Nazis did not have much control over the industrial capitalists in general, except in the emergency of war.

The traditional view that Nazi Germany practiced a state-capitalist and totally authoritarian political system is in fact inaccurate, since such a model of organization was not really established in Germany at the time. It should be said that this system in Nazi Germany was an authoritarian capitalism, but not an authoritarian capitalism, whose main characteristic was the effective organization of society as a whole, under conditions in which the various social acts and the mobilization of resources were primarily aimed at satisfying capitalist purposes in the pursuit of profit.[122]

Instead of relying on political parties and general elections to control the government, Japan relies on a top-down approach, dominated by the Emperor and a strong military ministry, relying on internal planning of a series of assassinations, coups and other terrorist incidents, waging wars of aggression to expand its power and influence, and establishing a military-fascist dictatorship.

Japan's "constitutional monarchy" is a constitution in which the monarch is the subject, and the constitution is only the means by which the monarch manages the country, not a check on the monarch. On the contrary, the constitution should not only protect the emperor, but also specify a mechanism so that the emperor's power is not restricted in any way. The Emperor is the "Head of the Empire", who appoints the Cabinet of Ministers and must be loyal to him at all levels; the Emperor is the "Grand Marshal" of the army, directly commanding and directing the army, with no interference from the Government or Parliament; the Emperor may summon or dissolve Parliament and may issue bulls in

---

[122] *Currency Wars 2: Jin Quan Tiandi,* edited by Song Hongbing, China United Publishing House, 2009, p. 175.

lieu of laws; Parliament has only an assisting and advisory role to the Emperor. It can be seen that the Emperor of Japan had more power than Hitler, and there are laws that clearly state this. Of course, the law is the law, and the actual power of the emperor still depends on the game between the emperor himself and the plutocrats, political parties and the army.

The Japanese military power bloc, based on the political foundation after the Meiji Restoration, became the power center of the government after two foreign wars, the Sino-Japanese War and the Russo-Japanese War, and occupied a special political position. There are two pillars of military power, one is the implementation of the principle of the separation of powers between the military government and military orders and the independence of command, which has greatly strengthened the political status of the military, with reference to Germany. Secondly, Japanese law expressly stipulates that the Minister of Land and Navy in the Cabinet must be an active soldier and establishes the legal basis for the military's interference, which will inevitably lead to the Cabinet's collapse if the military resists; the Military Order of 1907 makes it clear that only the Minister of Military Affairs has to give his consent in matters of command, bypassing the Prime Minister. This system allows political parties and the Government to have no control over military power, while the Ministry of the Army can appoint ministers to the Cabinet of Ministers at the will of the military and directly control the affairs of the State and the survival of the Cabinet. Just as in the "Taisho Coup", the resignation of the Minister of War easily brought down the Kouwang Cabinet of Nishionji, which was not satisfied with the military.

During the Meiji Restoration era, the country's goal was to build Japan into an industrialized nation in a generation. Japan, on the other hand, is a country with a thin base and a late start, and the only way to develop its economy is to be guided by the government and to invest the nation's efforts. In this way, Japan has formed several large monopolies closely linked to the government, and the interests of the monopoly capitalists are often combined with those of the state, and the capitalists often use a cooperative attitude to implement state policy.

Party political activity in Japan relied on the system of nomination of genros in its early years. There are two thresholds that political parties need to cross in order to form a successful cabinet, the first being the nomination of the patriarch and the second being an election victory. Rather than trying to win the support of the electorate through their own platforms and propaganda, the parties are trying to figure out how to win the hearts and minds of the patriarchs. When the patriarchs left one by one, the party cabinets, lacking popular roots and platforms, were helpless in the face of the actions of the hardline military ministry.

A constitutionally protected imperial power, a strong army, cooperative capitalists, and weak political parties all made the Emperor's path to militaristic despotism even smoother than Hitler's.

Hirohito also proved to the world that he was superior to Hitler – the Emperor's ability to control and agitate his grassroots subjects. These included low ranking officers, ronin and peasants. When a cabinet minister, bureaucrat or senior officer in the army does not listen to his command, he directly mobilizes the people at the grassroots level and the officers at the lower levels to fulfil the Emperor's will by "subordinating the top".

Hirohito, with the help of his royal patriarchs, began grooming young officers and bureaucrats early on. As early as 1921, while traveling in Europe, he received and gained the allegiance of young Japanese officers such as Tetsuyama Nagata, Toshiro Obata, and Ninji Okamura, who later formed the "Baden-Baden Eleven", an organization that Hirohito challenged the military patriarchs to, among whom Ninji Okamura, Hideki Tojo, and Kenji Tohohara were central to the Japanese military expansion.

Hirohito established a teaching center in the palace to control and train young officers and bureaucrats, which took on the rather obscure name of "university diao". For junior officers and fledgling bureaucrats, it was a great privilege to be able to listen to discussions in the sacred palace, where few who stayed would betray the emperor, and where friendships made between classmates would continue throughout life, and where their alliance had a major influence on Japanese politics after World War II.

He worked for many years with Yuhito's close associates, was a loyal assistant to the head of Japan's largest gang, the Black Dragon Gang, and worked as a spy in China for 10 years. Around him were gathered the followers of Greater Asiaism, spies and nationalists representing all classes. He was known as the "spiritual godfather of militarism" and the "Goebbels of Japan," and was a practical man who could eat both black and white.

Under the guidance of Dr. Okawa, various "doctrines" that he found useful were added to the curriculum of the university. Confucianism, weapons development, development of contingency plans, restructuring of the army and geopolitical doctrine, etc. The Emperor's chief advisor gave a course on the status of the Emperor, explaining the various duties of the royal family, the role of these duties in reconciling the Emperor's differences with his loyal cronies, and the necessity of not allowing the public and public opinion to tarnish the Emperor. The lectures were even given by members of the paramilitary system, such as secret police, commercial spies, drug dealers, brothel owners, terrorists and interrogation experts, who are in the front line of the "construction of fascism".[123]

In addition to nurturing talent, the Emperor also supports pulling in gangs and fascist organizations such as the Black Dragon Society and the Blood League, allowing them to bait public opinion and purge the opposition with assassinations and coups.

Founded in 1901, the Black Dragon Society is the center of the Japanese nationalist movement and the home base of the Japanese ronin, more powerful than any other group. At that time, a Japanese cabinet was formed, and no one could do it without the approval of the Black Dragon Society's big brother, Head Yamanaman. The Black Dragon Society also made a splash in the Sino-Japanese War and the Russo-Japanese War. Cooperation with the Japanese military has since intensified, in conjunction with the army's invasion of China and the launching of the Pacific War.

The Blood League is a right-wing Japanese terrorist organization founded by the fascist monk Inoue Nikkai, whose main members are students and rural youth. Inoue was a former spy in China and returned to Japan in the 1920s with his old friend Dr. Okawa. He and his disciples attempted to overthrow political parties, plutocrats and the privileged class by assassination to achieve the fascist system of "common rule of the people" in Japan. Both Finance Minister Junnosuke Inoue and President Takuma Mitsui, who were involved in the "dollar arbitrage trap", died at the hands of the Blood League's guns.

---

[123] *The Conspiracy of the Emperor of Japan*, by Bergamini (USA), Commercial Press, 1984, pp. 458–459.

With the clandestine cooperation of these organizations, the Emperor, in a short span of one year, used the "Great Shift" to manipulate the political situation in Japan behind the scenes, repeatedly resorting to conspiracies, assassinations and war tactics, so that political parties were wiped out, plutocratic capitalists fell on deaf ears, and the international community was silent and held the imperial power in its hands. His achievements have been far beyond the reach of Daishō, catching up directly with Meiji.

> *"This puts an end to the experiment of a democratically elected government in Japan. The murder of Inuyeongyeol has effectively put the Aizyoukai out of sight. For 13 years thereafter, while the Japanese continued to vote regularly, their votes were meaningless – at best, they were just unrealistic views on issues that were publicized at the time. In the years that followed, now that the plutocrats had willingly become the cogs in the machinery of the country's military rectification, the only possible resistance to the military plan that Hirohito inherited from his imperial ancestors was from the 'militarists' of the army.*
> *When the last grenade exploded, the smoke cleared; the last taxi drove to a halt in front of the secret police building; and the last bluff of the Nishiyonji temple's final intimidation ploy was brought down by Hirohito town, the total number of dead was just four. A year later, when Hitler seized power, he had to assassinate 51 of his political enemies and set fire to the German Reichstag. Hitler's name then immediately became synonymous with the devil throughout the world; while Hirohito remained unrecognized after his 'triple conspiracy' coup – still a mysterious figure under the cover of religiously tinged precepts and still, on the surface, a complete paragon of decent manhood. He took advantage of being an emperor who could draw on thousands of years of experience in conspiracy."*[124]

On February 26, 1936, when more than 1,000 Japanese subordinate officers and soldiers shouted for the overthrow of the plutocracy and the bloody cleansing of Tokyo by overthrowing the corrupt bureaucratic politicians, the world-shaking "February 26" mutiny completely crushed the forces that had dared to fight against the Emperor.

---

[124] Ibid., p. 663.

The Nishiyonji temple was among those who were assassinated, but in the end the coup d'état soldiers spared him out of a "sudden act of kindness". At this moment, the Saiyuanji Gongwang completely understood, this was a kind of the sternest warning from the highest level, he was not an opponent of Emperor Hirohito at all, it was impossible for the constitution to constrain the emperor, and it was difficult for the golden power to overcome the imperial power!

From there, Japan opened the Pandora's Box of World War.

CHAPTER VII

The Dream Breaks of the Golden Mausoleum

Why was the Exchange Parity Fund the second central bank in China at that time? Why were the four great families able to seize astonishing wealth through French money? Why is forex liberalization a bad decision to launch at the wrong time? Why did the Chinese Communist Party's "financial infiltration" hasten the fall of the Chiang Dynasty? Why did Chiang Kai-shek ultimately lose the currency war?

The French currency reform of 1935, which unified China's currency, accelerated Japan's war of aggression against China. As soon as the war broke out, there was an immediate shortage of foreign exchange and the base of the French currency was severely weakened. Chiang Kai-shek had to rely on Anglo-American loans to stabilize the currency and hold out against the war. Britain and the United States took full advantage of Chiang Kai-shek's plight, using the foreign exchange parity fund as a platform for foreign exchange loans, and in one fell swoop took away the central bank's power.

After the victory of the war of resistance, the four great families used monetary means to ruthlessly plunder the wealth of the Great Backland and the fallen areas, losing the hearts and minds of the people. At a critical time when the economy was recovering and monetary stability should have overwhelmed, Song introduced a misguided monetary policy at the wrong time, which was foreign exchange liberalization, the consequences of which led to hyperinflation and the collapse of French credit.

The Golden Round Voucher was supposed to clean up the mess of the French currency, but unexpectedly it created an even bigger mess that ended up burying the Jiang dynasty.

Banker's Death

On an early morning in August 1938, a civil aviation flight departed from Hong Kong airport and headed straight west to Chongqing. The plane had just flown over Zhongshan in Guangdong, when the captain suddenly noticed a fighter jet burrowing out of the clouds not far away, and the Japanese sun flag painted on the fuselage flanks was frightening – it was a Japanese fighter jet that had been ambushed! In a short while, another fighter appeared on the flank of the Japanese plane, followed by the third, fourth and fifth, and the people on the civilian flight immediately tensed up, and they fell into an air trap set by the Japanese.

The captain, seeing that the situation was not good, pulled the joystick violently and stabbed his head into the thick clouds in an attempt to escape the Japanese ambush; five Japanese planes immediately came up in a fan formation, and the machine guns fired their tongues at the civilian aircraft. In less than a minute, the civil aviation flight was knocked out of flight, pulling black smoke and plummeting down, and all the pilot could do was do everything he could to force the plane down into the water field.

Fortunately for the driver, it worked. The passengers who were still alive struggled to climb out of the cabin and scattered. One of the passengers had just taken two steps when he remembered that he still had an important briefcase in his cabin and immediately turned to grab it. At this point, Japanese warplanes swooped down, sweeping down on all life that was still alive. The passenger who had just returned to the cabin was tragically shot and killed.

The brave passenger was a Chinese banker named Hu Penjiang, the chairman of the Bank of Communications. There is also another heavyweight banker, Xu Xinliu, chairman of Zhejiang Industrial Bank, one of the "South Three Banks".

It was no coincidence that the Japanese fighter jet had stumbled upon this civilian aircraft and shot it down. In fact, Japanese spies have been closely monitoring the whereabouts of several Chinese bankers in Hong Kong for a long time, they used a beauty trick to get the flight information of Hu Penjiang, Xu Xinliu and others from the mouths of Hong Kong and British officials, as a result, the Japanese Air Force sent elite fighter jets to intercept halfway between Hong Kong and Chongqing.

It seems that the Japanese air force and spy groups need not make such a big deal out of it, if only to assassinate two Chinese bankers. In fact, it's not just these two bankers that Japan is trying to assassinate, it's the important mission that they have!

At this point, the two bankers' purses were carrying the fate of the Chinese French currency, which would ultimately determine the fate of the country.

In November 1935, China completed its monetary reform, abolishing the 400-year-old silver standard, nationalizing silver and making French currency the only legal tender in China. The four great families, Jiang, Song, Kong and Chen, gained the most from this series of monetary reforms. Among the Four Banks, the Song family controlled the Bank of China; the Kong family ruled the Central Bank; the Chen and Song families shared the Bank of Communications; and the Peasant Bank was Chiang's preserve, with underworld brothers such as Chiang Kai-shek and Du Yuesheng sharing the huge opium profits financed by the Peasant Bank. In the "Two Councils", the Kong family took over the Central Trust Board and monopolized the foreign trade and arms business; the large pie of the Postal Reserve and Exchange Bureau was shared among the families. The "Central Cooperation Treasury", which was later established, was the world of the Chen family. Foreign exchange, China's most scarce financial resource, is monopolized by the Song and Kong families. Of course, the biggest boss is still Chiang Kai-shek.

As Chiang developed from military centralization and political centralization to financial centralization, the national government's ability to control the nation's economic resources increased dramatically. Through the financial system, the four major families monopolized almost all heavy industry, infrastructure, trade and foreign exchange, realizing the pattern of monopoly of gold power. Foreign banking power in China has had to shift from direct to indirect control, from monopolizing the Chinese financial system to sharing power with the four major families. Objectively speaking, the four major clans have been given the possibility to evolve into the Japanese plutocracy system, and the national government has gradually tightened its grip on the financial high frontier.

In the former China, the monetary landscape was divided; now, the advent of French currency has unified the world and put an end to the disorder of the Chinese monetary system. The unification of the currency, in turn, promoted the formation of a unified domestic market and stimulated the development of national industry and commerce. After the French currency reform, and in the 20 months leading up to the outbreak of the war, "for the first time in its history, China experienced exchange rate stability",[125] thus greatly boosting China's foreign trade capacity, and the Chinese economy began to emerge from the shadow of the Great Depression and set itself on a steady growth path. Had the United States not unilaterally set off the "silver tide", China would probably have been one of the countries that emerged from the world economic depression earlier.

The success of China's currency reform has greatly stimulated Japan, especially the Japanese military, which has a strong impulse to conquer China.

The basic premise of Japan's grand strategy of "conquering the world first conquers China" is that China is weak and fragmented. Now that China has reformed its currency system and unified its currency issue, this is a very dangerous signal for Japan. Japan's own Meiji Restoration began with monetary unification and gradually improved its financial high frontier, and eventually, with the strong support of its own finance, it was on a fast track to complete industrialization within a generation.

U.S. diplomatic sources are keenly aware of this,

> *"Japanese military personnel have the belief that China's program of national unification, economic development and military improvement, which has progressed and achieved clear success in recent years, has become a threat to Japanese security. The postponement of the action currently under way to destroy that programme only means that it will be difficult to do so later."*[126]

Even more annoying to Japanese military personnel is the fact that the French currency has chosen the policy of being pegged to the pound and the dollar to keep the currency stable, thus effectively rejecting the possibility of yenification of the French currency. In May 1936, the

---

[125] *China's Financial and Economic Situation from 1927 to 1937*, (U.S.) Yang, China Social Science Press, 1981, p. 317.

[126] United States Foreign Documents, vol. 1937.3, pp. 545–547.

"Sino-US Silver Agreement" was signed, and the United States purchased 70 million ounces of silver from China in gold, and borrowed $25 million in 50 million ounces of silver, and deposited the gold and the US dollar into the Chinese government's account in the Federal Reserve as a reserve for the issuance of French currency, and stipulated that the exchange rate between the French currency and the US dollar was 30 cents to 1 French currency. This agreement tied the French currency firmly to the pound and the dollar.

A group of lieutenants and majors in the Japanese Army and the Kanto Army immediately came to the sobering realization that the result of this move by the Chinese government was to bring China into the pound and dollar zone and to bring China into a community of destiny with the Anglo-American forces, thus excluding Japan from the game entirely. Japan's Undersecretary of State for the Ministry of the Army, Furusho, accused China of currency reform and "no agreement on Japan, a neighboring country with strong political and economic ties... It is obvious that Japan has abandoned its pro-Japan policy, so it is hard to ignore it when it is relying on the stability of the Eastern powers". Even the Japanese Ministry of Foreign Affairs, which has been called "pigeonholing", said that China's implementation of monetary reform is "contemptuous of Japan's position and therefore cannot commit", and that the Japanese side "will resolutely reject it and, although resorting to force, will prevent its realization".[127] The Kanto army's response to the monetary reform was to speak directly from the artillery. As soon as China announced its monetary reform programme on 3 November, the Kwantung Army immediately sent infantry, tanks and field artillery units on 15 November to assemble at the Shan Customs front, ready to drive into the territory and expand its military aggression against China. At the same time, the Japanese began to mobilize the so-called "Autonomous Movement of the Five Provinces of North China" and infiltrated North China in an attempt to transform it into a "Manchukuo".

Japan's logic is clear, and China's monetary reform in fact demonstrates that the national government is determined to "look outside" Japan's "Greater East Asian Co-Prosperity Sphere". Since China won't eat wine, we'll serve it to them!

---

[127] Historical Archives, No. 2, 1982.

The full outbreak of the Anti-Japanese War in 1937 was a major reason why China's French currency completely fell to Britain and America!

Through monetary reform, China's financial system, which had just stabilized, began to falter. War needs money, modern war needs more money. The national government had to use inflation to mobilize the nation's ability to wage war, which, to put it bluntly, was to have the Central Bank Mint's printers run at full power to print money. The key to maintaining the stability of the French currency is the exchange rate stability of the foreign exchange market, while the real exchange rate stability requires the free trading of foreign exchange. The war and inflation caused the population to start throwing out French currency in droves, snapping up dollars, pounds, gold and silver, and soon the national government was running out of foreign reserves.

In February 1938, after the pseudo-" China United Preparatory Bank" came out of the cage in North China, the foreign exchange market in Shanghai was rampant in the Japanese financial forces of the pseudo-finance hedging activities, the daily amount of foreign exchange purchases to the Central Bank, from the previous 50,000 pounds to 500,000 pounds soared![128] At the same time, the value of the French currency fell all the way down. From March to August 1938, the French dollar fell from 14 pence to 8 pence against the pound and from 30 cents to 16 cents against the dollar, a loss of half its value in five months!

Forced by the enormous pressure of foreign exchange rush, the national government abandoned the policy of free foreign exchange trading, managed by the central bank and implemented the "foreign exchange request and approval" system, that is, all applications for foreign exchange purchase must be approved by the central bank and then sold at the legal exchange rate. Shanghai and Hong Kong became two official foreign exchange markets, with the legal exchange rate being priced out of the market.

However, the restrictions on buying and selling foreign exchange immediately led to the emergence of a black market in foreign exchange

---

[128] *North China Express*, 6 April 1938.

in Shanghai, which in turn created a more violent impact on the value of French currency.

The credit of the French currency was at stake, and the only way to maintain its value and thus stabilize the financial system on which China's war of resistance depended was to borrow money from the United States and Britain. The borrowed pounds and dollars would be deposited into the Chinese government's accounts with the Bank of England and the Federal Reserve, and a "board" would be set up by the funders to manage the foreign exchange, with a view to stabilizing the value of the French currency by systematically dumping the pounds and dollars into the Chinese foreign exchange market and returning the French currency. When the war is over and the financial stability is over, China will regularly repay the pounds and dollars it has borrowed.

This money is called a foreign exchange parity fund, and the "board" that manages the parity fund is the parity fund committee. The Commission is essentially a semi-independent financial institution with the power to make decisions to intervene in the foreign exchange market independently, based on the fluctuations in the foreign exchange market at the time. Since French currency is a foreign exchange standard, the Commission's power to manipulate the exchange rate amounts to a certain degree of control over the issuance of China's currency. Moreover, any institution or individual wishing to obtain foreign exchange must apply to the Commission for approval and disbursement. In this way, the Equalization Fund is taking into its own hands the "foreign exchange request approval" authority previously exercised by the Central Bank. Furthermore, all monetary policy of the Chinese government must be submitted to the Equalization Fund Committee before it can be implemented, and the proposed Equalization Fund Committee, once implemented, will become the de facto central bank of China!

Xu Xinliu and Hu Penjiang, who were shot down by Japanese warplanes, were then recalled by the Chinese government to the wartime capital of Chongqing, where they were to travel to Britain and the United States to borrow money on behalf of the Chinese government for the Ping Lo Fund. Xu Xinliu and Hu Penjiang were also the best people to accomplish this mission. Xu Xinliu studied in England in his early years, returned to China and joined the banking industry, quickly rose to become one of the pillars of Jiangsu and Zhejiang plutocrats, and also served for a long time as the Chinese director of the International Bankers in China Council – Shanghai Public Tenants

Bureau of Industry, close contacts with the international financial community, is also the U.S. Treasury Secretary Morgan Sow's old friend, he represented China to London Financial City and Wall Street to talk about the parity fund, is simply not more appropriate. As the chairman of the Bank of Communications, Hu Penjiang was a resolute anti-Japanese faction in the Jiangxi and Zhejiang plutocrats, and had been blacklisted by Chiang Kai-shek and the Japanese military for vigorously financing the 19th Road Army in the Shanghai War. An anti-Japanese banker's demand for international monetary cooperation by insisting on the war was very persuasive in the circles of international bankers, in Western parliaments and in the media. The duo is arguably a golden pair.

This is why the Japanese must put these two Chinese bankers to death. Once the Sino-British and U.S. foreign exchange parity fund is established, the value of the Chinese French currency will be stabilized, which will fundamentally enhance the Chinese government's financial mobilization capacity for the war against Japan. And the Anglo-American holding of the parity fund is tantamount to bringing China firmly under their sphere of influence, which Japan, in its attempt to dominate China, will never tolerate. Therefore, Japan must do whatever it takes to stir up this matter, and even if it cannot be stopped, it must do its utmost to disrupt its pace and rhythm.

Xu Xinliu and Hu Penjiang can be said to have fallen on the front lines of the "currency resistance war".

Foreign Exchange Parity Fund: Second Central Bank

After much effort, by March 1939, the Chinese and British governments finally reached an agreement. The Chinese side by the Bank of China funded 3.25 million pounds, the Bank of Communications funded 1.75 million pounds, the British side by HSBC funded 3 million pounds, Standard Chartered Bank funded 2 million pounds, a total of 10 million pounds (about 50 million U.S. dollars, 1 billion French currency) to form the "Sino-British parity fund", all the pounds deposited by the Chinese government in the Bank of England's account, and formed the "Sino-British foreign exchange parity fund committee" to intervene in the exchange market, parity French currency operations.

At the end of May 1939, just two months after the start of the fund's operation, all the £2/3 bullets in the fund were already depleted. But in the face of war, the dreaded meat grinder of fortune, and the madness of french money, it was simply too much to bear. By mid-July, the Equalization Fund was out of money! The National Government's foreign exchange reserves also fell to their lowest point since the outbreak of the war of resistance, leaving the Central Bank with only $25 million in foreign exchange savings.[129]

In desperation, the Commission had to stop selling foreign currency twice, and the French currency inevitably depreciated so much that by October 1939, the French dollar had fallen to an all-time low of 4 pence.

At this point, the Americans struck.

In July 1939, Arthur Younger, U.S. advisor to the National Government Treasury, informed the U.S. Embassy that "the last three days have seen an extraordinary expenditure of the Equalization Fund, about half of which has been purchased by American Express and Citibank."[130] Even the always pro-US Kong Xiangxi was angry, he called the U.S. State Department directly on July 18:

> "The foreign exchange situation is becoming more and more serious, there is little left in the parity fund. Recently sold foreign exchange, most of which are foreign buyers to go. According to the reports received, a significant share of these were purchased by American Express, Citibank and other American businesses. This is not a friendly move by any means. Therefore, it is imperative that this matter be stopped as soon as possible."[131]

Kong Xiangxi's phrasing was so harsh that he almost cursed his mother directly.

At this point it was Hitler who stepped forward to give China relief.

---

[129] China and Foreign Aid from 1937 to 1945, p. 163.

[130] Telegram from Ambassador Jensen to the Secretary of State (18 July 1939), United States Foreign Relations Papers 1939, vol. 3, p. 684.

[131] *Monetary History of the Republic of China*, Series 2, Shanghai People's Publishing House, 1991, p. 458.

In September 1939, Nazi Germany blitzed Poland. On the same day, Britain and France declared war on Germany, the pound depreciated and the French currency appreciated in the Shanghai exchange market. By early 1940, the French currency had risen by 80 per cent against the pound and 50 per cent against the dollar. The Parity Fund Board took the opportunity to dump £4.2 million in French currency to buy back £4.2 million, equivalent to 40 per cent of the total amount previously sold.[132]

In early May, the Commission for the Equalization of Funds again stopped providing unlimited foreign exchange to the Shanghai exchange market and the French currency plunged against the pound. Two months later, the £10 million Sino-British parity fund is down to £2 million, effectively rendering it useless for the function of parity.

The Japanese dismantled Taiwan, the traitorous and bogus government dismantled Taiwan, the Americans also dismantled Taiwan, the speculators pushed for more fuel, and Europe was overwhelmed by the outbreak of war.

On 14 May 1940, Chiang Kai-shek telephoned President Roosevelt of the United States and pleaded:

> *"At present, Japan's military progress has been struck and the undeclared war has turned into an economic war. The recent announcement of the establishment of an issuing bank in Shanghai by a pseudo-organization, coupled with the increasingly dangerous situation in Europe, has put more and more pressure on our currency system, causing prices to rise, exchange prices to fall and the foreign exchange fund to fail to replenish, the economic situation will become weaker and more affected, leading to chaos and disorder."*[133]

The United States is still waiting for a "more favorable" offer, Chiang Kai-shek can hardly wait.

In June 1940, Song Ziwen himself went to the United States for help. At this time, American society is "isolationism" in power, the American people feel that there are two oceans to protect, whether the

---

[132] *Compilation of Historical Information on Chinese Banks (1912–1949)*, vol. 2, Archives Press, 1991, p. 1412.

[133] United States Foreign Relations Papers, 1940, vol. 4, p. 691.

Japanese or the Germans can do nothing for me, why do you have to build the bones of your own children for the Chinese and Europeans. Despite his foresight, President Roosevelt was also forced to proceed cautiously on the issue of aid to China under pressure from the popular vote. It wasn't until Wang Jingwei's pseudo-government was established and the Germans, who were in their prime, put pressure on the Chinese government to compromise with Japan, that Roosevelt, fearing that China couldn't bear to fall to Japan's side, let loose and agreed to lend China a foreign exchange parity fund.

After much haggling, the two countries finally reached an agreement on the Equalization Fund and its Management Committee in April 1941. On the same day, a new phase of the Sino-British Parity Fund agreement was reached. Subsequently, the three countries exchanged letters and merged the two equalization funds, with the United States contributing $50 million, the United Kingdom contributing 10 million pounds sterling (about $40 million) and China contributing $20 million, making a total of $110 million to form the new "China-United States-Britain equalization fund".[134]

The new Fund Committee has the power to review all US-China trade, in addition to the day-to-day operations of the foreign exchange market and the parity of French currency rates. Whoever does business between the United States and China must have a certificate of authorization from the Fund Board for the use of foreign currency before ordering goods from the United States to China. For all Chinese exports to the United States, the U.S. Government must produce a certificate from the Foreign Exchange Sales and Equalization Fund Board before the U.S. Government will allow its goods to enter customs. That is to say, this Equalization Fund Board is not only the central bank of China in essence, but also the highest foreign trade management body in China!

Americans have a much bigger appetite than the British!

It is, of course, the Americans who play a leading role in this committee. Under the terms of the Equalization Fund Agreement, the U.S. Commissioners are to report all decisions and plans of the Commission to the U.S. Department of the Treasury at any time.

---

[134] Secretary of State Hull to Ambassador Jensen (28 April 1941), United States Foreign Relations Papers 1941, vol. 5, p. 637.

Approval from the U.S. Treasury Secretary or the Federal Reserve must be obtained before the Commission can use the funds for operations such as investment or refinancing. Moreover, the Bank of China, the Central Bank and the Equalization Fund Board must report regularly on the use of the Fund to the United States Treasury for its "reference".

Let's take a look at this list of the Chinese members of the Sino-US ESF Management Committee: Chen Guangfu, Tse Tak Mao and Pei Zu Yi. Chen Guangfu graduated from the Wharton School of the University of Pennsylvania in his early years and is a prominent figure in the plutocracy of Jiangsu and Zhejiang. The official identity of the Dongting Xi family was that of the Director of the Central Banking Bureau, while the real power he represented was the "Eight Nations Allied Army" of foreign banks. Pei Zu'ie was born in the Sheng Xuanhuai family of the Han Ye Ping company, and later joined the Bank of China, becoming Song's confidant and acting as Song's agent in the Equalization Fund.[135]

As can be seen from the composition list of this committee, it is a core organization under the leadership of international bankers, with buyers and sellers working closely with bureaucratic capital to control China's financial sovereignty.

In order to support this institution, the US government even decided to freeze all private funds between China and Japan in the US, followed by the UK and the Netherlands, which to some extent calmed the market hedge and reduced the pressure on the Foundation to sell. The United States Treasury Secretary, Mr. Morgenthau, spoke highly of the role of the Equalization Fund, saying that it helped the Chinese Government to organize its finances and conduct economic warfare against the currency of the puppet regime.[136] U.S. Ambassador to China Jensen even argued that "without this loan, the Chongqing government would have collapsed."[137]

---

[135] *Shanghai Times*, (Japan) by Shigeharu Matsumoto, Shanghai Century Press, 2010, pp. 90–91.

[136] *Xinhua Daily*, 10, 17 May 1941.

[137] Song, Z. Wenzhuan, Wang Song, Hubei People's Publishing House, 2006, p. 154.

Yet neither Morgantho, nor Jensen, expresses a deeper meaning, and that is that a flat fund is indeed a good thing, good in the sense that it can control China deeper and work better for it!

Kong Xiangxi's dollar fortune

In December 1941, just four months after the opening of the Sino-American Anglo-Pac Fund in Hong Kong, the Pacific War broke out. The U.S. Congress, thoroughly enraged by Pearl Harbor, decided in early 1942, in an atmosphere of shared hatred, to provide a huge loan of $500 million to the Chinese government, which had persisted in the war, to help improve its ability to fight against Japan.

Back in the day, the U.S. currency issue was only $9.6 billion, and all of a sudden it gave China $500 million! At that time, the Chinese government's annual revenue was only 1 billion French francs, and at the official exchange rate, 500 million US dollars was equivalent to 10 billion French francs, which was the sum of China's 10-year fiscal revenue! And this loan, with no time limit for repayment, no interest requirement and no additional conditions, is the only "three-nothing" loan in the history of Chinese foreign debt.

For Americans, this loan appears on the surface to be an absolute money-losing deal, but it's actually a million bucks! The $500 million would greatly strengthen China's morale and ability to fight against Japan, and the harder China fights, the smaller the number of American casualties on the Pacific front.

And Wall Street has long been framing the strategic landscape of the post-war world currency. From the perspective of monetary strategy, the $500 million "capital" will bring four major returns: first, the loan will immediately pull the United States military industry to rapidly expand the scale of production, and at the same time drive the revitalization of a large number of industries such as steel, mining, machinery manufacturing, transportation, shipbuilding, automobiles, aircraft and other industries, to get out of the plight of the Great Depression, greatly improve the unemployment rate of up to 18%, enhance domestic consumption capacity; second, the loan will completely dollarize China's monetary system, so as to firmly control China's economic lifeline at the height of currency issuance; third, and so on, the European "Marshall Plan" and other regional economic assistance plans, will greatly expand the circulation of the dollar, strengthen the integration of resources of the dollar on a global scale; fourth, the expansion of dollar power will eventually replace the British pound to establish the future hegemony of the world currency, when the world countries compete for dollar loans, the international reserves of the dollar and trading currency status will be established. After the war, the U.S. would impose an annual "mint tax" on countries in the form of additional dollar bills for 70 years!

You always have to pay! The architects of the dollar currency strategy have discovered that the "dollar reserve" amounts to a disguised tax and is a "super-tax" that the world can't get rid of and that won't stop for generations! What's not to like about such a lucrative business?

Half a billion dollars is a huge windfall for the national government! The four great families have spent a lot of effort to eat milk and bear countless scoldings, only to seize the financial power originally held by Jiangsu and Zhejiang plutocrats into their own hands, and built a "four banks and two bureaus" financial centralized power system, as a result of a few years of effort, inadvertently by the PingZhu Fund Committee seized the power. In private, I hated it, but because I had no hard currency in my hands, and because I had dollars and pounds in my hands, I had to hold my tongue. That's great, there's $500 million in the Fed's account to draw down at any time, so why keep a flat-rate fund committee with only $100 million in it like it's a grandfather?

So, under the leadership of Kong Xiangxi, the establishment of the Central Bank Foreign Exchange Management Committee, immediately the management of this amount of foreign exchange into the hands of the right to sit back on the real "central bank" position. At the beginning of the establishment of the Central Bank Foreign Exchange Management Committee, Kong Xiangxi falsely appointed Chen Guangfu, Sidemar and other members of the Parity Fund Committee as members of the Foreign Exchange Management Committee. However, Chen Guangfu issued a letter of resignation just after receiving the appointment, and Xi De Mao only appointed an agent to represent Xi Jia as a member of this foreign exchange management committee, his own ass is still sitting in the office of the flat fund committee.

With the change of the general environment, when the Wall Street bigwigs discovered the essence of "dollar reserves", they began to "grasp the big and put the small", what each of the China-US trade management issues and foreign exchange use authority approval and so on sesame green bean-like trifles, is not enough to bother it. Thus, the Equalization Fund Board gradually fell out of favor. The members have also had to "keep up with the times", and close to the Central Bank Foreign Exchange Management Committee.

When Kong Xiangxi suddenly made a fortune, what to do with the money became a matter of urgency. So how exactly is it in your best interest to spend?

It was not long before the programme came out: $100 million in savings funds; $100 million in public debt; $220 million to buy gold from the United States; $50 million to buy all kinds of goods in the United States; and the rest of the money to pay for all kinds of expenses, including handling fees, transportation costs, insurance, etc.

The so-called "US dollar savings fund" was set aside by the Ministry of Finance of the National Government from April 1942 to deposit $100 million into the Central Bank as a fund. The "four rows and two bureaus" are stored in French currency in United States dollars at the rate of 1 United States dollar to 20 French dollars. The minimum denomination of the savings certificate is US$10, and the term of the certificate is 1 year, 2 years and 3 years, with interest rates of 3%, 3½% and 4% per annum, respectively, with the principal and interest payable in US$ on maturity.

The so-called "U.S. dollar bonds" were issued by the Ministry of Finance of the National Government with a guarantee of US$100 million from April 1942 onwards. Those who subscribed to the national debt bought the bonds in French currency at the rate of 100 French dollars to 5 to 6 U.S. dollars and began to repay the debt in 10 years starting from 1944. Such bonds can be bought and sold as collateral, can be used as a deposit in official business, and can be used as a reserve in banks.

It sounds beautiful, but the people, including industrial and commercial enterprises and banks, are frightened by the "glorious tradition" of competing with the people for profits and issuing debts, from the Beijing government to the national government, and they are not sure whether they can pay the principal and interest when due. However, at the beginning of 1942, there was a parity fund and 500 million U.S. dollars pie backed by the French currency was once strong, the black market price of the U.S. dollar and the official price is not much difference, there is not much room for arbitrage, so whether it is the U.S. dollar savings fund or the U.S. dollar public debt, at the beginning there were very few respondents, had to use "persuasion", "amortization", "collocation" way to forcefully promote. The "four banks and two bureaus" were instructed to "amortize" two types of investments to the public, and all borrowers from the "four banks and two bureaus", irrespective of the public or government, were forced to convert 5 to 20 per cent of the loan amount into US dollar savings certificates. The "four lines" themselves had to subscribe to $2 million in United States dollar savings certificates, and even ordered provinces to "match" them to purchasers in a similar way when selling food.

The fate of U.S. dollar public bonds is not any better, the credit record of the government was not good, after the war even the stock exchange was closed down, the legal trading of public bonds no longer existed, and now suddenly issued a new kind of public bonds, still claiming to repay the principal and interest in dollars? The public believes that the central bank and the Ministry of Finance are a group of people who have come to fool the people.

In the face of such a situation, the "Four Union General Office", the highest financial regulatory body of the National Government, had no better way to do it than to use the method of promoting US dollar savings certificates to promote US dollar public bonds, in addition to "persuasion", "amortization" and "collocation", the central bank, the Bank of China, the Bank of Communications and the China Farmers' Bank were also forced to subscribe to US$2 million of public bonds each for promotion.

However, the Minister of Finance and President of the Central Bank, Kong Xiangxi, has learned from his predicament to make a fortune.

If other people don't know the details of the US dollar public debt, how else can Kong Xiangxi not know? The $100 million used to set aside for the issuance of public debt is in the Federal Reserve's account, and the debt is not a problem at all. What's more, how can you blame the finance minister and the president of the central bank? And there is no telling how long it will be before the war is over, and as long as there is a war, the French currency will certainly depreciate, and the arbitrage space between the official and black market prices will increase considerably over time, and there is no telling how much money will be made on that one hand alone! What is finance? Kong Xiangxi is finance; what is regulation? Kong Cheung-hee is the supervisor! Just do it. Just as it became clear to everyone that they were eager to buy

U.S. dollar bonds, Kong ordered the central bank's treasury bureau to stop selling U.S. dollar bonds from October 15, 1943 on the pretext that they were sold out.

Is it really all sold out? According to the recollection of Chen赓雅, a member and director of the Yunnan Provincial Branch, by October 1943, there were still 50 million U.S. dollars of public bonds that had not been sold, but Kong Xiangxi ordered that they be terminated and purchased by the Central Bank Business Bureau.[138] In fact, the central bank's business bureau didn't buy it all; Kong Xiangxi himself bought $11.5 million in US dollar bonds! The bonds were purchased by Kong Xiangxi at the official price of US$1 to 20 French francs, while the average price of US dollar bonds for the month was about 250 French francs to US$1. With this one move alone, Kong Xiangxi and his henchmen had embezzled more than 2 billion French coins!

And that's not all. After doing this job, Kong Xiangxi's appetite became so big that he wanted to eat the entire $50 million public debt. However, Kong Xiangxi's power is so great that he can only temporarily deceive all the people, or always deceive some people, but not all the people forever. There was no impervious wall, and when Kong's actions were exposed to public opinion, there was an outcry!

Huang Yanpei, Fu Shih-nian and a group of "royal historical officials" of the National Senate, at the National Senate in July 1945, jointly put forward the questioning of the sale of U.S. dollar public bonds for private fraud, Fu Shih-nian also collected a large amount of original information and evidence of the case of Kong Xiangxi U.S. dollar public bonds, and intended to formally submit it to the Senate for discussion, must play a hand "American-style democracy", shedding all the cuts, but also to pull down the royal pro-country relative, pro-American plutocrat Kong Xiangxi.

However, on the eve of the official meeting of the National People's Political Consultative Conference, Chiang Kai-shek's secretary of the room, Chen Bray, came to the door, and "pleaded" with Fu Shih-nian, asking Fu Shih-nian to "take the overall situation into account", not to give the "friendly countries" and "reactionaries" to attack the government's veracity, to believe that the Chiang chairman

---

[138] *The Kong Xiangxi I Know*, edited by Wen Si, Beijing, China Literature and History Press, 2003, p. 145.

will be impartial, in the hope that the file of the Kong Xiangxi case can be brought to Chiang Kai-shek's residence first, "the seat of the committee to see in advance".[139] Of course, this dossier is bound to end up "missing" forever. Afterwards, although Kong was forced to resign from power, but he was not subjected to any judicial investigation, nor was he subjected to any criminal prosecution, and the money he had embezzled was not used, and was lost in the pile of historical documents.

Chiang Kai-shek was clearly trying to shield Kong Xiangxi, in fact, the four great families that rule the national government, Chiang, Song, Kong and Chen, none of them are clean.

As early as 1943, the Asian Wall Street Journal estimated Song's wealth at $70 million, with investments in General Motors and DuPont, and it was clear that it was impossible to make that much money from his salary as finance minister, president of the Central Bank, chairman of the Bank of China and other national public offices. When American political writer Merle Miller interviewed failed re-elected President Harry S. Truman in 1953, Truman vigorously charged that it was Song and Kong Xiangxi and others who were planning to secretly embezzle US government aid to China. Truman became more and more agitated, and finally, unable to restrain himself, blurted out,

> *"They're thieves, every damn one of them ... They stole 750 million out of the 3.8 billion dollars we sent to Chiang Kai-shek. They stole the money and invested it in São Paulo, Brazil, and real estate right here, in New York!"*[140]

The dollars they took from them will eventually have to be repaid by the hard work of ordinary Chinese people to create wealth. What they are stealing, in fact, is not American taxpayers' money, but the hard-earned money of ordinary Chinese people. Such a government is not a "national government", but a wealth squeeze machine for the four great families of Jiang, Song, Kong and Chen to extract the blood and sweat of the people!

---

[139] *Kong Xiangxi Biography*, by Shen Guoyi, Anhui Wenyi Press, 1994, p. 274.

[140] Madame Chiang Kai-shek, a Power in Husband's China and Abroad, Dies at 105, *New York Times,* 25 October 2003.

Such a "national government" is bound to be abandoned by the people sooner or later!

The financial version of "Lurking"

In the autumn of 1939 in New York, Chen Guangfu interviewed a young man in a Chinese restaurant, only to see that the young man had a hint of sophistication. He is sharp-eyed and quick-witted, and he is fluent in English when it comes to Chen Guangfu's questions. Chen Guangfu secretly nodded his head, really is the assistant secretary of the United States Treasury Department and director of the currency department, his old friend Bai Laodou personally sponsored the young talent, really is the next generation of fear. Chen Guangfu immediately made a decision to hire the young man in front of him as his secretary and focus on cultivating him.

This young man, Ji Chaoding, is from Shanxi, has a PhD in economics from Columbia University and is a fellow of the Pacific International Institute. What is not well known is that he is an old member of the Chinese Communist Party who joined at the height of the White Terror in 1927. It was under the one-line leadership of Zhou Enlai in terms of party organizational relations. His brother, Ji Chaozhu, who would later represent New China as Under-Secretary-General of the United Nations.

While being sent by the organization to study in the United States, through the organizational relationship between the Communist Party of China and the Communist Party of the United States, Ji Chaoding befriended Edler, an official in the Office of Monetary Policy Research of the U.S. Treasury Department who joined the Communist Party of the United States in 1935. Later, Adele introduced Ji Zhaoding to the powerful man in the U.S. Treasury, Bai Laodou. As a member of the Council on Foreign Relations (CFR) at the time, Baird saw that Ji Chaoding was a rare talent from China and introduced him to the Pacific International Institute as a fellow.

This Pacific International Society is extraordinary, founded in Honolulu in 1925 as a branch of the Council on Foreign Relations of the United States, and is composed of the elite of the Pacific Rim countries, including Central America and Japan. It is funded by the Rockefeller Foundation and the Carnegie Foundation, and is controlled by a Wall Street coalition representing the interests of the Morgan and

Rockefeller families.[141] Also contributing to the organization are Mobil Oil, American Telephone and Telegraph, IBM, General Electric, Time Magazine, J.P. Morgan, Citibank, Chase Manhattan Bank, and other institutions with ties to Wall Street.

As the main U.S. representative of this body, Treasury's powerful figure, Assistant Secretary of the Treasury Robert White, has his own set of opinions on the institutional design of the postwar international financial order. In order to avoid the recurrence of tragedies such as the Great Depression, he believed that an international equalization fund should be established with the participation of the major countries of the world, with a minimum amount of $5 billion, to be paid by Member States in the prescribed shares, which would be determined on the basis of their gold foreign exchange reserves, balance of payments and national income, and that the fund should be set aside to issue a separate currency unit, the Unita. Each yunit is equal to 10 United States dollars or 137 grams of pure gold (1 gram = 0.0648 grams of pure gold), the yunit is pegged to the United States dollar and gold, the currencies of all Member States are to maintain a fixed parity with the yunit, and the currencies of Member States may not be devalued without the vote of 3/4 of the members of the Fund. In addition, discriminatory measures such as foreign exchange controls and bilateral settlements were eliminated, and short-term credit was provided to Member States to address their balance-of-payments deficits.

This was the predecessor of the International Monetary Fund (IMF), which today rules the global financial order, and the International Parity Fund (IPF) program proposed by Whitehead, which eventually went down in the history of international monetary and financial history under the name "White Plan".

White Lauder and the U.S. Treasury Department, which proposed the IAF program, desperately needed a test field to test how well their program was working. In order to stabilize its currency, China took the initiative to send Xu Xinliu and Hu Penjiang to the United States in August 1938 to negotiate the establishment of a Sino-US parity fund; however, the two Chinese bankers were shot down by Japanese warplanes before they had time to fly out of China. In the second month of the tragedy, the national government, which was in dire need of U.S.

---

[141] Carroll Quigley, op. cit., p. 947.

assistance, quickly sent Chen Guangfu to continue negotiations in the United States.

This was supposed to be something the U.S. Treasury wanted, but due to the strength of the U.S. isolationist forces and the Chinese government's inability to lend directly to the Chinese government. So Chen Guangfu, who is familiar with the political climate and business practices in the United States, suggested that the U.S. Treasury Department give loans for trade promotion to a U.S.-registered company, the China Global Import and Export Corporation, using this platform as a transition for the future establishment of a parity fund, whose records the U.S. government can check at any time. These loans are guaranteed by Chinese natural resources, including tung oil, tin, tungsten, etc., that the United States lacks. Exporting these resources will allow China to build up vital industries with minimum defense capabilities, such as trucks, automobile transportation, communications, modern mining machinery and modern processing plants.[142] Subsequently, Chen Guangfu engaged in intensive negotiations with U.S. Treasury Secretaries Morgenthau and White Lauder, culminating in the first $25 million "tung oil loan" agreement in late 1938.

Both Laodou Baek and Chen Guangfu, who are eager to establish the China-US parity fund, know full well that this "tung oil loan" is just a preview of the future establishment of the China-US parity fund, Laodou Baek needs to install "his own people" to the China Global Import and Export Corporation as soon as possible, Chen Guangfu also needs a competent person who can handle the daily business of the company, but also maintain close communication with the U.S. Treasury Department. Just at this time, Ji Chaoding appeared. The first job that Chen Guangfu arranged for Ji Chaoding was to write the "tung oil loan" report.[143]

In 1944, he represented the U.S. government at the Bretton Woods Conference, and after using his "White Plan" to defeat the Keynesian

---

[142] K. P. Chen Papers (Chen Guangfu Papers) [R]. Columbia University Collection, New York, p. 4.

[143] *The Reminiscences of Chen Guangfu* (English oral memoirs) [A]. Chinese Oral History [Z]. Chen Guangfu, Special Collections, Columbia University, New York, p. 109.

Plan on behalf of British interests, he was "double-crossed" by the FBI on suspicion of Soviet espionage. Shortly thereafter, White Lauder, who had penetrated the nerve centers of the global capitalist brain for deep lurking, inexplicably died.

As the war deepened, China's foreign trade routes were almost entirely cut off by the Japanese army, and there was virtually no foreign trade to speak of. Since there was no need for China Global Imports and Exports, Chen Guangfu returned to China with Ji Chaoding to take up the position of director of the newly established China-US Anglo-Indonesian Parity Fund Committee. Ji Chaoding also became the Secretary General of the Equalization Fund Board, as a matter of course. The main members of the Equalization Fund Committee, such as Chen Guangfu, Sidachem and Pei Zuoyi, are all financial bigwigs with several positions, each with their own bank "mouths", each with a large task, for the daily work of the Equalization Fund Committee can not be personally, so the daily operation of the fund is all in the hands of Ji Chaoding. And the parity fund at that time was almost equivalent to China's de facto central bank, this deep lurking "spy", can really be described as a high level of authority.

What's even more amazing is that Ji Chaoding not only made a name for himself on the Equalization Fund Committee, but soon became the Secretary General of the Foreign Exchange Management Committee under the control of Kong Xiangxi. It turns out that in his position, Ji Chaoding was acutely aware that between the two committees, especially between Chen Guangfu and Kong Xiangxi, the scales of power would sooner or later tilt towards the latter, and in order to lurk deeper, he had to take advantage of the contradictions between the two and adjust his strategy in time to move into Kong Xiangxi's camp. Although Chen Guangfu's talent, personal virtue and charisma are far superior to Kong Xiangxi's, although more than two years of living together have made him and Chen Guangfu already have a deep affection, although turning his back on Chen Guangfu causes Ji Chaoding pain in his heart, but for greater justice, there are things he must do.

After the Japanese invasion of Hong Kong, the Equalization Fund, which had been open for business in Hong Kong, had to move to Chongqing, the capital, where it was located in the Central Bank building. The staff of the Equalization Fund, including Ji Chaoding, live in the buildings of the Kongxiangxi compound in Fanzhuang on the north bank of Chongqing. Ji Chaoding occupied the "favorable terrain" and was able to make daily contact with Kong Xiangxi. With the worldly connections of the two powerful Shanxi families, Kong and Ji, Ji Chaoding soon became a regular guest of the Kong family, playing bridge with Song Anling every week and getting so close to Kong that he called him "Old Uncle". Soon after, he was appointed by Kong Xiangxi as the Secretary General of the Foreign Exchange Management Board.

In Kong Xiangxi's calculations, Ji Chaoding was a deadbeat with the American member of the Equalization Fund Board, Edelardo (the American Communist who lurked in the U.S. Treasury), and also had close ties with the U.S. Treasury (can it not be close? (The U.S. Treasury Department is full of "communist spies"), and there is "someone above" in the White House (no wonder McCarthy is so mad), when the $500 million "three no's" loan is in place, it is right to replace Chen Guangfu with Ji Chaoding to deal with the Americans and kick Chen Guangfu out completely. Ji Chaoding is also a Shanxi hometown, and after drinking American foreign ink, has close ties with the American upper echelons, and is also superb in business ability, so the "trustworthy, reliable, and useful" cadre does not need to who else? How could Kong Xiangxi have imagined that the Jizhao Ding would be a member of the Communist Party with such a background! Ji Chaoding soon became the confidant of Kong Xiangxi and won his supreme trust, so much so that he gave all his expensive suits that he hadn't worn to Ji Chaoding. When the Equalization Fund Committee was dissolved in February 1944, Ji Chaoding immediately became the director of the Foreign Exchange Management Committee.

By this time, Ji Chaoding had become the de facto maker of the national government's monetary policy! With great power in his hands, Ji Chaoding was about to strike.

Bankruptcy of the French currency: the consequences of foreign exchange liberalization

On August 15, 1945, Emperor Hirohito of Japan gave an edict declaring the unconditional surrender of Japan. The news came and the nation rejoiced that the Chinese people, at the cost of 35 million lives, had finally won this decisive battle that would determine the fate of the Chinese nation. At this point, it is imperative for the national government to take over the fallen areas and to restore and develop the national economy.

Kong Xiangxi, who was in charge of finance during the war, stepped down because of the US dollar public debt case, and was replaced by Song Ziwen as administrative president and finance minister. Back on the stage at the heart of managing the country's economy, Song found himself facing a real mess.

A history of a national government is a history of war. First, the Northern Expedition, then the "Communist", and then the warlords of various local power factions, followed by the Anti-Japanese War, which basically did not stop for several years, the war had long been fought to the end of the people's poverty, and the government's normal financial and tax revenues were shrinking, and it was not enough to make ends meet. The national government was able to rely on the support of the Jiangsu and Zhejiang plutocrats to issue public debt in the early days. After 1935, the financial power of the Jiang and Zhejiang plutocrats was basically seized by the four major families of Jiang, Song, Kong and Chen, and the government of Jiang has repeatedly defaulted on its debts and credit is extremely poor, making the public debt increasingly lacking. After the outbreak of the war of resistance, they had to live on foreign debt. Yet for a country of this size, dealing with a war of this magnitude, resorting to foreign aid can only be a stopgap measure. In a desperate attempt to finance military and political expenses and cover the fiscal deficit, Chiang Kai-shek was more inclined to let the national banks advance money, and after 1945, the central bank's advances to the government always amounted to more than 60% of government expenditure!

The central bank is no Ali Baba either, and by chanting a mantra you can turn into wealth out of thin air. Faced with the Government's insatiable appetite, the Central Bank had only one trick left: to start the machine to print money. Nowadays, this trick has a memorable and puzzling name, "quantitative easing".

The central bank recited its "quantitative easing" mantra, the result of which was the awakening of a demon called "inflation", while Song Ziwen's policy of looting the fallen zone with the exchange of 1 yuan of French currency for 200 yuan of counterfeit currency opened the corks of the demon's imprisonment. Soon, this demon would turn the Nuzhu District into an earthly purgatory.

In order to stabilize the economic order in the fallen areas, the invading Japanese army followed its strategy of "war for war" by announcing the exchange of one Japanese military ticket for one French dollar for every territory it captured, thus excluding French currency from the fallen areas. When Wang's regime was established, the issuance of pseudo-CRP vouchers, which exchanged 1 yuan of pseudo-CRP vouchers for 2 yuan of Japanese military tickets, actually devalued the currency by half. After the restoration, Song Ziwen surprisingly announced the exchange of French coins for pseudo-CBNs at a ratio of 1:200, which means that a white collar in the fallen area with a monthly salary of 10,000 yuan can still maintain a monthly income of 10,000 yuan after the Japanese fight; after the establishment of Wang's pseudo-regime, there was only 5,000 yuan left, but the life can still be lived; but it was not easy to survive until the restoration, all-night orgies, and the next day woke up suddenly to find his monthly income is only 25 yuan left! Where did the rest of the $9975 go? Forcibly deprived by the government and taken to fill the budget hole.

"Think of the center, hope for the center, and the center will suffer even more." Song's monetary policy has caused the people of the fallen areas to really cry for the sky and the earth. But the good thing is that it's finally back to light, no more wars, and a few years of hard work with your pants tightened will always make you feel better. And yet the common people were suddenly hit with a bigger pain – inflation! The market prices soar day by day, the original Nationalist Party, those who receive the big officers, as well as the speculators in the rear, find themselves holding the French currency in the fallen zone is really valuable, 1 yuan in the wallet to get to the fallen zone can be used as 200 yuan of money, who does not take advantage of this! A swarm of people seem to run to the fallen areas to rush to buy supplies, originally after the devastation of the war, the supply of materials is extremely scarce, coupled with the rush to buy the wind, prices like a rocket immediately soared up.

As a result, the national government has lost the hearts and minds of the people as it has taken the wealth of the fallen areas.

This is the fallen zone, so will things be better at the big back?

After 1942, the national government issued U.S. dollar public bonds and gold public bonds, many people bought public bonds, originally thinking that these two batches of public bonds had U.S. dollars and gold for preparation, credit will not be a problem, and can also support the country to fight the war and hedge the risk of inflation, why not? He took the coffin book and ate it all into some US dollar and gold bonds, expecting to get his share of dollars and gold when he won the war. As a result, the war was finally won, but all that was expected was a notice from the government that the gold bonds were to be received at 60% discount and the US dollar bonds were not to be received in US dollars. The government is blatantly robbing people of their wallets! And the vicious inflation in the fallen zone has now been extended to all parts of the country, and the big back market is a day at a price. There is already a dark tide of hatred among the common people towards the government.

Song Ziwen, who is high up in the world, does not think about the life of ordinary people, his mind is spent on how to accumulate "hard currency" as soon as possible through various means of wealth accumulation. With the money that Kong had scavenged from his predecessor, Song Ziwen already had about 900 million dollars in foreign exchange and gold in his hands.

Under Ji Chaoding's orchestration, Song believed there was enough capital already to launch a turnaround financial reform – foreign exchange liberalization.

Originally, the credit basis of French currency is the exchange rate stability generated by the free exchange of French currency and foreign exchange in the foreign exchange market, which is also the so-called "exchange standard system" is the main point. However, under the special circumstances of the war of resistance, in order to prevent the Japanese from using French currency to buy foreign exchange and then using foreign exchange to buy strategic goods, the national government froze the free exchange of French currency to foreign exchange. At the end of the war, Ji Chaoding lobbied Song Ziwen to continue to maintain foreign exchange control, which was not conducive to the stability and long-term stability of the national currency system, nor was it consistent with the principles of liberalization set forth in the Bretton Woods system. Ji Chaoding insists that if China wants to develop, how can it not keep up with the international scene? How could it be contrary to the international practice of the "Bretton Woods Consensus"? So, foreign exchange controls must be liberalized and the foreign exchange market must be liberalized!

Thus, in February 1946, "the Central Bank of Foreign Exchange Management Interim Measures" was introduced, providing that the Central Bank to 500 million U.S. dollars in preparation for the issuance of French currency, the dollar and the exchange rate of French currency from 1:20 to 1:2020, gold and foreign exchange trading freely again, and by the central bank to set up a parity fund at any time to carry out market regulation, to maintain the stability of the French currency.

However, in the face of fierce inflation, the official exchange rate is depreciating faster and the black market rate is depreciating even faster! The black market in foreign exchange continues to be a hot commodity for speculators, and the French currency is taking an increasing hit. The plunge in the value of the French currency, on the other hand, did not have the effect of stimulating exports and increasing foreign exchange generation that Song had expected. Because of the great destruction of the world war on the productivity, China can not make anything decent to export, industrialized countries other than the United States was reduced to rubble, the demand for raw materials in China has also plummeted, which makes the export of foreign exchange to become a pipe dream, and the Chinese people really need some commodities, domestic production capacity can not meet, before the foreign exchange control, domestic businessmen want to import can not be, now the foreign exchange is liberalized, can be justified to find the central bank to approve foreign exchange to buy foreign goods, this will be a single shot and can not be collected. Eight months after the foreign exchange liberalization reform, the central bank's consumption of dollars, pounds and gold from foreign exchange sold on imported goods and other government uses, net of export earnings, reached $400 million! The amount of foreign exchange funds available to the central bank was reduced by 60 per cent in one fell swoop. Song Ziwen took a bad look at it and hastily devalued the French currency to 1 US dollar for 3,350 French dollars, with the result that nothing was gained except to stimulate inflation to rise further.

The economy was depressed, the civil war was lost, and the whole of China was throwing French coins around and snapping up foreign exchange and gold.

At this time, Song Ziwen is like a red-eyed gambler, his "right-hand man" Ji Chaoding not only help him "ideas", "think of ways", but also super powerful execution. Song Ziwen, under his lobbying, concluded that the liberalization of foreign exchange had reached a critical "breakthrough stage", and that to advance would be to reap full credit, and to retreat would be to die without a place of burial, not only the complete collapse of personal credibility, but also the "ruin of the Party's great cause".

Minister Song, look how blue the sky is! Keep going, don't look both ways, walk over and you will melt in that blue sky...

Song Ziwen, like being hypnotized, will spend $220 million that year to buy back 6.28 million taels of gold, in the market to wildly throw back the french currency, he does not believe that such a scale of gold selling can not suppress the momentum of the french currency plummet.

It really didn't hold down!

By February 1947, Song Ziwen had sold more than 3.3 million taels of gold, while the official exchange rate of French currency had fallen to 12,000 francs to one dollar! The black market price would be impossible to see.

Had to, Chiang Kai-shek personally, on February 16, 1947, introduced the "Economic Emergency Measures Program", once again banned gold trading and foreign exchange circulation, the central bank no longer sell and only buy gold.

The government's credit collapsed. 50 years later, Chen Liff published his memoirs in Taiwan, and sadly blamed Song Ziwen's erroneous monetary policy for the ruin of the "party state": "Our (monetary) policy makes the rich people become penniless, penniless people, and even penniless... In other words, we have turned the people into the proletariat... Isn't this paving the way for the Communist Party? What kind of financial expert is Song (Song Ziwen)? ... Chiang Kung trusted Song too much, always thinking that Song was an expert in finance (and listened to Song on all financial matters), when in fact some things belonged to common sense and had nothing to do with experts ... (and) all these foolish tricks were bad ideas by Ji Chao Ding for Song." In the midst of his anger, Chen Liff titled the section of his memoirs "The Success of the Ji Dynasty's Conspiracy against the State".[144]

Ji Chaoding's series of monetary "dumb moves" combination punch, did not the KMT's suspicion? Not really. Ji Chaoding's recommendations for the national government's financial policy were implemented precisely because they fit the mentality of those in power. For these policies themselves are tailored to enrich the four great

---

[144] *A Study of Success and Failure*, by Chen Liff, Zhengzhong Books, 1994, pp. 388-340.

families from their immediate interests. As long as they can fatten up the four great families, for them, the Ji Chao Ding is not only innocent, but also meritorious.

In fact, the Kuomintang had lost the civil war since the failure of Song's foreign exchange liberalization reforms in February 1947, which triggered a gold rush and vicious hyperinflation.

The Last Struggle for the Golden Ticket

Hyperinflation illustrates only one problem, and that is the complete abandonment of government paper money by the people. The bankruptcy of the French currency has its roots in a severe fiscal deficit, with government spending 10 times more than taxes! The printing of banknotes became the main means of covering the deficit, so that paper credit would soon go bankrupt. When the people stopped trusting paper money, prices rose even faster than the rate at which money was printed; in the first half of 1947, the issue of paper money tripled while the price of rice rose sevenfold, the people stopped being willing to exchange commodities for paper money, and commerce and production shrank due to the lack of credible inflation, thus further weakening government revenue. People have treated paper money as a hot potato, once it is in their hands, it is immediately thrown out and exchanged for physical products, so that prices soar and hyperinflation is out of control. At the same time, hyperinflation has led to a loss of confidence in the Government, increased resentment of the lower and middle classes against the authorities, and a rise in riots and insurrections.

And the root cause of the fiscal deficit was the all-out civil war waged by Chiang Kai-shek. War depletion severely depleted the national government's finances, and by 1947, the national government's military expenditures accounted for half of the fiscal expenditures! The constant defeats on the battlefield added to the people's suspicion of government paper money. In this vicious circle, the fiat currency headed for its ultimate collapse.

In order to clean up the mess of the French currency, Ji Chaoding also urged the government to reform the yuan. Now that the French currency has no more credit, a new currency must be issued to rebuild the credit of the currency. JI Chaoding quotes from the classic, telling the story of how Germany's Shachter replaced the Weimar mark with the land rent mark, thus reversing Germany's super-inflation in the

1920s. He spoke from the top and listened to the senior officials nod their heads frequently. Thus, on August 20, 1948, Chiang Kai-shek carried out what was described as the world's largest monetary reform – the reform of the Golden Circle.[145]

The core of the gold round is the gold round as the currency, with 40% of gold, silver, foreign exchange and 60% of state assets as collateral, to issue a "fully prepared" new currency, with an issue limit of 2 billion; stop the circulation of French currency, and exchange 1 gold round for 3 million French francs to recycle the old currency; receive all the people's gold, silver and foreign exchange for a limited period of time, the people are not allowed to own gold, silver and foreign exchange, and violators are confiscated and confiscated. At the same time, people's deposits abroad must be registered and declared, failing which they are sentenced and their property confiscated.

It's basically open fire robbery. Ordinary people are not foolish enough to hear that the government is about to introduce a new currency, and people who have long lost trust in the government immediately jump at everything they can buy.

The Grand Gazette reported on October 7:

> *"The market in Beijing is getting worse and worse, and a rush to buy is pervading the city. The rice and wheat grain store has been empty for nine out of ten rooms, the black market for cigarettes, the number of changes in a day. Why do members of the public meet and ask questions like 'how do I get it? Daily necessities and the like are oddities."*

The situation in the capital city of Nanking was not good either. *The Central Daily News* reports,

> *"In the capital today, after a rush wind, the market is empty of everything... Housewives can no longer buy anything they need in the morning from small vegetable vendors. Pork has long been extinct, fish, shrimp, chicken and duck, also followed the pork 'retired' up, Nanjing's vegetable market, is the standard vegetable market, in addition to the gentry to seek high prices to the black market, the public can only naturally follow the vegetarianism."*

---

[145] *General History of China's Finance*, Volume 4, edited by Hong Jia, China Finance Press, 2008, pp. 506–507.

In Shanghai, where the market is at its most prosperous, the rush to buy is also the response to the Golden Yuan. The November 1948 issue of *Haiguang* Monthly described the Shanghai rush:

> "It happened to be Sunday, and the rush of Shanghai people was excited. Nanjing Road was unusually lively, with people moving around as if ants were moving, only to see a swarm of people carrying bags and bags of goods on the road. The four major companies, department stores, silk shops and cotton shops were packed with people who could be said to have some purchasing power left over. In general, small households compete to buy rice, oil, sauce, sugar, soap and other daily necessities from grain, soybean paste gardens, firewood shops and southern goods stores. For ten days in a row, the shop windows were all empty. Walking into shops large and small is like entering a cold temple, and although there are tourists, there is no Bodhisattva. They ran all over the street, lined up everywhere, or to the head, can not care about the feet, either worried about rice, or worried about vegetables, worried about firewood. Shanghai, known as the international business port, was actually born paralyzed."

Chiang Kai-shek's promise of "full preparation" was nothing more than a scam, as 40% of his gold and silver foreign exchange was already insufficient, and 60% of his marketable securities were just a front, while the National Government used the short-shares of several state-owned enterprises as reserves, and no one even bothered to issue shares of these enterprises, whose prices were calculated at high prices. Even so, the vowed ceiling for the issuance of 2 billion gold notes was immediately breached, reaching 8.3 billion by the end of the year; in January 1949, 20.8 billion; in April, 5 trillion; and in May, an astonishing 68 trillion!

Provinces have moved away from the centralized gold circulars and issued their own silver and copper dollars. By the time the PLA fought the Yangtze River, the national government's monetary system had completely collapsed, its finances were completely paralyzed, the army was on the verge of collapse, and the Chiang dynasty was on its last legs.

The famous American scholar Fei Zhengqing later analyzed that the small amount of money left in the hands of the most anti-communist urban upper middle class was tied up in the golden vouchers, and the last bit of support from the common people for the cause of the Kuomintang also went up in smoke, as did the golden vouchers.

The heavyweight "bad idea" that Ji Chaoding participated in the design of the "Golden Yuan Reform" has finally killed the "Party State"!

After the complete loss of public confidence, the "party-state" was so poor that it was left with nothing but money, and finally returned to Taiwan with 2.5 million taels of gold.

Money is the system of wealth distribution in a country, and to make a move on the currency, to make a loss, will change the flow of wealth in society, thus intensifying social conflicts, undermining the credibility of the government and losing public morale. Currency is again the circulatory system of the national economy, and its corruption will disrupt the economy, paralyse the finances, destroy trade and subvert the market. Ji Chaoding injected the super virus of "competing with the people for profits" directly into the KMT's monetary bloodstream, which circulated throughout the economy, directly accelerating the collapse of the KMT regime. From this point of view, the killing power of the Ji Dynasty Currency War was no less than the millions of male soldiers on the battlefield!

Why Chiang Kai-shek Lost the Currency War

Currency issuance is the most important power in human society, and the most hidden and difficult to navigate. Money drives the wheels of the economy, money governs the scales of politics, and money steers the pace of war. The emperors of ancient times, who have discovered the secret of monetary power, have had the first chance to win.

A unified currency is a prerequisite for the consolidation of power; without a unified currency, there is no unified finance, a unified political map is difficult to achieve and a unified military force cannot be established. Whether it was the success of the Meiji Restoration in Japan or the failure of the Qing Dynasty's "foreign affairs movement", the unification of the currency was a key factor in success or failure. Both Mao Tse-tung and Chiang Kai-shek recognized the importance of a unified currency, which led to the National Bank of the Soviet Union and the Central Bank of Nanjing, both of whose primary responsibility was to hold the power to issue currency.

The most important difference between the Soviet currency and the French currency and the gold notes is who the monetary power actually serves. The Soviet currency serves the people, Chiang Kai-shek's currency serves the four major families; the Soviet currency grows in practice, Chiang Kai-shek's currency decays in the foreign theory; the Soviet currency is a public instrument of the regime, Chiang Kai-shek's currency is the private power of the four major families; the "Red Army ticket" 13 days of issuance and recovery, focusing on credit, the "golden circular ticket" 9 months to issue 34,000 times more, the purpose is to loot.

There is another important difference between the Soviet currency and Chiang Kai-shek's currency, and that is whether the currency can be issued independently. Soviet monetary independence, Chiang Kai-shek's currency to the nostrils; Soviet currency to eliminate the intervention of foreign capital forces, Chiang Kai-shek's currency has become the U.S., Britain and Japan powers hunting for the fat sheep; Soviet currency no foreign equalization fund of the dictates, Chiang Kai-shek's currency will be the central bank and foreign exchange management of the financial sovereignty of the surrender; Soviet currency no foreign advisory committee of the commentary, Chiang Kai-shek's currency is the British and American members of the direct approval power.

Another difference between the Soviet currency and Chiang Kai-shek's currency is whether it is based on the principle of practice. The builders of the Soviet currency had no profound monetary and financial theories, Chiang Kai-shek's monetary decision-making level was full of ink; the Soviet currency was full of flexibility and flexibility in dealing with the run-off, Chiang Kai-shek's currency in the foreign exchange market was completely crushed by the gold rush; the Soviet currency courageously tried to price standardization to stabilize prices and people's hearts, Chiang Kai-shek's currency was stuck in gold, silver and securities issuance preparation, but repeatedly deceived the people eventually led to vicious inflation.

Why did Chiang Kai-shek lose the currency war?

This is because his monetary power has only the welfare of a very few rich people in mind, defying and trampling on the interests of the poor majority, with the end result that his regime, along with his currency, can only be abandoned by the majority!

CHAPTER VIII

The birth of the renminbi

Why did the anti-Japanese base lose the right to issue currency before the "South Anhui Incident"? Why did the "price standard" North Sea Dollar succeed? Why is the yuan able to beat hyperinflation? Why must China pay off the Soviet Union's foreign debt as soon as possible?

As early as the anti-war period, the base began the financial innovation of issuing currency with "material reserves", this kind of currency in the complete absence of gold and silver foreign exchange as reserves, maintaining the stability of the currency and prices, which at that time the world generally used to issue currency with gold reserves, which was a world-renowned situation. The Chinese Communist Party's monetary practice is far more avant-garde than Western monetary theory. More importantly, the feeling of doing it with your own hands is not on the same level as the theoretical exploration on paper.

Zhang Yuyan, a renowned financial scholar, once commented on the monetary practices of the anti-Japanese base and the liberated areas:

> *"We are not surprised to find that, despite the differences in scale and complexity, the issues of dollar hegemony, euro creation and eurozone expansion, financial liberalization, currency wars, and the internationalization of the renminbi that people talk about today have been encountered, discussed, and beautifully handled by the former frontier governments, especially the bank governors. If one of the greatest challenges facing China today comes from the monetary and financial spheres, the wonderful history of the local Communists of a few decades ago, who were courageous enough to practice, accumulate experience, make use of laws and sum up scientifically, may tell us much. This includes in particular those such as the mint tax theory and the closely related 'circulation domain' theory and inflation theory."*

The emergence of the renminbi marks the complete unification of the Chinese currency. Apart from the subjective reasons for the effectiveness of the measures, the objective factors are that China's economy has achieved four major balances within a short period of time: a balanced budget, which broke the root of inflation; a balanced currency, which fixed the source of currency stability; a balanced supply and demand of goods, which took advantage of speculative forces; and a balanced foreign exchange, which stopped the path of currency panic.

The renminbi is not pegged to any foreign currency, which fundamentally eliminates the possibility of foreign capital forces getting into China's financial system. The fully independent and self-issued RMB firmly guards China's financial high frontier.

The Frontier's God of Fortune

On a winter night in early 1941, Nan Hanchen, deputy minister of the United Front Work Department of the CPC Central Committee, was walking hurriedly on his way to Yangjialing in Yan'an. An hour earlier, he had just received an urgent notice from Mao Zedong and had come in hot pursuit. Looking at the lights of the Yangjialing kiln in front of you, you feel extra warm in the cold night.

After a brief exchange of pleasantries, Mao Zedong gave a straightforward account of the difficult situation in the border area. From 1940 onwards, Japan intensified its surrender campaign against the Kuomintang, and there was constant friction between the Kuomintang government and the BALU and the New Fourth Army.

After that, the Chiang Kai-shek government cut off financial allocations and aid to the border areas. At the same time, a policy of "blockade" and "siege" has been adopted for the border areas, prohibiting goods from entering and leaving the border areas, claiming that "not even a pound of cotton or a foot of cloth can enter the border areas". And the frontier region has been experiencing severe disasters since 1940, resulting in 30 years of unprecedented agricultural decline. The border area is in extreme financial difficulty, it can be said that the military and political personnel have no food, clothing, cover, paper, to the point of poverty.

Mao Zedong said to Nan Hanchen, the situation is very serious, Jiang, the chairman of the committee does not give us a meal, we can not open the pot. But we can't jump off the cliff, we can't disband, we have to do it ourselves.

Faced with the economic woes of the border region, how could Mao have thought of Nan Hanchen?

It was because Nan Hanchen had a wealth of revolutionary experience and a wide range of contacts. In particular, in the early 1930s, when he was secretary-general of the Shaanxi provincial government, he assisted provincial chairman Yang Hucheng in rescuing Shaanxi from the economic crisis that followed the Great Drought, putting all aspects of Shaanxi in order and supporting government personnel and the 50,000 Northwest Army with financial revenues. The central government decided to make him the finance director of the Shaanxi-Ganning border area, to be "a clever daughter-in-law who can cook without rice", to solve the problem of the border area 40,000 to 50,000 military and political personnel to dress and eat.

Nan Hanchen was ordered to be the big steward of the border area in a crisis. South Hanchen's top priority is to find food, without food for the army not only can not fight, even survival is a problem. The situation was indeed quite serious, the Grain Bureau warehouse had been scraped to the ground and the administrator carefully picked up a grain of rice from the ground before gathering a pot and cooking a New Year's Eve meal for the chief from the centre.

After careful investigation, Nan Hanchen found the crux of the problem. At the beginning of the war of resistance, with the small size of the demobilized cadres and the army in the border areas and the high level of external assistance, the Government implemented a policy of rest and recuperation and benefiting the people, with little collection of food from farmers. But as the number of military and political personnel increased, the number of horses rose and the need for food grew, but the frontier governments were still reluctant to collect food from the people, which caused the difficult situation in 1941.

Nan Hanchen believed that if government finances always emphasized "benevolent rule" without taking into account the actual needs of the revolution, it would become "the benevolence of Xiang Gong of Song". The Chinese nation is at a critical juncture of life and death, the people of the border areas should make strong contributions and have money. In 1940, the Government needed 140,000 koku of food, but only 90,000 koku were collected, and the people found it unbearable to borrow food from the people twice and buy it once, because of the difference.

Nan Hanchen calculated a detailed account and concluded that under the policy of rest and recuperation, on the one hand, the burden on the peasants was very light; the 90,000 stone grain levied in 1940 was only about 6 percent of the annual production, while under the national government, the burden on the peasants in Sichuan was 10 times that of the border areas! On the other hand, farmers have food in their hands. He visited many of the farmers in the New Year's Day are wrapping dumplings, and before the Red Army arrived in northern Shaanxi, nine out of ten households without overnight food, compared to the situation is simply a world of difference.

After careful consideration, Nan Hanchen decided decisively to levy 200,000 stone of public grain and 26 million kilograms of public grass in 1941, and declared to the peasants that all the grain borrowed before would be returned and not borrowed again the following year.[146]

Subsequently, the Ministry of Finance took the initiative to organize a large number of cadets and staff of the Party School to go to the counties to explain to the masses that they must have an army in order to defend their country and that they must have military food in order to have an army. The border areas are the brightest and happiest areas of China, and the happiness of the people in the border areas was created and protected by the Communist army. The army has to protect the people and the people have to supply the army; without food, the army cannot survive.

Through propaganda, the collection of grain and grass work has been the understanding and support of the people, the collection of sufficient grain and grass to basically guarantee the supply of the border areas, so that the border areas overcame the imminent difficulties. Later, Nan Hanchen took into account the fact that after the Land Revolution, there was not much difference between the rich and the poor, and proposed a progressive tax system for agriculture based on the actual harvest of each household, so that most farmers would bear the

---

[146] *The First Central Bank Governor of the Founding Kingdom* – Nan Hanchen, Deng Jialong, China Finance Press, 2006, p. 57.

agricultural tax, more out of more, less out of less, fair and reasonable, and everyone contributed to the war of resistance.

The food problem has been alleviated, but daily necessities, such as cotton, are still in short supply and can only be brought in from outside the border areas, while the Kuomintang has imposed a blockade. Nan Hanchen pondered bitterly about countermeasures, thinking that the only way to break the blockade was to find the materials needed outside and through trade. Through research and study, he found that northern Shaanxi has three treasures: salt, fur and licorice, but licorice is light and takes up space and is a pain to carry; fur production is limited and the border areas are not enough for themselves. Thus, salt became the only option.

At that time, salt in northern Shaanxi had a unique advantage. Since the War of Resistance, sea salt was controlled by the Japanese and could not be transported over, while other nearby salt-producing areas saw their production decrease year by year. The salt-producing areas of northern Shaanxi have been rising in status as the main salt suppliers in the northwest. With strategic goods such as salt, the frontier zone occupies the high point of trade.

In order to solve the problems of backward technology, low production and poor distribution conditions of salt farms, the Border District Finance Department set up a special Salt Bureau, responsible for the production and transportation of salt. The Salt Bureau organizes the army to participate in salt production to increase production; it buys salt from both the army and the people at a reasonable price; it encourages the people to transport salt; salt transporters do not pay the public grain for their freight income, but also get a share of the profits from the sale of salt; the Ministry of Finance allocates funds to renovate the roads along which salt is transported and to set up inn along the way to solve the problems of food, shelter, water and grass on the roads. These measures have mobilized enthusiasm on all fronts, and the masses refuse to rest even on the first day of the Lunar New Year in order to transport salt for profit.

The KMT first intercepted the salt shipped out of the border areas, but then could not stop it. In response to the KMT's plot, the Bureau of Salt Affairs in the border areas has implemented a unified purchase and sale of salt from the salt shippers and waited for the right time before promoting it. When the Salt Bureau heard that the surrounding salt-producing areas had been occupied by the Japanese, it immediately doubled the price of salt, and the KMT authorities began to hold on to it, but soon the Salt Bureau got accurate information that the KMT authorities were nearing the end of their salt stocks, and waited for them to come to their door. After more than 20 days, Yan Xishan took the initiative to go to the door to buy, and a few days later, Xi'an Hu Zonan could not hold back.

In this way, the government's plan to transport salt was completed smoothly, powerfully breaking the Nationalist Party's blockade and guaranteeing the supply of supplies in the border areas.

In order to bridge the trade between the Border Zone and the Guotong Zone, Nan Hanchen also found Xi'an's gang leader. In his early years, Nan Hanchen joined the revolution, and in order to mobilize the masses, he used to make friends with the three sects, and his qualifications in the club were old. At this time, when he arrived in Xi'an, the local leading elder brother all had to respect Nan Hanchen and listen to his command. Through them, Nan Hanchen mobilized the gang members in Hu Zongnan's army to send the border district souvenirs to Xi'an for sale, and then to buy medicine, cloth and other much-needed supplies for the border district, solving the border district's burning need.

In addition to the possession of strategic goods and the opening of trade channels, Nan Hanchen and Zhu Liji, the Governor of the Border District Bank, proposed to issue the Border District currency independently, take control of the currency issuance and support trade and economic development with their own currency, which enabled the Border District to overcome financial difficulties.

The frontier deficit exceeded $5 million in 1941, and after more than a year of effort, a surplus of more than $10 million was achieved in 1942. Nan Hanchen, who has never studied economics, is relying on the experience gained in practice and research, successfully made a return to the border area "can cook without rice for the smart daughter-in-law", saving the border area economy.

The hard rebirth of frontier currencies

"The struggle on the economic front behind the enemy is by no means less acute than on the military front. Our monetary policy

> *is also an important weapon in the development of production and in the war against the enemy."*[147]
>
> —Deng Xiaoping

In the spring of 1939, Lin Boqu, Chairman of the Shaanxi-Ganning Border District Government, received a letter from Kong Xiangxi, Administrative Dean of the National Government and Minister of Finance, questioning the Border District Government about the issuance and forced circulation of French coins in the denomination of 1 yuan and Kuang Hua shop price coupons.

Lin Boqu replied:

> *"The credit of French currency is very high and the circulation is smooth in the Shaanxi, Gan and Ningxia border district government, but there is a shortage of small amounts of coins, which affects the price of goods and hinders the livelihood of the ordinary people. Upon the request of the local Chamber of Commerce and Farmers' Association to the border district government, the Guanghua Store was allowed to issue 2 cent, 5 cent and 10 cent vouchers. The circulation is limited to the Shaanxi-Ganning border area. Since its issuance, it has been well-prepared, has gained the faith of the people and has not been forced by the armed forces to exercise things. Your Excellency listened to the report and it was completely untrue."*[148]

At that time, the French currency issued by the National Government was the legal tender of the Boundary District, and as Lin Boqu said, French currency was highly creditworthy and circulated smoothly, while the Boundary District only issued small bills with a denomination of one yuan or less, the Guang Hua Shop Price Coupons, which were neither compulsory in the Boundary District nor circulated to the Guotong District.

After the Xi'an Incident, the Kuomintang, pressured by the unanimous demand of the people of the country to resist the war, formed a national united front with the Communist Party against Japan.

---

[147] *Economic Construction in the Taihang Region*, Deng Xiaoping, Liberation Daily, 1943.

[148] Selected government documents of the Shaanxi-Ganning Border District, Series 1, Shaanxi Provincial Archives, Shaanxi Provincial Academy of Social Sciences, Archives Press, May 1986 edition, p. 230.

The Communist Party's democratic government of workers, peasants and farmers was renamed the Shaanxi-Gangying-Ningbin District Government and became a special administrative region under the jurisdiction of the Kuomintang. The Red Army was reorganized as the Eight Roads Army and became part of the National Revolutionary Army, receiving military pay from the Kuomintang government.

The Kuomintang financed its nemesis, the Red Army, which had lost money, and had to be recovered elsewhere, and control of the financial system in the border areas became the best target. According to the agreement signed by the two parties on the absence of banks in the border region, the French currency issued by the Kuomintang was designated as the only legal currency in the border region, and the banks in the border region did not operate openly, but only acted as cashiers for the Government, received the salaries paid by the Kuomintang to the eight-route army, and maintained the circulation of French currency.

This way the border government loses the right to issue money!

Without the right to issue money, it's like a person who has no hematopoietic function of his own and relies solely on blood transfusions to keep his body functioning properly. The BNP can cut off the money supply at any time, leaving the border areas in an economic crisis.

The money-playing Kong Xiangxi can't understand the mystery. However, the French coins supplied by the Kuomintang to the border areas are all 1 yuan or more of the main coin, which is too large for daily life. There was a lack of coins in circulation in the border areas, and the people had to replace the coins with stamps. It was only in June 1938 that the Boundary District Government and the Kuomintang Government made repeated attempts in vain that they began to issue the cost of coin vouchers in the name of Kwang Hua Shop, a cooperative affiliated with the Boundary District Bank.

What annoyed and frightened Kong was not the small bills issued by Bianchi, but the fact that Bianchi was secretly issuing his own currency in an attempt to restore its hematopoietic function and to create its own system independent of the Kuomintang's legal tender. Kong Xiangxi knew how much it had cost them to unify the French currency and economically eliminate the warlords. Therefore, if the Communist Party should have any signs of issuing money independently, it must be vigorously prevented and investigated to the end.

Since Lin Boqu's reply was reasonable, and the local banks in the provinces under the KMT's jurisdiction had already issued small amounts of supplementary coins, Kong had no choice but to let the "Guang Hua voucher fiasco" go to its end.

From 1935 to 1939, the value of the French currency of the Chongqing government was relatively stable and inflation was moderate, but as the war continued, the material consumption was huge, foreign aid was hampered, and the fiscal deficit began to rise sharply. In order to fill the deficit hole, the Chongqing government can only start printing money and engaging in "quantitative easing", as a result of which the French currency began to depreciate sharply and the inflationary devil began to rise.

After the Southern Anhui Incident, the Kuomintang government completely stopped financial allocations and aid to the border areas and imposed a comprehensive economic blockade. At the same time, the Chongqing government activated its monetary weapons, shoving sharply devalued French currency into the border areas for food and souvenirs, and passing it on to inflation. As a result, prices in Yan'an skyrocketed, the original retail price of 0.1 yuan a box of cigarettes, into 100 yuan to 300 yuan a box; the original retail price of 0.05 yuan a box of matches, rose to 50 yuan to 100 yuan. The masses are complaining, the economy and trade are shrinking and the currency problem is unusually acute.

At that time, Nan Hanchen's countermeasure was to ban the circulation of French currency in the frontier zone in the first place, to keep the right to issue currency and trade pricing firmly in his own hands, and to have the frontier zone banks issue frontier currency. The proposal was highly controversial within the party, with some opponents arguing that the border areas were already short of goods, and that if the border currency were to be issued again, wouldn't that mean high prices and serious inflation? The two sides were at loggerheads, and in the end, the secretary of the central secretariat, Ren Pil-Shi, took a position on behalf of the central government in favor of Nam Hanchen's proposal. This decision fully reflects the strategic vision of the top leadership of the Communist Party, whose understanding of the overall financial situation is no worse than that of the plutocrat Kong Xiangxi. Inflation is only a temporary hardship, and allowing French currency to circulate in the periphery will only make the periphery a poisonous place where there will never be peace.

The issuance of the side coins restored the blood-forming function of the side area; the expulsion of the French coins also allowed the side area to detoxify its body and ensure the unimpeded flow of fresh blood. By squeezing French coins out of circulation, it frees up space for the entry of marginal coins and expands their circulation area.

In March 1941, the Governor of the Border District Bank, Zhu Liji, who had studied economics at Tsinghua University for two years, took office. On the basis of a lot of research and studies, Richard Zhu found that since the border areas are in economically backward areas, and have not actively developed their own economy through allocations and foreign aid in the past, there is little tax revenue, and it is impossible to make up for the fiscal deficit caused by the loss of foreign aid in a short period of time by raising taxes significantly. Therefore, the issuance of credit money is the only means to overcome the fiscal crisis and expand production.

The issuance of border coins and the abolition of French coins are two sides of the same coin, and the French coins that have been replaced can be used to purchase goods from the Nationalist Party's jurisdictions, which can be described as "killing two birds with one stone". It would ease inflationary pressures in the frontier zone and further control price increases in the frontier zone by selling off inputs from the State-run zone. As the border governments have the power to issue currency, they are no longer helpless in the "currency war" with the Nationalist Party.

Another dilemma facing Jürgen is the need to issue money to stimulate economic development without allowing the currency to flood the economy and spiral out of control the already acute inflation problem. How exactly should the relationship between the volume of currency issued and prices be handled? He recognized that, "If the circulation of commodities is assumed to be constant, and the circulation of paper money increases, prices must rise. By the same token, the amount of money in circulation in the market is assumed to be constant, and a decrease in the amount of goods in circulation must be followed by an increase in prices".[149]

---

[149] A Collection of Essays in Memory of Zhu Lizhi, edited by the Party History Research Office of the CPC Henan Provincial Committee, CPC Party History Press, 2007, p. 112.

Thus, Jules proposed a two-pronged approach to inflation:

> "On the one hand, lend more money to industry, agriculture and transportation to promote production; on the other hand, develop credit as much as possible and reduce currency issuance so that the marginal currency does not go into inflation."[150]

A moderately tight monetary policy based on guaranteeing supply and supporting economic development, with the main objective of stabilizing the value of the marginal currency.

From 1941 to 1942, the border banks reduced the proportion of government financial loans by 11%, redirecting some of the cuts to commercial trade and production construction, and the loans to support salt exports alone amounted to nearly 10 million yuan. At the same time, savings and government revenues from salt sales are used to raise money back, reduce the amount of money in circulation and control inflation.

The stability and credibility of the currencies of the frontier zone are dependent on the "external" trade of the frontier zone, the growth of which is closely linked to the problem of the "exchange rate" between the French frontier currencies.

Shortly after the establishment of the Frontier Bank, the Government intervened administratively in the ratio of the frontier currency to the French currency due to the low creditworthiness of the frontier currency and the limited circulation, which led to the emergence of a black market in "foreign exchange". Jules believes that the problem of the black market in "foreign exchange" cannot be solved by simply banning and combating it. "Because under today's foreign exchange policy, the bank's French currency is only out, not in, and the black market can never be avoided."[151] Jules saw the problem for what it was. The coexistence of French coins and the temporary inability of the coins to fully redeem French coins are inevitable. Rather than administrative repression, the market should lead.

---

[150] Inflation and governance in the initial period of currency issuance in the Shanxi-Ganning Border Region, Gao Qiang.

[151] Financial Thought and Contribution of Comrade Zhu Liji, Song Linfei.

At the end of 1941, the Government of the Frontier Region established a currency exchange, in which frontier and French coins are publicly listed and freely exchanged, and the banks of the Frontier Region regulate the price of frontier and French coins according to market supply and demand, adjusting the time and regional surplus and shortage, with the aim of eliminating the black market and stabilizing the value of frontier coins and financial trade in the Frontier Region.

The establishment of the currency exchange has greatly facilitated the exchange of frontier and French currencies and has promoted the development of import and export trade in the frontier regions, in particular the export of salt and souvenirs. It also plays an important role in stabilizing the ratio of frontier currencies to French currencies, enabling frontier banks to combat currency speculation through the platform of the clearing house. The effect of credit enhancement of a frontier currency is achieved by making the frontier currency rise steadily in value. The result is that more and more people are willing to use and hold frontier coins, and frontier coins are becoming more and more widely available, gradually gaining the upper hand in the monetary struggle against French money.

After a year and a half of efforts to control the amount of money issued, develop the economy and increase the supply of goods, in the second half of 1942, prices began to rise at a lower rate than the increase in money issued, and the ratio of the frontier currency to the French currency also rose, from 325:100 in July to 209:100 in December, the frontier region made a welcome achievement in the suppression of prices and financial stability, and the frontier region's own currency stood on its feet.

Zhang Yuyan, a renowned financial scholar, commented on the monetary and financial achievements of the Shaanxi-Ganning Border Region more than half a century ago.

> *"We were not surprised to find that, despite the differences in size and complexity, the issues that are talked about today, such as dollar hegemony, the creation of the euro and the expansion of the eurozone, financial liberalization, currency wars, and the internationalization of the yuan, were encountered, discussed, and beautifully dealt with by the erstwhile frontier governments, especially bank governors. If one of the greatest challenges facing China today comes from the monetary and financial spheres, the wonderful history of the local Communists of a few decades ago, who were courageous enough to practice,*

> accumulate experience, make use of laws and sum up scientifically, may tell us much. This includes in particular those such as the mint tax theory and the closely related 'circulation domain' theory and inflation theory."[152]

The same currency war was repeated two years later in the Shandong base.

The "price standard" of the Beihai currency: financial innovation in the Shandong base

In August 1945, one day after the victory in the Anti-Japanese War, an American journalist was interviewing a cadre of the 8th Luftwaffe in the Shandong base.

> **U.S. Correspondent:** How can the currency of the Shandong base, which has neither gold, silver nor foreign exchange for issuance, maintain currency and price stability? It's an incredible miracle!
> **Eight Road Army cadres:** We have materials for distribution. You have 40% gold reserves and we have 50% of our material reserves.
> (The American reporter looked at each other puzzled.)
> **Eight Road Army cadres:** for every 10,000 yuan of currency we issued, at least 5,000 yuan was used to buy important supplies such as grain, cotton, cotton cloth, peanuts, etc. If prices rise, we sell them back into the currency and flatten prices. Conversely, if prices fall, we issue more currency and acquire supplies. We use these necessities of life to prepare for the issuance of money, which is far superior to gold and silver which are too hungry to eat and too cold to clothe.
> (American journalists ponder as they take notes.)
> **The Eight Corps cadre:** After the realization of the paper currency system, the value of the money represented was determined by the amount of it in circulation. Circulation increases 10-fold, and prices rise 10-fold if all else being equal. The reason why French and counterfeit coins are so devalued is that they issue paper money indiscriminately. Our prices are relatively stable because we properly control the amount of money in circulation.

---

[152] *Practice and True Knowledge* – Reading "The Financial Treatise of Richard Zhu", Zhang Yuyan.

> **AMERICAN JOURNALIST**: *That's an interesting point, if you could elaborate on it.*
> *(It took four hours of comparison with the American journalist for the cadres of the Eight Corps to get him to understand this.)*
> **American Reporter**: *Do you think the United States can have such a monetary system?*
> **Eight Way Cadre**: *The US now holds 2/3 of the world's gold and can still achieve a gold standard.*[153]

The cadres of the Eight Roads Army did not expect that, 30 years later, the United States was also forced to abandon the gold standard and also to control the amount of money issued to stabilize prices, and thus made Friedman's monetarist doctrine into a Western epistemology. But his theory was decades behind the monetary practice of the Shandong base. At the time of the interview, Friedman was still a PhD student at the university, a "thorough Keynesian", and was still far from a theory of money.

At this time, the Chinese Communist Party's monetary practice was far more avant-garde than Western monetary theory. More importantly, the feeling of doing it with your own hands is not on the same level as the theoretical exploration on paper. This is just like an MBA professor in a university who talks about how enterprises should be managed, but his knowledge is so great that it cannot be compared with the management practice of Wang Yongqing or Li Ka-shing.

After the reform and opening up, the "Friedmans" were once regarded as gods, despising the great achievements they had created with monetary practice, and lost in the fascinating aura of Western theories of all kinds, completely departing from the supreme principle of "practice is the only test of truth", which is really deplorable! Since learning American monetary thinking, the real purchasing power of the renminbi has shrunk severely over the past 30 years, and the enviable "super-duper" million yuan household in the early 1980s has now become the standard for China's "low-benefit households".

The true identity of an American journalist: an economist.

Eight Road Army cadres: Xue Muxiao, primary school culture, "graduated" from the Shanghai Prison "University", director of the Shandong Province Bureau of Industry and Commerce and host of

---

[153] *Memoirs of Xue Muxiao*, by Xue Muxiao, Tianjin People's Press, 2006, p. 170.

monetary policy, one of the founders of the new Chinese monetary system.

What kind of currency did Xue Muxiao come up with that made American economists come all the way to China like they were exploring nuclear secrets?

Originally, the Shandong base began issuing "Beihai coins" as a complementary currency to the French currency in 1938, but due to the base's lack of experience in issuing paper money, the Beihai coins were initially less creditworthy than the French currency.

At the time, the French currency was pegged to the British pound and the US dollar and was very strong in the various regimes. Not only did the Japanese hold large amounts of French currency to ensure the stability of the local currency, but the Japanese regime also issued counterfeit coins in the fallen areas and redeemed them in exchange for foreign currency or goods.

After the outbreak of the Pacific War, Japan confiscated Anglo-American financial institutions in China and could no longer use French currency to hedge foreign exchange. So they changed their tactics and used French coins to send billions of French coins from the areas under Japanese control to the Kuomintang and anti-Japanese strongholds to buy supplies. In 1942 alone, hundreds of millions of dollars of French currency flowed into the Shandong base. This has not only resulted in the flow of large quantities of material to enemy-occupied areas, but also in the number of French currencies in the territories far exceeding the market demand, the purchasing power of French currencies decreasing dramatically, the North Sea currency associated with it depreciating rapidly and inflation increasing. This is the same as the massive influx of dollars into China today, which has led to the excessive development of the renminbi while at the same time "hedging" Chinese products, resources and raw materials, thus leading to a decline in the purchasing power of the renminbi and rising prices.

The result of rapid inflation is that food prices in 1943 were 25 times higher than in 1941 in a country that traditionally believes in "food for the people"!

In early 1943, Xue Muxiao happened to be passing through the Shandong base to Yan'an, and was "detained" by the base leaders to help the base in the currency struggle against the enemy.

The government at that time, unaware of the laws of money and prices, allowed both French and North Sea coins to circulate, but prohibited counterfeit coins issued by the Japanese government. On the black market in the fallen zone, counterfeit coins are higher than French coins. The French coin is higher than the North Sea coin according to the place. Shandong used administrative means to compress the ratio of French currency and announced that the North Sea currency would be exchanged for French currency at a ratio of 1:2, which did not work at all.

After a lot of research, Xue Muxiao proposed that the only way to stabilize the value of the North Sea currency and the price of the base is to expel the French currency, so that the North Sea currency becomes the only currency in circulation in the base, the exclusive right to issue currency. The solution was to use the North Sea currency to crowd out and collect French currency, and to use the collected French currency to procure supplies from enemy-occupied areas and use those supplies to support the North Sea currency. The government sells the goods when prices rise, and the currency comes back, and prices naturally fall.

This approach does work. After the expulsion of the franc, prices did fall, but new problems arose. Prices have fallen excessively because the amount of North Sea coins is not sufficient to meet the demand for market circulation. At this time, the local government did not know that it should issue more currency to stabilize prices, but instead dumped the goods to bring back the currency, and in time for the agricultural products acquisition season, farmers rushed to sell, and as a result, prices plunged. Although the Bureau of Commerce and Industry immediately deployed to issue additional currency, it missed the opportunity to acquire agricultural products due to the weakness of the banks in printing money. The result of all three is that prices have fallen by half from when the French currency stopped. By the time of the spring famine, the Government did not have enough agricultural products on hand to return the "late" increase in currency, which led to another sharp rise in prices.

Xue Muxiao and colleagues realize that in the rural economy, the seasonality of currency issuance and the existence of a certain objective law of prices: autumn and winter increase the issuance of currency to buy agricultural products, spring sell agricultural products back to the currency, so that prices are basically stable, and stable prices are the mark of monetary credit, is the measure of success of the monetary system. It is in such monetary practices that they have created monetary financial innovations that are prepared for issuance with materials!

Xue Muxiao later recalled this history:

> *"The currency issued by the banks had to be handed over to the newly established Bureau of Commerce and Industry at half price for the acquisition of various agricultural products, which could be consumed at any time to stabilize prices. The currency that we issue is not reserved in gold, silver or foreign exchange, it is reserved in materials. As prices go up and down, the Bureau of Commerce and Industry is ready to take in goods and regulate the amount of money in circulation in order to keep the value of money and prices stable. At that time, the capitalist countries were on a gold standard and inflation was not a problem. This knowledge of regularity that we have acquired from practice may be a new discovery in the history of monetary doctrine."*[154]

The monetary system is described as a "price standard", which means that

> *"our currency is not tied to gold or silver, nor to French or counterfeit money. Our local currency is tied to prices, using the price index (not an index of a particular commodity, but the aggregate of several important commodities) as our criterion for determining how high or low the currency is."*[155]

After completing the monetary struggle to "expel the French currency and stabilize prices", the local trade struggle began, and the local Chamber of Commerce and Industry became the main trader.

"Strategic goods" and the trade war

Just as South Hanchen used salt as a "strategic trade weapon" in the Shaanxi-Ganning border area, the Shandong Industrial and Commercial Bureau used sea salt and peanut oil, two strategic goods that were urgently needed in the rich and enemy-occupied areas, as the main weapons in the trade struggle.

---

[154] Ibid., p. 166.

[155] Ibid., p. 169.

In the past, the government did not have a unified body to manage sea salt, and the salt merchants sold the salt by hand, exploiting producers and consumers at both ends. Sea salt was monopolized by the Trade and Industry Bureau, which drove out the salt merchants who were exploited in the middle, and the salt shops of the Trade and Industry Bureau purchased it uniformly, while reducing the salt tax, encouraging the people to join the production and transportation of salt, and ensuring their reasonable income. The Bureau of Commerce and Industry has developed a special marketing strategy whereby the closer to the enemy-occupied areas, the higher the price of salt, which has increased by 50 per cent in the areas bordering the enemy areas. This tiered salt price was cleverly designed to ensure a low salt price in the core of the stronghold, which was beneficial to the daily life of the population, and to increase the cost of salt in the enemy-occupied areas significantly, thus maximizing the income of the stronghold.

Peanut oil is a necessity in the Shanghai market, which the Bureau of Industry and Commerce buys and sells to Shanghai as a private businessman in exchange for industrial supplies needed on the ground, including paper equipment for printing money and military supplies. The Japanese in Shanghai knew the source of the peanut oil well, but had to covertly protect it because the Shanghai market needed it.

As a result of the favourable trade policy of the Directorate of Commerce and Industry, which has introduced the monopoly of strategic goods, the foreign trade of the territory has been greatly exceeded, thus providing a strong guarantee of the exchange of commodities urgently needed for the return of the territory. In this way, the Bureau of Commerce and Industry has been able to control the value of the North Sea currency and price stability, and actively supported the currency struggle.

Whoever controls the strategic goods controls the monetary settlement of the trade. The French currency is stable when using the French currency settlement, French currency depreciation and then use the counterfeit currency settlement, counterfeit currency depreciation according to the local limited material transactions must be completed with the North Sea coin, so that the enemy-occupied businessmen have to hold a certain amount of North Sea coin, and later these businessmen also realize that the North Sea coin than the enemy-occupied area currency stability preservation, so very happy to hold, North Sea coin so deep into the enemy-occupied area and take root. The Shandong base has discovered that the North Sea currency, as a "foreign exchange reserve" of the enemy zone, will be able to effectively mobilize the resources of the enemy zone for my use, which is a disguised "mint tax" benefit, which is almost synchronized with the design of the United States dollar international currency strategy.

If the older generation of currency and trade mavens were still alive and well today, they would not hesitate to pull off a nice financial combo punch based on core strategic goods under Chinese control, such as rare earth resources. Want to use Chinese rare earths? This is possible, provided that the RMB is used for trade settlement, thereby increasing the demand for international reserves of the RMB and accelerating the process of RMB internationalization.

Through the practice of currency and trade, the Shandong stronghold has changed from resisting the defensive war of French currency and protecting supplies to the strategic counterattack of expanding the circulation of North Sea currency and buying supplies from enemy-occupied areas, greatly improving the stronghold's ability to fight the currency war, making great contributions to the stronghold's financial income, making the Shandong stronghold the most affluent area among the liberated areas, and laying a solid material foundation for the victory of the war against Japan and the liberation war.

Early in the liberation war, at a financial work conference, when Bo Yibo met Xue Muxiao, he said that the Kuomintang sent 700,000 troops to make a focused attack on Shandong, the main force of the New Fourth Army moved to Shandong, the burden on Shandong was heavy. How many discharged military and political personnel does Shandong have to bear? Xue Muxiao asked Bo Yibo to estimate it, and Bo Yibo guessed that there were about 700,000 people, and Xue Muxiao laughed and replied that there were 900,000! Bo Yibo was very surprised after listening, he did not expect the financial strength of the Shandong base to be so strong.[156]

Xue Muxiao's practice in the Shandong base accumulated valuable experience in currency issuance, which provided an important basis for the independence of the yuan from gold and silver issuance a few years later.

---

[156] Ibid., p. 177.

In 1948, the CPC began discussing the yuan issuance policy, and Xue Muxiao's views on monetary independence were greatly questioned. Many economists from Yan'an at the time believed that, since the base had no reserves of gold and silver and was not supported by strong currencies such as the dollar and the pound, it was impossible to keep prices stable if the link with the French currency was severed again.

Xue Muxiao, on the other hand, used the experience of Shandong to prove that the value of money is fundamentally determined by the purchasing power of money, and can completely get rid of the association with gold, silver and foreign exchange. More critically, once the linkage occurs, the economy of the base will be vulnerable to the enemy.

> "In some regions (such as Central China), although the French currency has not been discontinued in previous years, they are constantly changing the ratio between the local currency and the French currency in order to maintain the relative stability of the local currency and prices because of the constant depreciation of the French currency. But in Shandong and Jinghiru, the currency struggle was won by deactivating the French currency and establishing an independent and autonomous local currency market."[157]

At the end of 1948, on the basis of summing up the experience of the past currency struggles of the various localities, the Chinese Communist Party began to issue a unified currency, the renminbi. The renminbi has no gold content and affirms its disassociation from gold and silver, with the exchange rate based primarily on the real purchasing power of the currency.

At that time, the Kuomintang took away all the gold and silver in the treasury, and if the yuan was pegged to gold and silver, the acquisition of gold and silver would increase the currency issue and prices would rise, a similar situation had already happened to the Kuomintang during the currency reform. So the Communist Party froze the pricing of gold and silver at the same time as the yuan was being issued, making it below the rate of price increases and below

---

[157] Ibid., p. 181.

international gold and silver prices. This was the beginning of China's gold and silver regulatory policy in the decades that followed.

More importantly, the Communist Party learned the lesson of the historical loss of monetary sovereignty of the Ming and Qing dynasties and the Kuomintang governments because they could not grasp the supply of silver and did not link it to gold, silver and foreign exchange, freeing itself from the monetary, economic and political control of China by Western powers with strong gold and silver reserves.

The independent issuance of the renminbi from gold and silver was a realistic choice at the time to free China from the monetary control of the Western powers, reflecting the important principle of pragmatism. Today, with the renminbi tied to the dollar, the dollar has to depreciate for a long time due to its excessive debt burden, and when faced with the loss of world currency status, the strategic posture of the renminbi will be very unfavourable if the dollar chooses in the future to be re-linked to gold in an "improved version of the gold standard" in order to strengthen the credit of the dollar, as China's gold reserves are seriously low.

Whether the future of the renminbi will be pegged to the U.S. dollar, or whether it will stand on its own to create a new model of currency issuance, will be a major strategic question.

The Yuan was born

In July 1947, the People's Liberation Army (PLA) turned to a strategic counter-offensive, and the liberated areas of Jinsui, Jincha and Hebei, and Jin-Hebei and Lu-yenyu gradually became one. The different currencies originally used in the liberated areas are now flooding into the unified liberated area market. Thus, many "monetary troubles" arose. In a unified liberated area, going out hundreds or even dozens of miles away would require switching to another currency.

Dong Biwu, who was in charge of financial work in North China at the time, experienced such trouble firsthand. He set out from Yan'an and went to inspect the base of Jincha and Hebei. When he was hungry and thirsty on the way, he stopped with his wife and children to rest under a large acacia tree by the roadside. Having eaten all the dry food they brought with them, the guard ran to the small and medium-sized grocery store in the village to buy some burnt cakes and roasted sweet potatoes. Who knew that when it came time to pay, there was a problem.

The seller of the burnt cake took the money and looked at it, not knowing where it was, the guard had to explain that it was the border currency of the liberated area of Shaanxi-Ganning. The seller of the burnt cakes looked over and over with the money several times before finally returning it and saying,

> "No, we don't spend this money here!" It turns out that only the currency of the liberated areas of Jincha and Hebei is used locally, and no other money is used at all!

The guards were helpless, took the money to a nearby public institution store to change, the institution store salesman also did not give change, attitude resolutely replied:

> "Jincha Hebei region only recognize Jincha Hebei border coin, other money tickets are not recognized, I received your money is also for nothing, who can do that stupid thing?"

At this point, Dong Biwu's wife said to the guard, "You don't need to hurry! I carry a piece of fabric with me for the kids, just take it and trade it in with people! I think it's enough to trade this fabric for a few burritos!"[158] Dong Biwu, the patriarch of the revolution, was forced by the currency problem to trade cloth for burnt cakes to feed his hunger.

At that time, the financial systems in the liberated areas were fragmented, not only in terms of currency, but also in terms of mutual taxation and trade protection. Some liberated areas, in order to reduce their trade deficits, have even increased the prices of local specialties by denying entry to goods from other liberated areas.

The Shandong stronghold has the most "strong" Haiyan, with the strongest issue of Beihai currency; the second strongest issue of Hebei banknotes in Jinji, Hebei and Luheyuan; and the weakest issue of Northwest agricultural currency in the Northwest because of the greatest shortage of materials and the need for large imports. As a result, there was confusion over the Jin-Hebei-Yu boycott of Haiyan in Shandong and the seizure of coal ordered by Ji Zhong in the south.

In his report to the Central Authorities at the end of 1947, Dong Biwu seriously criticized "the construction of tariff barriers, the

---

[158] *The First Central Bank Governor of the Founding Kingdom* – Nan Hanchen, Deng Garong, China Finance Press, 2006, p. 252.

suppression and boycott of regional currency, commercial competition, mutual friction, and forgetfulness of the enemy".

The unification of the financial work in the liberated areas, the establishment of banks throughout the liberated areas and the issuance of a uniform currency for use throughout the country has become an urgent matter. If we don't unify the currency and wait for Beijing's liberation, all the armies with their own banknotes will pour into Beijing and use them, and the market will be in chaos.

In order to issue a unified currency, there are two options: one is to draw on the Soviet Union's monetary reform of 1947 and, after the end of the Second World War, to exchange the new currency for the old, with a differential exchange rate of 1:10, at which time the more old currency is held, the greater the devaluation, so as to seize the opportunity to deprive some people of their monetary wealth and reduce the amount of money in circulation, thereby achieving the goal of monetary stability.

In fact, when Chiang Kai-shek took over the fallen areas after the war, the French coins were exchanged for counterfeit coins at 1:200, and the Soviet Union exchanged old coins at 1:10 for new coins, all of which were plundering the wealth of the old coin holders. By the same token, if the United States forces the RMB to appreciate, relative to the international purchasing power of dollar assets remains unchanged, if the ratio of 1:7 dollar to RMB suddenly becomes 1:6, this is equivalent to the RMB "exchanging the old for the new", at the moment of appreciation, the RMB "new currency" "replaces" the "old currency" with a ratio of 6:7, the result will inevitably be the loss of wealth of the "old currency" holders! This is the reason why the appreciation of the yuan is a "nominal appreciation" of the external and a real depreciation of the internal purchasing power.

From the point of view of protecting the interests of the people, Nan Hanchen argued that it was not appropriate for China to imitate the monetary reform policy of the Soviet Union.

Another option would be to merge and simplify the currencies issued in the liberated areas before issuing new ones when prices and currencies stabilize. At the same time, given the negative impact of the Kuomintang's monetary reform, it is important for the people to understand that the Communist Party is implementing a unified currency, not monetary reform, which is completely different from what the Kuomintang is doing. The KMT's monetary reform is a means to plunder the people's wealth with more severe inflation, with the result that prices soar, people's grievances boil over, and the economy collapses. The unification of the currency is intended to simplify and consolidate the monetary system in the liberated areas and to promote economic development and the exchange of goods, in the sole interest of the people.

On 1 December 1948, the People's Bank of China was established in Shijiazhuang, Hebei Province, with Nan Hanchen as General Manager, and the People's Bank of China banknote "RMB" was issued from that date.

In order not to prejudice the interests of the people in the process of currency unification, the Government has adopted the policy of "fixed parity, mixed circulation, gradual recovery and responsibility to the end" and has gradually recovered the currency issued in the liberated areas.

The Government has set a reasonable rate of exchange between the yuan and the currency of the liberated areas, based on the price levels in the liberated areas, and has stopped the issuance of currency in the areas, requiring banks in the areas to gradually withdraw the currency in accordance with the prescribed rate of exchange. In this way, economic relations between previously fragmented regions were rapidly adjusted. The emergence of the yuan has greatly facilitated the market circulation.

In order to dispel the people's fears that the currency of the liberated areas in their hands would not be ready for exchange and could be scrapped, the Government has pledged to be responsible not only for the new currency of the People's Bank, but also for the old currency previously issued by all liberated area banks. Later, the Government was not only responsible for recovering the currency issued during the war of resistance and the war of liberation, but also for recovering the currency, promissory notes and public debt issued during the land revolution at a reasonable rate of exchange. The interests of the people are fully protected from loss, thus establishing the credit of the yuan in society.

On the eve of the founding of the People's Republic of China, the government, through banking, fiscal collection and trade repossession, gradually recovered the currency issued by the liberated areas in Guan, laying a solid foundation for China's monetary reunification and successfully avoiding the chaos of the liberated areas' currencies in the capital city.

In 1950, after the domestic economic situation stabilized, the recovery of the Northeast currency began. Gao Gang, who presided over the work of the Northeast, wanted to engage in independence, had instructed the Governor of the Northeast Bank to propose to retain the Northeast currency, Nan Hanchen face to face questioned Gao Gang is what the attempt, Gao Gang only had to give up.

Thus, for the first time since 1911, China has achieved true unification of the national currency. Over the past 40 years, China's "currency secession" problem has been completely eradicated.

In addition to the gradual reunification within the liberated areas, in order to ensure the circulation of the yuan, the Government, drawing on the experience of "detoxification" by expelling French currency from its territory, has adopted different "detoxification" measures for the gold circulars, foreign currency and gold and silver in the area of circulation of the yuan.

The first is the resolute purge of French currency and gold bullion, the culprits of hyperinflation, which must be resolutely purged to pave the way for the RMB to occupy the market.

The second is the introduction of foreign exchange management. The abolition of the right of foreign banks to issue currency, the prohibition of the circulation of foreign currency and the implementation of uniform foreign exchange management. Foreign exchange and foreign currency must be deposited with the Bank of China, the sale or transfer of which is prohibited and is operated by the State Bank.

Once again, the circulation of gold and silver is strictly prohibited. Hyperinflation has caused gold and silver to circulate in the market and become the main object of financial speculation and a major obstacle to the RMB's occupation of the market. The Government strictly prohibits the circulation of gold and silver, stipulates that the purchase, sale and exchange of gold and silver shall be carried out uniformly by the National Bank, and that private purchase, sale and valuation are illegal. The gold and silver in the hands of the people are collected at an appropriate price and gradually concentrated in the national banks for use as international reserves.

However, when the renminbi was first issued, it could only solve the problem of unifying the country's currency before it could solve the problem of monetary stability; in 1949, the year of full victory in the war of liberation, fiscal expenditures soared, and the deficit had to be covered by the issuance of large amounts of renminbi, making inflation inevitable. During the year, there were several instances of inflation of varying degrees.

Inflation and speculative forces are like the relationship between fire and wind, fire without wind is not enough, and fire by wind, wind to help fire, then inflation will immediately escalate! At the heart of the fight against inflation is the fight against speculative forces.

In Shanghai, China's economic center, the government and speculative forces are engaged in a massive price war. The government, in the throes of inflation, finally took care of the speculators and achieved the stability of the yuan and prices.

The Battle of the Silver Dollar

On June 10, 1949, the streets around the Securities Building on Hankou Road in Shanghai were filled with the sound of clattering and jangling, with many people in long shirts and large silver dollars in their hands, constantly banging on each other, attracting the attention of passers-by and constantly quoting the price of silver dollars. They are the "silver bulls" who sell silver dollars in Shanghai. The Securities Tower is the center of speculative trading in Shanghai, with thousands of large speculators and hawkers gathered inside and out. They maintain close contact with their branch locations in all corners of the city through thousands of phones, manipulating the price of the silver dollar.

At 10 a.m., more than a dozen large military trucks sped by and stopped at the entrance of the securities building, jumping off a battalion of PLA soldiers and surrounding the building with water. The plainclothes of the public security officers who had already been ambushed in the hall and at all entry and exit routes also showed their identities and ordered all personnel in the hall to be inspected on the spot.

A spacious office on the sixth floor held 50 telephones and walkie-talkies, with phone lines that ran densely through the door and along the ceiling to the inside like cobwebs. The phones are ringing one after the other, interspersed with code words for speculative chips, constantly contacting the Hong Kong and Macau market calls. A blackboard hung on the wall, densely plastered with slips of paper, sorted by gold, US dollars, and silver dollars, with the day's buy and sell prices written in white chalk water marker below. A middle-aged man in a suit with his hair down, smoking a cigar and calling frantically:

> "It's up pretty good today, it's tripled in 10 days! Don't worry, the communists can't do anything about us. The other day, they threw 100,000 yuan in cash to suppress our momentum, but they didn't even hear a word. This is the Great Shanghai, not Yan'an. We are fighting them for silver dollars, not guns. Just relax and enjoy your stay in Hong Kong. Haha."

The middle-aged speculator was so stunned that he didn't even notice that his burning cigar had fallen on his lap.

From 10 a.m. to 12 midnight, public security officers searched the various speculative shops and registered the names and belongings of all those who had blocked the building, and then ordered all personnel to assemble in the ground floor lobby to listen to the Government representatives. A total of 2,100 people were gathered in the hall and, with the exception of more than 200 who were detained on the spot and sent to the Municipal People's Court on the basis of a pre-determined list, the rest were released after education.

Raided the Securities Building and won in one fell swoop. The Public Security Bureau has also followed the trail and arrested a large number of rogue silver dollar traffickers. Since then, the sound of silver dollars has never been heard in Shanghai.

This was the first battle of the Communist Party to liberate Shanghai and reorganize the economy – the "Battle of the Silver Dollar". The battle was commanded by a native of Shanghai, Chen Yun, director of the Central Finance and Economic Commission.

In the 12 years from the beginning of the war against Japan in 1937 to 1949, the currency issued by the Kuomintang government increased 144.5 billion times and prices soared like wild horses. Items that can be bought for 100 French dollars, 2 cows in 1937, 1 fish in 1945, 1 egg in 1946, 1/3 box of matches in 1947, no longer buy a grain of rice in May 1949.

The National Government issued 100,000 yuan, 500,000 yuan, 5,000,000 yuan and 10,000,000 yuan denominations of Golden Duan in May 1949, causing prices to rise wildly, 12,000,000 yuan per catty of meat and 1,000,000 yuan per stick of dough... Some people described the depreciation of the Golden Duan, saying that eating the first bowl of rice was a price, and by the time the second bowl of rice was eaten, the price had already risen!

The price of rice is not the same as the price of rice if you run slow or fast. This was still the life of a college professor back in the day, not to mention ordinary people. Fei Xiaotong's "Vernacular China", published in the late 1940s, is very short. Later, someone asked Ferrell why not write more of such a good academic work. His answer was that because of inflation, one must write and publish, publish and get paid for the manuscript, and when paid for the manuscript, run to buy rice. The process must not be disrupted and kept as short as possible, and by the time a large section is written, the manuscript fee will be worthless.

The devaluation of the gold bullion created a psychology of distrust of paper money and people were willing to use and keep hard currency such as gold and silver. In 1948, the number of people involved in gold and silver speculation in Shanghai alone was over 500,000.

The frenzy of speculation exacerbated inflation and spread from the Nationalist-ruled areas to the liberated areas. The Communist Party, on the other hand, had to resort to the issuance of renminbi to meet the living expenses of 9 million military and political personnel because of the military expenses of the PLA of more than 5 million, plus the full acceptance of the civil servants left behind by the Chiang Kai-shek government. From 1948 onwards, the issuance of renminbi increased dozens or even hundreds of times, which made the inflation left by Chiang Kai-shek not only uncontrolled, but also more and more intense. Without a solution to the problem of speculation, there can be no economic stability and the fledgling regime is bound to be seriously threatened.

Mao recognized that for the regime to be stable, prices must first be stabilized, and to stabilize prices, speculative activities and forces centered in Shanghai must be combated. Therefore, it was decided to establish the Central Financial and Economic Commission (CFEC) to unify the management of national financial affairs, under the command of Chen Yun, who has extensive experience in financial work in Shaanxi, Gan and Ningxia border areas and the northeast, Nan Hanchen and Xue Muxiao are the elite soldiers of CFEC.

At the time, various forces at home and abroad believed that the Communist Party could not solve the economic problems. U.S. Secretary of State Acheson argues that no government since the 19th century has been able to solve the problem of Chinese people eating. The view of Shanghai's businessman Rong Yiren at the time was that the Communist Party could fight a war with 100 points in military terms, 80 points in political terms on a united front, and only 0 points in economic terms.

On May 27, the day of Shanghai's liberation, the government announced that the renminbi would be the unit of measure, and that the ratio of the renminbi to the gold vouchers would be 1:100,000, and that the gold vouchers could circulate until June 5. Since the gold coupons were like scrap paper in the hearts of the people, some even used them to paste walls, the recycling was quickly completed.

But the renminbi still does not enter the Shanghai market. Although the government has explicitly prohibited the free circulation of gold, silver and foreign currency in the market, citizens living in fear of inflation for a long time still have the mentality that preserving banknotes is worse than preserving physical objects. Taking advantage of this fear of paper money, speculators ignored government decrees and concentrated on speculating in silver dollars, with some even threatening, "The PLA can get into Shanghai, but not the yuan."

Under their manipulation, only 10 days after the liberation of Shanghai, the silver dollar rose nearly two times, and drove up the price of the whole, the rice and cotton as a necessity of life followed by 1 to 2 times. At this point, the four major private department stores in Shanghai began to price their products in silver dollars and refused to accept the yuan.

The renminbi issued by the People's Bank was issued in the morning and returned almost entirely to the People's Bank in the evening. The credibility of the yuan and the government is seriously challenged. Chen Yun realised that the main opponent of the yuan was not the weak gold yuan, but the strong silver yuan.

In response, the people's government had resorted to selling silver dollars to stabilize the market. But as soon as the 100,000 silver dollars were thrown out, they were all eaten by speculators, not only did not stabilize the market, but the speculative wind grew more and more intense. Shanghai was too powerful for liquidity and speculators to stabilize the market by selling, and there was a silver dollar speculative crisis when the Japanese occupied Shanghai in 1937. The Japanese, trying to combat speculation by market means, shipped five tons of gold from Tokyo and dropped it into the sea, to no avail.

On the eve of the liberation of Shanghai, Chiang Kai-shek transported 2.7 million taels of gold, 15 million silver dollars and 15 million U.S. dollars. When the People's Government took over the Central Bank, only about 6,000 taels of gold, 30,000 taels of silver and over 1.5 million silver dollars were left. It's a little tricky to use the silver dollar sell-off to keep black market prices down. And with at least 2 million silver dollars in the hands of Shanghai citizens, the government does not have an absolute advantage in combating silver dollar speculation. If it doesn't stop, it may also attract hot money from all over the country and even Hong Kong and Macau to besiege Shanghai.

After weighing the pros and cons, Chen Yun decisively used an iron fist to seize the stock exchange and severely punish the speculators. In less than a month, the frenzy was calmed down, the silver dollar was completely withdrawn from the market, and the yuan began to gain a foothold in Shanghai.

But the speculators could not take it so easily, and when the silver dollar speculation failed, they pressed all their money into gauze and grain, to fight the government over daily necessities.

The Battle of Cotton

> *Whoever can explain China's achievements in managing inflation in the early years of the country's existence is enough to win the Nobel Prize in Economics.*[159]
>
> —Friedman.

On October 1, 1949, Mao Zedong solemnly proclaimed from the Tiananmen Gate Tower, "The Chinese people are standing up!" Only half a month later, with Shanghai and Tianjin leading the way, prices in the country began to soar, and in November, prices had already risen

---

[159] The "old sea returnee" who does not look at foreign affairs, Yang Bin, China Urban and Rural Finance News, 17 March 2006.

twofold from the end of July! The people were bent by inflation before they could straighten their backs.

This situation was already expected by Chen Yun. On the one hand, the war is still going on and military spending is so huge that the government has to make up for it by increasing currency issuance. On the other hand, the speculators who were suppressed by Chen Yun's iron fist in the battle for the silver dollar were not willing to lose, and placed their bets on the daily necessities of the people. Their plan was that the Communists would be able to confiscate silver dollars, and would they be able to outlaw the trade in grain and gauze? If the people could not buy food, they would go to the Communist Party to make trouble, and then the Communist Party would have to go to the speculators to buy food and cotton.

Where do they know that Chen Yun long ago figured out the key to stabilizing prices, that is, the government has the quantity of the main materials, "the people's hearts are not in chaos, in the city center is food". The strategy to deal with speculators, on the one hand, than to hoard supplies, on the other hand, to take a cauldron of their sources of funds, which is austerity!

Speculators made the fatal mistake of Hu Xueyan back in the day when the hoarding side called the government, but to not hold the power of currency issuance is to seek death!

The Central Finance Commission has organized and centralized the large-scale movement of grain, cotton and cotton cloth throughout the country. Chen Yun sent Cao Jiu Ru, the backbone of the National Bank of the Soviet Union that year, to the northeast to move grain. He personally instructed Cao Jiu Ru to sit in Shenyang and send a cart of grain to Beijing every day and hoard it at the altar of heaven, and must let the grain traffickers see that the grain hoard is increasing every day, and that the country really has grain in its hands, so the price increase will not be worth the loss. He also instructed the Soviet trade chief Qian Zhiguang to go to Shanghai, Xi'an and Guangzhou to adjust the stock of gauze in each place for unified action.

At the same time, a number of measures were taken to tighten the monetary situation, including the collection of taxes and the issuance of public debt. The capitalists were also ordered to pay their workers on time and not to stop production to transfer funds to speculative activities. State units are also required to deposit cash in the National Bank and not in private banks. Strict financial regulation of private firms. The People's Bank has also introduced "discounted savings" to absorb social idle funds. In this way, society's capital is gradually being sucked dry, while speculators, still unaware, continue to buy food and gauze at high interest rates on borrowed funds.

As of November 13, the state can call no less than 5 billion pounds of grain, the state-run Chinese spinning company mastered cotton yarn and cotton cloth up to half of the country's production, the People's Bank absorbed 800 billion yuan of social guanxi, speculators have been deep in the siege and do not know themselves.

At this time, Chen Yun believed that the basic conditions for stabilizing prices were already in place, and laid down 12 gold medals, making the final arrangements for the Great War by making rules to focus on price targets, concentrating materials, and combating speculators.

Starting November 20, Shanghai, Beijing, Tianjin, Hankou and other major cities of state-owned trading companies began to ship. The speculators, at the first glance, released supplies, no matter what the price, swooped in and ate them. This time, the state-owned company, while selling the goods, is actually gradually raising the price to move closer to the black market price. What kind of medicine is sold in this gourd? Does the government want to use the price hike to arbitrage too? They did not expect that this was Chen Yun's "snake out of the hole" trick to entice speculators to take out all the funds in their hands.

Speculators, based on past experience, the tight commodities can go up several rounds a day, not only to cope with the interest on borrowing, but also to make huge profits. They also can't think much about the motives of the state-owned companies to raise prices, and eat into them frantically at all costs, while the money in their pockets is unwittingly sucked dry. When the banks can't get the money, they take out loan sharks and even go out of their way to pay a staggering 50% or even 100% interest every day!

On November 24, the overall price level reached 2.2 times that of the end of July, which is precisely the price target set by Chen Yun, and at this level, the amount of goods in the hands of the State is equal to the amount of money in circulation in the market, and the time has come for the government to concentrate its efforts on a general attack on speculators!

On November 25, meanwhile, everywhere, state-run trading companies began a general sell-off of gauze and kept lowering prices.

The speculators began to dare to pick up the slack and continue to eat in. But the state company's supplies came in all over the place, and the money in the hands of speculators was drained in a few strokes. This is when speculators realize that the big thing is not good, and hurry to "cut meat" to sell the high price of hoarded gauze in the hands. The more they throw, the more they lose, the cotton market quotations like an avalanche of general downward spiral.

After 10 consecutive days of government selling, prices of commodities such as grain and cotton plunged by a total of 30–40%. Many speculators can't take it anymore and have gone bankrupt, and speculators in Tianjin have jumped to their deaths. Dozens of private wholesalers in Shanghai closed down at once, and cotton speculators lost a total of more than 25 billion yuan.

Three months later, Chen Yun used the same tactics, in the food war, on the negative corner of stubborn speculators to give the final fatal blow, from then on the speculative forces fell apart, in the subsequent 50 years, never again formed the climate, until 2010's "garlic you hard", "beans you play", "ginger you army".

Since then, prices have been gradually stabilizing, and the super-inflation that has been rampant in China for over a decade has finally been tamed!

The speculators in Shanghai were defeated and left with nothing to lose, lamenting, "The Communist Party is so powerful, we can't beat that little guy from the Commercial Press (referring to Chen Yun)!" The only consolation was that they lost to a fellow Shanghai resident who was more finicky and able to navigate the market than they were.

The heavy blow to speculative capital has completely subdued the Shanghai businessmen. Rong Yiren said that in June, the silver dollar tide, the Chinese Communist Party is using political power to suppress, this food and cotton war and completely use economic power can be stabilized, gave Shanghai business community a lesson.

In this battle for food and cotton, the government was not only able to respond proactively, but also to achieve its intended objectives in a planned and systematic manner. Both the general price index and the prices of major commodities are at the expected levels. The inflation that Chiang Kai-shek could not solve, the price of goods that the

Americans thought impossible to quell, was achieved in one fell swoop by Chen Yun and his colleagues, after precise calculations and strict execution.

The famous financier Zhang Naiqi, who was then an advisor to the China Finance Committee, once admired Chen Yun's timing in countering speculative forces:

> "At that critical moment, intellectuals like us would inevitably fall ill with subjectivism. I used to repeatedly suggest at the time to get down early and put pressure on the market. However, the head of the financial work (Chen Yun) is as calm and determined as ever, believing that the time is not ripe to prepare more strength based on the comparison of the quantity of currency and the quantity of goods. In the meantime, it may be useful to retreat a few more steps from the market position in order to take the initiative and launch a counterattack. Hindsight actually tells us that this strategy was exactly right. The economic counterattack began in mid-November, to Wufu cloth, for example, the market on November 13 was 126,000 yuan per horse, compared with 55,000 yuan on October 31, has risen more than double. That is to say, if the counterattack is carried out half a month earlier, two rags will not be able to absorb the money back in the same way as one half a month later. For example, after the enemy has reached a terrain that is absolutely advantageous to me, one division of soldiers can use the strength of two divisions of soldiers, and you will be able to defeat the enemy with certainty."[160]

In 1948, Chen Cheng recommended Zhang Naiqi to Chiang Kai-shek to become the Minister of Finance to save the situation. Chiang Kai-shek sighed and said, "I was going to use Zhang Naiqi, but he's not for me!" It could be seen that Zhang Naiqi's level, and Chen Yun was the top of the masters.

Mao Zedong considered the victory of this price defense battle to be of great significance, "no less than the battle of Huaihai". Once, when Bo Yibo reported to Mao Zedong on his work and talked about Chen Yun, he said, "Comrade Chen Yun presided over the work of the Central Committee of Finance and Economics very powerfully, and always had the courage to do whatever he saw fit." Mao replied, "I

---

[160] Zhang Naiqi, First Volume, Zhang Lifan, Huaxia Publishing House, 1997, p. 621.

haven't seen it in the past." The first time I said that, I took the pen in my hand and wrote the word "can" on the paper. Bo Yibo asked: "Does this word 'can' you wrote refer to Zhuge Liang's use of Liu Bei's compliment to Xiangyang in his "Former Division Table": 'The General Xiangyang, Shujun, who is a good military man, was tried in the past, and the former Emperor called it 'can'. Mao Zedong nodded his head and said yes.[161]

Judging by the fact that Chen Yun commanded the whole grain-cotton battle, his combination of a genius economist's spot-on insight and a super trader's mastery of detail and market timing is the perfect combination of Friedman and Soros.

No wonder it was once said that those who won the Nobel Prize in economics were not on the same level as Chen Yun, Xue Muxiao, Nan Hanchen and so on, because they did not have the opportunity to actually test their theories in the world's most populous country. Friedman and Samuelson, among others, focused on the free market, and Stiglitz emphasized government program regulation. As early as in the early years of the founding of the country, Chen Yun put forward the guiding principle of "big plan, small freedom" in economic work, emphasizing both government regulation and control and paying attention to the free market.

If there were veterans like Chen Yun, Xue Muxiao, and Nan Hanchen, would there still be the problem of today's uncontrollable high prices in China?

RMB: currency for the people

At the end of 1954, the CPC Central Committee instructed that "the existing yuan had lost its usefulness in calculation and had a negative impact on the psychology of the people in the country in terms of international perception". To further improve and consolidate the monetary system in our country, to organize the circulation of money, reduce the denomination of bills and facilitate their calculation and use". The central government approved the issuance of the new

---

[161] Bo Yibo, He Lipo, the first Minister of Finance of the new China.

renminbi in 1955, which was rescheduled to March 1, taking into account that two months of the beginning of the year fell on holidays.

With the introduction of the new yuan, two major issues must be resolved: first, whether the yuan is pegged to gold; and second, how the old and new currencies will be converted.

At a time when the world has a universal currency with a gold content, Chen Yun advocates that the RMB is not pegged to gold and does not have a gold content.

Why was Chen Yun so thoughtful in setting up the RMB gold content? It also involves the loss of Soviet Foreign Minister Gromyko.

On 30 April 1951, on Stalin's own initiative, the Politburo of the Soviet Communist Party Central Committee took a decision to revoke a decision of 5 April drawn up by the National Bank of the USSR on the exchange rate between the rouble and the yuan. The Governor of the National Bank and the Minister of Finance were given a warning, and Foreign Minister Gromyko was demoted to the rank of British Ambassador because Gromyko had infuriated Stalin on the exchange rate issue.

At the beginning of the new China, Mao Zedong and Zhou Enlai went to Moscow to negotiate and sign the Treaty of Friendship and Mutual Assistance with Stalin and other Soviet leaders, which established the strategic alliance between China and the Soviet Union in a legal form. The most hotly contested issue between the two sides was the exchange rate between the ruble and the renminbi, which the Soviet government had carefully prepared for.

The Soviet Union does not, and does not want to, determine the ruble's ratio to the renminbi on the basis of a composite index of the prices of major products, in accordance with normal international practice, but instead takes the approach of raising the ruble to depress the renminbi. The Soviets first established with China that the ruble to yuan ratio was calculated through the dollar. Immediately after Mao Zedong negotiated the general framework of the treaty and left the Soviet Union, they announced an increase in the exchange rate of the ruble against all foreign currencies, including the United States dollar, which in one fell swoop increased the purchasing power of the ruble by 30 per cent, thus greatly increasing the difficulty of the exchange rate issue in the Sino-Soviet trade negotiations. The representative of the Chinese side was very dissatisfied and expressed a dissenting opinion on the matter. However, due to China's eagerness to acquire Soviet material and technology at that time, it had to make concessions and compromises and set the exchange rate of the two currencies under unequal conditions, setting the ruble to RMB ratio at 1 ruble to RMB 9500.

Since then, the Chinese side has been trying to find ways to change this exchange rate, adopting the same approach as the Soviet Union, "treating people the way they were treated". In February 1951, the Soviet Ambassador reported that the Chinese Government had reduced the United States dollar exchange rate four times in a row since the end of 1950, and that since the ruble to the renminbi exchange rate was expressed in United States dollars, the reduction in the dollar exchange rate led directly to a decline in the ruble to renminbi exchange rate, from 1 ruble to 5720 yuan. The report estimates that the exchange rate between the ruble and the renminbi, based on the dollar, is about 20 per cent lower than the exchange rate based on the official price of gold acquired by the People's Bank of China. Therefore, a lower exchange rate of the dollar in China automatically leads to a lower exchange rate of the ruble against the renminbi is an anomaly and is politically and economically detrimental to the Soviet Union, especially since the settlement between the Soviet Union and China in 1951 will grow further and the situation will be even more detrimental to the Soviet Union.

> *"The Soviet Embassy suggested that the Soviet Ministry of Finance and the National Bank of the USSR should negotiate with China in order to determine the ratio of the ruble to the renminbi in terms of the price of gold, and on 5 April the National Bank of the USSR prepared a document on the exchange rate of the ruble to the renminbi, the details of which are not known, but which, according to the recollection of Dobrynin, then Ambassador to the United States, was more favourable to China. When Deputy Foreign Minister Zorin presented the document to Acting Foreign Minister Gromyko for review, Gromyko, out of an abundance of caution, did not dare to take his own decision and, believing that the exchange rate was not a major problem and would not disturb Stalin, shelved the document. Later, the Chinese and Soviet embassies pressed again and Zorin supported it, so Gromyko approved the*

> document without consulting Stalin. Stalin was greatly annoyed when he learned of this."[162]

Gromyko apparently did not fully understand the profound intentions of the great leader Stalin and made a big mistake in one fell swoop.

When Stalin integrated the Eastern European countries into the "socialist family" of the Soviet Union, he had a strategy for controlling them economically. Since all the Eastern European countries insist on issuing their own independent currencies, it's time to work on the exchange rate. The Soviet Union produced gold, which at that time accounted for about 2/5 of the world's production, so it deliberately set the gold content of the ruble at a very high level, far exceeding the actual purchasing power of the ruble. Take advantage of the exchange rate by using self-serving gold as a criterion in assessing the exchange rate. The Eastern European countries cried out in private, but no one dared to confront the hard-line Stalin to his face.

In the Sino-Soviet negotiations, Stalin used the same method against China, which led to the sudden appreciation of the ruble against the dollar after Mao left the USSR. Stalin calculated that China would not be too tough on the exchange rate when it had a request from the Soviet Union.

How could Stalin have set up a setup that Gromyko, who had only diplomatic brains but not economic brains, not be outraged! Chen Yun understands that China has taken advantage of the exchange rate, and if the gold content of the yuan is made public, it becomes a target for the Soviet Union to demand a redefinition of the exchange rate.

If the RMB does not specify a gold content, what exactly is the value of the currency based on? Chen Yun believes that the purchasing power of pre-war French currency is used as a reference system to assess the value of money from the observation of social practice. Since the price of the French currency has remained stable since its introduction in 1936, and the market has responded well to its moderate value, the new renminbi should be roughly equivalent to the purchasing power of one French currency in that year. On this basis, the exchange rate between the old and the new RMB should be 1:10,000.

---

[162] On Soviet economic assistance to China from 1950 to 1953, Shen Zhihua.

As for the conversion of old and new RMB, China has adopted the principle of no-difference conversion, and all holders of RMB, whether deposits or cash, are converted in a uniform manner. The ultimate effect would be a reduction of four zeros across all monetary units, as would prices, equivalent to currency replacement, not monetary reform, with no significant change in social wealth.

The issuance of the new RMB went very smoothly. Within the first 10 days of issuance of the new currency, 80% of the old currency in circulation is recovered. On June 10, 1955, the exchange of old and new currency was basically completed, the market responded well, prices were basically stable, and the people actively supported it. In just 100 days, China has quietly replaced the old currency with the new one, completely eliminating the vestiges of inflation from the Kuomintang era. From then on, the RMB began a whole new journey.

Apart from the subjective reasons for the effectiveness of the measures, the objective factor is that China's economy has achieved four major equilibria within a short period of time: a balanced budget, which broke the root of inflation; a balanced currency cashier, which consolidated the source of currency stability; a balanced supply and demand of goods, which copied the bottom of speculative forces; and a balanced foreign exchange, which eliminated the path of currency fear.

Only by having a completely independent currency can we talk about economic, political and military independence!

After the Opium War, imperialism controlled China's history by financial means through China's bought-and-paid bureaucratic bourgeoisie, and Mao Zedong, Chen Yun and others knew better than anyone. Over the past hundred years or so, foreign capital, foreign buyers, and bureaucratic landlords have formed a vast network of interlocking interests, and no matter which warlord is in power or which government is in power, they have to rely on and borrow from this network. They have colluded with each other, sheltered each other and exploited the people together. It was only in 1949 that China eradicated this vast network of tumours, even digging three feet into the ground to ensure that there would never be a future.

The renminbi's refusal to be pegged to any foreign currency is an attempt to cut off the infiltration and control of China by foreign capital forces from its financial roots, with the aim of completely controlling China's financial high frontier, which is the supreme financial strategy of the Chinese Communist Party!

In the early years of its founding, China faced sanctions from Western countries, led by the United States, and had to turn to the Soviet Union for money and technology.

> *"According to Soviet statistics, from 1950 to 1961 the Soviet Union borrowed 14 times from China, amounting to 1,818 million roubles, which also included 200 million roubles of military borrowing for the Korean War, at 2 per cent interest. Throughout the war against the United States and North Korea, the Soviet Union has never stated that the arms provided by the Soviet Union were war loans, but has always claimed that they were compensation for China's military contributions to defend the interests of the socialist bloc, a responsibility that the Soviet Union should assume. However, this part of the arms was later added to China's debt with a high interest rate."*[163]

In order to get rid of the Soviet Union's financial control, China had to repay the Soviet Union's loans as soon as possible and, in the absence of a strong state at the time, tightened its belt and established an extremely strict state budget system, thus ensuring the independence of the yuan. By 1965, China had finally repaid the Soviet Union's loans in full. At the end of this year, Foreign Minister Chen Yi proudly declared in a meeting with Japanese journalists that "China has become a country without any foreign debt."

The history of the yuan is the history of serving the people, the history of independence, the history of practice making miracles!

---

[163] *The Rise and Fall of the Ming and Qing Dynasties in 500 Years: Who Wrote the History in Five Hundred Years*, by Han Yuk-hai, Kyushu Press, 2009.

CHAPTER IX

Financial High Frontiers and the Internationalization of the RMB

In today's world, the smoke of currency wars has not broken, and the war drums in the distance are far from stopping. In the future, as the "debt cancer" of the United States spread, the "dragon body" of the dollar "Zhou Tianzi" will be increasingly weakened, followed by a currency "Spring and Autumn Warring States" era. Currency wars will become a norm in the world economy.

The dilemma of the yuan is that the foreign exchange account has in fact essentially "dollarized" the yuan. At the heart of the problems, such as the exchange rate crisis and foreign exchange reserves, is the deviation in the positioning of the currency standard of the yuan. The supreme purpose of the RMB is to serve the people, which requires significant innovation in the issuance of the RMB, and "broad price parity" would be an alternative. With the dollar constantly depreciating, the manner in which foreign exchange reserves are held needs to be adjusted accordingly.

In order for the RMB to stand out and implement the internationalization strategy, it should be laid out as a whole under the strategy of high financial frontier. The internationalization of the renminbi is not simply a matter of releasing the currency overseas, where the renminbi appears is where the national interest lies and where the monetary authorities regulate the new frontier. The prerequisite for the yuan to go out of the country is: it can be released, it can be collected, it can be seen and it can be managed.

The currency standard, the central bank, the financial network, the exchange market, financial institutions and clearing centres together constitute a strategic system of financial high frontiers. The main purpose of this system is to ensure the intensity and efficiency of the mobilization of money against resources. From the source of money created by the central bank, until the final acceptance of money customer terminal; from the dense network of money flow, to the clearing center of settlement; from the trading market of financial instruments, to the rating system of credit assessment; from the soft financial legal system regulation, to the rigid financial infrastructure; from the huge financial institutions, to efficient industry associations; from complex financial products, to simple investment finance, financial high frontier protects the monetary blood from the heart of the central bank, to the financial capillaries and even the whole body economic cells of the complete and efficient circulatory system.

Currency wars: the reincarnation of history

The cover of the October 2010 issue of The Economist magazine in the United Kingdom, which featured the beacon of the world's "currency wars" as if a new world war had begun. The media of various countries in the world immediately followed up and reported the "state of battle" of the "currency war", and various dignitaries, economists, international organizations and high-end forums entered the "battlefield" one after another.

Over time, calls for the "siege" of the renminbi exchange rate have been rising and falling in the West, and the pressure of strong public opinion seems to be overwhelming, as if the renminbi does not significantly appreciate against the dollar, there will be no way out of the plight of world economic imbalance, the economic recovery of all countries will eventually be thwarted, a trade war will sweep the world, and the tragedy of the Great Depression of the 1930s will be repeated.

Some U.S. economists have even thrown out that the financial crisis in the U.S. is all caused by the yuan. The undervaluation of the renminbi has led to China's trade surplus is too large, the Chinese love to save rather than spend money and buy U.S. Treasuries, causing the United States to be hit by China's cheap "hot money", making the U.S. long-term interest rates are low, ultimately inducing asset bubbles and financial crisis.

Under the pretext of trade imbalance, the crackdown on China's currency as a breakthrough, and then create chaos in China's economy, tainting China's financial system and eventually controlling China's financial high frontier, which has been repeated in China's recent history.

By the time the British arrived in wealthy China in the 19th century, they had successfully conquered more than 20 countries on the African continent, had Commonwealth dependencies such as Australia and New Zealand in Oceania, controlled Canada, Guyana, Jamaica, the Bahamas in the Americas, and in Asia, ruled large swaths of land from India (including Pakistan), Malaysia (including Singapore) to Myanmar. Under the British Empire's strategic approach to global colonization, China was too weak to be conquered by force in the face of a great nation of 400 million people. Therefore, to conquer China, one must first conquer its currency. The collapse of the monetary system would lead to the collapse of the financial high frontier, which in turn would lead to the disintegration of the country's financial capacity, the paralysis of political power and the disintegration of military power before China could eventually be used as a source of revenue for its colonies. Thus, the opium trade and the opium war were waged on the grounds of trade inequality, with the main thrust being against China's silver currency. The opium trade had brilliantly completed the destruction of China's silver monetary system, resulting in a massive outflow of silver from China, a deflationary "silver is expensive and money is cheap" in the country, a depressed economy, shrinking production, untold suffering of the people, intensifying social conflicts, a serious deficit in trade all year round, the country's finances failing to make ends meet, and a heavy tax burden that forced the people to revolt. The internal and external wars forced the Qing Government to incur huge debts to the great powers, mortgaged the main source of revenue for the central treasury such as customs duties, salt taxes and cents, and lost the financial high point of the central bank, resulting in the pricing power of trade, the autonomy of the railways, shipping, textiles, iron and steel and other foreign movements, and the loss of the right to finance military operations such as "sea defense" and "defense of the territory", eventually plunging the whole country into a tragic situation of semi-colonial slaughter.

In the early 1930s, just as the national government was about to complete the "abolition of two yuan", the silver standard currency system, the "four banks and two bureaus" and the financial centralization of monetary unification, to regain the financial high frontier, the Americans resorted to the same old trick again to strike at China's silver currency. Roosevelt unilaterally announced a massive acquisition of world silver, claiming that by buying silver in the market, he hoped to drive up the price of silver and increase the purchasing power of silver-dominated countries such as China, in effect forcing

China's currency to appreciate in order to dump its surplus commodities and destabilize its currency. The U.S. silver action caused international silver prices to soar, attracted by the rise in international silver prices, a large amount of Chinese silver "was exported". China is not a major silver-producing country, originally used for minting coins still need to import, at this time China's metal currency like a torrent of water rushing by, in 1934 only three and a half months, silver outflow has reached 200 million yuan. The U.S. kept buying silver, and by 1934, the price of silver in the London silver market had risen to twice what it had been before! The result is unexpected, silver outflow, the Chinese currency "was appreciated", the foreign trade deficit is increasing, foreign goods flood the Chinese market, Chinese exports are increasingly difficult. Silver outflows also caused deflation, bank credit decreased, interest rates rose, at that time in Shanghai was almost as high as the interest rate could not borrow money. At the end of 1934, the price of silver fell sharply, and the price of Shanghai's rental sector fell by 90%! People's hearts are floating in the market, bank runs are widespread, and banks and money banks are failing. This eventually forced the National Government to abandon the silver standard and turn to the British pound and the United States dollar to issue French currency based on the foreign exchange rate. After the outbreak of the war of resistance, in order to maintain exchange rate stability, only the establishment of foreign exchange equalization fund, the central bank and foreign exchange management power was handed over to the United Kingdom and the United States, again lost the financial high frontier.

Will this time, by forcing the yuan to appreciate, the United States be able to solve its trade deficit and unemployment crisis? The root cause of the U.S. trade deficit lies in the fatal inherent flaw in the design of the international dollar system, which makes it impossible for the U.S. sovereign credit currency to assume the functions of a world currency in a stable manner over time. In fact, no sovereign credit currency can do that. The world currency mainly carries the transaction function of international trade, if the United States trade surplus for a long time, the United States will necessarily net exports of commodities, the world dollar will flow back to the United States. As a result, international trade would shrink due to the lack of a trading currency, and all economies would experience a recession. Likewise, the continued development of international trade objectively requires the U.S. to export currency and import goods, so the existence of a U.S.

trade deficit is inherently predetermined, and the difference lies only in the object of the trade deficit.

Thus, the appreciation of the renminbi is unlikely to change the structural problem of the U.S. trade deficit, only to shift the target of the deficit from China to India, Mexico or other countries.

The appreciation of the yuan is equally unlikely to solve the unemployment problem in the United States. If the renminbi were to appreciate by 200%, not 20%, it would never be possible for the United States to start producing toys, clothing, hardware and electrical appliances on its territory, because the average labor cost in the United States is more than 10 times that of China!

The US policy makers and financial strategists are of course well aware of this, and the strategic focus of the high pressure to force the appreciation of the yuan is never trade and employment!

If history is anything to go by, this action should be in line with historical examples: in 1840, the British Empire used the opium trade to attack the silver of the Qing government; in 1935, the United States used the "silver wave" to attack the French currency of the national government; and this time, the United States used trade and unemployment as a pretext to attack the Chinese yuan.

The RMB Dilemma

> *"Wrong economic thinking makes it difficult to see where one's interests belong. Therefore, what is more dangerous than the benefits is actually the ideas."*
>
> —Keynes

There have been significant changes in the current renminbi issuance mechanism from the early years of the statehood. The overriding principle of China's financial strategy at that time was independence and autonomy, neither pegged to the Soviet ruble nor to the U.S. dollar, nor to gold under Soviet and Western control. After 60 years, China's economy is increasingly integrated with the world economy, and against this backdrop, it is inevitable that the RMB issuance mechanism will be adjusted accordingly.

However, since 1994, the increasing share of foreign exchange in the base currency of the renminbi has led to an increasing domination of the renminbi by foreign currencies, especially the dollar. So far, the foreign exchange share has become the main way of generating the RMB base currency. The so-called foreign exchange accounted for, to put it plainly, is the issuance of renminbi collateralized by the United States dollar, and through the amplification effect of the banking system, the vast majority of the 70 trillion renminbi in circulation in China's "issuance reserves" are actually dollar assets. The dilemma now is that the yuan has been largely "dollarized".

Under today's credit-money system, the value of money depends on whether the person who created it keeps his or her word. And the current U.S. is facing the worst unemployment crisis since the Great Depression of the 1930s, unbearably high indebtedness, an 18% real unemployment rate, sharply devalued real estate, severely shrinking pension accounts, 79 million "baby boomers" retiring over the next decade or two (half the size of the employed population), soaring future government health care pension spending, an irresistible worsening of the fiscal deficit, and a continued rise in private national debt, all of which translate into an unprecedented rise in American defaults, and an unprecedented decline in the value of those white slips that created the dollar. Defaults can be direct and overt, or indirect and covert, and the second round of monetary "quantitative easing" being pursued by the United States falls into the latter category.

The essence of the dollar is a currency that is issued against a debt. Behind every dollar in circulation is someone's debt to the banking system, and this note is actually a receipt for a debt, so everyone who holds dollars is a creditor of the dollar debt.

When the United States started printing money under the "unbelievable" name of "quantitative easing", the Federal Reserve, through the purchase of United States treasury bonds and bonds and notes held by financial institutions to carry out large-scale "monetization" of the huge debt of the United States. "Quantitative easing" has two meanings: first, it is on a much larger scale than normal, thus achieving debt dilution; and second, the quality of "monetized" bonds is significantly reduced, such as those issued by the "two houses", which are already substantially bankrupt. In this way, the large amount of additional dollars issued has greatly diluted the "gold content" of the claims in the hands of the original holders of the dollar, and at the same time, the "asset toxins" in the newly issued dollars has greatly increased, and the "new dollar" from the "quantitative easing" after the financial tsunami in the United States in 2008 is a typical inferior currency, which is why the main reason why gold, an honest currency has soared from $700 per ounce at the time of the financial crisis in 2008 to the current $1400!

How can the global financial order not be disrupted when the "gold content" of such claims is greatly diluted and the "asset toxin" is greatly exceeded by the poor quality of the dollar flooding the world? How can countries sit back and watch the impact of the "poor quality toxic dollar"?

Since 2008, "bad and toxic dollars" have been pouring into China, and the Chinese banking system has been settling foreign trade and direct investment and other dollars coming into China as RMB, and then selling them to the People's Bank of China. And the renminbi issued against them is the receipt of these inferior dollar claims, which end up in the hands of a large number of renminbi holders. The "dollar virus" is "transmitted" to the yuan through currency circulation. On the face of it, the dollar reserve assets are owned by the Government, but the final receipts for these assets are in the hands of the renminbi holders, so the actual owners of these "poor quality toxic dollar" assets are the Chinese people, and the Government is merely "holding them on behalf".

At this point, the United States began to flex its muscles and strongly demand the appreciation of the yuan.

If China has $2 trillion in foreign exchange assets and the RMB is worth 8:1 to the US dollar, then RMB 16 trillion has been issued against these assets and the receipts for these "toxin-overweight" US dollar assets have flowed into the Chinese economy and are widely held by the public through the amplification of the banking system. What will happen if the yuan is forced to appreciate to 6:1 under pressure from the US? To make an analogy, if $2 trillion can be exchanged for 16 trillion loaves of bread in the international market, then every receipt before the yuan appreciates can be exchanged for one loaf of bread. Now that the price of bread has suddenly changed to 16 trillion loaves of bread with 12 trillion new receipts, it seems that the purchasing power of the new receipts has increased as a result of the appreciation, but in fact when one uses this relationship to exchange bread, one suddenly finds that after the first 12 trillion receipts have taken 16 trillion loaves of bread, there are still 4 trillion receipts that cannot be exchanged for anything. The moment the RMB appreciated, forcing 12 trillion "new" coins to equal 16 trillion "old" coins meant that the purchasing power of the "old" coins against the stock of assets plummeted. This is as much a deprivation of wealth for the holders of old coins as Chiang Kai-shek's 1:200 exchange for counterfeit coins in the fallen zone and the Soviet 1:10 exchange for old rubles.

To make matters worse, as a result of the dollar's indiscriminate distribution, which has led to an increase in international commodity prices, $2 trillion could previously buy 16 trillion loaves of bread, and if only 10 trillion loaves can now be bought, the result is that the real wealth that can be claimed by 16 trillion old receipts has fallen from 16 trillion loaves to 10 trillion loaves, meaning that the real purchasing power of pre-appreciation yuan holders has shrunk dramatically.

This is why the RMB is "nominally appreciating" externally, while its real purchasing power is depreciating internally. When the renminbi is issued against the U.S. dollar, the depreciation of the U.S. dollar is eventually transmitted to the renminbi holder.

While the public eye is drawn to topics such as the trade balance or exchange rate manipulation, what's really going on is a revaluation of all of China's stock assets over the past 30 years, as a result of the appreciation of the yuan. The appreciation of the nominal international purchasing power of the renminbi has been accompanied by the depreciation of the purchasing power of the renminbi against a large stock of assets. This process will clearly cause inflationary pressures within China, especially in the area of asset prices. Compounding the problem is the fact that $16 trillion in receipts are base currency, and when the banking system amplifies them, the total amount of credit entering China's economy is even greater, with predictable inflationary effects.

While the benefits of the nominal increase in international purchasing power resulting from the sharp appreciation of the yuan will only gradually become apparent over the next few years, along with imports and overseas investments, the loss of foreign exchange reserve assets and the pernicious effects of asset inflation induced by the revaluation of large domestic stockpiles of assets are immediate.

The core of the appreciation game is that while the nominal international purchasing power of the renminbi increases, the real purchasing power of the pre-appreciation stock of renminbi at home is reduced, thus effectively diluting the "gold content" of renminbi holders' claims against the US dollar. It is important to emphasize here that it is not the Chinese government that ultimately owns the U.S. debt, but the vast majority of renminbi holders, and therefore the last person to pay for the U.S. debt is the Chinese people.

Without any suspense, the appreciation of the yuan is bound to trigger a larger influx of hot money, which will further strengthen inflationary pressures. Referring to the serious asset bubble caused by the forced appreciation of the yen in 1985, and the crazy rise in real estate prices and stock market frenzy triggered by the 20 per cent rise in the exchange rate of the yuan since July 2005, it is not difficult to see that the effect of the United States forcing the yuan to appreciate significantly is to kill two birds with one stone, one is to significantly reduce the real liabilities of the United States to China and the other is to stimulate the asset price bubble in China. The faster the renminbi appreciates, the stronger the impulse of renminbi speculators to cash in on dollar assets. When the toxic debts of the United States carried by the "bad toxic dollar" are more or less digested around the world, China's asset bubble may grow to a vicious state that is difficult to save. At this point, the U.S. may suddenly raise interest rates sharply, raising the banner of fighting global inflation and bursting the asset bubbles of China and other countries in one fell swoop.

Time is a key variable in war, and currency wars even more so. The United States needs the immediate and significant appreciation of national currencies to use the energy of economic recovery in other countries to help it dilute and spread the bad debt attached to the "bad toxic dollar". How can such a selfish act of beggar-thy-neighbour not be resisted and resisted by the nations of the world!

If China's asset bubble is stimulated large enough, its burst will be large enough to produce an explosion equivalent. So, how to save China's economy?

The Greek-Irish sovereign credit crisis, which is taking place in the euro area, is a "model". The euro countries have ceded the power of monetary issuance to the ECB, which, note, is an institution that transcends the sovereign states of the European Union and is not accountable to the European Parliament, not to the voters of each country, not to mention to the governments, which will act according to their will. At this point, the ECB will have the power to kill or kill countries with sovereign credit crises by imposing a series of harsh conditions on fiscal taxes, national liabilities, budget size, pensions, health care, retirement insurance, etc., which it will force countries to implement, and if they do not agree, they will not get the euro currency!

When problems arise in China, it is likely that the International Monetary Fund (IMF), the future "world central bank", will step in. The terms of the rescue are imaginable on the heels of a "shared" currency issuance, a series of "impermissible" currency issuance conditions, "supervision" of China's "exchange rate" and fiscal tax policy implementation, in other words, the need to cede control of the financial high frontier.

This situation, which today seems similar to a sci-fi scenario, will always be just sci-fi if coped with properly.

Broad price standard: alternative to the yuan

The RMB's predicament stems from the misalignment of the currency standard, and the RMB should and must take China's economic development as its basic starting point, and neither the US dollar nor any foreign currency should have a drastic impact on the RMB's currency value. If, in the 1930s, the North Sea currency issued by the Shandong base could be used as a reserve for currency issuance and financial innovation, thus stabilizing prices, prospering the economy and greatly enhancing the economic strength of the base; if, in the 1950s, the issuance of the RMB could be completely avoided from being pegged to any foreign currency and the "price standard" was adopted, which also achieved a high degree of price stability and rapid economic recovery, then there is no reason why the RMB cannot be more innovative today and go down a path completely different from that of the United States and the West.

In the 1930s, the National Government's French currency adopted an "exchange rate standard" of the pound sterling and the United States dollar, thus losing the right to fix the currency, and the National Government's central bank could only "look up to the British and the United States" and had to reserve large amounts of the pound sterling and the United States dollar to ensure exchange rate stability, which proved to be an unworkable path.

The supreme principle of a country's monetary standard is to ensure "price stability" so as to serve the people's livelihood and the stable development of the economy. Of course, today's price stability is a far cry from the 1950s, when people's income from wages and social resources were poorly monetized and the prices that mattered to the population were mainly the basic price of food, oil and salt. In modern society, people's incomes and assets have risen dramatically, and people's concerns about prices have long ceased to be the prices of food and simple daily necessities, and have become more concerned with the prices of assets and social services such as health care, education and old age. The new major part of the money supply, however, does not go directly to the consumer market for frenzied purchases; it necessarily goes to the asset or social services sector, where the money would have been invested if not consumed.

A monetary system that takes into account the interests and well-being of the people at all times should adopt the stability of "broad prices" as the benchmark for currency issuance and the "broad price" standard of the yuan. Only when the masses of the people see that the prices of bread, milk, vegetables and pork today are roughly the same as they will be ten years from now, and that the prices of assets such as real estate, education, health care, pensions and social services are similarly essentially stable, will their interests be effectively guaranteed, and such a currency will surely win the full trust and genuine affection of the masses of the people.

"Broad prices" can be sampled by categories and subregions based on the prices of assets of most interest to the people (such as real estate, stocks, gold and silver, etc.), social services (medical care, education, old age, etc.) and daily life (such as the current CPI, etc.), with different weighting coefficients, which are regularly published by statistical offices. The central bank's monetary operations can be fine-tuned around this "broad price" index.

Only by addressing the principle of the RMB first can we talk about eradicating other problems.

One of the big problems created by the pegging of the yuan to the dollar is the huge foreign exchange reserves. In fact, there is no "law of the heavens" that requires foreign exchange reserves to be issued as collateral for RMB. By cutting off the direct relationship between foreign exchange and the issuance of renminbi, the issue of foreign exchange can be completely solved, which in turn requires the courage and daring of financial innovation.

If a "foreign exchange equalization fund" is set up, which will issue special "foreign exchange bonds" on national credit and raise RMB funds to replace the central bank's role as "buyer of last resort" of foreign exchange in China's banking market, it can block the channel of foreign exchange into the balance sheet of the central bank and eliminate the substantial increase in base currency investment just for the purpose of acquiring foreign exchange. At the same time, this "foreign exchange bonds" can also greatly enrich the variety of the bond market, for insurance companies, banks, funds and other institutions to provide new investment options.

The main responsibilities of the "Foreign Exchange Equalization Fund" include: market intervention in foreign exchange emergencies; adjustment and stabilization of the exchange rate in accordance with trade demand; and, as the largest concentration of foreign exchange, lending to institutions that demand foreign exchange, so long as the proceeds from lending exceed the cost of issuing "foreign exchange bonds", the Fund will naturally be profitable. The Fund itself does not make direct foreign exchange investments, which can be outsourced to CIC or other newly established foreign exchange investment institutions, or even conduct institutional tenders around the world; it only deals with foreign exchange investment management companies as a lender.

As for the central bank's share of foreign exchange already in existence, it can be resolved gradually in batches by means of asset swaps. For example, in order for the State to vigorously develop medical and health institutions and thoroughly improve the difficulty of access to medical care in China's cities and villages, the Ministry of Health can commission the Medical Fund to issue medical bonds to raise funds to vigorously develop medical and health institutions nationwide; similarly, the new bond types issued by the State, such as the National Innovation Bond, the Employment Promotion Bond, the SME Revitalization Bond, the Low-rent Housing Bond and the National Resource Reserve Bond, can be used to replace the central bank's foreign exchange assets in batches, and the foreign exchange gained can be used to import advanced medical equipment to help medical and health institutions, introduce technology patents to help innovation and employment, and introduce environmentally friendly and energy-saving technologies to improve the energy-saving and environmentally friendly quality of housing.

In addition, more foreign exchange assets, after being replaced by similar assets, do not necessarily have to go overseas to invest in financial assets, these foreign exchange can be used to buy back stakes in foreign companies that are very profitable in China. Since the reform and opening up, many foreign-owned enterprises have formed a strong monopoly in key industries that are the lifeblood of China's economy, which is by no means a blessing for China in the long run. Rather than investing in a foreign country where you are not familiar with, you should invest in a local foreign company that knows its roots, and there are no barriers to market environment, legal policy, or government regulation. The advantage of this is that these foreign-funded enterprises have already formed a market monopoly with high profits, and equity investment in them will have a higher probability of success, to put it bluntly, they will share power and profit, which not only guarantees the security of foreign exchange reserves investment, but also achieves the effect of monitoring the market monopoly of foreign-funded enterprises, as to whether these enterprises are willing to cede equity, this is the technique of commercial negotiations and government persuasion. Generally speaking, one can't twist one's arm, and as long as the government is determined to do it, there is no deal that cannot be made. If the timing, location, people and all the circumstances of the situation can not do a good job, then the foreign exchange reserves to invest in overseas equity and financial assets, the idea of the early to cancel, the domestic good assets are unstable, in the case of overseas away, can you buy good assets? A little brainstorming will tell you it's no good.

When the foreign exchange reserves are gradually replaced from the central bank's assets, the issuing reserves of the RMB will be gradually replaced from the increasingly depreciating dollar assets to China's key industries and the strong emerging productivity of people's livelihood, the RMB will be increasingly in line with China's own economic development, truly achieving the highest principle of the RMB to serve the people. Gradually reduce dependence on foreign currencies and achieve the independence of the issuance of the renminbi.

Important features of a good currency

Money is something that is both familiar and foreign to the average person. Familiarity is because people use money every day, unfamiliarity is because people don't understand how money comes to be. Simply put, money is a receipt for wealth, and it can only be issued with wealth as collateral. So what is wealth again? Wealth is the various goods and services that are created through people's work.

People give society the proceeds of their labour, and society gives them receipts of wealth as proof. The reason for the acceptance of such receipts is that people can use them to go to society when they need them to redeem the fruits of other people's labor that they need.

The receipt of such wealth constitutes the basic means of exchanging ownership of wealth in society. Thus, money determines the distribution and flow of wealth in society. If anyone can tinker with money, he will be able to change the ownership of wealth unnoticed, and to manipulate the value of money is to quietly transfer the wealth of society.

It is precisely because money is the central means of distributing wealth in society that the most central foundation of money is the moral principle of who it really serves. In Western monetary theory, the question of the moral principles of money is evaded, which is precisely the most inescapable problem of money.

Without the moral principle of money, there would be no basis for a just distribution of wealth in society. A society that lacks a just system of distribution is bound to condone the theft and even pillage of wealth. Few people realize that the root cause of widespread social injustice and divisions between rich and poor actually lies in immoral monetary principles.

On the basis of the moral principle of money, any good money must also meet the following conditions.

—The integrity of monetary sovereignty.

—Good monetary credit.

—High currency availability.

—Good currency stability.

—Easy access to currency.

—High currency acceptance.

Monetary sovereignty is the ability of a country to have complete control over its own monetary policy, over which other countries' currencies have no decisive influence, such as the pound sterling in the 19th century and the dollar in the 20th century, and over which other countries have essentially no say.

Monetary credit means that currency issuers never go back on their word and are trusted by the public. A counter-example is the "quantitative easing" of the United States dollar, which has been criticized by all countries, but which continues to be unconventional, with the indiscriminate issuance of dollars as a disguise for bad debts. And then there is Chiang Kai-shek's French coins and gold notes, which have failed to keep their word and repeatedly deceived the public, ultimately ending up in a fate of being completely abandoned, destroying the currency and losing the country.

The usability of money is reflected in its ability to buy the goods it needs, and a currency, no matter how much it claims to be worth, does not have the usability of money if it cannot buy the things it needs. If a consumer needs to buy oil, he can buy it in dollars, but not in yen. The less restrictive the currency is when buying goods, the more usable it is.

Currency stability is the ability of a currency to preserve its purchasing power, such as the pound and the dollar during the gold standard era, both of which were able to keep their purchasing power essentially stable for hundreds of years, with a pound in 1664 able to buy the same amount of beef 250 years later, and a dollar in 1800 able to buy essentially the same amount of bread by 1939, a good sign of purchasing power stability. In 1971, the dollar was decoupled from gold, and 39 years later, its purchasing power shrank considerably, with a dollar losing about 90 percent of its purchasing power.

Easy access to money is also important, and without adequate financial infrastructure, access to money will be relatively costly and time-consuming. If someone traveling overseas needs to get the RMB, it's basically impossible because not all banks have the RMB in storage and the time and cost to get it would be staggering.

The acceptability of money is, in essence, how large the currency's circulation area is and how wide the population is willing to accept it. Holding RMB in hand is not a big problem in Hong Kong, and it is still possible to walk in Southeast Asia, but in other places, it will be very difficult. This is particularly true in the area of international trade. Currency swaps are a good way to go, but there's a long way to go.

If the yuan is to become a world currency, the above issues must be taken seriously. To be sure, the gap remains wide. In addition to the fact that there is a huge gap between the strength of the currency and the international currency, another important factor is that China is very much lacking the mentality to become an international currency. This is evident in the exchange rate exchanges between China and the United States.

Lousy creditors and arrogant debtors

General Kim Il Nam of the National Defense University once made an impressive remark: "What does strategic deterrence mean? One, you have to be strong, two, you have to be determined to use that strength, and three, you have to convince your opponents that you dare to use your strength!"

The central purpose of war is the plundering of wealth, and monetary warfare is more "civilized" than traditional warfare in that it is achieved by means of the plundering of wealth without bloodshed. The only way to stop currency wars is to convince the party that started them that the costs of starting them outweigh the benefits of them.

On October 13, 2010, at the World Knowledge Forum in Seoul, South Korea, two world-class scholars, Paul Krugman and Neil Ferguson, engaged in a heated debate on whether the U.S. Treasury bond market can withstand a Chinese sell-off.

In Harvard professor Ferguson's view, the centerpiece of the Fed's upcoming second round of money printing is a larger monetization of debt, and the biggest hidden worry is that investors in U.S. Treasuries will lose confidence in them, triggering a sell-off.

Krugman, for his part, argues that the key to the second round of money-printing is to force savers to spend money to stimulate economic recovery, or they will have to suffer the consequences of eroding wealth. As for U.S. creditors such as China are not worth worrying about, and the U.S. fiscal deficit is not a problem, he argues that creditors are unlikely to abandon U.S. national debt. He even stressed that even as these countries sell off U.S. Treasuries, the Federal Reserve can take it all in stride.

While Ferguson expressed concern about the possibility of creditors dumping U.S. Treasuries, Krugman felt it didn't matter; did Krugman's optimism really hold up?

In the United States economic recovery did not reveal a clear danger signal, the sudden announcement of the "second round of quantitative monetary easing" policy really seems very abrupt, what is the reason for the United States to make such a serious shock to the global foreign exchange market choice?

The root cause is the collapse of credit expansion in the United States, where highly indebted American consumers and businesses have lost $13 trillion in wealth since the 2008 financial tsunami, with official unemployment rates approaching 10 per cent and real unemployment rates reaching 18 per cent. In 2009, US private sector credit contracted by $1.8 trillion.

If we liken the economy to a huge waterwheel, then credit expansion is the water that drives the economic gears. When credit expansion stagnates or even contracts, the turning of the economic gears stops or reverses. A positive turn of the economic gears creates wealth, and a reversal is like a meat grinder that devours wealth.

The private sector's credit expansion began to collapse, triggering panic in Bernanke, who himself was an expert on the Great Depression of the 1930s and had made it clear that he would never sit back and watch the "horrors" of deflation return. His long-standing vow was that if there was such a sign, his response would be to "borrow money, print money, spend money" and even scatter money from helicopters to get people to spend money and fight "horrible deflation" with "horrible inflation" to the point of earning him the nickname "Bernanke on a helicopter".

It was this logic that kept the U.S. economy growing in 2009, when U.S. private sector credit contracted and U.S. federal and local government indebtedness began to soar, with an expansion of $1.8 trillion that offset the private sector credit collapse. However, the current situation is that the stimulus for government credit expansion has largely been exhausted, the strength of the US economic recovery is at its end, and the violent expansion of government debt has not been effective in activating the restart of private sector credit expansion.

That's where the second round of money printing comes in. By monetizing the debt, the Fed is once again injecting credit expansion stimulants into the economy.

So, Krugman's confidence seems to make sense. Since the Federal Reserve is determined to print $600 billion to buy treasury bonds in full force, it should not be a major shock to the treasury bond market if China sells some of its bonds. But Ferguson's thinking is more long-term, the financing of about half of the size of U.S. Treasury bonds depends on foreign investors, while China holds nearly one-third of the world's foreign exchange reserves, China as one of the largest buyers of U.S. Treasury bonds, its enormous capital strength and psychological potential, will have a significant impact on the investment climate of the U.S. Treasury market. In the event of an unexpected event, China's behavior, and even psychological cues, have the potential to create an uncontrollable chain reaction that could trigger a disaster in the treasury bond market.

As of June 2010, the U.S. federal government's total debt has passed the $13 trillion mark. The U.S. national debt is now at 90 percent of GDP, and if it were to reach 150 percent of GDP, there would be a significant risk of hyperinflation. A report to Congress by the U.S. Treasury Department indicates that the size of the U.S. national debt could climb further to $19.6 trillion by 2015.

To be sure, if the United States were to add $6.6 trillion in national debt over the next five years, $3.3 trillion of that would have to be financed by foreign investors, and China, which holds nearly one-third of the world's total foreign exchange reserves, could be expected to contribute its share.

There is no need to imagine China selling US Treasuries, one only has to speculate about the consequences if China stops buying US Treasuries, that is, the US will have to rely on a third or even fourth round of money printing, and the scale will be larger than ever. If this second round of money printing has already hit the world's foreign exchange markets so hard that currency wars have been fought, can one imagine what the next one will look like? At that time, would anyone else be willing or brave enough to hold dollar assets?

Between China and the United States, a reversed creditor-debtor relationship has actually been formed, one that has rarely been seen in world history as distorted and deformed. The largest debtors impose a series of harsh conditions on the largest creditors, and are quick to threaten them with punishment.

The creditor's passivity was not due to a lack of strength, but rather a lack of determination to use that strength, at least not to convince the debtor of it.

In addition to the factors of the currency itself and its mentality, the establishment and improvement of the core financial infrastructure must be taken into account in the path of the RMB's internationalization.

Clearing centre: the "router" of the financial network

> "We have always envisioned that if you wanted to cripple the U.S. economy, you would first cripple its payment system, banks would revert to inefficient manual money transfer operations, commerce would revert to the primitive state of barter and debit, and the nation's level of economic activity would plummet like a free-falling stone... The Federal Reserve's electronic payment system transfers up to $4 trillion in currency and securities between banks and around the world every day... I doubt that the hijackers of 9/11 had in mind the power to substantially disrupt the financial (clearing and payment) system (the power)."[164]
>
> —Greenspan.

In the world of the Internet, the router is a central part of the free, orderly, accurate and efficient flow of information through the network. With millions of computers simultaneously sending and receiving information from each other, the flow of information would present complete chaos without the path guidance of a router.

The flow of money through the network nodes of finance also requires the "router" of the financial network, which is the clearing and payment system.

From the "transfer system" pioneered by the Ningbo Money Bank in the Qing Dynasty, to the "big exchange bank" system implemented by the Shanghai Money Industry Association, from the clearing system of the central bank, to the payment and settlement system of the Federal Funds Transfer System (Fedwire) in the United States, the "Global Interbank Financial Telecommunication Association" (SWIFT) and the "Pan-European Automatic Real-Time Gross Settlement Direct Transfer System" (TARGET) in Europe, from the Visa credit card to the bank card clearing center of China UnionPay, the flow of money for a moment is also inseparable from the operation of clearing and payment systems.

The key to the clearing system is that every transaction of funds will leave a trace here, if followed, through the current data mining technology, will be able to discover the laws of the money account, the

---

[164] *The Age of Turbulence*, Alan Greenspan, the Penguin Press, p. 2.

information of the account owner, and even consumption habits, and these information has a significant value.

Rothschild, who had presented Churchill in 1939 with an analysis of Germany's strategic materiel purchases, had pioneered an unorthodox but highly visionary way of thinking about the military through an analysis of the financial system. The Rothschild Family Bank branches in various countries collect a wide variety of financial transaction information, which contains key data on all types of purchases and transactions in Germany. All purchases of goods by the Nazi government, as long as they are transacted through the banking system, are under the control of the Rothschild family banking system. Rothschild's meticulous analysis of this financial data led to key information such as the scale of German purchases of military materiel and weaponry, concluding that the Nazis were carrying out military expansion plans. Churchill's war office applauded the young man's novel research ideas. It was this report that led to Rothschild's successful entry into the British Intelligence V Bureau, Part B, in 1940, primarily for commercial counterintelligence work.[165]

It was using bank transaction records and clearing data in the bank network, as well as relevant information from the owners of trading accounts, that the Law family analyzed and researched and estimated the time and scale of Germany's preparation for war.

The power of financial "data mining" was actually proven 70 years ago, and when combined with today's supercomputers and large, complex data mining software technology, the traces of financial activity left behind by clearing centers will reveal even more secrets behind the money.

That's where Visa and China UnionPay compete for clearing rights! It's never just a matter of business profits, it's a matter of core national financial secrets!

Within China, foreign credit cards are prohibited by Chinese law from building their own payment and clearing systems, so there is no way to keep the core financial data of customers in China confidential. Such legal provisions, of course, make Whisky companies furious. But

---

[165] *Currency Wars: 2 Jinquan Tiandi*, edited by Song Hongbing, China United Press, 2009.

if they are allowed to go deep into China to issue hundreds of millions of credit cards and build their own clearing system, the money will be made small, and the key is that data will be available on every credit card transaction for hundreds of millions of people in China, and the consequences will be unthinkable. Imagine that with every swipe you make, your bank account, the store where you buy the item, the amount of the transaction, the time of the transaction, and so on, all of your transactions are being watched dead in the eyes of others. The other side then collect your bank account information, real estate information, stock trading information through other channels, when this information is powerful data mining tools splicing and analysis, hundreds of millions of people's financial property secrets will be mastered, even what brand of wine you love to drink, smoke what brand of cigarettes, drive what model of car, wear what brand of clothing, favorite places to travel, like which airlines and other information will be leaked. In a word, what a life it would be like to have all the details of your life potentially scrutinized and analyzed! As small as personal privacy, as big as state secrets, or the business activities of enterprises can not withstand such "mining" and "analysis". The economic and strategic value of this data may be more valuable than the secrecy of strategic nuclear weapons!

Currently, the battle between Visa and UnionPay is focused on whose clearinghouse customers with dual cards actually go to in their overseas transactions. If you go through the Visa clearing channel, the transaction details of all cardholders will be captured by Visa's data clearing network and deposited in a huge data centre "on demand".

If the Chinese military does not dare to rely on the U.S. GPS satellite positioning system or Europe's Galileo system to navigate and locate its own missiles in the event of war, who can guarantee that in the event of war or financial gaming, the financial transaction data of Chinese customers will not be used for other purposes by clearing centers in Europe and America?

The construction of a financial high frontier must include the establishment of an independent and autonomous global financial clearing and payment system, just as China independently developed its own Beidou system. Without its own financial "router", when China's money flows beyond its borders, there is no reliable guarantee of information security, let alone the hidden and suddenness of funds in the commercial war. In fact, many domestic financial institutions have been defeated in bets and fights in foreign financial markets, and should be considered from the perspective of whether there is a possibility of leakage of funds in the course of offshore flows.

The internationalization of the renminbi by no means means means means that everything will be fine if the renminbi is released, and the "extracorporeal circulation" of the currency needs to strengthen the regulation of funds. The United States has a very strong ability to monitor international financial transactions, no matter what country, no matter whose account is used, no matter what time, as long as there are any funds in bank accounts with hostile countries of the United States, as long as it is not a cash transaction, it can hardly escape the "eyes of the United States"! It is through its control of the global clearing system that the United States has opened this "legal eye". Imagine what State and commercial secrets could not be uncovered if this "eye" was not only on the bank accounts of terrorist States, but was interested in monitoring the bank accounts of certain States or companies? At the time of the 1997 Asian financial crisis, Mahathir had complained that no one knew where the hedge fund money was coming from and how the offensive against Asian currencies was being launched. That is invisible to Malaysia. How can the "eyes of the law" of the United States not see?

How can this war be fought if the world clearing system is not mastered, and in the event of a currency war, the other side, supported by the clearing system, as if by spy satellites, will be able to see clearly the full arrangement of its troops?

If the yuan goes out of the country, if the clearing centre is not mastered, it will become "released, invisible and unmanageable", and the problem will be troublesome. Also during the Asian financial turmoil, Thailand's baht and Hong Kong's Hong Kong dollar were both freely convertible currencies, the difference being that the baht was heavily scattered across Southeast Asian countries, while Hong Kong's currency was concentrated only in Hong Kong. When Soros began to quietly collect the baht in Southeast Asia, the Central Bank of Thailand went unnoticed and finally Soros launched a sudden and powerful offensive and the baht quickly lost.

In Hong Kong, Soros is ready to do the same thing again. When he collected a large amount of Hong Kong currency, he was soon discovered by the HKMA, which turned the sneak attack into a strong attack. The HKMA used the tactic of substantially raising the overnight lending rate, which greatly increased the cost of the Soros attack on the

Hong Kong dollar, and finally forced back the financial predator and preserved the Hong Kong dollar. One important difference between the Thai baht and the Hong Kong dollar is that Thailand was caught off guard by not being able to monitor the movements of the baht circulating abroad, while the Hong Kong dollar is concentrated in Hong Kong, which is well within the authority of the authorities and difficult for financial predators to sneak up on.

The currency standard, the central bank, the financial network, the exchange market, financial institutions and clearing centres together constitute a strategic system of financial high frontiers. Under this system, from the moment money is created by central banks, to the moment it enters the global financial network, flows through the world's clearing houses, is present in international markets, changes hands between the accounts of national financial institutions, and eventually flows back to central banks, each link in this monetary cycle must be under close protection and monitoring. The governing body of the currency must have a clear idea of what state the currency is in in the course of the international grand cycle, who is the ultimate demander of the currency, how he intends to use it, through what channels and in what manner he is using it, whether these transactions fit into the normal sphere of business, who his counterparties are, and other important information.

If the RMB is to go global, it is imperative to establish an independent, strong, efficient and secure global RMB clearing system, while at the same time strongly supporting the global expansion of UnionPay cards.

The Global Financial Network of the RMB

> "Throughout the 19th century, Jewish bankers, starting in Germany, quickly pounced on the world, forming a Jewish financial conglomerate with the Rothschild family at its core, These families formed a group warfare posture, with each other's horns, intermarriage and interlocking interests, gradually forming a vast and dense financial network, which was increasingly difficult for outsiders to break into."[166]

---

[166] Source: Ibid.

Clearly, China has lost the best historical opportunity to build a financial network that spans the globe. Although China's state-owned banks rank among the world's financial institutions in terms of market capitalization, China's banks have few international branches. Without a global financial network, it is impossible to build a financial circulation system that connects the central banks that create the RMB with the aorta and capillaries of the end customers that use the RMB.

The internationalization of the RMB is not just a matter of scholars sitting around talking about it, it is simply a matter of national central banks increasing their RMB reserves or using the RMB for trade settlement. This is far from achieving control over the channels of RMB circulation, as the end-users of the RMB cannot be reached and have to rely on financial networks that are already firmly controlled by international financial groups.

What makes China free to use the resources of online channels that international bankers have spent nearly 300 years fighting through the financial markets to create? There is a channel fee to enter someone else's channel. Whenever there is money flowing through the network, it has to be paid for and will continue to be paid for generations to come. If China's financial high frontier strategy does not reach out to the world, control of the renminbi circulation domain remains in the hands of others.

Who holds the world's channels of credit and capital flows, who is the real game changer! Channel is king in the financial market is even more bloody truth.

China's state-owned banks are finding it more difficult to go abroad to build global financial networks. An insertion in the established world financial network would inevitably come under siege from vested interests. Governments, under pressure from these groups, are bound to resort to various means of restraint, prevention, delay and so on to prevent China from building a global financial network. The economic stakes are enormous, but also the core interests of the financial strategy are at stake. Western agitators of free trade and open markets will be "in for a treat" in this key area.

Currently, there are two models for state-owned banks to build global networks, one is the Bank of China model and the other is the ICBC model. Using its long history, particularly its nearly century-long accumulation of international business, Bank of China has more than 30 branches worldwide, many of which existed before 1949.

Nevertheless, efforts by Chinese banks to open more branches in other countries in recent years have not been so smooth, because the world's financial resources have long since completed the era of "horse racing", and those who come after will not be easy to share this big pie. But the advantage of the Chinese banking model is the ability to have complete control over branch operations, and such network nodes can be trusted 100 percent. ICBC's model is to merge banks from other countries abroad, for example, the acquisition of Standard Bank of South Africa can be a successful model. In recent years, ICBC has significantly expanded the number of overseas branches through overseas mergers and acquisitions, with a strong tendency to dominate and overwhelm Chinese banks. This model has the advantage of being "fast". Its problem is how to effectively integrate the resources of the local bank for my use, which includes corporate culture, personnel arrangements, debt settlement, adaptation to local laws and regulations, etc. As for the future of the two models, it is still difficult to judge the merits and demerits, which will take time to test.

From the development history of world finance, the first thing that finance serves is trade, and the financing and exchange of trade has become an important way of financial expansion. HSBC was established in China to have a colonial "Bank of England", to provide financial services for foreign banks to trade in China, and in fact to exercise the powers of a central bank.

Today's Chinese goods have long been sold to all corners of the world, and China is a world-class superpower in the scale of foreign trade, but China's financial institutions have yet to keep up with the pace of international trade. While Chinese goods are on the shelves of countries around the world, Chinese financial institutions are still far away in China. In the process of global expansion, Chinese trading companies and all kinds of enterprises have almost no access to local financial services from domestic financial institutions, they have to rely on local banks or multinational banks to manage all financial services, exchange, credit, deposits and other huge profits have fallen into the pockets of others. In terms of the total scale of China's imports and exports, the huge scale of financing and the profit opportunities involved are indeed a "must-contend place" for financial players.

Another more realistic development path for large state-owned financial institutions is to follow the model of Japanese integrated trading houses. In Japan's general trading companies, financial institutions such as banks and insurance companies and industrial companies maintain a close open-space synergistic battle posture, bundling in and rolling development. China should follow the principle of reciprocal openness, and all countries with financial institutions in China must be open to Chinese financial institutions, which can start with financing for Chinese enterprises and trading companies overseas and gradually penetrate into local economic activities.

Given the speed and efficiency with which this strategy is being pursued, it is feared that the task of establishing a global financial network will not be effective in the short term.

In addition to the model of the regular army, the guerrillas are also playing a partisan game, developing financial networks on the ground "behind enemy lines", in order to break the current financial network impasse.

One of China's great strengths is the global community of Chinese businessmen who have taken Chinese goods to all corners of the world. Encouraging and supporting local people to establish various financial institutions, providing them with credit support, and using their trade channels to establish financial channels has the same significance as when the Shanxi Ticketing Company was born from the Shanxi Commercial Company. Since these trading companies have been operating locally for a long time, are familiar with the business environment, and have a solid customer base, many of them have the possibility of transforming into financial institutions, like the big boss of the Shanxi Rishengchang Ticketing Company, Lei Lütai. Just as in foreign businesses, Jews open banks, Koreans open shopping malls, Chinese open restaurants, the entrepreneurial crowd can often produce a convergence effect, once a person succeeds, will immediately form a demonstration effect. Can you be sure that the Chinese do not have the talent to create local financial institutions? With the right financial support, these entrepreneurs are likely to create a new financial network model and become the contemporary "Shanxi Ticket", and be able to "connect the world".

Ultimately, these financial networks will provide a variety of financial services to Chinese businesses and locals in the country and will be subject to financial regulation in the country where they are located. They can offer mortgages, trade remittances, deposit money and other intermediate business to locals. China's financial institutions maintain credit relationships with them, both to nurture these vast networks of financial tentacles overseas and to extend financial operations, and to make the domestic headache of foreign exchange reserves more effective.

Since five revolutionaries, such as Mao Zemin, who had only a primary school education and no financial experience at all, were able to create such an incredible miracle as the Red Central Bank, today, among the Chinese businessmen all over the world, there are both international students with doctorates and experience in large financial institutions, as well as many hardworking and hard-working entrepreneurs who started their business from scratch, the organic combination of the two may create a new group – a large group of overseas Chinese bankers that has never been seen before.

The spread of this model could help China build its own RMB circulation network and extend such financial tentacles to any corner of the world.

As China's surplus capital begins to expand globally for lack of investment opportunities at home, huge and hungry capital will be searching the world for mines, forests, farms, water resources, patented technologies, factories, research institutes or medical high technology, and large numbers of local Chinese bankers will become a great treasure trove of human resources.

The reason why China's table tennis is so dominant is because hundreds of millions of Chinese are involved in this torrent. As the new high frontier for China's future development, the emergence of a large number of entrepreneurs will be an essential link. It may be too hard to open a bank in China, but it's relatively easy overseas. In the field of financial entrepreneurship, Jews are Chinese role models. Who says that only Jews under heaven can be in finance? Once the Chinese people understand the enormous benefits of finance, with the corresponding financial support, they also have the potential of "a star can start a prairie fire".

One day, when overseas Chinese talk about starting a business, they will say, "I found an investment, why don't we open a bank?"

The day will come sooner or later when China becomes a world financial power!

The infrastructural dangers of the financial high frontier

In contemporary society, where computer technology is highly advanced, financial activities are increasingly dependent on electronic information and network technologies. A large number of security hazards remain hidden in this core financial infrastructure.

Today's technology is sufficient to remotely activate the power supply and wiretap the phone with the phone turned off; the CIA can read hard disk data through the computer CPU, emitting weak electromagnetic waves that can non-contactively intercept and steal computer data from a few meters away. In such a highly insecure, electronic society, China's financial system is arguably still quite indifferent to potential security threats.

Almost all financial institutions in the country currently use foreign host hardware systems and operating system software, and for the most core data storage, most use foreign database software, which, even if all applications are developed independently, is still far from sufficient to ensure the security of financial data. It's no longer news that Microsoft has left a dark door in the operating system, and what does the surprising sensitivity shown by the US to Lenovo's acquisition of IBM laptops suggest? When national security repeatedly becomes a key obstacle to China's acquisition of U.S. companies, people may simply dismiss these claims as news media hype or trade protection rhetoric and not seriously consider the reasons behind it.

What is perfectly technically feasible is to open the back door to the host hardware system, and in emergency and special cases, may be remotely activated or closed. In terms of the host operating system software, it is even more possible to make a big impact, because of the secrecy of the source program, domestic financial institution users are unlikely to be aware of the various "small programs" that may exist in the underlying system running programs. The problem is even bigger with the database, where all the key information, such as the number of deposits in the customer's bank account, is kept. Some sleepy "Trojan horses" can be planted unknowingly in the source program of the database software.

If an irresistible event occurs one day, these dormant "Trojan horses" and closed dark doors may wake up and open. Some programs may suddenly go "crazy" and delete all deposit data from bank accounts, and the programmers may not be able to tell whether the accounts belong to the military or civilian, commercial or personal, government or institutional. When the army is about to send out planes, tanks or cars, it suddenly finds that the money in the account is missing and cannot pay for the operation of the military machine; when people wake up overnight to go to the bank to withdraw money, they are told that there is no money in the account; when the company is ready to buy goods, the cheque is returned; when the government pays the salary, it is not possible to punch money into the cards of civil servants. Can one imagine how to respond to emergencies of all kinds with such a collapsed financial system?

When a financial institution starts a backup system in an emergency, it finds that the backup system uses the same hardware, the same software and the same database, and ends up with the same problems.

Always put up your own fence first, and financial security is not just an empty phrase: "You can't have a heart of harm, but you can't have a heart of prevention". The insidious disease must first be eliminated before it occurs.

The advent of the "Spring and Autumn and Warring States" era of money

The whole activity of human society is to do two things, one is to create wealth and the other is to distribute it. The efficiency of wealth creation and the balanced distribution of wealth determine the trajectory of civilization. Without the creation of wealth, there is no distribution of wealth.

If the real economy, centered on labour, production, technology, natural resources and trade, is primarily responsible for the creation of wealth, the distribution of wealth takes two forms: a financial distribution system consisting of money, credit, fiscal taxes, financial instruments and financial markets, and a violent distribution system consisting of war, pillage, fraud and colonization.

There are two ways of owning wealth, large to the state and small to the individual, either by creating it through their own labour or by sharing it through the distribution system. A strong nation and a harmonious society must seek a stable equilibrium in the setting of the rules of the game for the creation and distribution of wealth.

In the final analysis, wealth is the organized and efficient use of natural resources by human beings, through the process of labour, to create a variety of products and services that meet the final needs of society.

Labor keeps people in good living and working habits; labor keeps people's excitement centered around how to reduce production costs, use advanced technology, and increase production efficiency so that more products can be produced; and labor keeps and continues to improve the ability to create wealth. In fact, the creativity of wealth is far more important than the possession of wealth itself.

In the 16th and 17th centuries, the powerful Spanish Empire once owned 18,000 tons of silver and more than 200 tons of gold, accounting for 80% of the world's total gold and silver, which can be said to be the world's richest. The world is working for Spain. When a country has so much wealth, the wealth itself will erode that country's ability to create wealth.

In 1545, Spanish manufacturers had a six-year backlog of orders from the New World in their hands. Under the protection of a powerful military force, these overseas orders could only be produced by Spain, with high profits at hand, and the immense wealth possessed by Spain had deprived its manufacturers of the desire and pressure to eat hard work and engage in arduous production activities. The British textile industry, Dutch shipbuilders, Italian farms, and Nordic fishing boats all started to engage in hard and dirty labor production.

Spanish manufacturers, on the other hand, put their own trademarks on their final products for export to various countries, forming the earliest models of OEM and outsourced production. As a result, the hard-working and courageous Englishmen, in their labour, improved their productivity, strengthened their wealth and creativity, and eventually ousted the Spanish Empire, with its vast wealth, extravagance, indiscriminate expansion, shrinking production, financial bankruptcy and unemployment, from the throne of world domination.

At the end of the 19th century and the beginning of the 20th century, the British Empire, which had been founded on manufacturing, had achieved a global maritime military and financial hegemony that was unprecedented in its history. In Africa, Britain's sphere of influence covers most of the continent, with as many as 21 countries subjugated to the British Empire, and vast quantities of raw materials and natural resources at Britain's disposal; in the Middle East, Britain controls most of the region, from Palestine and Saudi Arabia to Iran and Iraq, and holds the source of oil in the Middle East; in Asia, Britain rules large areas from India (including Pakistan), Malaysia (including Singapore) to Myanmar and Hong Kong, China, with vast human resources, natural resources and strategic corridors all under British control; in Oceania, it is backed by Commonwealth dependencies such as Australia and New Zealand as industrial raw materials; in the Americas, Canada, Guyana, Jamaica, the Bahamas and others provide the British Empire with endless strategic supplies from naval bases to natural resources.

The British Empire, the global hegemon, was once again faced with the same choice as the Spanish Empire, whether to continue to create wealth through its own hard work or to use its military and financial hegemony to "share" the fruits of others' work. Wealth itself has once again corrupted wealth creativity. The wealthy British, tired of boring and hard work, began to invest massively in the United States, exporting industrial production technology, leaving the Americans to do the hard work, enjoying the huge returns on their own investments, and beginning the "good life" of profit-seeking capitalism. At this time, Britain determined the world's cost of capital, monopolized world resource prices, controlled the flow of global orders, divided world market demand, and protected trade shipping lanes. With these five strategic high points firmly at the throat of the United States, the United States will always be the global production plant of the British Empire, and the shareholders controlling the plant will be British capital. In a word, the UK positions itself as the organizer of the global market, while the US is merely the producer. As long as there is no large-scale war to subvert the whole world, Britain has nothing to fear from the United States trying to "usurp power".

As a result, the two world wars completely threw the British Empire's dream of a "sun that never sets" into the museum of history.

History is always surprisingly similar. "In 1971, when Nixon announced the de-linking of the dollar from gold, the United States had a huge hegemony of wealth that Spain and Britain could not even dream of, and that was the dollar issue! Spain, with its wealth, had to travel far and wide to plunder gold and silver; the British Empire had to invest in "honest pounds" in order to obtain the privilege of profit; and the United States today has easy access to the rich and cheap natural resources and labour products of the world simply by printing dollar bills. This unprecedented hegemony of wealth has an irresistible allure, it has made all honest labor superfluous, it has stimulated the unprecedented expansion of the game of greed for wealth, it has overturned the hard-won spiritual system of the Puritans who founded the United States, it has dismantled the industrial base of the United States as a power, it has exacerbated the worldwide division between rich and poor, and it has become the real source of the 2008 global financial crisis!

Many believe that America's current problems are merely technical, that the American system has a strong capacity for self-correcting, and that like the various crises in American history, America has eventually managed to get through them. In fact, the crisis in the United States is not an institutional one, but a more serious one, namely, the gradual erosion of an entire nation by vast and easily acquired wealth, with a consequent loss of enthusiasm for hard work and an irreversible damage to wealth creativity. The long and widening trade deficit, which began in 1971, has shown relentlessly that Americans produce fewer and fewer products that can be exchanged with other countries, and the staggering global minting tax revenues and huge investment gains that accompany the privilege of issuing the dollar have allowed the United States to continue exporting its own industry, not unlike the behavior of Spain and Britain in those years. The high profits have been achieved while dismantling the wealth creation capacity of their people.

In the United States in the 1950s and 1960s, the most respected people in society were scientists and engineers; in the 1970s and 1980s, doctors and lawyers; and since the 1990s, Wall Street financiers. If a good college student going into Wall Street makes far more money than being a scientist or engineer, who else in this society wants to work hard research jobs and a boring factory life? Can the US export doctors, financiers and lawyers to other countries? Maybe it can, and that's expensive medicine, inferior financial products and protracted claims legal services.

As the lead washed away, the world suddenly discovered that the United States, once a great carrot and stick, was now left with only a bare stick, perhaps $57 trillion in various liabilities, and a potential shortfall of $100 trillion in Medicare and Social Security funds, and that these unpayable debts had formed a huge "debt lagoon". The world will eventually ask: what is a $14 trillion economy going to do to pay off these huge debts that are 10 times over? Not to mention that these debt rollovers are increasing at a much faster rate than the growth of the economy.

As Harvard University professor Neil Ferguson pointed out in the December 2009 cover article of *Newsweek* in the United States, "The Decline of Empire": historical experience shows that when 20 per cent of a country's fiscal revenue is spent on debt servicing, the country's finances are in serious crisis.

Spain: Between 1557 and 1696, a heavy debt burden led to 14 defaults on the national debt.

France: in 1788, on the eve of the French Revolution, 62 per cent of fiscal revenues were spent on debt servicing.

Ottoman Empire: in 1875, 50 per cent of government revenues were used to pay debt service; British Empire on the eve of World War II: 44 per cent of revenues were used to pay debt service.

These once-unbeatable empires eventually fell under the cross of excessive debt. What causes excessive debt? It boils down to a decline in wealth creativity and a rise in the cost of sustaining the empire's existence.

The easier a nation's wealth comes, the less enthusiasm it has to create it through hard work, and the great wealth corrupts wealth creativity, which is perhaps the dialectic of history.

By 2035, the U.S. national debt as a percentage of GDP will reach 200%. By that time, a whopping 46% of US coffers would be spent on debt servicing, which is what Britain faced in 1939! It was then that the British Empire began its descent into decline.

As the US debt problem worsens, the dollar will eventually go into decline. With the future of the dollar "Zhou Tianzi" is gradually becoming seriously ill, and with it is bound to come the era of the rise of the currency "Spring and Autumn five hegemon" and "Warring States seven male". A world-wide battle for currency will gradually kick off over the next 1/4 century.

CHAPTER X

The Glory and Dreams of Silver

Silver is synonymous with money in over 50 languages. Silver was once a major currency in many countries around the world. In the more than 50 years from the Opium War to the end of the Qing Dynasty, China was repeatedly defeated in various wars, signed more than 1,000 unequal treaties, and the cumulative compensation amounted to 1 billion taels of silver. Why don't Westerners, who have always loved gold, plunder China's gold in the first place? In the 1930s, the United States purchased most of the world's silver at high prices, and in the 1960s, at the height of its official and private silver reserves, the United States suddenly began to abolish the monetary function of silver, for which the unexplained President Kennedy was killed for opposing the abolition of the silver currency. Thereafter, the U.S. government began selling silver in bulk. After so many years of fighting, spending so much money, even robbing and buying so much silver, just gathered almost, but began to sell it all to the cheap like a piece of broken metal. Up to the Fed, down to some of the big banks are doing blank silver on a massive scale in various ways to desperately keep the price down. Why exactly is this?

This chapter will unravel the amazing mysteries involved. By dissecting the past, present and future of silver, you will not only be able to satisfy your curiosity and curiosity, but you will also be able to appreciate a major investment opportunity that you have never encountered in your life.

The next 20 years will be a time of radical change in the world monetary system. It is an era when the two plates of debt currencies, represented by the dollar, and honest currencies, represented by real gold and silver, collide violently. As a result of their collision, one of them gradually fell, while the other one rose to the sky and rose to prominence. In the midst of a violent collision between the dollar and gold and silver, the wise man should put his money on the rising side.

It will take your investment to the pinnacle of returns just like the rise of the Himalayas!

September 18, 2008, 2:00 p.m., the world financial system almost collapsed!

Due to information asymmetry, the Chinese were almost completely unaware of the catastrophe facing the wealth of the people of the world at that moment. Yes, this is not the "dream space" of science fiction blockbusters, nor is it a disaster rehearsal of the financial system, but a financial nightmare that really happens in reality! The world has been sleepwalking through the ghost of the collapsing dollar, but the vast majority of people still don't even know it!

This is the most horrific mega-bank run in modern history! To this day, the details of what happened on this day are kept strictly confidential.

The earliest to reveal this was US Democratic Congressman Paul Kandrzynski, who leaked the shocking news in February 2009 while doing a talk show on C-SPAN TV in the US.

> "At 11 a.m. Thursday (September 18, 2008), the Federal Reserve discovered that up to $550 billion in the U.S. money market had been 'run wild' by international investors within 1 to 2 hours.
> The Treasury Department opened the bailout window in an emergency and immediately pumped in $105 billion to try to stem the frenzied money-smuggling frenzy, but they quickly realized that it simply wasn't going to help. What we are facing is an electronic banking run.
> The Treasury Department decided to halt all transactions, urgently freeze all accounts, and declare the U.S. government to guarantee the safety of $250,000 of funds in each account to stop the spread of panic.
> If they don't take these measures, by 2:00 p.m. the entire $5.5 trillion in the U.S. money market will have been squeezed out and the U.S. economic system will have completely collapsed, and within 24 hours the world economic system will have completely collapsed.
> If that happens, the economic landscape and political system of the United States as we know it will be turned upside down."

In a radio interview in Tulsa, Oklahoma, U.S. Senator James Inhfe mentioned that then-Treasury Secretary Paulson, while exhorting members of Congress to pass bills related to the bailout of Wall Street, even threatened that if members of Congress voted against the bill, there could be major social unrest in the United States and the government would have to declare military regulations.

Total military control of American society? It's a scene one can't imagine at all, I'm afraid. What kind of crisis would lead society into such a mess? This is the dollar crisis!

To understand that a run on the U.S. money market will lead to a dollar crisis, we must first understand the significant role of the money market in the U.S. economy.

Unlike Chinese companies, U.S. companies rarely turn to banks for short-term lending, either because of cumbersome procedures or high fees. When businesses need short-term borrowing for less than 270 days, they often use short-term commercial paper to finance directly in the money market. These commercial paper notes are a type of debit note, generally based on corporate credit, and are simple and convenient to issue. Even if an enterprise needs money that day, it can get cash that afternoon by notifying commercial paper dealers to issue "debit notes" early in the morning. Therefore, enterprises tend to distinguish between the short-term costs of payroll, procurement of raw materials, transportation and storage, rent, utilities, and other expenses for the operation of the company, and the financial needs of the company's medium- and long-term development, short-term funds mainly rely on commercial paper financing, long-term capital is often invested in the capital market with higher returns in order to mobilize the full effectiveness of every penny in the company's account. It is safe to say that millions of companies in the United States cannot function without commercial paper and money markets for a single moment on a daily basis. In addition to commercial paper, short-term government bonds, federal funds, bankers' bills of exchange, repurchase agreements, large depository receipts, and other types of short-term paper rely on the money market to trade.

If the $5.5 trillion U.S. money market were to be completely dried up in a matter of hours by a mad rush of international investors, the cash flow to almost every company and business, financial institution, federal and local government in the United States would be completely disconnected in an instant, and within 24 hours, we would see an astonishing sight.

—The financial markets of the United States collapsed, stocks plunged, bond prices plunged, financial institutions across the country were suspended, banks could not operate, ATMs stopped withdrawing money, and corporate and individual accounts of banks were frozen completely.

—Panic-stricken crowds lined the banks, irate customers cursed and a few militants began to smash the ATMs.

—The production, logistics, transportation, procurement, and warehousing systems of many companies are crippled because the companies are unable to pay the various costs.

—There is a cash rush in major supermarkets because consumers can't swipe their cards to make purchases.

—Government servants, police officers, and the masses take to the streets together and traffic is basically paralyzed because they cannot get paid and their cars cannot be fueled. Families without cash in hand are unable to purchase food and medicine. The angry crowd began to riot.

—Schools, hospitals, office buildings are in a situation of lack of electricity and water because of the inability to pay for electricity and water, and power plants and water companies are shut down because they cannot pay for the raw materials they produce.

—Large numbers of U.S. fighter jets can't get airborne, warships can't sail, tanks, cars can't run because money in military accounts is frozen due to the suspension of short-term government bond financing.

—The U.S. government declared a state of martial law in the country.

Twenty-four hours later, the disaster began to spread throughout the world. Financial markets around the world opened one after the other, and after learning the shocking news from the United States, the prices of all financial products collapsed across the board. The financial institutions of various countries' financial transactions and liquidation are in complete chaos, China's exporters can't get the money and refuse to ship the goods, the Middle East's oil exports are halted due to lack of money, Russia's food exports are announced to be terminated, India's overseas call service centers are not answering the phone, the European Central Bank has declared a state of emergency and tightened the monetary base, a number of European government bond refinancing fails and announces the freezing of civil servants' wages, European workers demonstrate strikes, the world's major airlines have cancelled flights ...

When the world financial markets fell into the aforementioned reverie on September 18, investment institutions immediately acted, and while trying to seize a glimmer of escape, they instinctively pounced on the "Noah's Ark" of the monetary disaster – gold and silver!

Gold in September 18, before and after the breath of each ounce skyrocketed nearly $100, a record in the history of the gold market; silver is soaring more than 20%, making all investors dumbfounded. While other commodities, including other precious metals, were generally weaker on the same day.

In other words, when there is a real major crisis in the world monetary and financial system, the instinct is not to grab oil, steel, copper or zinc, but to go straight to gold and silver. There is no doubt that gold and silver immediately present their long forgotten monetary attributes in the face of this monetary disaster!

Gold needless to say, since the financial tsunami, there has been a general acceptance of its monetary properties. What's really amazing is the silver! Like gold, silver is the true monetary metal, although its monetary properties were only silver on September 18, 2008, but with the decline of the dollar's "son of the week", silver's monetary properties will rise to the forefront, and its light will be directly on the dazzling gold.

Silver's past is not unfamiliar to the Chinese, who, as the world's largest silver currency country, were once at the heart of the world's economic and trading system. However, today's countrymen have a vague understanding of what great strategic opportunities the future of silver will bring to China.

Not only was silver once the world's currency, but silver will create significant strategic opportunities for China's rise!

Silver: The World Currency of the Past

In 1621, a Portuguese merchant wrote: "Silver flowed all over the world until it reached China. It stayed there, as if to its natural center."

The main business of the Europeans in the 16th and 17th centuries in world trade was to sell silver, gold and commodities backwards, because they had nothing to sell in the thriving Asian markets, mainly because their own products were not competitive.[167]

China has used silver as its main currency in circulation since the Ming Dynasty, when China itself was not the world's leading silver producer, so why did the Ming Dynasty choose silver as its currency? And where does Chinese silver come from?

Silver became the main currency of the Ming dynasty not by voluntary choice, but as a result of the situation being stronger than man. Pre-Ming Dynasty Song, Gold, and Yuan all tried to replace precious metals with paper money as their main currency, and the results were surprisingly similar. Due to the iron law of human greed, once money is divorced from its commodity properties, it loses its natural rigid constraint and the wealth-grabbing of massive indiscriminate paper money to cover fiscal deficits ends in vicious inflation, tax depletion, fiscal collapse and empire collapse. The early years of the Ming Dynasty also tried the previous dynasty's paper money experiment, issued Ming Bao banknotes, until 1522, the paper currency depreciated to the original 2‰, inflation rampant, public discontent boiled over. The Ming government was finally forced to abandon the paper money system in favor of a return to the metal money system. After nearly 500 years of experimenting with the paper money system from Song to Ming, history has come to the ultimate conclusion: it is not reliable.

The metal currency in front of the Ming dynasty in the choice of gold, silver, copper, gold is too expensive, and copper is too cheap, so silver as the only candidate, became the real "people's money".

The question is, where does a silver-starved China go to get a lot of silver to use as currency? The answer is world trade.

If the world trading system is figuratively likened to a giant waterwheel system, the currency is the torrent that drives the waterwheel gears. The larger the money supply, the faster the turnaround of water trucks, and the greater the scale of world trade.

---

[167] *Silver Capital*, (German) Frank, translated by Liu Beicheng, Central Compilation Press, 2008.

From the 16th to the 19th centuries, the currency that drove the world's trading system was silver.

In 1581, the Ming dynasty, Zhang Juzheng in the country began to implement "a whip law", from the law of service and the field, from the government to ensure that the desire for servitude, gradually the focus of the service from the household to the field mu, and the final settlement of taxation currency is silver, thus creating a huge silver public demand.

Coincidentally, the discovery of huge silver mines in Peru and Mexico by the Spaniards in 1545 and 1548 respectively, together with the export of silver from Japan, constituted a powerful force driving the wheels of world trade.

At the time, China's most powerful industry was tea, porcelain and silk, and there were few decent competitors in the world market. China's porcelain exports to Europe account for 50% of all porcelain exports, so much so that China's name in the world is the English word "China" for "porcelain". Silk is also a heavyweight export from China, and "more silk is exported from China than one would think," he said. A thousand quintals are exported annually to the Portuguese Indies and the Philippines, which are filled with fifteen large ships, and countless silks are sent to Japan..."[168]

In the early 17th century, the price ratio of gold and silver was 1:5.5 to 1:7 in Guangzhou and 1:12.5 to 1:14 in Spain, and the price of silver in China was twice that of Spain. Spanish merchants, who had just discovered a huge silver mine in the Americas, were overjoyed to discover this huge currency arbitrage space, and hordes of European merchants boarded ships bound for China with the huge amounts of silver they had plundered from the Americas. It was this silver-gold arbitrage impulse that spurred the gigantic, incomparable wheel of world trade to begin turning at full speed.

Although Europe began the Industrial Revolution in the 17th century and machine production significantly reduced production costs, their main product, textiles, was not competitive in China. On the one hand, the long-distance shipping has greatly increased transportation costs, and on the other hand, China's long-term and sustained

---

[168] Source: Ibid.

investment in inland river shipping, especially the Grand Canal, has effectively reduced the transportation costs of local commodities in China, thus greatly increasing their competitiveness.

More importantly, the Chinese textile industry had reached a considerable production scale in the late Ming and early Qing dynasties, with Western missionaries estimating that by the end of the 17th century, there were as many as 200,000 weavers in and around Shanghai, and as many as 600,000 spinners providing yarn. The industrial scale effect and low transportation costs almost eliminated the opportunity for European products to compete in China, a phenomenon that continued until the mid to late 19th century.

Under this situation, the merchant ships of Europe mainly transported commodities is the silver of the Americas, after arriving in China, exchanged silver for Chinese porcelain, silk and tea, and exchanged "expensive silver" for "cheap gold", and then transported to India to purchase Indian goods, and finally loaded with oriental goods and gold back to Europe, and made a lot of money.

For nearly 400 years between the 16th and 19th centuries, the Europeans were primarily engaged in the plundering of American silver and international pours. It is no exaggeration to say that the plundering of American silver was the first barrel of gold in Europe's development. And the center of world trade at that time was clearly in China, which exported goods and imported currency, thus establishing a silver-based monetary system. The way to prove that China was the world trade center of the time was simple, the silver never left China once it arrived and became a major part of the Chinese money supply until the British started selling opium to China.

It is estimated that from the discovery of the American silver mine in 1545 to 1800, the Americas produced a total of 133,000 tons of silver, of which 75 percent (about 100,000 tons) went to Europe, which eventually sent 32,000 tons of silver to China through Asian trade. When silver shipped directly to China from the Americas and silver exported from Japan to China are added, China has gained 48,000 tons of silver through world trade.[169] Interestingly, the 68,000 tons of American silver that flooded into Europe (minus the 32,000 tons shipped to China) brought a prolonged period of inflation, while the

---

[169] Source: Ibid.

48,000 tons of silver that entered China did not cause the apparent inflation of the Ming and Qing dynasties for one reason only, China's commodity economy at the time was far more developed than Europe's, and the increase in currency stimulated a substantial increase in commodity supply, which effectively offset the inflationary pressure.

After 1935, Chiang Kai-shek abolished the silver standard, the French currency reform and the issuance of gold notes triggered super-inflation again and eventually lost power.

Looking back at history, if there was any currency in those 400 years that could be called the world's currency and thus propelled the wheels of world trade, silver would be the only candidate.

Can dollar bills keep their value?

What is money? What is wealth? This issue is primary to recognizing the nature of the dollar. An important characteristic that distinguishes great thinkers is their special sensitivity and profound reflection on important things that are commonplace and ignored by the common man. "The apple falls on the ground", a phenomenon so commonplace that people have not cared about for millennia, has inspired in Newton's mind an epiphany of gravity. The concept of "time", which was so common that it could not be more common, resonated in Einstein's mind and eventually led to the birth of the theory of relativity. For thousands of years, people have been living in a money society, and many people who have been busy their whole lives to earn money, how many people can quietly take a serious look and think deeply and carefully, what is "money"?

There is no doubt that there are really that many people in this world who have explored the question of what money is. Unfortunately, instead of producing great financial and monetary theories that rival the laws of gravity and relativity, these explorations have become more and more confusing. For unlike the purely physical concepts of "time" and "gravity", money is heavily influenced by the unmeasurable variable of human greed. Scholars have come up with a variety of monetary theories that are incompatible and contradictory. The bankers, however, took advantage of the opportunity to muddle through, taking the entire Western financial system from theory to practice and gradually leading it astray, to the point where it finally went off the rails and lured the entire world into a huge financial crisis.

The concept of money in the classical sense is fairly clear. Money is a special commodity that already exists, has a stable value and can be used as a medium of exchange. It has the following characteristics: limited quantity, easy to measure, easy to exchange, not easy to counterfeit, market accepted, and can be stored for a long time. Many goods that meet these characteristics can become "money". The commodity that fits best with these definitions and characteristics is the best "money". Gold and silver are the incomparable and best "money" that people in different countries, cultures and regions, both at home and abroad, have chosen after thousands of years of repeated comparison and practice. They can be used as storage for value because they all have a specific intrinsic value in their own right and are waterproof, fireproof, corrosion resistant, and hard wearing for a long time. Because they are portable, easy to carry, divide and measure, and difficult to counterfeit, they can be the most convenient and trusted medium of commodity exchange. Because they are stable and easy to measure, they are best suited as a measure of value. Since they are commodities of real value that already exist, they are the most reliable "money" that does not require any guarantee, does not require any coercion and will not be invalidated by force majeure such as change of government, change of law, economic crisis, natural or man-made disasters, etc. Moreover, the more the time of turmoil, the more the gold and silver became the "Noah's Ark" for people to protect their wealth. As the saying goes, "The vicissitudes of the sea and the currents reveal the hero's true character". Because of this, gold and silver is the highest form of "money", is well-deserved, the people of the "king of money".

What is wealth? The essence of wealth is the various goods that people create through their labour. Money represents the "right of claim" to the fruits of such labour. Everyone in society should have the "right to claim" the fruits of others' work by selling the fruits of his or her own work. When this "claim" is transferred, it acts as a "means of payment"; when a certain "claim" is universally accepted, it becomes a "medium of exchange"; when the holder of the "claim" chooses to delay its fulfilment, it fulfils the function of a "store of wealth"; and finally, when the "claim" is required to be fulfilled, it is able to obtain intact the equivalent labour of others, then the "claim" is a good "measure of value". Together, these four factors form a perfect correspondence between money and wealth. In fact, of the four functions of money, the most central is the function of the "store of wealth". The more intact the currency is with the ability to delay the encashment of wealth, the more important the "scale of value" will be, the more popular it will be in the market and the more liquid it will be, thus becoming a high-quality "medium of exchange" and "means of payment". The complete abolition of the commodity attributes of money would lead to a dysfunctional and dysfunctional "store of wealth". Any currency, once removed from the iron law of the commodity nature of money, is ultimately subject to constant devaluation. Gold and silver represent "money in the classical sense", the highest level of monetary pursuit.

Historically, empires have been in cycles of rising power, with developed economies, vibrant trade and military power, expanding imperial boundaries, stable currency purchasing power, expanding currency circulation and low interest rates on loans. As the ruling class decayed, internal conflicts within the empire intensified, production capacity declined, external conquests continued, fiscal expenditures increased dramatically, and tax revenues gradually fell short, resulting in the increasing combined cost of keeping the empire afloat. At this point, empires often begin by devaluing their currencies in an attempt to relieve fiscal pressure. The monetization of fiscal deficits, whether it is the dilution of the gold content of money in ancient times or the "quantitative easing" of money in modern times, is the source of inflation.

The most essential "invention" of contemporary Western monetary theory is the replacement of gold and silver, real money that does not lose its value through default, with credit money as collateral for debt. They abolished the silver standard by first looting the silver from the countries of the world where it was the main currency, either through war or the opium trade. This was followed by the initial establishment of a world currency exchange system by pegging the world's currencies to the United States dollar and the dollar to gold. And then decoupling the dollar from gold, thereby abolishing the gold standard. Let the French currency, represented by the US dollar, become the world's reserve currency, unencumbered by gold and silver. We now use the US dollar, a currency without any definition of real value, which is called "currency" in English, the basic meaning of which is liquidity. It is only a medium that facilitates the "flow" of commodities. The medium itself has no value. It can be paper money, it can be a check, it can even be a number in a computer. It is a voucher that is temporarily used to exchange value. It is essentially a note of indebtedness that does not guarantee that it will actually be redeemed 100 percent of its original value in the future. Because it is a note of indebtedness, the note of indebtedness becomes a white note if someone else cheats. Nowadays, when people have gradually forgotten that gold and silver are the most reliable real money for thousands of years, they often confuse the two concepts of credit money, such as a note of indebtedness, with money, thinking that this note is money. To earn money is to earn this kind of debt, and to save money is to save this kind of debt. In fact, under the credit-money system, these notes that one earns and saves presumably to be honored have full value when they are not in default, only partial value when they are in partial default, and nothing when they are in full default.

Experiments with pure paper money often yield surprisingly good results in the early days, but eventually these notes are reduced back to their original value, which is the cost of paper! The system of pure paper money is, by its very nature, an experiment in testing the greedy nature of man. Whether the power to issue money is in the hands of the Government or private individuals, and regardless of the social system of the country in which monetary policy is implemented, this does not change the nature of the problem, which is whether the inherent greed of human nature is worthy of trust or not! The whole history of mankind has shown that greed, anger and rage are the inability of human nature to transcend itself. If we look closely at the manifestations of infants who are completely untainted by the social atmosphere, we will find that their greed, anger and rage are in fact already in the beginning.

This is the root cause of the fact that we have never been able to find any kind of paper money that preserves its value in the history of human civilization.

From 1023 to 1160 A.D. in the Northern Song Dynasty, the reserve for currency issuance was reduced from 1/3 to 1/60, and by the end of the Southern Song Dynasty, inflation was 20 trillion times higher! The finances collapsed completely, the country's ability to mobilize for war dried up, and the dynasty fell apart.

The Golden Dynasty issued paper money for more than 70 years, and prices rose 60 million times, until the people's hearts and minds were in turmoil and wealth creation was lost.

At the end of the Yuan Dynasty, the price of rice rose to more than 60,000 times its original value, and the banknote system completely collapsed, the Yuan government was unable to control finances and taxes, and the country was declining in strength and eventually perished.

The Ming experiment with a purely paper currency system lasted for another 150 years, and by 1522, the Ming Bao banknotes were devalued to 2 per cent of their original value, and inflation was rampant. The Ming government was forced to abandon the paper currency system and restore the silver currency, and the empire was maintained until 1644.

In 1716, the first French paper money experiment by John Law led to the collapse of France four years later; in 1790, the second paper money experiment after the French Revolution, with inflation of 13,000% five years later, resulted in a public upheaval that led to Napoleon's rise to power; and the third pure paper money experiment in 1937, with the franc depreciating by 99% 12 years later. The French have only self-deprecatingly said that the French have two traditions: one is that surrender is particularly rapid; the other is that the currency depreciates particularly rapidly.

The Weimar Republic of Germany's paper currency mark experiment came to the end of its life in four years, from 1 dollar to 12 marks in 1919 to 4.2 trillion marks to 1 dollar in 1923.

If the greedy nature of mankind had not changed, the dollar today would simply be repeating history.

The Fed's "magic plan": let the gold soar

The Fed, like all Western central banks, likes to operate behind the scenes. They guard against government intervention, they hate Congress to intervene, they hate the people to know the details, and they claim to keep monetary policy independent, as if the currency of society as a whole is their private property and must not be coveted by others.

The Federal Open Market Committee (FOMC) of the Federal Reserve's decision on interest rate policy, the word "public" is really ironic, because they do not intend to disclose the content of the eight meetings a year, but wait until five years later to "declassify", and the content of these meetings have been filtered or "repair" has been. The United States Sunshine Act of 1976, which explicitly requires organizations, including the Federal Reserve, to make detailed and unmodified stenographic and original recordings of all official meetings immediately available to the public, has misled Congress for 17 years, from 1976 to 1993, by claiming that their original minutes were destroyed and that only the "repaired" minutes were retained. Only five

FINANCIAL HIGH FRONTIERS

years later could the public guess at the details of the discussions that took place on the floor of the meeting from the "filtered" minutes.

Aside from focusing on issues like interest rates, the Fed's bigwigs are quite interested in one thing, and that's gold.

(Federal Reserve Open Market Committee minutes, May 18, 1993)

> **Angell**: *I think that's how things might go. I don't think we should raise rates by 300 basis points, but if we do, I'm pretty sure the price of gold will start a violent and rapid (decline). Gold prices are going to fall so fast that you have to go to the gold ticker screen to witness it all. If we raise interest rates by 100 basis points, the price of gold will surely turn down, unless the situation deteriorates beyond what I can imagine. If we raise interest rates by 50 basis points, I don't know what will happen to the price of gold, but I'm sure I'll be very curious about it (laughs)... People will say that the price of gold is going up because the Chinese are starting to buy, which is the silliest view. The price of gold is largely determined by those who have no faith in the fiat system and who own gold to escape paper money in a time of danger. Now if annual gold production and consumption is only 2% of the total gold stock, then a 10% change in gold production and sales per year will not have too significant an impact on the gold price. However, attitudes towards inflation will change (gold prices).*
> **Greenspan**: *If we're dealing with market psychology, then the (gold) thermometer we use, when measuring (inflationary expectations) temperature, also changes the temperature itself. I raised with Mr. Mullins the question of how the market would react if the Treasury were to sell a small amount of gold in the market. It's an interesting thought experiment, and if the price of gold changes, it suggests that (gold) this thermometer is not just a tool to measure (inflationary expectations), but that it will also change the underlying psychology (of the market's expectations of inflation).*
> *(Minutes of the December 1994 meeting of the Federal Reserve Open Market Committee)*
> **Jordan**: *I think the main issue we're facing right now is inflation expectations. This clearly reflects the lack of a nominal (monetary) anchor for our (the dollar). This means that political claims of maintaining a strong dollar will help. If we can achieve a true gold standard state without actually using gold anyway, then we have to get the idea of dollar purchasing power stability (deeply embedded) in people's minds. With time, the short-term*

problems we now face (inflationary expectations) will become easier to deal with.
(Proceedings of the July 1995 meeting)
Greenspan: *I think I got it (laughs)! You told me that the SDRs issued from the Treasury (on the Fed's balance sheet) offset their (Treasury's) liability to the Fed, which was purely an asset swap, so Treasury's liability to the public was reduced by the same amount simultaneously. Is that right? That, in turn, solves Mr. Jordan's problem at the same time (laughs).*
Jordan: *Can I talk about my opinion on that? (In the 70's) the same effect was achieved when we raised the price of gold from $35 an ounce to $38, all the way to $42.22. As a result of these two so-called (dollar) "devaluations", the Ministry of Finance received a windfall of $1 billion to $1.2 billion. My question is, when we monetize SDRs, at what price should it be? You say I have an asset on my balance sheet, but I don't know its price.*
Greenspan: *(The price of the SDR) is about $42.*
Truman: *is $42.22, which is in line with the official price of gold.*
Jordan: *Are we using the official gold price for SDRs?*
Greenspan: *Are you saying that we can raise the price of gold to reduce public debt pressure? This would indeed lead to a significant reduction in public debt.*
Jordan: *I was going to try not to mention it, the public was actually afraid that someone would want to do it.*
Greenspan: *It's a pity it's too late, as we've just mentioned.*
Jordan: *5 years from now (declassification period for minutes), the public will know about it.*

From the dialogue of these Fed bigwigs, we can clearly see that gold has always been a "heart disease" of international bankers. Historically, playing with paper money inevitably goes through three stages: playing with strength, playing with confidence, and playing rogue! When the empire was strong and wealthy, and the creativity of wealth was strong enough to ensure the commodity cashing power of paper money, paper money had a bottom. When the empire's overextended power fails to keep pace and its financial resources become dwindling, the "acrobatics" of 10 bottles with 5 caps must be played, paper money cannot fully cash in commodities, inflation begins, and the stage of confidence play begins. By the time the empire's wealth has been emptied and only an empty shelf remains, the paper currency loses credibility and hyperinflation strikes, at which point the empire has no choice but to play rogue.

From the founding of the United States to 1971, the dollar is playing the stage of strength, once accounted for half of the global GDP of the strong industrial production capacity to ensure the credit of the dollar, so the dollar dares to link with gold, because its export capacity is enough to earn back gold in other parts of the world, just as China through 400 years of world trade, a small half of the global silver will be absorbed into China, the same, at this time the gold and silver as honest currency, in the economy to play a good role in the rational distribution of wealth, thus stimulating further economic development, the economic cycle in a virtuous state.

1971 to 2008 financial tsunami, the dollar entered the stage of playing confidence, 1971 is the turning point of the dollar, the United States can not afford the world countries launched a gold squeeze attack, only to give up the dollar and gold link, the essence is the United States trade deficit, wealth outflow and wealth creativity decline, Americans can not produce enough goods needed by other countries to balance the huge imports, over time, the financial overload, the dollar can no longer carry the gold honest currency support. At this stage, international bankers are most concerned about the so-called confidence in the dollar. They have invented a system of economic "black talk" to modify the nature of the problem, such as "inflationary expectations", "quantitative easing of monetary policy", "asset re-inflation", etc. In fact, in the words of ordinary people, the dollar is "gross". What is even more bizarre is that they actually imagined how to achieve the "gold standard without gold", it seems that the Federal Reserve or change to engage in magic can play their speciality. However, in November 2010, the President of the World Bank, Mr. Zoellick, actually suggested that the world should consider a return to a "modified gold standard", a "gold standard without gold", is this really a historical "coincidence"?

In 2008, the global financial crisis that originated in the United States marked the third phase of the dollar – playing rogue! The most important feature of this phase is that the United States is trying to lie on the debt, using the means of forcing the currencies of other countries to appreciate sharply, in the name of "global economic rebalancing", accusing other countries of "manipulating the exchange rate". Even more interesting is the discussion by Greenspan and others of letting the price of gold soar and the dollar depreciate sharply, thus "offsetting" the pressure on the US debt. They have long understood the true value of gold, that is, gold is the "honest money", because of its children, the real price, so in the monetary system bears the "final means of payment". However, they have been promoting the "gold uselessness theory" to other countries around the world, systematically and permanently "brainwashing" academia, and playing "strong dollar" word games with people and markets, so as to achieve the goal of "the idea of dollar purchasing power stability (deeply embedded in people's minds)".

Gold and silver are like pressure gauges that measure inflation expectations, and in the world of paper money centered around the dollar, the more banknotes are printed, the more inflationary pressure is exerted in the pressure cooker of the market. The price of gold and silver, as the only credible pressure gauge, must be "effectively regulated", which is what the Western central banks have been doing since the 1990s to suppress gold and silver prices. When the market for gold and silver acts as the most honest and fair currency, it will be very difficult for bankers to want to cheat. And without the gold and silver restraint, things are very different. The dollar, for example, is now issued by the Federal Reserve and is not only the French currency of the United States, but also the world's leading reserve currency. But its monetary policy is completely irresponsible, issuing as much as it wants, without the need for UN Security Council approval or congressional approval. There is no regard for the interests of creditors worldwide. Bankers are neither subject to so-called democratic elections, nor to press scrutiny, nor to legal constraints. As the saying goes, "I don't care who makes the laws as long as I control the right to issue the currency of a country." Total lawlessness.

It is often said that "absolute power leads to absolute corruption." Actually, corruption isn't the worst thing. What can a few bankers who are corrupt day in and day out, corrupt night in and night out, do to the whole society? The most frightening thing about absolute power is not that it makes people corrupt, it makes people crazy! The ambition and appetite of the monopolistic financial predators of the monopoly on currency issuance will be so inflated that the whole of humanity will suffer as a result. Bankers have been able to fool the people of the world with all sorts of "industry black talk", control currency issuance at will, periodically create all sorts of bubbles and economic crises, collapse national finances through currency wars and, on top of the ruins of the global economy, reconstruct a new system of a unified world currency controlled by a tiny minority, and ultimately enslave all of humanity by controlling the world currency.

However, the international bankers have also made the worst case scenario, that sooner or later the pressure cooker is going to blow, and once the lid of the cooker goes up with a "bang", the soaring price of gold will also significantly reduce the debt of the West, which holds a lot of physical gold. By June 2010, the global central banks combined gold reserves of 30462.8 tons, of which Europe and the United States have a total of 21898.5 tons (including the IMF under European and American control), accounting for 72% of the total gold reserves.

Greenspan's whimsical idea of diluting debt pressure on the dollar by letting the price of gold soar may seem plausible at first glance, but I am afraid they underestimate the risk that "water can carry a boat and it can overturn it". Once the price of gold is completely out of control, the price of dollar-denominated gold assets on the U.S. balance sheet can certainly skyrocket, and the corresponding pressure on paper currency liabilities is significantly reduced. But the problem is that the global hyperinflation caused by the dramatic depreciation of the dollar will fundamentally upend the credit of the dollar, and who wants to continue to hold US bonds and dollar assets? Can the superpowers we know today still exist without the dollar's ability to mobilize global resources in general?

In 1948, Chiang Kai-shek's reform of the Golden Yuan, which eventually caused the price of gold assets on the balance sheet of the Kuomintang government to soar, was followed by the indiscriminate issuance of the Golden Yuan, which led to the rejection of paper money and the reintroduction of "Yuan Da-tou" transactions in various places. Ultimately, the super-inflation created by the indiscriminate issuance of paper money has brutally plundered the people's wealth, with the consequence that the people have abandoned the gold vouchers, as well as the Kuomintang government that issued them. When the Kuomintang retreated to Taiwan, as when John Law fled Paris that year, they took with them not fine printed paper money, but heavy gold and silver!

Balancing the dollar's liabilities with a gold spike would be a final act of madness that would bring not the stability of the dollar, but rather its destruction.

Meanwhile, another key variable is overlooked in the Greenspan's magic equation, and that's silver!

Gold and silver 1:16 historical super-stable structure

The ancients said, "If gold is the sun, silver is like the moon." In many ancient civilizations, there were 13 months of the year, 28 days a month. Thus, the earliest gold to silver ratio is 1:13.

Over the course of 5,000 years, the ratio of gold to silver has remained essentially stable at 1:16. The ratio of gold to silver reserves in the earth's crust is approximately 1:17, and, coincidentally but not surprisingly, the ancient intuition and historically formed ratio of gold to silver is quite similar to the results of modern scientific investigations.

This ultra-stable structure of the gold-silver ratio can be effectively explained in terms of both geology and market supply and demand. Although there is a certain degree of arbitrage space between Europe and Asia in the gold and silver ratio, but it is all in the form of the Asian region "silver expensive and gold cheap" formed by the eastward flow of silver and gold westward expression. In between this dynamic balance, Europe prefers gold, while Asia prefers silver. In the history of Europe, whoever could control the channels of East-West trade could take advantage of the difference in the ratio of gold and silver in Eurasia to carry out huge arbitrage transactions of 50 to 100 per cent, thus reaping huge commercial profits and dominating the fate of the continent.

With the great discovery of silver in the Americas, the huge supply of 133,000 tons of silver briefly caused some fluctuations in the gold-silver ratio over the course of 250 years, but as the massive world trade between East and West was digested, gold and silver eventually returned with historical inertia to the magic equilibrium of 1:16. Although silver and gold prices began to fluctuate sharply after the turn of the twentieth century, this was largely due to the adoption of the gold standard in most countries and the abandonment of silver currencies, which led to a "surplus" of silver for some time. As the world's largest silver standard country, China's silver currency lasted until 1935 and the United States' silver currency (U.S. government silver bills and silver coins) remained in circulation until 1965. By 1971, the ratio of gold to silver fluctuated around 1:23.

In 1971, the United States unilaterally announced the decoupling of the dollar from gold, and the "dollar" became the "no gold". This was the first major experiment in human history in which the whole world came together to enter the era of pure paper money, and it continues to this day. The pure paper money system completely abolished the commodity properties of money, and the wealth storage function, which was the core element that formed money, was completely lost.

The indiscriminate issuance of purely paper dollars has led to worldwide price dislocations, including serious distortions in the gold-silver comparative system. The gold-silver ratio has been severely distorted from a steady 1:16 over 5000 years to 1:60!

Is it less gold?

World gold stocks have increased from about 30,000+ tons in 1940 to about 150,000 tons today, about a fivefold increase in 70 years!

Is it more silver?

World silver stocks have fallen from about 300,000 tons in 1940 to about 30,000+ tons today, down to $1/10^{th}$ of that year!

The current silver stock is only 1/5 of the gold stock if measured by weight, which means that silver is far more scarce than gold!

This huge difference stems from the massive industrial demand for silver. Starting in 1942, the industrial consumption of silver began to greatly exceed the production supply, and over the decades, silver maintained a supply-demand balance with 5,000 years of accumulated inventory. Demand currently exceeds supply by about 4,000 tons per year. Based on the current net silver consumption, the existing 30,000-plus tons of silver stocks will only be enough to last another 7 to 8 years, and the silver on the ground that mankind has accumulated for 5,000 years will be eaten up by industrial demand!

So, how much silver is left in the ground?

In 2005, a U.S. Geological Survey survey indicated that silver would be the first metal in human history to be mined away for about 12.3 years. Considering that two-thirds of current silver production comes from companion mines such as copper, lead and zinc, it is difficult to increase silver production significantly due to the constraints of other mining inputs. While there is still silver in the earth's crust to be mined, it has mining value only at a much higher price due to technology and cost. At the end of 2009, the latest USGS statistics indicate that the world's silver reserves were 400,000 tons. Based on the current year's mineral production of 21,400 tons, it can be mined for 18 years.[170] Silver provided by minerals will account for the lion's share of the total supply, as silver provided by government sales and scrap recycling has declined significantly in recent years. The total world demand for silver is now about 27,700,000 tons per year,[171] and if it is all supplied by mineral silver, the total world reserves of 400,000 tons would only guarantee a 14-year supply. Considering that the silver industry is rapidly expanding its applications, the consumption of silver is expected to rise sharply in the future, by which time the 12.3 or 14 year mining deadline will be significantly advanced.

Given the historical ratio of the current gold price ($1350 per ounce) to the silver price, the ratio should be 1:16, i.e. $84 per ounce, to be considered reasonable. And the historical ratio of gold to silver has been determined by how much they are. In ancient Egypt, silver was scarce and its price was comparable to gold. More silver was later discovered and gold became relatively scarce. Things are scarce, so gold is worth more. With this further analysis, there are currently about 400,000 tons of minable reserves of silver in the world, and with the existing stock of about 30,000 tons, the total amount of silver is only about 430,000 tons. Gold stocks are rising because they are rarely consumed for industrial purposes, and are currently generally estimated at 160,000 tons. According to the statistics of the United States Geological Survey as of the end of 2009, the world's recoverable reserves of gold are about 47,000 tons, the total amount of the two together is about 207,000 tons of gold. The ratio of total gold to total silver is 20.7:40, or about 1:2. This means that the total amount of silver is much less than in the past and should be priced at 1/2 the price of gold, not 1/16. At the current gold price of $1,350 per ounce, the price of silver should be $675 per ounce! And the current market price of silver is only around $25 an ounce. In other words, a little bit of non-bubble counting would leave silver with 27 times more upside right now. Over time, silver will decrease further, with a 1:1 ratio of gold to silver, and further down the line silver will total less than gold. This means that silver's potential to appreciate in value over the next decade or so is likely to be extremely thrilling!

---

[170] U. S. Geological Survey, Mineral Commodity Summaries, January 2010. Silver.

[171] Silver Institute, Demand and Supply in 2009.

Silver on the shoulder: both a monetary and industrial metal

The ancient Phoenicians discovered early on the miraculous function of silver to sterilize wine, and they put the wine in silver bottles to preserve its freshness, a secret that still lives on in the famous wineries of today. Sailors in the British Empire put silver coins into their own drinking water tanks during their long sea voyages to keep the water from decaying. Ancient Greek physicians first discovered that silver had a significant effect on wound healing and could prevent disease. Ancient Chinese monarchs used silver chopsticks to test for toxicity in their food. Silverware was widely used in the tableware of European aristocrats because bacteria could not survive long on sterling silver surfaces, while wooden tableware was a favorite of bacteria, and stainless steel tableware could not resist the growth of bacteria. Despite the widespread contemporary use of antibiotics to kill bacteria, the problem of bacterial resistance to antibiotics has long plagued the medical community.

For a long time, the miraculous killing effect of silver on bacteria and viruses has not been studied in depth. It was only recently that the principle of silver killing bacteria was figured out. Silver in water can form trace amounts of silver ions that adsorb bacteria, destroying the enzymes on which they depend, causing the bacteria to die quickly. According to research, silver ions can kill more than 650 bacteria in a matter of minutes, 113 times more effective than ordinary antibiotics, and without any resistance.

In health care, the number of people cross-infected by bacteria and viruses in European and American hospitals alone is in the millions each year, and the follow-up problems of resistance from the heavy use of antibiotics are enough to make the health insurance system unsustainable. Hospitals in the UK have started using cleansers and protective creams containing silver ions to avoid the problem of cross infection. Hospitals in the United States have also begun to use gauze, masks, surgical sheets and room interiors containing silver ions in large quantities to avoid cross-contamination.

The industrial demand for silver in the 21st century is brewing even more explosively, and in recent years, more silver has been used in technology patents worldwide than in any other metal.

If green technology will be the main engine of the world's economic development in the coming decades, silver consumption in this area will see a blowout growth.

Application of silver in the field of new energy

Silver has the best light reflection efficiency and polish of any metal and is an essential core component in solar concentrator applications. At the same time, silver is an excellent catalyst, and when mixed with semiconductor materials, the efficiency of solar energy conversion to electricity can be greatly improved, and energy output can be increased by 12%. The rapid development of solar technology will generate thousands of tons of silver demand worldwide every year.

Batteries will become the core element of the green era, and silver batteries will be the best candidate to replace traditional lithium batteries. Its duration is 40% higher than that of lithium batteries, and there is no risk of lithium batteries exploding. 95% of the parts can be completely recycled, which has important environmental value. Silver batteries have an extremely wide range of applications in computers, cell phones, hearing aids, medical devices and all mobile electronics. Applications in spacecraft, deep-sea detectors, torpedoes, missiles, submarines, etc. are highly promising.

The widespread civil use of silver batteries is still in its infancy, but represents the future trend of a new generation of environmentally friendly battery technology. Considering the extent of widespread use of battery technology, the total increase in demand for silver will be staggering.

2017, 25.9 billion RFID chips will use silver

The rapid global expansion of radio frequency identification (RFID) technology will take silver applications to a whole new level. The tremendous use of RFID technology for tracking and location was described in the introduction to chapter 6 of The Currency Wars, in which a micro-coupled circuit and antenna are embedded in the RFID chip to receive electromagnetic waves emitted by the card reader, and the energy carried by the electromagnetic waves forms a current in the coupling coil and "reads out" the unique ID information on the chip, which is then transmitted back to the card reader by the antenna. In this way, a card reader, about a few hundred meters away, is like a remote ID detection radar that can confirm that the chip is within its detection range. Once these remote ID detection radar, forming a network as small as shops and schools, as large as community cities or even the whole country, the world, then the existence of this huge network of all RFID chip carriers, will be located and tracked in real time, the Internet of Things technology is based on RFID technology.

In July 2010, Walmart announced that it was beginning to use RFID extensively to manage its large inventory to reduce costs. Once it works well, Walmart will have full RFID adoption across its 3,500 U.S. stores, and its global suppliers will be required to use the same technology to interface with Walmart's inventory system.

According to the U.S. company IDTechEx predicts that RFID chips will grow at a staggering rate of 93% per year in rapid expansion worldwide. By 2017, the world's annual production of RFID chips will reach an appalling 25.9 billion pieces! And 10.9 milligrams of silver is used on each chip, which is completely unrecoverable due to its tiny content.

U.S. timber protection field will consume 2,400 tons of silver per year in the future

On 11 September 2003, the United States Senate Committee on Forests and Public Lands Management introduced the Public Lands Output Study Act. The bill seeks to replace the currently widely used copper-containing wood preservation technology, which produces toxic compound salts of copper arsenate and copper acetate that are so harmful to the environment that they have become a growing concern in the United States. Silver has a natural antiseptic effect as a wood preservative that resists termite infestation, spore fungus growth and decay, aquatic hosts, and other insect parasitism and reproduction. The vast majority of homes in the U.S. are made of wood, and once this technology is officially introduced into the U.S. wood preservation market, the U.S. wood preservation sector alone will consume 2,400 tons of silver annually!

Apparel applications will be one of silver's biggest future needs

Silver is a natural inorganic antimicrobial material, inorganic silver antimicrobial material has the characteristics of persistence, longevity and broad spectrum, good heat resistance, high safety, does not produce chemical resistance.

Silver-ionic materials are commonly used in the desert combat uniforms of the U.S. Army for sterilization and deodorization. The same is true for sportswear, as the large amount of bacteria in sweat is a major source of all kinds of odors and lesions, and silver kills most of them. The silver lined garments keep their smell fresh and healthy even when they sweat heavily from strenuous outdoor sports but cannot be cleaned for long periods of time. In the clothing sector alone, silver has become the largest single application, consuming 1,200 tons of silver per year.

This number is just the beginning of Silver's entry into the apparel space. Imagine the demand for silver if 1.3 billion Chinese clothing consumers also start wearing healthy clothing containing silver ions and 1 billion Indian people join the trend!

In the field of food packaging, packaging materials such as food, beverages and milk containing silver ions can greatly extend the shelf life. The use of silver ion sterilization materials in drinking water filters has also begun, while swimming pools across the U.S. are abandoning chlorine gas sterilization, which has serious side effects, in favor of silver sterilization materials.

Currently, global industrial consumption of silver is around 30,000 tons per year, and the huge emerging silver consumption market is just beginning to draw the curtain.

One major difference between silver and gold is that silver has a wide range of industrial uses and, as a result, silver has a much larger industrial consumption than gold. Another important feature of silver is in various applications in the industrial field, the vast majority of them are trace applications, such as mobile phone integrated circuits containing several cents worth of trace silver, LCD large screen color TVs are also plated with trace silver, almost all household electronic devices are not difficult to find trace silver applications. Such trace silver applications, even in the face of a 10-fold spike in silver prices, would hardly make a noteworthy impact on the price of their final product.

In addition, the characteristics of silver used in trace amounts in industry have resulted in silver being lost forever as it cannot be effectively recovered after industrial applications.

Silver's excellent variety of properties and huge application space make it the most price explosive of all metals!

People who cannot understand the monetary properties of silver tend to refer to it as an industrial metal, a clearly misleading designation. Do people change the monetary properties of gold when they discover that it can be used for dentures? Rather than harming silver's rare and precious qualities in the slightest, the large number of industrial uses and small amounts of non-recyclable consumption are important evidence of its greater investment value. The exact term for silver should be a rare monetary metal that has a lot of industrial uses.

What did the price find?

Neither the historical ratio of gold and silver, nor the market supply and demand, nor inflation, can explain the fact that silver today costs $25 per ounce far less than it did in 1980 at $50! What kind of mysterious force has been able to seriously distort the price of silver to the extent that it is now?

For a long time, because gold and silver have a natural monetary bloodline relationship, its historical value is more stable than thousands of years, this solid connection has long been deeply embedded in the memory of civilization, it crosses the era, crosses the country, crosses the religion, crosses the geography, crosses the ideology, far more durable than the international bankers artificial "strong dollar" in people's minds. It is known that silver, like gold, is the best quality "money" and that silver is more widely available than gold. Because the daily life of clothing, food, housing and transportation, mostly small transactions, while gold is generally used for very large transactions. So silver is not only real money, but it's better money than gold in terms of liquidity. In order to protect the enormous benefits of the issuance of the dollar, bankers would have to break free from the gold and silver currencies, which would have to be abolished. If you want to abolish gold and silver money, you must first abolish silver, because silver is closely connected with the daily life of the people. Thus, the strategy of the international bankers is: to conquer money, you must first conquer gold; to conquer gold, you must first conquer silver!

Nowadays, although the dollar has been willingly usurped the "monetary throne" of gold and silver, but the "false emperor" is after all a fake, international bankers are always unrealistic, because as soon as any crisis winds up, people will immediately think of gold and silver. International bankers really "hate gold and silver so much they are scared to death". His mentality is very similar to that of Wang Mang, who usurped the throne in Chinese history and hated to kill all the people surnamed Liu in the world. Silver is like Prince Liu Xiu, who has been hunted down by the "Wang Mang of the banking world" for decades now. This "hunt" is the price suppression, they want people to think of silver as a common metal, a common industrial material. If we can't forget that silver has been the "king of money" like gold for thousands of years, then the international bankers first drove it out of the monetary palace – the central banks. The price of silver was then deliberately and drastically depressed, reducing it to the status of a "common man", who, along with copper, iron, lead and zinc, roamed the streets of common goods.

The silver market is much smaller than the gold market plate, through the large-scale "naked shorting" means to depress the silver price, while using the low-priced silver rope to drag the gold rally off the hook wild horse, is really a high leverage and highly effective price control strategy. Just suppressing the price of silver will enable the global financial casinos centered on dollar bills to bring perpetual windfall profits to the international bankers who run them!

From 1990 to 2003, the price of silver has been nearly $50 per ounce from 1980, was all the way down to just $4 to $5 per ounce. Just when silver was at its most depressed, some insightful people saw the investment opportunity created by the severe undervaluation of silver. The investment fund managed by the famous "stock god" Warren Buffett bought nearly 130 million ounces of silver in tranches between 1997 and 1998. It accounted for 1/4 of the world's annual silver production at the time, essentially copying the bottom of silver for decades. It is puzzling why Buffett prematurely sold off all of his silver in 2006. His average buy price is $6 per ounce and his sell price is only $7.50. Buffett himself admits that the deal was not done beautifully. "I bought early and sold early. That was my mistake. Speculation is the craziest in the end." Very coincidentally, just shortly after Buffett sold all of his silver, the first silver-traded fund created by Barclays was also approved to open on a US stock exchange in 2006. The company is also a member of the Board of Governors of the United States of America. The sale is not without suspicion. As for what kind of shady dealings Barclays has had with Warren Buffett, it is not known.

Another person with a particularly keen sense of the silver market and a far-reaching influence is Ted Butler. Butler has been a commodity futures trader since 1971, when he worked for Merrill Lynch, and in the mid-1980s, one of his clients asked him, "What is the reason why the silver market is in short supply, but the price of silver hasn't risen for years?" In order to explain the reasons for this to his clients, Butler began to study the silver futures market. But he was also puzzled, he learned that silver is really in short supply, but can not explain why the silver price just does not rise. Later, with his years of experience in the commodity futures market, he discovered that the amount of blank silver made in the market was always much greater than the supply of spot silver. It turns out that there are institutions that are artificially driving down the price of silver. So he reported this market manipulation to the US Commodity Futures Trading Commission (CFTC). But the authorities replied that there was no problem and ignored it. Butler is a stubborn man, and he insists on doing what he thinks is right to the end, and he persistently reflects it to the authorities, to no avail. Then came the Internet, and from 1996 Butler began using the Internet to expose the truth that the price of silver had been artificially suppressed. He publishes a detailed analysis or commentary on the silver market almost every week online. As a result of his long years of persistent research and commentary on the silver market, Butler gradually became the most influential authority in the field. He considered the manipulation of the silver market to be "the worst capital conspiracy ever". In addition to continuing his numerous petitions to the U.S. Commodity Futures Trading Commission, he also called on investors at large to join forces to fight the manipulation of the silver market. After years of effort, the crimes of several major banking giants in illegally suppressing the silver (and also gold) market are being exposed more and more, causing widespread concern in the world. After nearly two years, the U.S. Commodity Futures Trading Commission has finally opened an investigation into this.

In response to the CFTC's investigation, Butler said in an exclusive interview that despite the willingness of those involved to address the issue, the problem of silver market manipulation is too great. So much so that it's hard to come up with a solution that doesn't cause a huge upheaval.

For two decades, participants in the world's precious metals markets have been sweating through lawsuits and public debates about the manipulation of gold and silver prices. As mentioned in *Currency Wars*:

> "On April 14, 2004, the Rothschilds, who had dominated the world gold market for 200 years, unexpectedly gave up their rights to price the gold market. In an unprecedented move, silver market big brother AIG voluntarily relinquished its pricing rights in the silver market on June 1. Are the Rothschilds really bearish on gold? If so, why not quit in 1999 when gold prices hit all-time lows, but instead quit in 2004 when gold and silver prices were in full swing? The other possibility is that the price of gold and silver will eventually get out of hand... Set aside any relationship with gold early, and no one can blame the Rothschilds if, 10 years from now, the price of gold and silver does go terribly wrong."

Now the price of gold and silver is really "something", the price of gold continues to set new all-time highs, has been close to 1,400 dollars, while silver has exceeded 30 years highs, more than 25 dollars, compared with the time, gold and silver prices have risen nearly three times!

That's right, the big brother of the silver market here, AIG, is the world's largest insurance company that was bailed out by the US government in the 2008 financial tsunami. After AIG, the main manipulator of the silver market became Bear Stearns. Just the day Bear Stearns collapsed on March 17, 2008, silver hit its highest price since 1980 – $21.

Founded in 1923, Bear Stearns is the fifth largest investment bank on Wall Street and one of the nation's leading securities trading firms, and on March 15, 2008, the 85-year-old investment bank, which experienced the Great Depression of the 1930s and many economic ups and downs, suddenly announced a severe cash shortage. That day, the Federal Reserve and JPMorgan Chase joined forces to provide emergency financial assistance to Bear Stearns. On March 14, 2008, the price of silver shot up from $17 an ounce to nearly $21 after nearly a month of gains. The fact that Bear Stearns can't afford to cover its positions to resist is, I'm afraid, another important reason why it has suddenly declared a severe cash shortage. The sight of being forced to close positions would not only leave all the money it had spent on blank silver unprofitable, but it would also potentially send silver prices immediately out of control and trigger a surge in gold prices and a plunge in the dollar. The Federal Reserve sees a bad situation and comes to the rescue. Bear Stearns was given a 28-day loan, which was made to Bear Stearns by the Federal Reserve through JPMorgan Chase, but the risk of the loan was borne by the Federal Reserve. It was also the first time since the Great Depression of the 1930s that the Federal Reserve had lent in this way. On March 16, 2008, JPMorgan Chase & Co. announced its acquisition of Bear Stearns after the Federal Reserve agreed to "underwrite" a $30 billion loan to support JPMorgan Chase & Co. on March 16, 2008, saving the company from a serious silver price crisis.

Immediately after JP Morgan's acquisition of Bear Stearns, a new round of brutal repression of silver prices began, following the established policy of international bankers to suppress silver prices. Beginning on March 18, the day after JPMorgan Chase took over for Bear Stearns, silver prices began a sudden plunge. By March 20, in just three days, the price of silver had plummeted from $21 per ounce to $17.50 per ounce, and all of silver's one-month gain was lost. Since then, JPMorgan Chase and HSBC joined forces to continue to hunt down silver, by August 2008, the two held a total of 85% of the net short position in silver, the silver market in these two banks joined forces to fight all the way down, August 15 fell below $13, late October to early December, surprisingly fell to $9 per ounce or so, back to the 2006 price level.

It all naturally doesn't escape the eyes of silver market analyst Butler. Why is there a significant increase in banks making blank silver positions? Butler questioned the CFTC and members of Congress on this several times, and finally, the explanation he received was that it was because JPMorgan Chase had taken over Bear Stearns. Until then, Butler and all the silver investors have been unclear on the question of who exactly is the biggest short in the silver market because the identity of the participating traders is not disclosed on the futures trading reports. Butler's market analysis reports have always been described in an unnamed way, and it was only then that it dawned on Butler that Bear Stearns and JPMorgan Chase were the culprits in the suppression of silver prices. Butler's revelation of the insider's story caused a strong reaction in the market and sparked public outrage among silver investors. This led to the CFTC's investigation of JPMorgan Chase, followed by a number of investor lawsuits against JPMorgan Chase and HSBC for their illegal manipulation of the silver market.

In the majority of investors under increasing pressure, in September 2010, JPMorgan Chase announced that in order to meet the requirements of the new U.S. financial regulatory bill "Dodd-Frank Wall Street Reform and Consumer Protection Act, stop self-employment, laying off about 20 commodity futures traders in London, these people traded in the variety of silver, including silver, as a result of the silver market sounded, the price immediately exceeded 21 U.S. dollars, breaking the March 17, 2008, the fall of Bear Stearns set a high point. Since 1980, silver prices exceeded the record high twice, both and the main manipulator of the silver market in big trouble, is history really full of interesting coincidences?

It's worth noting that a lot of the big moves on the silver market have been made from London, as has AIG, as has JPMorgan Chase, largely to stay out of trouble with US regulators.

The manipulation of the price of silver is well known as the case of the American tycoon Hunt brothers who hoarded silver in the 1970s and failed miserably. Through this case, textbooks repeatedly teach that market regulation works, that manipulation of the futures market is over forever, and that anyone who wants to manipulate the price of silver again, the Hunt brothers, is a lesson from their past.

In fact, the manipulation of silver prices is not limited to the hoarding of silver price increases, but should include the price suppression effect of large-scale "naked short selling" silver. For the latter, the U.S. Futures Trading Authority has not previously investigated it seriously. That is to say, the governor can set fires, but the people cannot light lamps. It makes sense to be a blank silver, but a long silver is a must!

As in the case of gold, pricing power in the world silver market has always been in the hands of the Wall Street-London axis. The New York Futures Exchange is responsible for "paper silver" pricing, while the London Bullion Market Association (LBMA) determines the pricing of "physical silver", and with the cooperation of both parties, silver prices have always looked grey in the face of inflation. In this way, the so-called monetary properties of silver seem like a joke, even the most common metal can effectively combat inflation, silver does not even have this ability, how can we talk about monetary properties? Silver has been thoroughly demonized as a common industrial metal.

Note that in people's minds, industrial metals and base metals can almost draw equivalents.

That's what ordinary people think is inexplicable when they hear about silver investing at first glance! International bankers have cleverly created prolonged weakness in silver prices and have taken full advantage of this psychological effect to mask the monetary nature of silver, thus making the gamble on the dollar system bigger and better.

The economic laws of supply and demand that determine prices are like the three Newtonian laws of physics, an untouchable iron law. Industrial demand is a nail in the coffin, it is difficult to have room to tamper, so the suppression of silver prices will only be from the artificially increased supply to solve the problem. Depressing silver prices can effectively curb investment demand for silver, and it is the potential investment demand that will be triggered by silver's monetary attributes in an increasingly inflationary world economic ecology that will be the focus of future silver supply and demand. If the supply of physical silver is insufficient, the ideal effect of "oversupply" of silver can also be achieved by creating an amazing supply of "paper silver". And it is along this line that the Wall Street-London axis is manipulating silver prices.

Silver Market: The Game of 1 Bottle Cap and 100 Bottles

The fractional reserve system was originally a system of "amplification" of money used by the banking industry, whereby every dollar created by the central bank, when deposited into the banking system, can be amplified 10 times by the banking system for credit output. The more bottles there are with one lid, the more difficult it is to play the game and the more likely it is to go wrong. At their craziest, these institutions play with the idea that one lid has to cover 50 bottles, and the slightest hiccup will be all over the place.

If the 1:50 cover game eventually led to a serious financial crisis, the silver vs. gold market game played even crazier, the ratio is 1:100!

Behind every ounce of physical silver in the current world silver market, there are 100 ounces of paper contracts of all kinds claiming to own it! After a 100-fold amplification, "physical silver" seems to be both supply and demand, frequent trading, market boom, in this super bubble "physical silver" market, the price has finally been reasonably "discovered", this is the extremely low silver price, and it seems that the supply of silver can seem endless. It's a genius idea to use 99% of your imaginary "paper silver" trading volume to fully trade around 1% of your physical silver price. As long as 99% of the people who hold "paper silver" do not come to ask for physical silver, the game can rest easy. What ultimately determines the price of silver is the international bankers' never-ending lack of dollars, not the true supply and demand of silver.

Ironically, even in the London gold and silver market, where "physical silver" is traded, the vast majority of transactions are not delivered "physically", but are transferred through "paper silver", which is "physical". Such accounts have a scientific name and are called "non-physical accounts". As defined by the London Bullion Market Association: "It is an account with no specific block of metal to which it corresponds; what the client has is a commitment to the block of metal... The transaction is delivered on the account by the borrowing and lending parties based on the borrowed balance. The account owner does not directly own a specific block of gold or silver metal, but is secured by the metal inventory of the dealer where the account was opened. The customer is the owner of the (gold and silver) without physical confirmation." Of these, the last sentence is the most truthful, as the owner of "paper and silver" is in fact "the owner of (gold and silver) without physical confirmation".

On March 25, 2010, the U.S. Commodity Futures Trading Commission held a hearing in Washington to investigate possible price manipulation in the silver market, the magnitude of which was highlighted in the minutes.

(The parties are debating whether the large number of short-selling contracts in the US silver futures market constitutes price manipulation.)

> ***O'MALLEY*** *(Commissioner, U.S. Futures Trading Commission): Do you think that when silver futures expire, if the buyer demands physical delivery of the silver, does that pose a problem for the short-selling side?*
> ***Klinsky*** *(former head of commodities research at Goldman Sachs): No, I'm not worried at all. Because it has always been so for decades. Another reason is that some other mechanism (when a physical claim for silver is honoured) can be used for cash delivery; thirdly, many people are aware that almost all the short positions in the silver and gold markets surveyed today are hedging risk, and the futures short contracts are hedging the risk*

of buying (physical gold and silver) in the (London physical) OTC market. So I really don't think any risk exists.
A ludicrous problem arises here, when a buyer asks for spot silver, and the seller, who has nothing in kind in his hands, asks if he can lose money, which is itself a breach of contract! Since the time and place of delivery and the color and quantity of the goods are specified in the futures contract, anything that cannot be done in accordance with the contract is a breach of contract, and Klimstchen does not consider it a risk! What's even more ridiculous is the logic of his first one, the previous Ponzi scheme went off without a hitch, so there's nothing to worry about now. Immediately following, Douglas of the Gold Antitrust Association took the field.

Douglas: *We're talking about hedging the spot market risk with futures, but if we look at the spot market, the London Bullion Market Association, they trade 20 million ounces of gold a day on a net basis, which equates to $22 billion, about $5.4 trillion a year... You can see from the London Bullion Market Association's website that there is no physical substance behind these so-called 'non-physical account' trades. They are traded in partial preparation and you can't trade on that scale because there isn't that much (gold and silver) on the planet. So those who are short in the (US futures market) are actually hedging their paper exposure with pieces of paper in the (London gold and silver) market.*
(8 seconds of silence)

Here, Douglas points to the crux of the matter, which is why those who do blank silver futures on Wall Street are running to the London over-the-counter (OTC) physical market to "hedge" the so-called risk. The reason for this is that the U.S. futures market has clear regulations for futures contracts and anyone doing blank silver must have a 90% identified spot source or be suspected of market manipulation. The London gold and silver OTC market, known as the "physical market", trading is "no physical" account, but the London Gold and Silver Market Association is a "self-regulatory" organization, fully believe that everyone is "conscious", so does not rigidly require participants to take out real gold and silver to inspect the goods, and the OTC market is an opaque market, no one knows exactly what things in the transaction, the transaction price is how much. So Wall Street silver manipulators can make a big play in London, they use the so-called "physical transactions" of the London market to get the U.S. regulators to explain why the big shorting on Wall Street is a reasonable hedge, thus avoiding the U.S. regulation, play the game of "reasonable" hedging of the paper with the paper piece risk.

London's so-called "physical silver" market, where approximately 125 million ounces of silver are traded daily, has a vault of just 75 million ounces of real silver for delivery. The New York futures market is open for about 800 million ounces of silver contracts, but it actually has only 50 million ounces of spot silver available for delivery. The total physical volume of silver available for delivery in the London and New York silver markets is approximately 120 million ounces. According to the Bank for International Settlements in June 2009, the derivative balance of the "other precious metals category" (overwhelmingly silver) was $203 billion, equivalent to 12 billion ounces of silver (about 20 years of total silver minerals)!

What is unfolding before our eyes is a super virtual silver market, a market manipulated by price, a market highly leveraged, a market that is already on the verge of a spot run!

Silver manipulation investigation

On March 25, 2010, the U.S. Futures Trading Commission's hearing on silver price manipulation focused on the manipulation of the gold and silver markets since September 2008. Sixteen people were invited to testify at this hearing, including regulators, exchange officials, banks, dealers, brokerage firms, investors and others. Among the most powerful was the testimony of London precious metals trader Andrew McCall about JPMorgan's manipulation of silver prices.

In a bizarre twist, on March 26, McCall and his wife were "accidentally" involved in a car accident in London, England, and were admitted to hospital. According to eyewitnesses who were walking on the road at the time, "a car came slanting down the side road and hit his (McCall's) car". When the witness attempted to stop the vehicle that had attempted to flee, the driver accelerated violently and the witness hurriedly dodged out of the way and was nearly hit, followed by the vehicle that hit two other vehicles in the process of fleeing. In the course of an emergency police pursuit, a helicopter was also called, which led to the arrest of the perpetrators, the details of which have not yet been made public.

Who was McCall to stand up to the silver manipulation shadows, and why did he fall prey to this? The World Gold Antitrust Association

(GATA) reported on March 23, 2010 that "London precious metals trader Andrew McCall had contacted Gold Antitrust Association head Andry Douglas, and a (silver) trader at JPMorgan Chase provided McCall with first-hand information about the manipulation of the precious metals market and boasted to him about how JPMorgan Chase was profiting from this manipulation." After obtaining this information, McCall reported the crime to the U.S. Futures Trading Commission Enforcement Division in November 2009. He describes in detail how JPMorgan Chase sent signals to the market to suppress the price of silver, and how numerous traders in the market recognized these signals and profited greatly in the process of short selling silver with JPMorgan Chase. Specifically, JPMorgan Chase generally selects key timing points such as option expiration dates, non-farm payrolls data release dates, U.S. futures market silver contract rollover dates and other significant events that occur.

In an email dated January 26, 2010, McCall explained to the U.S. Futures Trading Commission that when JPMorgan Chase started doing blank silver, "we traders closely watched their (JPMorgan Chase's) 'signals' prior to major moves. The first signal was the smaller (silver) volume that appeared in Asia. As a trader, we made a windfall profit, but I didn't want to be in a rigged market and in criminal activity (to make money). For example, if you look at today's open, you'll see that about 1,500 contracts were sold at the same time, while buyers were only 1/5 to 1/10 of a percent. Maybe you can check out for yourself who is behind the short sellers. Note that in just 10 minutes, 2,800 lots of the contract instantly crushed the buying power. This cannot be normal commodity trading in search of the best price."

To further illustrate his allegations, McCall had sent an e-mail alert to Erud Ramirez, senior investigator in the Enforcement Division of the United States Futures Trading Commission, on 3 February 2010 that the silver market would be "hit" two days later, on 5 February. In the email McCall wrote: "Precious metals traders in London are aware that JPMorgan Chase began discussions in March about clearing out as many short positions as possible before the (silver short position) limit. I feel sorry for those who are not in the loop that huge amounts of wealth will change hands on this day, which, in my opinion, is the result of the U.S. Futures Trading Commission's misguided definition of illegal market manipulation."

In an email on February 3, McCall "predicted" to the U.S. Futures Trading Commission that the silver market would appear two days later.

"Non-farm payrolls data will be released at 8:30 a.m. ET. There will be two scenarios at the moment, both good and bad data, with silver (and gold) prices falling sharply in a massive short selling operation aimed at breaking through technical support lines. While I have no doubt that I will profit from this manipulation, this example shows how easily the market can be manipulated by a few traders when highly concentrated position situations are allowed (by the US Futures Trading Commission). The first scenario is that bad news comes out (poor employment data), which is good for gold and silver because (bad economic news) will weaken the dollar, precious metals will attract investors, and (gold and silver) prices will move higher. This process will last for a short time (1 to 5 minutes), and then thousands of new short sale lots will emerge, (short sale attacks) which will completely destroy the new buying contracts and send precious metal prices plummeting below key technical support points. The second scenario is good news (better-than-expected employment), which would result in an immediate sell-off of massive short-selling contracts and an immediate plunge in (silver) prices. Those who go long will be immediately hit by the stop loss line and the price will fall below the technical support point. In both cases, it's the two major shorting majors (JPMorgan Chase and HSBC) who step in and reap the windfall. Those of us who will be 'invited' to join in on the (silver price's) decline."

The market sentiment on February 5th was exactly in line with McKell's "prediction"!

On 9 May 2010, the *New York Post*, a mainstream United States media outlet, reported heavily on the opening of a dual criminal and civil investigation by the United States federal government into JPMorgan Chase's manipulation of the silver market under the headline "Federal Government begins investigation into JPMorgan Chase's silver trading". "The Futures Trading Commission is in charge of civil crime investigations and the Department of Justice began investigating criminal offenses, according to sources who wished to remain anonymous. The investigation was wide-ranging, with federal officials looking at JPMorgan Chase's precious metals trading records at the London Gold and Silver Exchange Association, a physical (silver) trading market, as well as their trading in (silver) futures and derivatives at the New York Mercantile Exchange. According to a report from the Treasury Department's Office of Monetary Control, JPMorgan Chase added a total of $6.76 billion in silver derivatives in the last three months of 2009, equivalent to 220 million ounces (about 6,800 tons of silver)... It is alleged that in the operation of doing blank silver, JPMorgan Chase acted to suppress the price of silver by massively shorting silver option contracts or physical silver."

The *New York Post*'s report strongly rocked the world silver market, with the price of silver smelling 6.5% higher in one day! A few days later, JPMorgan Chase issued a statement: "JPMorgan Chase is not under investigation by the Justice Department for criminal or civil silver trading."

If the Hunt brothers hoarded 200 million ounces of silver to push up the price of silver is a major case, then, in today's silver futures and derivatives market at every turn 12 billion ounces in front of the masterstroke, the Hunt brothers are only afraid to make such a big name for themselves and shame difficult to be.

Curiously, like the news of the near-collapse of the US currency market on September 18, 2008, the silver price manipulation case of the century does not seem to have attracted much interest from the US mainstream media.

On October 26, 2010, at a hearing held by the U.S. Commodity Futures Trading Commission, Chairman Chilton stated, "Some market participants continue to resort to fraudulent means to influence and control the price of silver, and this dishonesty, which is not in good standing, must be severely investigated." The commission is conducting a two-year, high-profile investigation into the silver market.

Meanwhile, two of the largest banks that manipulate the silver market are being sued in court by investors, based on a wealth of evidence gathered. International media reported on October 27, 2010 that JPMorgan Chase and HSBC were accused of hoarding large short-term short positions in order to manipulate silver futures prices. Investors claiming to trade silver futures and options contracts on the New York Metal Exchange said the two banks conspired to depress silver futures, inform each other of large trades, and use large positions to issue orders to influence the market. This monopoly and market manipulation have caused serious damage to investors' interests. The investors claim that the two banks also arranged for so-called mock trading orders, in which large orders are submitted that are not executed, but which, after having an impact on prices, are withdrawn before they are to be executed. Investor submissions show that JPMorgan Chase and HSBC together held a net short position of 85 percent of silver in

August 2008 and $7.9 billion in precious metal derivatives by the first quarter of 2009.

As of 24 November 2010, at least 25 lawsuits had been filed against the two banks.

It remains to be seen whether the two big banks will eventually be brought to justice. As we all know, the bane of this global financial crisis is on Wall Street, right here at the Federal Reserve. But they are too big to fall, too big to be bound by law, and the golden power of the capitalist era and the kingly power of feudalism are both above the law. JPMorgan Chase is one of the largest banks in the United States, with financial derivatives worth a whopping $70 trillion. Its downfall would have triggered a much worse shock than the collapse of Lehman Brothers Bank. It's not too late to beg for it to fall. How dare you serve it with torture? Yet the laws of the market are iron-faced and ruthless. No matter who it is, defying the laws of the market will not escape the final punishment. The suppression of the silver and gold markets violates the iron law of supply and demand. In a silver market where demand is increasing, supply is dwindling, and resources are being depleted, it is impossible to go long and short with impunity. The larger the scale, the longer the time, the heavier the punishment.

Silver market on the verge of a massive run

While there are no illusions about whether US courts can sanction financial giants like JPMorgan Chase and HSBC, the incident has made investors around the world appreciate the value of silver anew. The price of silver is so low, not because it and cabbage go together, but as a result of being desperately hunted down by some super heavyweight financial giants like AIG, Bear Stearns, JPMorgan Chase and HSBC. Silver is the Federal Reserve at all costs to get rid of the "dollar trick", at the same time, silver will be in the near future in the investment market to shine in the "Cinderella". When investors all over the world understand this, silver, a "generation of pride", will immediately attract "countless heroes to bend the waist" in the market.

After entering 2009, silver and gold joined forces, just like the Soviet Red Army of that year, after tenaciously holding Stalingrad, finally ushered in the moment of a great counterattack against the dollar. Up and down from $9 per ounce at the end of 2008, all the way to about $18 per ounce in August 2010. From late August 2010, the price of silver began to hit $18 per ounce, all the way up to $30 per ounce. In less than 3 months, the rise was as high as 61%, superimposed a 30-year high, attracting world attention.

As more and more investors discovered the tremendous investment value of silver, people began to compete for very limited physical silver resources. According to the World Silver Association, the world's total silver production in 2009 was about 889 million ounces, and the manufacturing industry had to use up about 730 million ounces, and the remaining 137 million ounces were eaten up by investors after mining companies reduced their hedging requirements, and investment demand in 2009 jumped 184% from 48 million ounces in 2008! Looking at current trends, investment demand for silver will rise more in 2010 than in 2009.

The current stock of silver available on the world market is about 700 million ounces, worth a total of about $17.5 billion at the current price of $25 per ounce. Such a tempting and very small market, once locked on the market's radar, would be inevitable with the onslaught of global money, and a spike in prices would be inevitable.

Butler is far more discerning and patient than Buffett when it comes to silver's value-added potential. Butler argues that it is because of the artificially low price of silver by a few big banks that the average investor has encountered a once-in-a-lifetime investment opportunity, and that the market's supply and demand will ensure that the buyers of silver will eventually prevail over the big banks that are shorting it. Developments appear to be confirming several of the eventual explosive increases in silver prices that Butler had envisioned that year.

The first scenario is the effect that the forced unwinding of short sales contracts by the big banks has on the silver market. When the market discovers silver's potential to increase in value, and the influx of buyers keeps pushing up the price of physical silver, the short sale contracts of the big banks will come under tremendous pressure to deliver. Forcing them to either pay physical silver when due or to buy an equal number of contracts as the short sale, i.e., forced to close their positions. Currently, the total amount of contracts made on the New York Futures Exchange alone for blank silver is equivalent to 550 million ounces. It is equivalent to selling 79% of all silver spot on the world market. Where is the short side going to find so much silver spot to sell without bleeding the book?

The second scenario is the impact of forced restitution of leased silver on the price of silver. Since more than 20 years ago, multiple central banks have been suppressing silver prices by dumping large amounts of silver on the market by renting it out. Why is there a move to rent out silver? Because some silver mines are unable to deliver on time for various reasons, they first rent silver from gold and silver spot trading banks to ensure on-time delivery. When the silver is later mined it will be returned at the original amount, plus 1% or less interest. By the same token, gold and silver spot trading banks can also lease silver from central banks. The central bank, on the pretext that the silver piled up in warehouses could not generate interest, happily leased out large reserves of silver, at least at 1% interest. And the gold and silver spot trading banks, having leased the spot silver, dumped the vast majority of it into the market to cash out. The cash proceeds were then used to purchase government bonds with a yield of 5 per cent. After returning 1% interest to the central bank, a solid 4% can be earned. In this way, the central bank and the gold and silver spot-trading banks have suppressed the prices in the silver market without showing a trace.

Butler estimates that probably hundreds of millions or even billions of ounces of silver have flowed into the market in the last 20 years by renting out this form. Theoretically, the leased silver would eventually have to be returned to the central bank. However, most of this silver had already been used as industrial materials and could not be returned in its original form. Once the price of silver was finally overwhelmed and surged, the central bank began to demand the return of the renter, who had to buy back an equal amount of physical silver from the market. This physical silver is in addition to the other large pool of spot silver that was shorted on the New York Mercantile Exchange. Buying back this silver spot will be a huge blow to silver prices. If that happens, the price of silver alone could punch up to $500 per ounce. This is a big reason why the gold and silver spot-trading banks that lease silver are desperately trying to suppress the price of silver.

The third scenario is the impact of the panicked reserves of industrial users on silver prices. Silver is a raw material with thousands of uses. It is a critical material in many products, but in small quantities, a characteristic that keeps the demand for silver from falling as prices rise, the so-called rigid demand. With the surge in investment demand, more than 30,000 tons of inventory will be quickly depleted, and the new silver mineral cycle of several years, but also mostly associated with the mine, far from water to quench the near thirst. In this way, silver will be out of stock, and for longer and longer, from a few days to a few weeks, and later, possibly as long as a few months. The factory's production line can not be stopped because of the silver out of stock, so the enterprise must be prepared for the rainy day, to pre-empt the reserves, which will inevitably lead to the silver price soaring.

Looking at the reality of the years since the 2008 financial crisis, both the deflation in the US and Europe and the inflation in Asian countries have been good for gold and silver in general. Because gold and silver are denominated in U.S. dollars, the deflation in the U.S. and European countries, may leave the Asian people threatened by inflation to buy gold and silver with large amounts of money in their hands, at this time the price of gold and silver soared. On the other hand, in order to resist deflation, the U.S. and European countries will prompt the Federal Reserve to carry out further quantitative easing and print more money, affected by the depreciation of the dollar, gold and silver prices will inevitably continue to rush higher.

Silver is a fantastic investment variety, and in times of inflation or deflationary financial crisis, it appreciates as much as gold does as the dollar depreciates. After the economic recovery, silver will again exhibit its industrial raw material characteristics due to the large industrial demand, which will appreciate with the supply and demand relationship. This is a unique dual advantage that no other investment breed has.

Today's world silver market is staggeringly small, with just 30,000 tons of silver stocks above ground worldwide, worth just 120 billion yuan, much smaller than the size of the Agricultural Bank of China's listed financing. At present, the world silver market, the ratio of physical and "paper silver" extreme disparity to 1:100, 100 ounces of "paper silver" behind the transaction, only 1 ounce of physical support, if the financial market 1:50 high leverage eventually led to the financial tsunami sweeping the world, then the silver market than this ratio is double again has reached the edge of the danger of a run at any time.

An extremely distorted, highly leveraged, very small silver market with the power to seriously shock the world financial system!

When Greenspan et al. explored in 1995 that the skyrocketing gold price could effectively reduce U.S. debt, they were certain they could win. Because the United States and Europe control a total of central banks with gold reserves of more than 20,000 tons, has the unquestionable pricing power of the physical gold market, coupled with the Wall Street-London axis of gold futures and other gold derivatives market has absolute control, they can fully achieve a controlled rise in the price of gold, and cover the dollar "establishment" retreat, in a substantial reduction in government debt, at the same time, continue to maintain the status of the dollar world currency hegemony, to achieve a soft landing of the dollar crisis.

However, they overlook one important variable, and that is silver.

Because of the historical inertia of gold and silver prices and the huge psychological interaction energy of the market gold and silver, if the world silver prices suddenly and violently rise, will disrupt the rhythm of gold prices, runaway silver prices inspired by the risk aversion of the world financial market will be like a mountain of fire bull formations, directly impacting the gold market feet. As physical silver runs out, the New York silver futures market will see widespread defaults and severe delays in delivery, as industrial users of silver begin to urgently stockpile raw silver, as investment clients of silver rush to withdraw their own reserves from the spot, and as panicked silver futures holders rush to demand delivery of spot silver.

Investors desperate for physical silver will instantly squeeze out 50 million ounces of physical deliverable silver on the New York futures trading market. After being completely disappointed in the New York "paper silver" market, people immediately began to flock to the London "physical silver" market in droves. However, they immediately discovered that the largest market for so-called "physical silver", with only 75 million ounces of spot, turned out to be "no physical account", and that the vast majority of silver owners were simply "unidentified (gold and silver) owners".

Meanwhile, the horrible news in the silver market will induce a run on the gold market, and don't forget, it's also a 1:100 superb bottle cap game.

With New York and London's silver and gold markets crippled one after another, world financial markets would immediately be in a real panic. This panic from the heart would be unprecedented. That's when the world suddenly discovered that the original gold and silver were the cornerstones of the world's credit-money skyscraper buried deep in the ground, and that once that cornerstone shakes, the even larger bond market, stock market, money market, foreign exchange market, and the $50 trillion financial derivatives market built on top of it all will shake even more violently!

At this point, financial markets around the world began calling for government bailouts.

At this time, the European and U.S. governments can not do anything about it, silver, after all, can not get a "quantitative easing" paper can be changed out. European and American governments have long since sold out of their previously huge silver inventories, thus losing the most important bargaining chip that directly affects market prices. Even if the European and American governments ordered the forced confiscation of private silver, as President Roosevelt did in 1934 when he ordered U.S. citizens to surrender all their gold, it would not help, because the entire stockpile of silver above ground level is nothing more than 30,000 tons, which is still far from enough to handle the scale of the run.

In a pinch, there's another trick, and that's emergency silver mining to quell the world's silver run. However, when the government ordered emergency silver mining, it took at least five years from resource exploration, additional equipment, and expanded production to a significant increase in total supply, and the cucumber greens went cold.

At this point, the eyes of the world will be on China. Because the largest producer and exporter of silver in the world today is China! What a huge international political and financial lever that would be! And what a strategic opportunity this will be!

People's War in Silver

China is now the world's largest silver producer, with a total annual production of about 10,000 tons, of which 5,000 tons are used to generate foreign exchange for export, and until 2008 China had an export tax rebate policy to encourage silver exports. That 5,000 tons of silver is enough to make up for the 4,000 tons of silver shortage caused by world industrial demand, allowing the Wall Street-London axis of the gold and silver market to keep the 1 bottle cap to 100 bottle trick going!

Exporting silver to generate foreign exchange? It's a mind-boggling thought! It's like trading real money for fake money, and there are government subsidies for export tax rebates! From early 2009 to October 2010, the price of silver skyrocketed from $11 to $23 per ounce, doubling with more to go! The real purchasing power of the dollar over the same period has been declining, repeatedly "quantitative easing" under the dollar river day by day, the second recession clouds are again dense. In one year and nine months, 8,000 tons of silver exports "recovered" is nearly 20 billion yuan of wealth loss! Also brought in are more dollar bills with no way to go but to buy US Treasuries!

It is extremely strategically short-sighted to treat silver as a general industrial commodity export! To exchange the ever-rising and increasingly scarce currency, silver, for the daily devaluation of the never-quite-dollar paper currency is to lose not only wealth itself, but also the high point of the financial strategy of the great powers.

Silver not only used to be money, it still has the function of money. With the increasing risk of the dollar, euro, yen and other paper money today, silver has a clear hedge against the risk of the entire credit and currency system. This is also the fundamental reason why silver prices soared by 20% a day on September 18, 2008, when the dollar system had a collapse crisis.

On July 30, 2008, China finally abolished the 5 percent export tax rebate on silver, a policy that is undoubtedly correct, but whose starting point is still to ease the contradiction of China's excessive foreign trade surplus. This shows that the relevant sectors are not thinking from a financial perspective when formulating trade policies. In the absence of an overall national financial strategy, contradictory and uncoordinated policies are inevitable.

When considering a silver strategy, it should be viewed on the same level as gold. Regardless of how the rest of the world now views silver, in the United States dollar, "the son of the week" is declining in today's world, national currencies will inevitably appear "Spring and Autumn five hegemon" and "warring states seven male" situation. Silver will be a hot hard currency in the future, a trend that will become more pronounced as the dollar declines.

If China maximizes the circulation of the renminbi as one of the high points for building a strong financial frontier, then there is a need to comprehensively revisit the great financial strategic value of silver and gold.

In fact, to squeeze the international silver market, it doesn't need to be on the scale of RMB 120 billion at all, as long as domestic investors eat up all of the 5,000 tons of silver China exports each year to generate foreign exchange, using RMB 25 billion is enough. That alone is enough to shake up the world silver price system. The silver market available in New York and London is nothing more than 125 million ounces (about 3,900 tons) of silver, basically only enough to cover the difference between supply and demand for one year of industrial consumption, physical delivery of silver will be very difficult and defaults on futures contracts will be difficult to avoid.

What is the concept of 25 billion yuan? It's something that a few stock funds can do.

If there are 10,000 people, $2.5 million of silver will be purchased in kind per person (about 450 kg at $5.6 per gram).

Or 1 million people, each of whom purchased 25,000 yuan of silver in kind (about 4.5 kg).

Or 10 million people, each purchasing $2,500 of silver in kind (about 0.45 kg).

The world silver market is likely to trigger a chain reaction of runs.

What investors need to understand is that you are not buying silver, you are selling dollar bills! Silver is savings, silver is investment, silver is the faithful insurance of wealth, silver is the currency of the common people! Not only are you investing for individuals, but you are casting a veto vote against the world financial hegemony! It's a self-defensive retaliation against the international bankers who stole China's wealth! Such an investment is beneficial to the country, to the people and to oneself!

Gold is a bow, silver is a drawn string, the will of the people is an arrow, and the bullseye is international monetary hegemony!

If the common people have any chance of changing the course of history, if the people can rise up against the world's financial hegemony, if the general public is not willing to be "sheared" in various crises, if the people are really the driving force behind history, then action is more convincing than any words!

The long-awaited enthusiasm for silver investment in China has erupted like a volcano since the gradual opening of silver investment channels in 2010. Following the bumper harvest of investing in gold, there has been a boom in silver investment across the country.

More and more people are aware of the value of silver, which not only carries the genes of Chinese history and culture, but also carries the burden of reality, it is not only a reliable tool for the people to protect their wealth, but also an effective means to counteract the hegemony of the world currency.

Silver, the greatest opportunity of your life!

Acknowledgements and Reflections

The autumn nights in Fragrant Hill are quiet and bland. On the terrace of a teahouse, the moonlight flowed and the breeze was gentle. A group of like-minded young people, often giving up holidays and weekends, have come together to study and discuss the impact and role of finance in China on various areas of society over the past century. This group is the study group members and volunteers of Currency Wars 3. After a day of intense research work, we often discuss and sort out our thoughts here at ease.

Zheng Yingyan, the only girl in the study group, is affectionately known as "Little Goddess". Because her eyebrows are so different from those of the Middle-earth, they often remind one that her ancestor was most likely a Persian princess. She is a mixture of humor, eccentricity, and maverickness, and she has a "god" that one can never find the right English equivalent. Her knowledgeable, spot-on approach to detail has earned her the title of "The Greatest Picker of All Time". Discussing the initial draft, she said unflinchingly, "What is this? Overturned and restarted! I'm not going to be able to read it, and so will the reader! Too deep, too obscure, too many clues, too many names, too many terms to remember, too many to understand! Can't ordinary people read it, is your book still worth anything?" I was surprised by her rebuke of the manuscript on behalf of the reader, who used to write only for his own pleasure and rarely for the reader's feelings. I was deeply touched by her concept of the reader's reading experience. So, twice, three times, four times, adjust the structure, change the text, reason the clues.

Yang Wei, who never argues head-on with anyone, has a Gemini personality that shines through in him. He was always euphemistic and polite in expressing his views. Lao Yang is a hardcore brother I grew up with, and we were almost all together from kindergarten to the United States on the other side of the ocean. He came to the U.S. a year before me and has a far richer learning and working experience than others, from biology to computers to MBA to investment banking. In particular, his experience at Fuji Bank in Japan and Schroders in Hong Kong, China, has given him direct experience of the financial markets in the United States and Asia. Thus, he undertook the heavy work of screening and cross-validating Japanese data. During the last four months, he also studied in depth the financial problems of the Soviet Union, the border areas and the liberated areas, and then Lao Yang said that after studying the financial innovations of the Chinese Communist Party, he was so impressed that he wanted to hand in an application for membership.

Miao Gang, who is typically known to frown and shake his head, said, "This data is not necessarily reliable, a secondary source must be found." As soon as he finds an important clue, Miao Gang is instantly transformed into a different person, sometimes frowning and dancing, sometimes speaking righteously from the Three Emperors all the way to the end of the world, displaying the amazing eloquence of a Beijing man. We have always thought that he should participate in the People's University debate team, and later legend has it that Miao just studied finance at Columbia University in the United States from Mondale, but also practiced a hard English kan fu. In addition to his talent for speaking, Miao Gang is also very sensitive to numbers, and in the "quality control" part of his gate-keeping, data proofreading and information sources have been greatly improved.

The most impressive thing about Xue Xiaoming is his unpretentiousness and simplicity, which is characteristic of Northwesterners. The doll-faced boy also gets into a facepalm with his opponent when his point of view is challenged and he gets emotional, but often doesn't prevail because of his slow speech. This graduate student in the School of International Relations, who is a diligent student, a strong reader of English and passionate about financial and historical research, has made significant contributions to the collection and collation of materials.

Currency Wars 3 examines financial issues in recent Chinese history. From 1840 to 1949, there is a vast array of finance-related material to be consulted. From the imperial court records, the emperor's approval, the archives of the Republic, foreign and provincial newspapers, secret telegrams from foreign missions, the records of bond issuance in the international financial market during the same period, the activities of major financial families in China and abroad, the statistics of foreign debt, customs duties, salt tax, tax rate statistical reports, the declassified files of various countries, the confessions and statements of the parties concerned, and of course, hundreds of books of financial and monetary history and biographies of people are inevitable. At this time of the year when the leaves of Fragrant Hill are in full bloom, everyone forgets all the troubles of the world and roams in the vast ocean of historical data with all their hearts.

The greatest contribution to this book is also made by the general readership. In my tweets, countless bloggers have enthusiastically offered suggestions and, of course, a lot of fair-minded criticism. It was the tremendous encouragement and anticipation from these colleagues and friends that allowed me to persevere in the end.

I've always had a belief that one's worth is not in what is the same as others, but in what is different from others. The process of researching and writing the "War on Money" series of books, which has been challenging, arduous and frustrating, yet passionate, uplifting and open-minded, has become an integral part of my life. In the smoke of the world's currency wars, I would like to be a faithful recorder of history.

I have always considered myself a very lucky person, and having the support and help of so many friends has often made me passionate. At the same time, I am calm and objective in the face of many controversies. I feel like I have found the source of the most value and creativity in my life. It is not painful to not eat or drink or sleep when one is doing what one is most gifted at, because one is trying to contribute value creatively to society. In fact, everyone in the world is born with some kind of gift, and one's greatest happiness is to be able to discover one's gift as early as possible. And the sad thing about most people is that they don't know, or give up on their gifts. It seems to me that the whole point of educating, reading, working and living is to find one's gift, it is innate, it is immutable, and to explore and discover it will be a lifelong task.

I would also like to thank my wife and daughter, without your long and unreserved support and encouragement, I would not be who I am today.

Finally, I would like to dedicate this book to all readers who are concerned about the fate of China.

Author.

Late 2010, Xiangshan, Beijing

Other titles

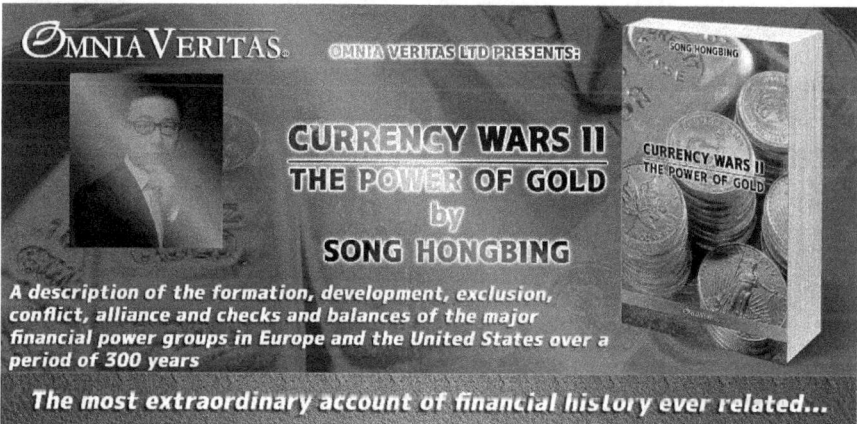

FINANCIAL HIGH FRONTIERS

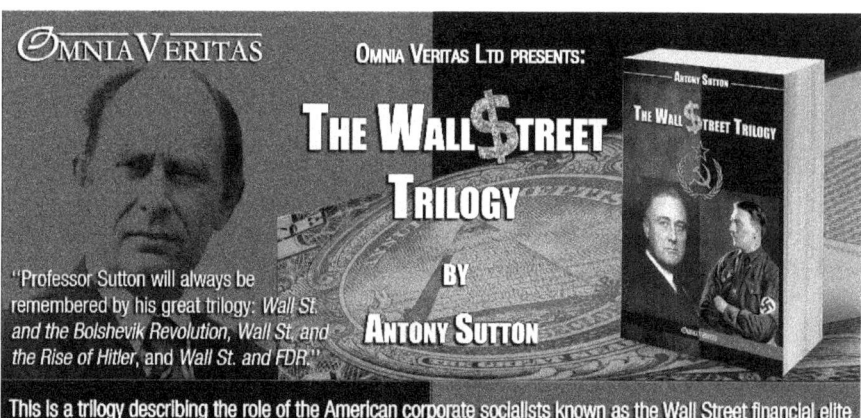

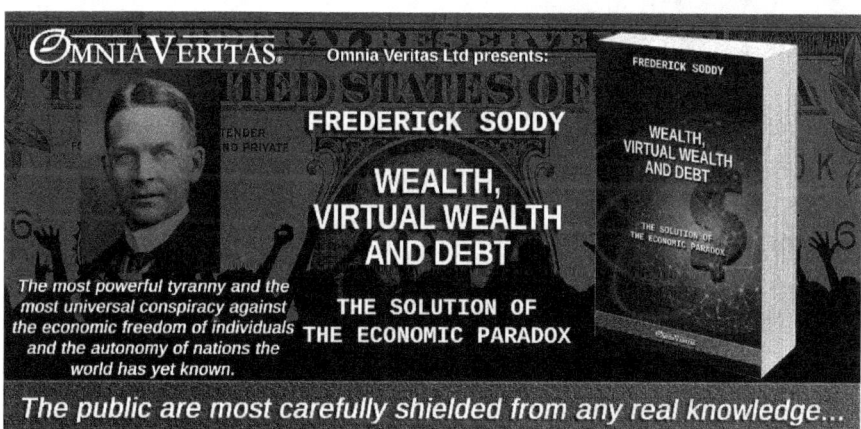

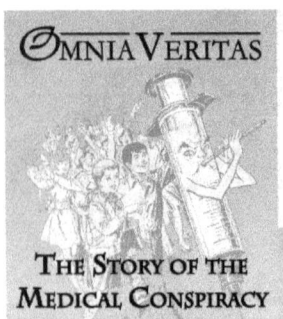

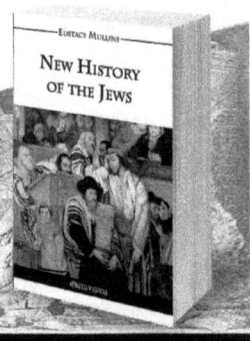
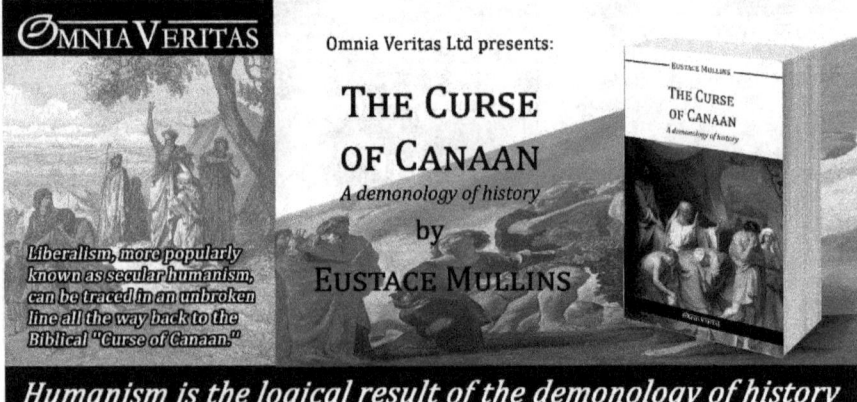

FINANCIAL HIGH FRONTIERS

Omnia Veritas Ltd presents:

THE RAPE OF JUSTICE
by EUSTACE MULLINS

American should know just what is going on in our courts

Omnia Veritas Ltd presents:

THE SECRETS OF THE FEDERAL RESERVE
by EUSTACE MULLINS

HERE ARE THE SIMPLE FACTS OF THE GREAT BETRAYAL

Will we continue to be enslaved by the Babylonian debt money system?

Omnia Veritas Ltd presents:

THE WORLD ORDER
OUR SECRET RULERS
A Study in the Hegemony of Parasitism
by EUSTACE MULLINS

The peoples of the world not only will never love Big Brother, but they will soon dispose of him forever.

The program of the World Order remains the same; Divide and Conquer

www.ingramcontent.com/pod-product-compliance
Lightning Source LLC
Chambersburg PA
CBHW071310150426
43191CB00007B/577